AMERICAN LITERATURE
for Life and Work

Elaine Bowe Johnson, Ph.D.
Associate Dean
Language and Literature Division
Mt. Hood Community College
Gresham, Oregon

Christine Bideganeta LaRocco
Integrated and Applied Curriculum Consultant
English Instructor
Arlington, Virginia

SOUTH-WESTERN EDUCATIONAL PUBLISHING

Project Manager: Laurie Wendell
Production Coordinator: Tricia Boies
Editor: Timothy Bailey
Marketing Manager: Carolyn Love
Senior Designer: Elaine St. John-Lagenaur
Vice President/Editor-in-Chief: Peter McBride

Product Development, Design and Production Services:
Learning Design Associates, Inc.
Columbus, Ohio

Cover Photography Credits: Man sawing wood, laptop computer, woman, CD, and watch and glasses atop book—Images provided by © 1994 Photodisc, Inc.; American flag—© International Stock; wood background—LDA, Inc.

ACKNOWLEDGMENTS

"Barba Nikos" by Harry Mark Petrakis. Reprinted from *A Writer's Work, A Writer's Life,*
    copyright Harry Mark Petrakis and Lake View Press, Chicago, IL, 1983.
"Ben Franklin: A Man Who Didn't Waste Any Time Watching TV" by Irwin Unger, Ph.D. From
    Instant American History by Irwin Unger, Ph.D. Copyright © 1994 by Byron Preiss Visual
    Publications, Inc. Reprinted by permission of Ballantine Books, a Division of Random
    House Inc.

Continued on page 336

Copyright © 1997
by SOUTH-WESTERN EDUCATIONAL PUBLISHING
Cincinnati, Ohio

ISBN: 0-538-64279-3

I(T)P
International Thomson Publishing

South-Western Educational Publishing is a division of International Thomson Publishing Inc.
The ITP trademark is used under license.

1 2 3 4 5 6 7 KI 02 01 00 99 98 97 96

Printed in the United States of America

For Tom, Thom, and Roussel and in memory of Elaine Larson

Elaine B. Johnson

The authors and editors of *Literature for Life and Work* gratefully acknowledge the following educators for their insightful reviews of literature selections, sample lessons, and manuscript:

Nancy Barker
Norwood High School
Cincinnati, OH

Ken Brown
Lakeland, FL

Audie Cline
California High School
Jefferson City, MO

Randy Gingrich
Hughes High School
Cincinnati, OH

Donna Helo
Rayne High School
Crowley, LA

Dorothy Hoover
Huntingdon Area High School
Huntingdon, PA

Judy Kayse
Huntsville High School
Huntsville, TX

Marcia Lubell
Yorktown High School
Yorktown Heights, NY

Carter Nicely
Old Mill High School
Arnold, MD

Jan Smith
Upsala Area Schools
Little Falls, MN

Alice Jane Stephens
Triton Central High School
Fairland, IN

Ruth Townsend
Yorktown High School
Yorktown Heights, NY

Joe Banel
Nelson Canada

Susan Freeman Carson
South-Western College
  Publishing

Dr. Willard Daggett
International Center for
  Leadership in Education, Inc.

Special Contributors

Frances Caldwell
Educational Consultant
Portland, OR

Douglas Dickston
Developmental Education Instructor
Mt. Hood Community College
Gresham, OR

TABLE OF CONTENTS

To the Student:

When you first looked at this book, you probably thought, "Oh, sure, I've seen this kind of textbook before. It's just another collection of readings with predictable questions for me to answer."

But this textbook differs from any you have used before because everything in it connects with your own experiences, interests, and ambitions. All the poetry, fiction, and nonfiction, both classical and modern, were chosen because they deal with life experiences shared by people of all times and places.

This book takes you seriously. It asks you to develop the art of thinking. It encourages you to apply what you read in a way that affects your daily life. That's what makes it unique. We hope you enjoy it and discover the excitement of connecting literature to life and work.

The literature is arranged in units under a common theme. Our goal was to allow you to read about experiences and ideas that matter in your lives. Once the literature was chosen, we then set out to challenge you with real world assignments that connect the course with your experience.

The assignments in the "Exploring," "Understanding," and "Connecting" sections invite you to express your own views, to share them with others, to work on teams, and to make a significant difference in your community. You learn best when you connect learning to your own experiences and knowledge. The assignments invite you to learn not only by studying, but also by becoming involved in activities in the real world. You learn to write, read, and

think critically by doing work that joins academic material with everyday life.

Expect some changes in your classroom. The lessons emphasize practical writing for the real world, where there is no room for a misspelled word or missing comma. Meeting the high standards of business is not the only new thing. Working in groups with other students to prepare different parts of a document may also be foreign to you. However, collaborative writing is common in the world of work. Workshops in the back of this text will give you practice in moving from school assignments to workplace tasks.

Our approach to writing assignments trains you in skills you'll actually use in your lifetime as an individual, a family member, worker, customer, and consumer. You will practice the reading, writing, listening, and speaking skills expected of you by employers, clients, colleagues, neighbors, businesses, and the person on the other end of the phone. Whether you go on to college, vocational school, the military, special training, or the world of work, the exercises in this book will prepare you for success.

This book will help you discover how much you already know. We challenge you to become involved in your English class this year in a new way and because of one simple fact: you'll be using these communication skills every day of your life.

Elaine B. Johnson

Christine B. LaRocco

UNIT ①

LIBERTY AND AUTHORITY

Since the United States declared itself a free and independent nation in 1776, its citizens have grappled with the question of individual liberty. Politicians, Constitutional scholars, and community groups continue to debate whether limits should be placed on liberty and, if so, what kinds of limits?

Everyone wants to be free. This longing for freedom is powerful. It can influence behavior, cause conflict with authority, and even provide incentive for social movements and political change. The selections in this unit demonstrate different ways of pursuing liberty and reacting to authority.

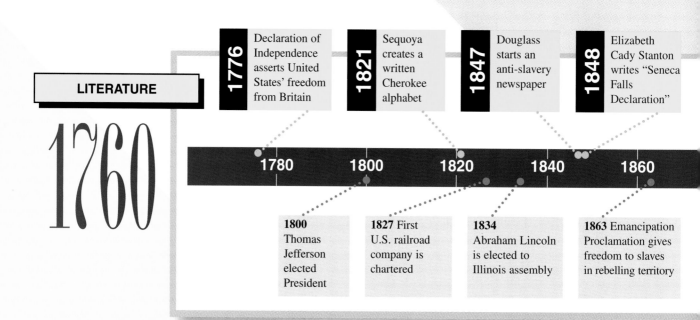

LITERATURE

1760

1776 Declaration of Independence asserts United States' freedom from Britain

1821 Sequoya creates a written Cherokee alphabet

1847 Douglass starts an anti-slavery newspaper

1848 Elizabeth Cady Stanton writes "Seneca Falls Declaration"

1780 1800 1820 1840 1860

1800 Thomas Jefferson elected President

1827 First U.S. railroad company is chartered

1834 Abraham Lincoln is elected to Illinois assembly

1863 Emancipation Proclamation gives freedom to slaves in rebelling territory

1910 Dr. Williams begins practicing medicine in his hometown, Rutherford, New Jersey

1962 William Stafford wins the National Book Award for poetry

1983 Voigt receives Newbery Medal for *Dicey's Song*

1900 1920 1940 1960 1980

2000

1892 Emil Behring invents vaccine for diphtheria

1953 Department of Health, Education, and Welfare is created

1964 U.S. Congress passes the Civil Rights Act

1973 Military draft ends in the United States

LIFE and WORK

The Declaration of Independence

EXPLORING

• • • • • • • • • • • • • • • • • •

Most people have to obey someone. For example, supervisors, teachers, and parents often give direct orders. Have you ever been treated unjustly by someone in a position of authority over you? Discuss the kinds of behavior you think unfair or unjust. Write a definition of injustice as you understand it.

THEME CONNECTION...
FUNDAMENTAL FREEDOMS

The Declaration of Independence asserts that God created all human beings and gave them the right to live, be free, and seek happiness. People create governments to protect their basic rights. If a government takes away these fundamental rights, the people who called it into being are entitled to get rid of it. The Declaration states that since Britain's King George III tyrannizes the colonies, the colonies therefore have the right to "dissolve the political bands which have connected them with another [to Britain]" and to form a new government for a new nation.

TIME & PLACE

The Continental Congress of 1776 asked Thomas Jefferson, Benjamin Franklin, and John Adams to prepare a document explaining the need for independence. Though Jefferson and Adams had very different political views, they worked together for the greater good of the colonies to create this document. Jefferson wrote the draft; Franklin and Adams revised it slightly.

Congress approved the revised document on July 4, 1776. Ironically, fifty years later, on July 4, 1826, both Jefferson and Adams died.

THE WRITER'S CRAFT

ARGUMENT

Jefferson's job in The Declaration of Independence was to persuade the world that the colonies had no choice but to separate from Britain. Jefferson's argument is divided into four parts. **First:** He explains why separation from Britain is necessary—King George III denies the very rights he should protect. **Second:** A list of the King's tyrannical acts follows, along with a condemnation of the "pretended Legislation" of the British Parliament. **Third:** The colonies asked the British "to disavow these usurpations" and got nowhere. **Fourth:** He concludes: since the British "have been deaf to the voice of justice," separation is necessary.

The Declaration of Independence

Thomas Jefferson

The Unanimous Declaration of the Thirteen United States of America

In Congress, July 4, 1776.

 hen in the Course of human events, it becomes necessary for one people to dissolve the political bands which have connected them with another, and to assume among the powers of the earth, the separate and equal station which the Laws of Nature and of Nature's God entitle them, a decent respect to the opinions of mankind requires that they should declare the causes which **impel** them to the separation.

We hold these truths to be **self-evident**, that all men are created equal, that they are endowed by their Creator with certain **unalienable** Rights, that among these are Life, Liberty and the pursuit of Happiness. That to secure these rights, Governments are instituted among Men, deriving their just powers from the consent of the governed, That whenever any Form of Government becomes destructive of these ends it is the Right of the People to alter or to abolish it, and to institute new Government, laying its foundation on such principles and organizing its powers in such form, as to them shall seem most likely to effect their Safety and Happiness. Prudence, indeed, will dictate that Governments long established should not be changed for light and **transient** causes; and accordingly all experience hath shown, that mankind are more disposed to suffer, while evils are sufferable, than to right themselves by abolishing the forms to which they are accustomed. But when a long train of abuses and **usurpations**, pursuing invariably the same Object **evinces** a design to reduce them under absolute **Despotism**, it is their right, it is their duty, to throw off such Government, and to provide new Guards for their future security.—Such has been the patient sufferance of these Colonies; and such is now the necessity which constrains them to alter their former Systems of Government. The history of the present King of Great Britain is a history of repeated injuries and usurpations, all having in direct object the establishment of an absolute Tyranny over these States. To prove this, let Facts be submitted to a candid world.

He has refused his Assent to Laws, the most wholesome and necessary for the public good.

He has forbidden his Governors to pass Laws of immediate and pressing importance, unless suspended in their operation till his Assent should be obtained; and when so suspended, he has utterly neglected to attend to them.

He has refused to pass other Laws for the accommodation of large districts of

> ● ● ● ● ● ● ●
> We hold these truths to be self-evident, that all men are created equal…
> ● ● ● ● ● ● ●

impel—to force or drive to an action

self-evident—needing no explanation, obvious

unalienable—unable to be taken away

transient—passing away quickly

usurpations—the act of seizing without legal right

evinces—shows clearly

despotism—unlimited power or authority

FOCUS ON... MATH

One of the many contributions Jefferson made to American society was the application of the decimal system used in the monetary system of the United States. What are the advantages of a decimal system? Describe how Jefferson's system works.

◆ ◆ ◆ ◆ ◆ ◆ ◆ ◆ ◆ ◆ ◆ ◆ ◆ ◆ ◆ ◆ ◆

inestimable—too valuable to be measured

annihilation—complete destruction

tenure—the time during which something is held

people, unless those people would relinquish the right of Representation in the Legislature, a right **inestimable** to them and formidable to tyrants only.

He has called together legislative bodies at places unusual, uncomfortable, and distant from the depository of their Public Records, for the sole purpose of fatiguing them into compliance with his measures.

He has dissolved Representative Houses repeatedly, for opposing with manly firmness his invasions on the rights of the people.

He has refused for a long time, after such dissolutions, to cause others to be elected; whereby the Legislative Powers, incapable of **Annihilation**, have returned to the People at large for their exercise; the State remaining in the mean time exposed to all the dangers of invasion from without, and convulsions within.

He has endeavored to prevent the population of these States; for that purpose obstructing the Laws for Naturalization of Foreigners; refusing to pass others to encourage their migration hither, and raising the conditions of new Appropriations of Lands.

He has obstructed the Administration of Justice, by refusing his Assent to Laws for establishing Judiciary Powers.

He has made Judges dependent on his Will alone for the **tenure** of their offices, and the amount and payment of their salaries.

He has erected a multitude of New Offices, and sent hither swarms of Officers to harrass our people and eat out their substance.

He has kept among us in times of peace, Standing Armies, without the Consent of our legislatures.

He has affected to render the Military independent of, and superior to, the Civil Power.

He has combined with others to subject us to a jurisdiction foreign to our constitutions, and unacknowledged by our laws; giving his Assent to their Acts of pretended Legislation:

For quartering large bodies of armed troops among us;

For protecting them, by a mock Trial, from punishment for any Murders which they should commit on the Inhabitants of these States;

For cutting off our Trade with all parts of the world;

For imposing taxes on us without our Consent;

For depriving us, in many cases, of the benefits of Trial by Jury;

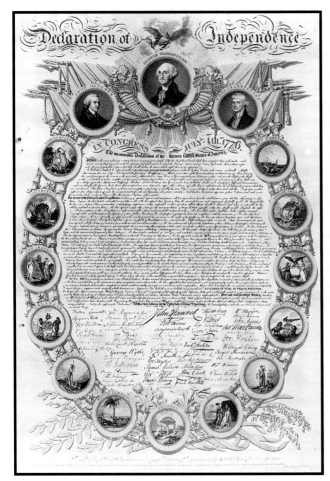

SPOTLIGHT ON... USING LOGIC

Thomas Jefferson was very precise in his wording of the Declaration of Independence. He allowed logic and reason to guide him. Practice the following guidelines as you use logic.

1. Use available information to draw logical conclusions about a situation.
2. When presented with an argument or a set of facts and conclusions, determine which conclusions logically follow from the facts.
3. Discover what, if anything, seems to link two or more objects, events, or people. Use this information to draw conclusions.

For transporting us beyond Seas, to be tried for pretended offences;

For abolishing the free System of English Laws in a neighboring Province, establishing therein an **Arbitrary** government, and enlarging its Boundaries, so as to render it at once an example and fit instrument for introducing the same absolute rule into these Colonies;

For taking away our Charters, abolishing our most valuable Laws, and altering fundamentally the Forms of our Governments;

For suspending our own Legislatures, and declaring themselves invested with Power to legislate for us in all cases whatsoever.

He has abdicated Government here, by declaring us out of his Protection, and waging War against us.

He has plundered our seas, ravaged our Coasts, burned our towns, and destroyed the lives of our people.

He is at this time transporting large Armies of foreign Mercenaries to complete the works of death, desolation and tyranny, already begun with circumstances of Cruelty and **perfidy** scarcely paralleled in the most barbarous ages, and totally unworthy the Head of a civilized nation.

He has constrained our fellow Citizens taken Captive on the high Seas to bear Arms against their Country, to become the executioners of their friends and Brethren, or to fall themselves by their Hands.

He has excited domestic **insurrections** amongst us, and has endeavored to bring on the inhabitants of our frontiers the merciless Indian Savages whose known rule of warfare is an undistinguished destruction of all ages, sexes, and conditions.

In every stage of these Oppressions We have Petitioned for **Redress** in the most humble terms. Our repeated Petitions have

arbitrary—not guided by rules or law

perfidy—breaking faith, treachery

insurrections—rebellions or uprisings

redress—correction or satisfaction

been answered only by repeated injury. A Prince, whose character is thus marked by every act which may define a Tyrant, is unfit to be the ruler of a free people.

Nor have We been wanting in attention to our British brethren. We have warned them from time to time of attempts by their legislature to extend an unwarrantable jurisdiction over us. We have reminded them of the circumstances of our emigration and settlement here. We have appealed to their native justice and **magnanimity**, and we have **conjured** them by the ties of our common kindred to disavow these usurpations, which would inevitably interrupt our connections and correspondence. They too have been deaf to the voice of justice and of **consanguinity**. We must, therefore, **acquiesce** in the necessity, which denounces our Separation, and hold them, as we hold the rest of mankind, Enemies in War, in Peace Friends.

We, therefore, the Representatives of the United States of America, in General Congress, Assembled, appealing to the Supreme Judge of the world for the **rectitude** of our intentions, do, in the Name, and by the Authority of the good People of these Colonies, solemnly publish and declare, That these United Colonies are, and of Right ought to be Free and Independent States; that they

● ● ● ● ● ● ●

…these United Colonies are, and of Right ought to be Free and Independent States…

● ● ● ● ● ● ●

are Absolved from all Allegiance to the British Crown, and that all political connection between them and the State of Great Britain, is and ought to be totally dissolved, and that as Free and Independent States, they have full Power to levy War, conclude Peace, contract Alliances, establish Commerce, and to do all other Acts and Things which Independent States may of right do. And for the support of this Declaration, with a firm reliance on the Protection of Divine Providence, we mutually pledge to each other our Lives, our Fortunes and our sacred Honor. ❖

ACCENT ON...
DESKTOP PUBLISHING

● ● ● ● ● ● ● ● ● ● ● ● ● ● ● ● ● ●

Jefferson and his contemporaries worked laboriously not only writing and editing the Declaration of Independence, but also making clean, handwritten copies to distribute to all of the colonies. Word processing computer technology would have enabled Jefferson to disseminate the Declaration of Independence in a much quicker fashion. If possible, create portions of this document using a word processing program that has several different fonts. Then choose a font that best characterizes the words Jefferson wrote and word process the first page of the Declaration.

UNDERSTANDING

1. Find in the first paragraph of the Declaration of Independence the reason this document is being written.

   The colonists did not like the treatment they received from Britain. Think of times when the decisions someone else made negatively affected your life. Formulate clear, reasoned arguments in a letter to persuade that person to change his or her mind. *Workshop 10*

2. The second paragraph of the Declaration says certain truths are self-evident. Make a list of these truths, and next to each, write why you think each is, or is not, self-evident.

   Write your own Declaration of Independence, arguing for freedom from a situation, person, or condition you consider unjust. Be sure to follow the four-part order of Jefferson's work. *Workshop 1*

3. The phrase "He has" repeatedly precedes criminal acts of King George III. The word "For" repeatedly introduces wrongs by the British Parliament. Working with several classmates, name two acts among those listed that you think people would most condemn if they happened today. Write the reasons for your view. From these reasons, formulate a thesis for a brief speech that will persuade others of your position by giving sound reasons and using repetition to gain force.

4. Most people expect certain fundamental rights to be honored at work. Interview parents, students, and people in various occupations to discover the rights they connect with their work. Ask them to define "rights." Then ask them what they think their responsibilities are as employees. Make a chart for each occupation mentioned. In one column list "Rights" and in the other "Responsibilities."

CONNECTING

1. The colonists declared their independence only after exhausting all available political channels. Community groups and individuals also follow procedures to bring about changes. To see how these changes occur, attend a school board, city council, or town hall meeting. Note who runs the meeting, how to get an item placed on the agenda, and what issues are discussed. Do presenters use reason and logic as Jefferson did? Does the tone of the presentation affect the outcome of the decision? Write your findings in a one-page observation report. *Workshop 3*

2. Jefferson said that all men—not women—are created equal and have fundamental rights. Interview your parents, aunts, uncles, and grandparents. Keep a list of the rights they think women once lacked. Read articles about the rights women still lack. Make a colorful, poster-size chart or table that illustrates the different rights possessed by men and women over the past 100 years. *Workshop 20*

The Use of Force

EXPLORING

Think of a conflict that you have had with a person in authority, perhaps a parent, teacher, employer, or policeman. What began the conflict? How did you argue your position? Did you win or lose? What advice would you give to another student in the same situation? How would you "replay" your own situation to correct any mistakes you may have made?

THEME CONNECTION...
RESISTING AUTHORITY

"The Use of Force" presents a battle of wills. A child exercises her freedom to maintain her privacy and keep her secret. The adults around her use their authority and power to force her to submit. This story shows that when authority demands to have its way, both the oppressor and the oppressed suffer.

TIME & PLACE

"The Use of Force" takes place in the United States at the turn of the century, a time when doctors still made housecalls, $3.00 was considered a large sum of money, and the diphtheria vaccine was yet to be developed. Until this vaccine made possible widespread immunization against diphtheria, epidemics regularly swept the United States. Victims were usually under 10 years of age, and often they died. Symptoms of diphtheria included a sore throat, fever, and swollen neck glands. A gray membrane formed over the tonsils and in severe cases blocked the breathing passages.

THE WRITER'S CRAFT
PUNCTUATING FOR MEANING

William Carlos Williams wants the reader to feel the doctor's urgency in this story. He punctuates his sentences unconventionally to convey this feeling. The first two sentences could be four, but Williams uses commas rather than periods so that the reader experiences a sense of breathlessness right away.

The Use of Force

William Carlos Williams

 hey were new patients to me, all I had was the name, Olson. Please come down as soon as you can, my daughter is very sick.

When I arrived I was met by the mother, a big startled looking woman, very clean and apologetic who merely said, Is this the doctor? and let me in. In the back, she added. You must excuse us, doctor, we have her in the kitchen where it is warm. It is very damp here sometimes.

The child was fully dressed and sitting on her father's lap near the kitchen table. He tried to get up, but I motioned for him not to bother, took off my overcoat and started to look things over. I could see that they were all very nervous, eyeing me up and down distrustfully. As often, in such cases, they weren't telling me more than they had to, it was up to me to tell them; that's why they were spending three dollars on me.

The child was fairly eating me up with her cold steady eyes, and no expression to her face whatever. She did not move and seemed, inwardly, quiet; an unusually attractive little thing, and as strong as a **heifer** in appearance. But her face was flushed, she was breathing rapidly, and I realized that she had a high fever. She had magnificent blond hair, in **profusion**. One of those picture children often reproduced in advertising leaflets and the **photogravure** sections of the Sunday papers.

She's had a fever for three days, began the father, and we don't know what it comes from. My wife has given her things, you know, like people do, but it don't do no good. And there's been a lot of sickness around. So we tho't you'd better look her over and tell us what is the matter.

As doctors often do I took a trial shot at it as a point of departure. Has she had a sore throat?

Both parents answered me together, No . . . No, she says her throat don't hurt her.

Does your throat hurt you? added the mother to the child. But the little girl's expression didn't change, nor did she move her eyes from my face.

Have you looked?

I tried to, said the mother, but I couldn't see.

As it happens, we had been having a number of cases of **diphtheria** in the school to which this child went during that month and we were all, quite apparently, thinking of that, though no one had as yet spoken of the thing.

Well, I said, suppose we take a look at the throat first. I smiled in my best professional manner and asking for the child's first name I said, come on, Mathilda, open your mouth and let's take a look at your throat.

Nothing doing.

Aw, come on, I coaxed, just open your mouth wide and let me take a look. Look, I said opening both hands wide, I haven't anything in my hands. Just open up and let me see.

Such a nice man, put in the mother. Look how kind he is to you. Come on, do what he tells you to. He won't hurt you.

> ● ● ● ● ● ● ●
> I could see that they were all very nervous...
> ● ● ● ● ● ● ●

heifer—a young cow

profusion—a great supply

photogravure—a process for printing

diphtheria—a contagious disease marked by the formation of a false membrane, usually in the throat

FOCUS ON... SCIENCE

In his essay, Williams describes trying to obtain a throat culture in order to test for diphtheria. Before the 1920s, when immunization with diphtheria vaccines became available, diphtheria epidemics swept across the United States and Europe. Diphtheria is caused by a bacterium that usually infects the tonsils, upper throat, and breathing passages. Research and then write two or three paragraphs that describe the process used to identify the diphtheria bacterium, including the laboratory work involved in processing a throat culture as well as the treatment used to cure this serious disease.

◆ ◆

culture—a growth of bacteria

contemptible—deserving scorn, despicable

ensuing—following

abject—hopeless, spiritless

At that I ground my teeth in disgust. If only they wouldn't use the word "hurt" I might be able to get somewhere. But I did not allow myself to be hurried or disturbed, but speaking quietly and slowly I approached the child again.

As I moved my chair a little nearer, suddenly with one catlike movement both her hands clawed instinctively for my eyes and she almost reached them too. In fact she knocked my glasses flying and they fell, though unbroken, several feet away from me on the kitchen floor.

Both the mother and father almost turned themselves inside out in embarrassment and apology. You bad girl, said the mother, taking her and shaking her by one arm. Look what you've done. The nice man. . . .

For heaven's sake, I broke in. Don't call me a nice man to her. I'm here to look at her throat on the chance that she might have diphtheria and possibly die of it. But that's nothing to her. Look here, I said to the child, we're going to look at

• • • • • • •
Look here, I said to the child, we're going to look at your throat.
• • • • • • •

your throat. You're old enough to understand what I'm saying. Will you open it now by yourself or shall we have to open it for you?

Not a move. Even her expression hadn't changed. Her breaths however were coming faster and faster. Then the battle began. I had to do it. I had to have a throat **culture** for her own protection. But first I told the parents that it was entirely up to them. I explained the danger but said that I would not insist on a throat examination so long as they would take the responsibility.

If you don't do what the doctor says you'll have to go to the hospital, the mother admonished her severely.

Oh yeah? I had to smile to myself. After all, I had already fallen in love with the savage brat, the parents were **contemptible** to me. In the **ensuing** struggle they grew more and more **abject**, crushed, exhausted while she surely rose to magnificent heights of insane fury of effort bred of her terror of me.

The father tried his best, and he was a big man but the fact that she was his daughter, his shame at her behavior and his dread of hurting her made him release her just at the critical moment several times when I had almost achieved success, till I wanted to kill him. But his dread also that she might have diphtheria made him tell me to go on, go on though he himself was almost fainting, while the mother moved back and forth behind us raising and lowering her hands in an agony of apprehension.

Put her in front of you on your lap, I ordered, and hold both her wrists.

But as soon as he did the child let out a scream. Don't, you're hurting me. Let go of my hands. Let them go I tell you. Then she shrieked terrifyingly, hysterically. Stop it! Stop it! You're killing me!

Do you think she can stand it, doctor! said the mother.

> ...the worst of it was that I too had got beyond reason.

You get out, said the husband to his wife. Do you want her to die of diphtheria?

Come on now, hold her, I said.

Then I grasped the child's head with my left hand and tried to get the wooden tongue depressor between her teeth. She fought, with clenched teeth, desperately! But now I also had grown furious—at a child. I tried to hold myself down but I couldn't. I know how to expose a throat for inspection. And I did my best. When finally I got the wooden spatula behind the last teeth and just the point of it into the mouth cavity, she opened up for an instant but before I could see anything she came down again and gripping the wooden blade between her molars she reduced it to splinters before I could get it out again.

Aren't you ashamed, the mother yelled at her. Aren't you ashamed to act like that in front of the doctor?

The Use of Force

Get me a smooth-handled spoon of some sort, I told the mother. We're going through with this. The child's mouth was already bleeding. Her tongue was cut and she was screaming in wild hysterical shrieks. Perhaps I should have **desisted** and come back in an hour or more. No doubt it would have been better. But I have seen at least two children lying dead in bed of neglect in such cases, and feeling that I must get a diagnosis now or never I went at it again. But the worst of it was that I too had got beyond reason. I could have torn the child apart in my own fury and enjoyed it. It was a pleasure to attack her. My face was burning with it.

The damned little brat must be protected against her own idiocy, one says to one's self at such times. Others must be protected against her. It is social necessity. And all these things are true. But a blind fury, a feeling of adult shame, bred of a longing for muscular release are the operatives. One goes on to the end.

In a final unreasoning assault I overpowered the child's neck and jaws. I forced the heavy silver spoon back of her teeth and down her throat till she gagged. And there it was—both tonsils covered with membrane. She had fought **valiantly** to keep me from knowing her secret. She had been hiding that sore throat for three days at least and lying to her parents in order to escape just such an outcome as this.

Now truly she was furious. She had been on the defensive before but now she attacked. Tried to get off her father's lap and fly at me while tears of defeat blinded her eyes. ❖

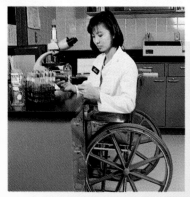

ON THE JOB
MEDICAL LAB TECHNICIAN

A medical laboratory technician usually needs at least two years of post-secondary education, with a concentration of classes in biology and chemistry. Experience in computer technology is also helpful. Lab technicians make cultures of body fluid or tissue samples to determine the presence of bacteria and other micro-organisms. They also may examine blood samples and provide test data to help in the diagnosis and treatment of disease.

ACCENT ON...
HEALTHCARE FOR CHILDREN

As a young physician, William Carlos Williams made house calls. Today, doctors see children in their offices. What is the impact of a doctor's office on patients, especially children? Discover how doctors care for children between the ages of 6-12 who must come to their offices for treatment. Draw partly on your own recollections. Arrange to visit the office of a general practitioner or pediatrician to study its atmosphere. Write a brief description of the office you visit, detailing types of games, activities, books, or other diversions that might comfort children or pass the time. Notice furniture, supplies, and equipment. Include diagrams of the physical layout of the waiting and examination rooms. Interview nurses to find out how long patients are kept waiting.

UNDERSTANDING

1. In a group, keep track of the doctor's thoughts, actions, and words to Mathilda and her parents from the time he first arrives at their home until he says, "Will you open it now by yourself or shall we have to open it for you?" Divide your paper into into three categories: *Private Thoughts, Actions,* and *Spoken Words.* Categorize what the doctor says and does under these headings.

   With your group, define the word "professional" as it refers to an employee's behavior. Using your lists, argue in a paragraph that the doctor does, or does not, behave professionally during the early part of the story. ***Workshop 12***

2. Find passages in the story that show the doctor's professionalism beginning to crumble. What stresses were on the doctor? Why did he fight and not give up? Many companies reward employees for being praised in a customer's letter. Think of a professional person, store clerk, waiter, or other worker who has behaved professionally towards you. Write a letter of appreciation to the person's employer describing his or her excellent treatment of you.

3. Explain Mathilda's behavior. What fears does she seems to have? What words or behavior might convince her to cooperate? What would you have said or done had you been present to convince Mathilda to open her mouth?

   Brainstorm to identify jobs that call for workers who can keep calm in any crisis. Write a letter of recommendation for a friend you think would do well in one of these jobs. ***Workshop 11***

A LAST WORD

When a conflict turns emotional, it is easy to lose control, as the doctor did when examining Mathilda. How would you maintain self-control if someone tried to prevent you from doing something you strongly believed was necessary?

CONNECTING

1. This story is well known. Do you think it should be included in the curriculum of a medical school? Interview a doctor to find out if she has read this story. If not, give her a brief summary. Ask the doctor you interview if she feels this story would offer any insights to medical students. What could they learn from the story? Also, ask the doctor to define "professionalism" in medicine. Then find out whether medical schools teach "professionalism" to doctors in any formal way. Report your findings to your class. ***Workshop 12***

2. Gather information from as many sources as possible about three occupations related to medicine. What jobs exist? What education do they require, what duties do they entail, and how much do they pay? Write a brief report on the feasibility of making a living at each of these jobs. Make a graph or chart that shows the salary range. You may wish to do additional research on a medical occupation that especially interests you. ***Workshop 20***

The Price of Liberty

- *from* Narrative of the Life of Frederick Douglass, An American Slave, Written by Himself
- The Gettysburg Address

EXPLORING

● ● ● ● ● ● ● ● ● ● ● ● ● ● ● ● ● ● ● ●

Students go to school to get an education. The purpose of education is to help students make the most of their potential—their potential to acquire knowledge and skills and to develop character. Education serves the economic and social well-being of each person and of the entire nation. Since education is essential to personal well-being, how would you feel if you were no longer permitted to attend school?

Another crucial component of personal and national well-being is freedom. Some modern commentators have suggested that the twentieth century is the century of wars. To what extent has freedom been an issue in these wars? Under what circumstances do you think a country should be willing to fight for freedom?

THEME CONNECTION...
STRUGGLES FOR FREEDOM

Frederick Douglass understood the immense importance of literacy in a democracy. Education, he wrote, invests man with "power that shall open to him the treasures of freedom." Abraham Lincoln says the Civil War was being fought to bring about "a new birth of freedom. . . ." Liberty comes with responsibilities to educate oneself and to guard against any threats to freedom.

TIME & PLACE

Frederick Douglass wrote his autobiography in 1845, seven years after he had escaped from slavery. Until 1865, it was illegal in many states to teach slaves to read and write, since this would make slaves "unfit" for slavery.

By the time the Civil War broke out in 1861, Douglass was an advisor to President Abraham Lincoln. Douglass convinced the president to make the abolition of slavery a primary issue of the war. Though Lincoln does not directly address this issue in his speech, he does commemorate the soldiers who died in its cause. Lincoln delivered his speech in November 1863 at Gettysburg, Pennsylvania, the site of one of the war's bloodiest battles.

THE WRITER'S CRAFT

REPETITION

Douglass and Lincoln both use repetition to emphasize their points. Douglass employs a simple, direct style, often repeating the same sentence structure to underscore the diligence with which he learned to read and write. Lincoln repeats key words and phrases: "We cannot dedicate—we cannot consecrate—we cannot hallow this ground. The brave men . . . have consecrated it. . . ." These words touch our feelings as they recur throughout the address.

● ●

from *Narrative of the Life of Frederick Douglass, An American Slave, Written by Himself*
Learning to Read and Write

Frederick Douglass

 lived in Master Hugh's family about seven years. During this time, I succeeded in learning to read and write. In accomplishing this, I was compelled to resort to various **stratagems**. I had no regular teacher. My mistress, who had kindly commenced to instruct me, had, in compliance with the advice and direction of her husband, not only ceased to instruct, but had set her face against my being instructed by anyone else. It is due, however, to my mistress to say of her, that she did not adopt this course of treatment immediately. She at first lacked the **depravity** indispensable to shutting me up in mental darkness. It was at least necessary for her to have some training in the exercise of irresponsible power, to make her equal to the task of treating me as though I were a brute.

My mistress was, as I have said, a kind and tender-hearted woman; and in the simplicity of her soul she commenced, when I first went to live with her, to treat me as she supposed one human being ought to treat another. In entering upon the duties of a slaveholder, she did not seem to perceive that I sustained to her the relation of a mere **chattel**, and that for her to treat me as a human being was not only wrong, but dangerously so. Slavery proved as injurious to her as it did to me. When I went there, she was a pious, warm, and tender-hearted woman. There was no sorrow or suffering for which she had not a tear. She had bread for the hungry, clothes for the naked, and comfort for every mourner that came within her reach. Slavery soon proved its ability to **divest** her of these heavenly qualities. Under its influence, the tender heart became stone, and the lamblike disposition gave way to one of tiger-like fierceness. The first step in her downward course was in her ceasing to instruct me. She now commenced to practice her husband's precepts. She finally became even more violent in her opposition than her husband himself. She was not satisfied with simply doing as well as he had commanded; she seemed anxious to do better. Nothing seemed to make her more angry than to see me with a newspaper. She seemed to think that here lay the danger. I have had her rush at me with a face made all up of fury, and snatch from me a newspaper, in a manner that fully revealed her apprehension. She was an apt woman; and a little experience soon demonstrated, to her satisfaction, that education and slavery were **incompatible** with each other.

From this time I was most narrowly watched. If I was in a separate room any considerable length of time, I was sure to be suspected of having a book, and was at once called to give an account of myself. All this, however, was too late. The first step had been taken. Mistress, in teaching me the alphabet, had given me the *inch*, and no precaution could prevent me from taking the *ell*.

The plan which I adopted, and the one by which I was most successful, was that of making friends of all the little white

About the Author

Born into slavery in Maryland in 1817, Frederick Douglass escaped to freedom in Massachusetts in 1838. Though he feared recapture, from 1841 until 1845 Douglass lectured openly against slavery. In 1845 he wrote his autobiography and spent the next two years in Britain seeking support for the abolitionist cause. Upon his return, Douglass founded the *North Star* anti-slavery newspaper and aided the Underground Railroad, a network of people who helped slaves escape to freedom. After the Civil War, Douglass was named a United States marshal of Washington, D.C., and in 1889–1891, he served as the ambassador to Haiti.

stratagem—a trick or scheme

depravity—corruption or evil

chattel—property

divest—to take away from

incompatible—incapable of existing at the same time or place

ell—a unit of length equal to 45 inches

SPOTLIGHT ON...
BRINGING ABOUT CHANGE

In the excerpt from his autobiography, Fredrick Douglass adopts a plan to learn how to read and write. When trying to bring about a change, whether it is to improve your own skills or improving your community, you should plan carefully. Use the following steps as a starting point:

• Lay out your plan in a logical manner.
• List specific ways and means for success.
• Itemize the resources needed in time, money, and human effort.
• Plan ways to acquire resources.
• Review your plan periodically and update it if necessary.

boys whom I met in the street. As many of these as I could, I converted into teachers. With their kindly aid, obtained at different times and in different places, I finally succeeded in learning to read. When I was sent on errands, I always took my book with me, and by doing one part of my errand quickly, I found time to get a lesson before my return. I used also to carry bread with me, enough of which was always in the house, and to which I was always welcome; for I was much better off in this regard than many of the poor white children in our neighborhood. This bread I used to bestow upon the hungry little urchins, who, in return, would give me that more valuable bread of knowledge. . . .

The idea as to how I might learn to write was suggested to me by being in Durgin and Bailey's shipyard, and frequently seeing the ship carpenters, after hewing, and getting a piece of timber ready for use, write on the timber the name of that part of the ship for which it was intended. When a piece of timber was intended for the larboard side, it would be marked thus—"L." When a piece was for the starboard side, it would be marked

thus—"S." A piece for the larboard side forward, would be marked thus—"L.F." When a piece was for starboard side forward, it would be marked thus—"S.F." For larboard aft, it would be marked thus—"L.A." For starboard aft, it would be marked thus—"S.A." I soon learned the names of these letters, and for what they were intended when placed upon a piece of timber in the shipyard. I immediately commenced copying them, and in a short time was able to make the four letters named. After that, when I met with any boy who I knew could write, I would tell him I could write as well as he. The next word would be, "I don't believe you. Let me see you try it." I would then make the letters which I had been so fortunate as to learn, and ask him to beat that. In this way I got a good many lessons in writing, which it is quite possible I should never have gotten in any other way. During this time, my copy-book was the board fence, brick wall, and pavement; my pen and ink was a lump of chalk. With these, I learned mainly how to write. I then commenced and continued copying the Italics in *Webster's Spelling Book*, until I could

FOCUS ON...
PHOTOGRAPHY

FOCUS ON...
PHOTOGRAPHY

Many of the people and events of Douglass's and Lincoln's times were captured in photographs, and news photography as we know it today began in the mid-1800s. In the United States, Mathew Brady was the unofficial photographer of the Civil War, recording the horror and anguish of battle. Through his pictures, we see the ravages of war on real human beings in unforgettable clarity. Find some examples of his photography in history books. Based on these photographs, how do you think photographs help to shape public opinion about war? Compare his photographs with pictures from the Vietnam War, the war in Bosnia, or the civil strife in Rwanda. How does photography help shape public policy?

make them all without looking on the book. By this time, my little Master Thomas had gone to school, and learned how to write, and had written over a number of copy-books. These had been brought home, and shown to some of our near neighbors, and then laid aside. My mistress used to go to class meeting at the Wilk Street meeting-house every Monday afternoon, and leave me to take care of the house. When left thus, I used to spend the time in writing in the spaces left in Master Thomas's copy-book, copying what he had written. I continued to do this until I could write a hand very similar to that of Master Thomas. Thus, after a long, **tedious** effort for years, I finally succeeded in learning how to write. ❖

tedious—tiresome

ACCENT ON...
PRINTING
TECHNOLOGY

One reason Douglass wrote his autobiography was to give final form to personal details and stories he had been using in his talks and lectures at anti-slavery rallies. Many people have fascinating life stories to tell, but they don't write them in part because they have no idea how the publishing industry works. If you were going to write your life story, how would you find a publisher? What length would you recommend for the book? What would you include for cover art? What type of paper would you use? Would you include pictures in color? How many copies would you issue at the first printing? What marketing and sales strategy would you use? Write up your proposed plan and explain what technical solutions you would include.

The Gettysburg Address

Abraham Lincoln

About the Author

Abraham Lincoln (1809–1865) holds a cherished, honored place in American history. He is considered one of the most important leaders in modern times for his unwavering belief in democracy and for his ability to hold the United States together during the greatest test it ever faced. He became a lawyer, public servant, and eventually President. He helped abolish slavery and proved himself as a daring military leader. Lincoln's Gettysburg Address, Second Inaugural Address, and many other speeches, essays, and letters are evidence of his great writing ability.

Four **score** and seven years ago our fathers brought forth on this continent a new nation, conceived in liberty, and dedicated to the proposition that all men are created equal.

Now we are engaged in a great civil war, testing whether that nation, or any nation so conceived and so dedicated, can long endure. We are met on a great battlefield of that war. We have come to dedicate a portion of that field as a final resting place for those who here gave their lives that that nation might live. It is altogether fitting and proper that we should do this.

But, in a larger sense, we cannot dedicate—we cannot **consecrate**—we cannot **hallow**—this ground. The brave men, living and dead, who struggled here have consecrated it far above our poor power to add or detract. The world will little note nor long remember what we say here, but it can never forget what they did here. It is for us, the living, rather, to be dedicated here to the unfinished work which they who fought here have thus far so nobly advanced. It is rather for us to be here dedicated to the great task remaining before us—that from these honored dead we take increased devotion to that cause for which they gave the last full measure of devotion; that we here highly resolve that these dead shall not have died in vain; that this nation, under God, shall have a new birth of freedom; and that government of the people, by the people, for the people, shall not perish from the earth. ❖

score—twenty

consecrate—to make or declare sacred

hallow—to make holy

UNDERSTANDING

1. Douglass writes of his master's wife, "Slavery proved as injurious to her as it did to me." In what ways was she injured?

   Education should do more than fill the head with facts. In a group, decide on the benefits an education should provide. Write an essay about the purpose of education by collaborating on the thesis and the major points to cover. ***Workshop 1***

2. Douglass learned without the help of trained teachers and a classroom. Infer from the text why he was so passionately motivated to learn: What does his denial of an education say about society at the time?

   Many people develop skills or knowledge without formal instruction. Write a set of simple instructions explaining how to do something you taught yourself or learned outside of school. Use graphics to help readers understand the text. ***Workshop 4***

3. Lincoln begins and ends his speech by reminding listeners of the principles upon which this nation was founded. What are these principles? Do your friends and family live by them? Use specific examples to support your position.

   Outline a short speech that addresses a specific event, action, or person that either threatens to weaken or offers hope of strengthening the principle that *all persons are created equal.* Use repetition as Lincoln did to emphasize key points.

4. How many times does Lincoln refer to women? A speaker today would not use the phrase "all men are created equal" because the term "men" excludes women. Gender-fair language is the rule in the workplace. It is no longer appropriate to use *chairman*, *spokesman*, or *foreman* because women may hold these positions. Make a list of five sexist words, such as *stewardess*, and write a non-sexist synonym for each. Compare your list with those of others in the class. Then prepare a pamphlet containing a glossary of non-sexist terms. ***Workshops 20 and 21***

A LAST WORD

What price are you willing to pay for liberty? Would you have the dedication Douglass and the soldiers who fought at Gettysburg exhibited? Is freedom worth the price they paid?

CONNECTING

1. School is not the only place that provides opportunities to learn. What other educational opportunities exist for people in your area? Prepare a pamphlet describing things people can learn outside of school and indicating where they can find instruction. ***Workshops 20 and 21***

2. In many occupations, employees make oral presentations. Many theme park employees and flight attendants deliver memorized speeches. Think about the kinds of oral communication required in jobs you have held. Collaborate to research the kinds of oral communication required by a cross-section of occupations. Compile your findings in a notebook that lists your discoveries. ***Workshop 19***

Train Time

EXPLORING

Do you think one person can make a positive difference in a community? If a *community* is a group of people sharing common interests, in what communities are you a participant? For instance, your classroom is a community, just as your home, your school and your city are communities. In what ways do you participate? What influence do you have as one voice in a community?

THEME CONNECTION...
VALUING FREEDOM

Today many of us take our freedoms for granted, such as our freedom of religion, freedom of speech, and so on. However, many people in the history of the United States have not had the same freedoms and rights. Westward expansion in the 1800s and 1900s deprived Native Americans of many rights. Some Native Americans are still fighting today to regain these rights.

TIME & PLACE

Written in the 1930s, "Train Time" appears to have taken place on the Flathead Reservation in Montana, where the author was born. Like the author, the main character Eneas is probably a Flathead, a member of the Salish-speaking tribe in western Montana.

At the time the story takes place in the 1920s or 1930s, the railroad had already established itself as an integral part of Anglo-American culture; at the same time it helped to break down the culture of Native Americans.

THE WRITER'S CRAFT

FLASHBACK

Usually stories unfold in chronological order, moving in a straight line from first events to last. In the story that follows, however, the author uses a flashback technique. A *flashback* is an interruption in a natural time sequence to describe earlier events. This technique also occurs in movies and allows an author to present the beginning of a story in a dramatic way. As you read, think about why the author decides to have Major Miles remember the past as he stands waiting for the train.

Train Time

D'Arcy McNickle

n the depot platform everybody stood waiting, listening. The train has just whistled, somebody said. They stood listening and gazing eastward, where railroad tracks and creek emerged together from a tree-choked canyon.

Twenty-five boys, five girls, Major Miles—all stood waiting and gazing eastward. Was it true that the train had whistled?

"That was no train!" a boy's voice explained.

"It was a steer bellowing."

"It was the train!"

Girls crowded backward against the station building, heads hanging, tears starting; boys pushed forward to the edge of the platform. An older boy with a voice already turning heavy stepped off the weather-shredded boardwalk and stood widelegged in the middle of the track. He was the doubter. He had heard no train.

Major Miles boomed, "You! What's your name? Get back here! Want to get killed! All of you, stand back!"

The Major strode about, soldierlike, and waved commands. He was **exasperated**. He was tired. A man driving cattle through timber had it easy, he was thinking. An animal trainer had no idea of trouble. Let anyone try corraling twenty to thirty Indian kids, dragging them out of hiding places, getting them away from relatives and together in one place, then holding them, without tying them, until train time! Even now, at the last moment, when his worries were almost over, they were trying to get themselves killed!

Major Miles was a man of conscience. Whatever he did, he did earnestly. On this hot end-of-summer day he perspired and frowned and wore his soldier bearing. He removed his hat from his wet brow and thoughtfully passed his hand from the hair line backward. Words tumbled about in his mind. Somehow, he realized, he had to **vivify** the moment. These children were about to go out from the Reservation and get a new start. Life would change. They ought to realize it, somehow—

"Boys—and girls—" there were five girls he remembered. He had got them all lined up against the building, safely away from the edge of the platform. The air was stifling with end-of-summer heat. It was time to say something, never mind the heat. Yes, he would have to make the moment real. He stood soldierlike and thought that.

"Boys and girls—" The train whistled, dully, but unmistakably. Then it repeated more clearly. The rails came to life, something was running through them and making them sing.

Just then the Major's eye fell upon little Eneas and his sure voice **faltered**. He knew about little Eneas. Most of the boys and girls were mere names; he had seen them around the Agency with their parents, or had caught sight of them scurrying behind tipis and barns when he visited their homes. But little Eneas he knew. With him before his eyes, he paused.

He remembered so clearly the winter day, six months ago, when he first saw Eneas. It was the boy's grandfather, Michel Lamartine, he had gone to see. Michel had contracted to cut wood for the Agency but

About the Author

Born on Montana's Flathead Reservation, D'Arcy McNickle (1904–77) was first educated, like the main character in "Train Time," in a traditional boarding school. McNickle became a university professor after attending the University of Montana, Oxford University in England, and the University of Grenoble in France. As a professor of anthropology at the University of Saskatchewan in Canada, McNickle studied Native American experiences, customs, and history. He helped found the National Congress of American Indians and won fame for his short stories and novels about Native Americans.

exasperated—annoyed or irritated

vivify—to give life to

faltered—hesitated; spoke or moved in an unsteady fashion

FOCUS ON...
HISTORY

Many events during this period of United States history made life difficult for Native Americans. Using reference books or on-line database services, gather information on other groups of people who were forced from their homes. Choose from the following groups: Native Americans; Japanese-Americans, Jews, and Poles during WWII; Bosnians in Eastern Europe; Palestinians in the Middle East; and South American Indian tribes. In an essay, describe the groups of people, the reasons for their relocation, and the result of the relocation. You may also wish to prepare a map that illustrates the location of the groups before and after they were forced to move.

◆ ◆ ◆ ◆ ◆ ◆ ◆ ◆ ◆ ◆ ◆ ◆ ◆ ◆ ◆ ◆ ◆ ◆

ponderous—large, heavy, or lumbering

sustenance—food or nourishment

had not started work. The Major had gone to discover why not.

It was the coldest day of the winter, late in February, and the cabin, sheltered as it was among the pine and cottonwood of a creek bottom, was shot through by frosty drafts. There was wood all about them. Lamartine was a woodcutter besides, yet there was no wood in the house. The fire in the flat-topped cast-iron stove burned weakly. The reason was apparent. The Major had but to look at the bed where Lamartine lay, twisted and shrunken by rheumatism. Only his black eyes burned with life. He tried to wave a hand as the Major entered.

"You see how I am!" the gesture indicated. Then a nerve-strung voice faltered. "We have it bad here. My old woman, she's not much good."

Clearly she wasn't, not for wood-chopping. She sat close by the fire, trying with a good-natured grin to lift her **ponderous** body from a low seated rocking chair. The Major had to motion her back to her ease. She breathed with an asthmatic roar. Wood-chopping was not within her range. With only a squaw's hatchet to work with, she could scarcely have come within striking distance of a stick of wood. Two blows, if she had struck them, might have put a stop to her laboring heart.

"You see how it is," Lamartine's eyes flashed.

The Major saw clearly. Sitting there in the frosty cabin, he pondered their plight and at the same time wondered if he would get away without coming down with pneumonia. A stream of wind seemed to be hitting him in the back of the neck. Of course, there was nothing to do. One saw too many such situations. If one undertook to provide **sustenance** out of one's own pocket there would be no end to the demands. Government salaries were small, resources were limited. He could do no more than shake his head sadly, offer some vague hope, some small sympathy. He would have to get away at once.

Then a hand fumbled at the door; it opened. After a moment's struggle, little Eneas appeared, staggering under a full armload of pine limbs hacked into short lengths. The boy was no taller than an ax handle, his nose was running, and he had a croupy cough. He dropped the wood into the empty box near the old woman's chair, then straightened himself.

A soft chuckling came from the bed. Lamartine was full of pride. "A good boy, that. He keeps the old folks warm."

Something about the boy made the Major forget his determination to depart. Perhaps it was his wordlessness, his uncomplaining wordlessness. Or possibly it was his loyalty to the old people. Something drew his eyes to the boy and set him to thinking. Eneas was handing sticks of wood to the old woman and she was feeding them into the stove. When the firebox was full a good part of the boy's armload was gone. He would have to cut more, and more, to keep the old people warm.

The Major heard himself saying suddenly: "Sonny, show me your woodpile. Let's cut a lot of wood for the old folks."

It happened just like that, **inexplicably**. He went even farther. Not only did he cut enough wood to last through several days, but when he had finished he put the boy in the Agency car and drove him to town, five miles there and back. Against his own principles, he bought a week's store of groceries, and excused himself by telling the boy, as they drove homeward, "Your grandfather won't be able to get to town for a few days yet. Tell him to come see me when he gets well."

That was the beginning of the Major's interest in Eneas. He had decided that day that he would help the boy in any way possible, because he was a boy of quality. You would be shirking your duty if you failed to recognize and to help a boy of his sort. The only question was, how to help?

When he saw the boy again, some weeks later, his mind saw the problem clearly.

● ● ● ● ● ● ●
These children were about to go out from the Reservation and get a new start.
● ● ● ● ● ● ●

"Eneas," he said, "I'm going to help you. I'll see that the old folks are taken care of, so you won't have to think about them. Maybe the old man won't have rheumatism next year, anyhow. If he does, I'll find a family where he and the old lady can move in and be looked after. Don't worry about them. Just think about yourself and what I'm going to do for you. Eneas, when it comes school time, I'm going to send you away. How do you like that?" The Major smiled at his own happy idea.

There was silence. No shy smiling, no look of gratitude, only silence. Probably he had not understood.

"You understand, Eneas? Your grandparents will be taken care of. You'll go away and learn things. You'll go on a train."

The boy looked here and there and scratched at the ground with his foot. "Why do I have to go away?"

"You don't have to, Eneas. Nobody will make you. I thought you'd like to. I thought—" The Major paused, confused.

"You won't make me go away, will you?" There was fear in the voice, tears threatened.

"Why, no Eneas. If you don't want to go. I thought—"

The Major dropped the subject. He didn't see the boy again through spring and summer, but he thought of him. In fact, he couldn't forget the picture he had of him that first day. He couldn't forget either that he wanted to help him. Whether the boy understood what was good for him or not, he meant to see to it that the right thing was done. And that was why, when he made up a quota of children to be sent to the school in Oregon, the name of Eneas Lamartine was included. The Major did not discuss it with him again but he set the

inexplicably— impossible to explain

emerged—came forth

remorse—regret or anguish

wheels in motion. The boy would go with the others. In time to come, he would understand. Possibly he would be grateful.

Thirty children were included in the quota, and of them all Eneas was the only one the Major had actual knowledge of, the only one in whom he was personally interested. With each of them, it was true, he had had difficulties. None had wanted to go. They said they "liked it at home," or they were "afraid" to go away, or they would "get sick" in a strange country; and the parents were no help. They, too, were frightened and uneasy. It was a tiresome, hard kind of duty, but the Major knew what was required of him and never hesitated. The difference was, that in the cases of all these others, the problem was routine. He met it, and passed over it. But in the case of Eneas, he was bothered. He wanted to make clear what this moment of going away meant. It was a breaking away from fear and doubt and ignorance. Here began the new. Mark it, remember it.

His eyes lingered on Eneas. There he stood, drooping, his nose running as on that first day, his stockings coming down, his jacket in need of buttons. But under that shabbiness, the Major knew, was real quality. There was a boy who, with the right help, would blossom and grow strong. It was important that he should not go away hurt and resentful.

The Major called back his straying thoughts and cleared his throat. The moment was important.

"Boys and girls—"

The train was pounding near. Already it had **emerged** from the canyon, and momentarily the headlong flying locomotive loomed blacker and larger. A white plume flew upward—*Whoo-oo, whoo-oo.*

The Major realized in sudden sharp **remorse** that he had waited too long. The vital moment had come, and he had paused, looked for words, and lost it. The roar of rolling steel was upon them.

Lifting his voice in desperate haste, his eyes fastened on Eneas, he bellowed: "Boys and girls—be good—"

That was all anyone heard. ❖

ON THE JOB
• • • • • • • • • • • • • •
CARGO SUPERVISOR
• • • • • • • • • • • • • •

The railroad played a major role in the westward expansion of the United States. Today a railroad cargo supervisor uses a highly sophisticated tracking system to direct carloads of raw materials and finished goods across the country. She or he monitors the movement and schedules of trains as they pass through major rail hubs, picking up and dropping off cars as directed.

ACCENT ON...
COMMUNICATIONS TECHNOLOGY
• •

Eneas faced a future of separation from his home. Even if he had the tools to communicate, any message he sent would have taken days or weeks to reach his family. Working with Business Education students, discuss ways in which modern office technology would have enabled Eneas to keep in close touch with his friends and family. If possible, send an e-mail message or a fax.

UNDERSTANDING

1. What were the major's motives in sending Eneas and the others to boarding school? What do you think his intentions were? Cite examples from the text to support your answer.

   Think about situations in which you did something you thought was good or positive, but your actions had negative results. For example, you may have cooked dinner to help out your mother or father, but you ended up ruining the pan. Divide a sheet of paper into 3 columns. Label the first column *Action*, the second *Expected Result*, and the third *Actual Result*. Think of at least three situations, and label each accordingly. ***Workshop 6***

2. Major Miles considered Eneas a person of "real quality." Cite examples from the text that illustrate why Miles thought this. Discuss with your classmates what makes someone a person of "real quality."

   Portray yourself or a friend as a person of "real quality" in a letter in which you either apply for a job or nominate a classmate for student council. ***Workshop 11***

3.  The author of "Train Time" states "Major Miles was a man of conscience." Working in groups, define "conscience." Using your group's definition, find the parts of the story that illustrate how Major Miles was or was not a man of conscience. Discuss the impact of conscience on your classmates or colleagues at work. Write down three examples of home, school, or work situations where your conscience could affect the decisions you make. ***Workshop 12***

4. Cite evidence from the text to show what Miles thinks about doing one's duty. Compare your view of duty with that of Miles, and write a list of concrete examples from your own experience to support your position. Explain why these are considered one's "duty."

A LAST WORD

"Train Time" raises questions about individual freedoms, or rights. Which freedoms should everyone have? Have you ever seen someone denied his or her fundamental rights? Have you ever been in a situation when you had your rights unfairly taken from you?

CONNECTING

1.  Eneas and his grandparents need help. Discuss with your classmates ways in which help is provided to people in your community. Collect brochures or newsletters from two or three community service agencies. Which one is the most effective? Working in groups, discuss the information contained in the brochures as well as their formats and designs. Follow the model of the brochure you like the best to create brochures for a community service agency of your own. ***Workshop 21***

2. Major Miles had difficulty communicating with the children in this story. Written and oral communication are important in any occupation. Call the manager of a local business, and ask what written and oral communications skills are expected of the employees. Write down a list of these skills to share with your class.

Freedom

EXPLORING

• •

A 1960s song states that "Freedom's just another word for nothing left to lose." What do you think this definition means? Do people always have freedom to choose what they want to do? Do you have freedom of choice? On what occasions have you been unable to do what you chose to do?

THEME CONNECTION...
FREE CHOICE

The United States Constitution guarantees liberty to American citizens. Freedom of choice, however, is elusive. Old habits and unexamined beliefs limit free choice. The demands and expectations of others limit free choice. Even bad luck sometimes limits free choice. This poem considers just how free each person really is.

TIME & PLACE

This poem was written in the 1970s, a time when many Americans were wrestling with United States involvement in the Vietnam War. William Stafford became something of a standard-bearer for the generation of people who felt we should not fight in Vietnam. Stafford retained his pacifism throughout his lifetime.

THE WRITER'S CRAFT

DICTION

William Stafford is often compared to Robert Frost in his ability to attract a wide audience. Both poets use simple "diction," or words. Both poets avoid the difficult vocabulary that frightens some people away from poetry. This simplicity of diction, or word choice, should not be equated with unimportant subject matter. With his familiar words, Stafford deals with complex ideas.

Freedom

William Stafford

Freedom is not following a river,
Freedom is following a river
   though, if you want to.
It is deciding now by what happens now.
It is knowing that luck makes a difference.

No leader is free; no follower is free—
   the rest of us can often be free.
Most of the world are living by
creeds too odd, chancy, and habit-forming
   to be worth arguing about by reason.

If you are **oppressed**, wake up about
four in the morning; most places
you can usually be free some of the time
   if you wake up before other people. ❖

About the Author

A lifelong pacifist, William Stafford (1914–1993) was a prolific poet and critic who often used nature and the American West as a backdrop for his universal themes. Stafford grew up in Kansas and attended college there. He held a variety of jobs before and during World War II, including farm worker and laborer in oil refineries. As a conscientious objector, he was placed in a forest service work camp. After the war, Stafford became an English teacher and professor. His books of poetry have earned him recognition as an accomplished American poet.

creed—a set of fundamental beliefs

oppressed—crushed or burdened

FOCUS ON...
SOCIAL STUDIES

Stafford explores how much of our life is restricted, maintaining that neither leaders nor followers are free. In what ways throughout history have Americans been oppressed? Consider, for example, women's suffrage, job and housing discrimination, and other cases of oppression. Choose a particular example of oppression and write a two- to three-page report describing the issue and explaining how and to what degree the oppression has stopped or has been reduced. Use a case study approach to make your historical research come alive. Present your study to the class orally. Use visuals if possible.

◆ ◆

UNDERSTANDING

1. Consider all the things Stafford might mean when he says "Freedom is not following a river, / Freedom is following a river / though, if you want to." How is freedom described in the next two stanzas?

   As we freely follow a river, often what waits around the bend is unknown. However, we still take risks to see what will come next. List specific instances when you decided not to do something. List the times you wanted to "follow a river" and did so. What factors influenced your decisions to do or not do something? Using this material, prepare a graph, chart, or table that illustrates the times free choice keeps you from doing something or liberates you to do something. Note the kinds of influences that shaped your decisions. ***Workshop 20***

2. Examine lines 4 and 5 carefully: "It is deciding now by what happens now. / It is knowing that luck makes a difference." What do these lines say about people who make plans for the future? In what way are these people not free?

   Draw a line down the center of a piece of paper. On one side of the page, list things you feel you are *free to* do, such as travel, express opinions, and read what you please. On the other side of the page, list things you are *free from*, like being arrested without cause. Using these as prewriting, write an essay in which you compare and contrast these two forms of freedom. Try to come to a conclusion about the importance of freedom in your life. ***Workshop 9***

3. What do you think Stafford means when he says, "you can usually be free some of the time if you wake up before other people"? What freedoms do you have in the morning that aren't available to you at other times of the day? Write a short paragraph about how different times of the day, week, or year affect your freedom.

CONNECTING

1. Working in groups, use newspapers, magazines, television reports, and other sources to gather information about citizens' freedoms. Look for information that demonstrates both "freedom to" and "freedom from." Determine which parts of the world or the United States seem to be most and least free. Your information could result in a report to Amnesty International or some government official describing violations of civil liberties. ***Workshop 7***

2. Most of us are familiar with Constitutional freedoms, but we are often less aware of the freedoms maintained in state and local constitutions and charters. In groups, research the freedoms protected by your state or city governments. Read your state's constitution or your city's charter at the local library. Create a graphic that illustrates these freedoms in each. ***Workshop 20***

from Homecoming

EXPLORING

What would you do if you were left on your own for seven days in a strange city where you could turn to no one for help? You have paid in advance non-refundable rent for a room. Your room has neither running water nor food. You have only $5.00 to your name. Come up with a survival plan that uses your money well.

THEME CONNECTION...
ESCAPING AUTHORITY

In Chapter One of Cynthia Voigt's *Homecoming*, the four Tillerman children, ages 6, 9, 10, and 13, must rely entirely upon themselves. The oldest, Dicey, fears police and social workers because they might separate the children and place them in foster homes or orphanages. Dicey outsmarts a security guard and develops a plan to keep her family together and free.

TIME & PLACE

Homecoming (1981) is the first of thirteen novels by Cynthia Voigt. Many of her books, such as *Dicey's Song*, *A Solitary Blue*, and *Seventeen Against the Dealer* portray the Tillerman family. In *Homecoming*, set in the late 1970s, the children search for a place to call home. Abandoned by their mentally ill mother as they journey from their home in Provincetown, their first plan is to go to Aunt Cilla in Bridgeport. Since life with Aunt Cilla proves dismal, the children resume their journey in search of a true home. The novel portrays their many adventures on this quest.

THE WRITER'S CRAFT
REALISM IN FICTION

The term *realism* means that a story could happen. The story is believable, but not actually true. Realistic short stories and novels contain no miracles or supernatural figures. Instead, they take place in today's world, involve characters who look and act like real people, and deal with life's actual problems.

from *Homecoming*

Cynthia Voigt

Chapter 1

The woman put her sad moon-face in at the window of the car. "You be good," she said. "You hear me? You little ones, mind what Dicey tells you. You hear?"

"Yes, Momma," they said.

"That's all right then."

She slung her purse over her shoulder and walked away, her stride made uneven by broken sandal thongs, thin elbows showing through holes in the oversized sweater, her jeans faded and baggy. When she had disappeared into the crowd of Saturday morning shoppers entering the side doors of the mall, the three younger children leaned forward onto the front seat. Dicey sat in front. She was thirteen and she read the maps.

"Why'd we stop?" asked James. "We're not there yet. We've got food. There's no reason to stop." James was ten and wanted everything to have a reason. "Dicey?"

"I dunno. You heard everything she said, same as I did. You tell me."

"All she said was, *We gotta stop here.* She didn't say why. She never says why, you know that. Are we out of gas?"

"I didn't look." Dicey wanted some quiet for thinking. There was something odd about this whole trip. She couldn't put

About the Author

In most of her dozen or so books, Cynthia Voigt (1942–) writes of the relationships between adults and young people. She never takes sides but always tries to promote understanding. Voigt grew up in Boston and after college began teaching high school English in Maryland. In 1983, she won the Newbery Medal for children's literature for *Dicey's Song*, the sequel to *Homecoming*.

her finger on it, not yet. "Why don't you tell them a story?"

"What story?"

"Cripes, James, you're the one with the famous brain."

"Yeah, well I can't think of any stories right now."

"Tell them anything. Tell them Hansel and Gretel."

"I want HanselnGretel. And the witch. And the candy house with peppermint sticks," Sammy said, from the back seat. James gave in without a quarrel. It was easier to give in to Sammy than to fight him. Dicey turned around to look at them. Maybeth sat hunched in a corner, big-eyed. Dicey smiled at her and Maybeth smiled back. "Once upon a time," James began. Maybeth turned to him.

Dicey closed her eyes and leaned her head back. She put her feet on the dashboard. She was tired. She'd had to stay awake and read maps, to find roads without tolls. She'd been up since three in the morning. But Dicey couldn't go to sleep. She gnawed away at what was bothering her.

For one thing, they never took trips. Momma always said the car couldn't run more than ten miles at a stretch. And here they were in Connecticut, heading down to Bridgeport. For one thing.

But that might make sense. All her life, Dicey had been hearing about Momma's Aunt Cilla and her big house in Bridgeport that Momma had never seen, and her rich husband who died. Aunt Cilla sent Christmas cards year after year, with pictures of Baby Jesus on them and long notes inside, on paper so thin it could have been tissue paper. Only Momma could decipher the lacy handwriting with its long, tall letters all bunched together and the lines running into one another because of the long-tailed, fancy z's and f's and g's. Aunt

Cilla kept in touch. So it made sense for Momma to go to her for help.

But driving off like that in the middle of the night didn't make sense. That was the second thing. Momma woke them all up and told them to pack paper bags of clothing while she made sandwiches. She got them all into the old car and headed for Bridgeport.

For a third—things had been happening, all at once. Things were always bad with them, but lately worse than ever. Momma lost her checker's job. Maybeth's teacher had wanted a meeting with Momma that Momma wouldn't go to. Maybeth would be held back another year. Momma said she didn't want to hear about it, and she had ripped up every note, without reading any of them. Maybeth didn't worry her family, but she worried her teachers. She was nine and still in the second grade. She never said much, that was the trouble, so everybody thought she was stupid. Dicey knew she wasn't. Sometimes she'd come out and say something that showed she'd been watching and listening and taking things in. Dicey knew her sister could read and do sums, but Maybeth always sat quiet around strangers. For Maybeth, everyone in the world was a stranger, except Momma and Dicey and James and Sammy.

Momma herself was the fourth thing. Lately she'd go to the store for bread and come back with a can of tuna and just put her hands over her face, sitting at the table. Sometimes she'd be gone for a couple of hours and then she wouldn't say where she had been, with her face blank as if she couldn't say. As if she didn't know. Momma didn't talk to them any more, not even to scold, or sing, or make up games the way she used to. Except Sammy. She talked to Sammy, but even then they sounded like two six-year-olds talking, not one six-year-old and his mother.

● ● ● ● ● ● ●

...they sounded like two six-year-olds talking, not one six-year-old and his mother.

● ● ● ● ● ● ●

Dicey kept her feet on the dash, and her body slouched down. She looked out through the windshield, over the rows of parked cars, to where the sky hung like a bleached-out sheet over the top of the mall buildings. Bugs were spattered all over the windshield and the sky promised a heavy, hot day. Dicey slid still further down on the seat. Her skin stuck to the blue plastic seat covers.

James was describing the witch's house, listing the kinds of candy used for various parts of the building. This was the part James liked best in Hansel and Gretel, and he always did it a little differently from the time before. Picturing the almond Hershey bar roof and the shutters made of cinnamon licorice sticks, Dicey did fall asleep.

She woke covered with sweat from the hot sun pouring in through the windshield. She woke hungry. Maybeth was singing softly, one of Momma's songs, about making her love a baby with no crying. "I fell asleep," Dicey said. "What time's it?"

"I dunno," James said. "You've been asleep a long time. I'm hungry."

"Where's Momma?"

"I dunno. I'm hungry."

"You're always hungry. Go ask someone what time it is, OK?"

James climbed out of the car. He crossed to the walkway and stopped a man in a business suit. "Twelve-thirty," James reported.

"But that means I slept for more than two hours," Dicey protested.

FOCUS ON...
MATH

Dicey suddenly finds herself in charge of the family's financial resources. She must allocate money for food and transportation if she is to get her siblings safely to Connecticut. Plan out a trip for four to a destination of your choice. Figure out how to get there, how long it will take, what it will cost, and other specific details like meals, stops, and so on. Write a detailed travel plan complete with budget and schedule. Show how you will use your resources from beginning to end. You may wish to prepare a chart that shows your plan and a map that illustrates the course of your trip.

◆ ◆

"I'm going to eat," Sammy announced from the back seat. He opened the bag of food and pulled out a sandwich before Dicey could say anything.

"What do you want me to do?" James asked, looking into Dicey's face. His narrow little face wore a worried expression. "Want me to go look for her?"

"No," Dicey said (*Now* what had Momma gone and done?) "Sammy, give Maybeth a sandwich too. Let her choose for herself. Then pass the bag up here."

When everyone had a sandwich, and James had two, Dicey reached a decision. "We have to wait here for a while more," she said. "Then we'll do something. I'm going to take a walk and see if I can find her."

"Don't you go away too," Maybeth said softly.

"I'll be right where you can see me," Dicey said. "I'll stay on the sidewalk— see?—just like a path in front of the stores. Then maybe later we can all go into the mall and look in the stores. You'd like that, wouldn't you?" Maybeth smiled and nodded her golden head.

Dicey did her best thinking when she walked. On this warm June afternoon, she walked so fast and thought so hard, she didn't even see the people going past her. If Momma went past she'd say something, so Dicey wasn't worried about that.

She was worried that Momma had wandered off. And would not come back.

("You always look for the worst," Momma had often told her. "I like to be ready," Dicey answered.)

If Momma was gone . . . But that wasn't possible. Was it? But if she was, what could they do? Ask for help, probably from a policeman. (Would he put them in homes or orphanages? Wouldn't that be just what the police or some social worker would do?) Go back to Provincetown, they could go back home. (Momma hadn't paid the rent, not for weeks, and it was almost summertime, when even their old cabin, set off alone in the dunes, could bring in a lot of money. Mr. Martinez wasn't sympathetic, not when it came to money, not when it came to giving something away for free. He'd never let them stay there to wait for Momma.) They could go on to Bridgeport. Dicey had never seen Aunt Cilla—Great-aunt Cilla. She knew the name and address, because Momma had made her write it down four times, on each paper bag, in case something happened: Mrs. Cilla

Logan, 1724 Ocean Drive, Bridgeport, Connecticut. Aunt Cilla was family, the only family Dicey knew about.

The sun beat down on the parking lot and heated up the air so even in the shaded walkway Dicey was hot. The kids must be hot too, she thought, and turned to get them.

Momma must have gone away on purpose. (But she loved them, loved them all.) Why else the addresses on the bags? Why else tell them to mind Dicey? (Mothers didn't do things like going off. It was crazy. Was Momma crazy?) How did she expect Dicey to take care of them? What did she expect Dicey to do? Take them to Bridgeport, of course. (Dump it all on Dicey, that was what Momma did, she always did, because Dicey was the determined sort. "It's in your blood," Momma said, and then wouldn't explain.)

Anger welled up in Dicey, flooded her eyes with tears, and now she was swept away with the determination to get the kids to Bridgeport. Well, she'd do it somehow, if she had to.

Momma wasn't at the car when Dicey returned, so Dicey said they'd wait for her until the next morning.

"Where'll we sleep?" Sammy asked.

"Right here—and no complaints," Dicey said.

"Then Momma will come back and we'll go on tomorrow?" Sammy asked.

Dicey nodded.

"Where is Momma? Why's she taking so long?" James asked.

"I dunno, James," Dicey answered. Maybeth was silent, staring.

After a few minutes, Dicey hustled them all out of the car and trailed after them as they entered the mall.

> ● ● ● ● ● ● ●
> …now she was swept away with the determination to get the kids to Bridgeport.
> ● ● ● ● ● ● ●

The mall was built like a fortress around a huge, two-story enclosed street, where store succeeded store, as far as you could see. At one end of the central section was a cage of live birds in a little park of plastic trees and shrubs. The floor of their cage was littered with pieces of popcorn and gum wrappers. At the other end, the builders had made a waterfall through which shone different colored lights. Outside, beyond the covered sidewalk that ran like a moat around the huge building, lay the huge, gray parking lot, a no-man's-land of empty cars.

But here inside was a fairyland of colors and sounds, crowded with people on this Saturday afternoon, artificially lit and planted. Inside was a miniature city where endless **diversions** from the workday world offered everything delightful. If you had money, of course. And even without money, you could still stare and be amazed.

They spent a long time wandering through stores, looking at toys and records and pianos and birthday cards. They were drawn to restaurants that **exuded** the smell of spaghetti and pizza or fried chicken, bakeries with trays of golden doughnuts lined up behind glass windows, candy stores, where the countertop was crowded with large jars of jelly beans and sourballs and little foil-covered chocolates and peppermints dipped in crunchy white frosting; cheese shops (they each had two free samples), where the rich smell of aged cheeses mingled with fresh-ground coffee, and hot dog stands, where they stood back in a silent row. After this, they sat on a backless bench before the waterfall, tired and hungry. Altogether, they had eleven dollars and

diversion—something that gives pleasure by distracting one's attention from a problem or burden

exuded—displayed conspicuously

fifty cents, more than any one of them had ever had at one time before, even Dicey, who contributed all of her baby-sitting money, seven dollars.

They spent almost four dollars on supper at the mall, and none of them had dessert. They had hamburgers and french fries and, after Dicey thought it over, milkshakes. At that rate, they could have one more meal before they ran out of money, or maybe two more. It was still light when they returned to the car. The little ones horsed around in the back, teasing, wrestling, tickling, quarreling and laughing, while Dicey studied the map. People walked by their car, vehicles came and went, and nobody paid any attention to them. In parking lots, it's not unusual to see a car full of kids waiting.

At half-past eight, Dicey herded everybody back into the mall, to use the bathrooms they had found earlier. Later, Sammy and Maybeth fell asleep easily, curled up along the back seat. James moved up to the front with Dicey. Dicey couldn't see how they were both to sleep in the front seat, but she supposed they would manage it. James sat stiffly, gripping the wheel. James had a narrow head and sharp features, a nose that pointed out, pencil-thin eyebrows, a narrow chin. Dicey studied him in the darkening car. They were parked so far from the nearest lamppost that they were in deep shadows.

With her brothers and sister near, with the two youngest asleep in the back seat, sitting as they were in a cocoon of darkness, she should feel safe. But she didn't. Though it was standing still, the car seemed to be flying down a highway, going too fast. Even the dark inside of it was not deep enough to hide them. Faces might appear in the windows at any time, asking angry questions.

"Where's Momma gone?" James asked, looking out at the night.

"I just don't know," Dicey said. "Here's what I think, I think if she isn't back by morning we ought to go on to Bridgeport."

"On our own?"

"Yes."

"How'll we get there? You can't drive. Momma took the keys."

"We could take a bus, if we have enough money. If we don't, we'll walk."

James stared at her. Finally he spoke.

"Dicey? I'm scared. I feel all jiggly in my stomach. Why doesn't Momma come back?"

"If I knew, James, I'd know what to do."

"Do you know the way?"

"To Bridgeport? I can read a map. Once we get there, we can ask directions to Aunt Cilla's house."

James nodded. "Do you think she's been killed? Or kidnapped?"

"Rich people get kidnapped; not Momma. I'm not going to think about what might have happened to her, and I don't think you should, either."

"I can't help thinking about it," James said in a small voice.

"Don't tell Sammy or Maybeth," Dicey warned.

"I wouldn't. I know better. You should know I'd know better than that."

Dicey reached out and patted him on the shoulder. "I do know," she said.

James grabbed her hand. "Dicey? Do you think Momma meant to leave us here?"

"I think Momma meant to take us to Bridgeport, but—"

"Is Momma crazy?"

Dicey turned her head to look at him.

> …they could have one more meal before they ran out of money…

"The kids said so, at school. And the way the teachers looked at me and loaned me their own books and talked to me. And Maybeth. Craziness can run in families."

Dicey felt a great weight settle on her shoulders. She tried to shrug it off, but it wouldn't move.

"Dicey?"

"She loves us," Dicey muttered.

"But that's the only reason I can think of that might be true."

"There's nothing wrong with Maybeth. You know that."

"It runs in families. Hereditary craziness."

"Well, you don't have to worry about it, do you? You're the smart one, with A's in school and the science projects that get entered in the state contest."

"Yeah," James said. He settled his head back on the seat.

"Listen, I'm going to go to a phone and see where the bus station is and call them up to find out how much tickets cost. You lay low."

"Why?"

Dicey decided to tell him the truth. "Just in case. I mean, three kids in a car in a parking lot at night . . . See, James, I think we've got to get to Bridgeport and I just don't know what would happen if a policeman saw us. Foster homes or something, I dunno. I don't want to risk it. But one kid . . . and I'm pretty old so it doesn't look funny."

"OK. That sounds OK."

"We've got to get to Bridgeport."

James thought about that, then nodded his head. "I never listened much to Momma's talk about her. What will she be like, Aunt Cilla?"

"Rich," Dicey said.

"It would be a long walk," James said.

"Long enough," Dicey agreed. She got out of the car fast.

It was full dark, an overcast night. The parking lot was nearly empty; only two cars besides theirs remained. Dicey wondered how many cars were left in the other three parking lots that spread out from the other sides of the building. It felt as empty as all of space must be. She hoped there were cars in each lot. The more cars there were, the safer their car was for them.

Dicey headed confidently for the walkway, as if she had every right to be where she was, as if she had an important errand to run, as if she knew just where she was going. She remembered a telephone at the far end of the building. It wasn't a real phone booth, but a kind of cubicle hung up on the wall, with an open shelf underneath to hold the directory. James could probably see her from the car, if he looked for her. From that distance, she would look small.

SPOTLIGHT ON...
ACHIEVING
GOALS

Dicey's short-term goals are realistic and action-oriented. As you set and try to achieve your own goals in life, keep in mind the following:

1. Select one goal to work on at a time.
2. Make the goal specific.
3. List what resources you need or what you need to do to reach the goal.
4. Set check points to evaluate your progress in reaching your goal.
5. Acknowledge your achievement when you reach your goal.

The walkway was lit up, and the store windows were lit, so she moved through patches of sharp light. At the phone, she took out the directory to look up bus companies in the yellow pages. She ran her finger down the names, selected one that sounded local and reached into her pocket for change.

She heard footsteps. A man approached her, in a uniform like a policeman's, but tan not blue, and without the badge. He took his time getting to her, as if he was sure she'd wait, sure of his own strength to hold her, even at that distance. He moved like he thought she was afraid of him, too afraid to run.

"Hey," the man said. His shirt had the word "Security" sewn onto it. Where his belly sagged, the shirt hung out over his pants. He carried a long-handled flashlight. He wore a pistol at his belt.

Dicey didn't answer, but she didn't look away.

"Hey kid," he said, as if she had shown signs of running and he needed to halt her. He was heavy, out of shape. He had a pig-person face, a coarse skin that sagged at the jowls, little blue eyes and pale eyebrows, and a fat, pushed-back nose. When he came up next to her, Dicey stepped back a pace, but kept her finger on the number in the book.

"You lost?"

"Naw. I'm making a phone call."

"Where do you live?"

"Just over there," Dicey said, pointing vaguely with her free hand.

"Go home and call from there. Run along now. If you were a girl, I'd walk you over, but—"

"Our phone's broken," Dicey said. "That's why my mom sent me here."

The guard shifted his flashlight, holding it like a club. "Phones don't break. How's a phone break?"

"We've got this dog that chews things up. Slippers, papers, you know. He chewed the phone. The cord, actually, but it's all the same—the phone's broken."

"Are you bulling me?"

"I wish I was."

"What's your name kid?"

"Danny."

She felt funny, strange, making up lies as quickly and smoothly as if she'd been doing it all her life.

The man took a piece of gum out of his pocket, unwrapped it, folded it in half and stuck it into his mouth, chewing on it a couple of times.

"Danny what?"

"Tillerman." Dicey couldn't make up a new last name, except Smith and nobody would believe that even if it was true.

"You don't look more than ten. Isn't it late to be out?"

Dicey shrugged.

The guard grew suspicious. "Who're you calling?"

"The bus company. My sisters and me are going down to Bridgeport some time soon, to stay with my aunt."

He chewed and thought. "Sometime soon wouldn't send you out after ten at night to phone. What's the rush?"

"My mom just got back from the clinic and she's gonna have her baby, any day now the doctor said, and my aunt needs to know what time the buses arrive so she can meet us on Monday. So's we can take a bus it's good for her to meet. My mom asked me to come find out so's she can call first thing in the morning, before my aunt goes to church. It's hard for my mom to get around now—you know."

"Where's your father?"

"Gone."

"Gone where?"

"Dunno. He just up and went, way back, last winter."

The guard nodded. He reached in his pocket and pulled out the pack of gum. He offered a piece to Dicey, but she shook her head.

"Can I call now, mister?"

"Sure thing," he said. "I wouldn't have bothered you except that there've been

some windows broken around here. We think it's kids. I'm the security guard. I've got to be careful."

Dicey nodded. She inserted the coins and slowly dialed the numbers, hoping he'd go away. But he stood there and listened. Behind him lay the parking lot, a vast open space where occasional clumps of planted bushes spread long shadows over the ground. An impersonal voice answered. Dicey asked about tickets to Bridgeport, how much they cost.

"From where to Bridgeport."

Dicey grabbed at a name. "Peewauket." That was what the map said. She pronounced it Pee-Walk-It. The guard, listening, narrowed his eyes.

"From Peewauket?" the voice asked, saying it Pwuk-it.

"Yeah."

"Two dollars and forty-five cents a person."

"What's the rate for children?"

"The same. The charge is for the seat. Unless you've got a child under two."

"What time do buses run?"

"Every other hour, from eight to eight."

Dicey thanked the voice and hung up the phone. She stood with her arms hanging down at her sides, waiting for the guard to leave.

He was studying her with his little piggly eyes. He held his flashlight now in one hand and slapped it into the palm of the other. "You better get back now," he said and then added, "You didn't write anything down."

"I've got a good memory."

"Yeah? I'll give you a test." His body blocked the way to the safe darkness of the parking lot. "You don't remember anything

> ● ● ● ● ● ● ●
> The more cars there were, the safer their car was for them.
> ● ● ● ● ● ● ●

about broken windows in the mall, do you? For instance, just one for instance, at Record City."

"I don't know what you're talking about."

"I wonder about that. I really wonder, Danny. You said Danny, didn't you? Tillerman, wasn't it? You see, we figure it was probably kids did it, account of nothing's been stolen. Or maybe just one kid did it, that's what I'm thinking."

Dicey glared at him. "I said I don't know anything about that."

He put one arm out to bar her in, resting his hand against the side of the phone. "I can't think of why I should believe you. Nope, now I come to think of it, I don't think I do believe you. The only question in my mind is, what do I do with you?"

Dicey thought fast, then acted just as fast. She lifted her right knee as if to hit him in the groin where she knew it would hurt bad. He lowered his arm and stepped back, to protect himself. In that one second while he was off balance, Dicey took off. She sprinted into the

> ● ● ● ● ● ● ●
> You don't remember anything about broken windows in the mall, do you?
> ● ● ● ● ● ● ●

darkness of the parking lot. As soon as she was in the cover of the shadows, she turned left around the corner of the building, away from their car. He thundered after her.

Dicey ran smoothly. She was used to running on beaches, where the sand gave way under your feet and each thrust of your legs was hindered. Running over asphalt was easier. Dicey pulled away from her pursuer. His steps were heavy and his breathing was heavy. He was out of shape and too fat to catch up with her. She had time to crouch behind one of the little islands of green that decorated the parking lot. She had on a dark shirt and jeans, her face was tanned and her hair brown; she was confident nothing would give her away.

He stopped by the front entrance shining his flashlight out over the parking lot, like one bright eye. Dicey watched him. He listened, but his chest was heaving so much that she was sure he couldn't hear anything but the blood pounding in his ears. She smiled to herself.

"You haven't got a chance," he called. "You better come out now, kid. You're only making it worse."

Dicey covered her mouth with her hand.

"I know you now. We'll find you out," he said. He turned quickly away from the parking lot and looked further along the front of the mall. He hunched

behind the flashlight. He used the beam like a giant eye, to peer into the shadows. "There you are! I can see you!" he cried.

But he was looking the wrong way. Dicey giggled, and the sound escaped her even though she bit on her hand to stop it.

He turned back to the parking lot, listening. Then he swore. His light swooped over the dark lot, trying to search out her hiding place. "Danny? I'm gonna find you."

Dicey moved softly away on soundless sneakers through the covering shadows. He continued to call: "I'll remember your face, you hear? You hear me? Hear me?"

From halfway across the parking lot, safe in her own speed and in shadows, Dicey stopped. Her heart swelled in victory. "I hear you," she called softly back, as she ran towards the empty road and the patch of woods beyond.

Much later, when she returned to the car, James awoke briefly. "Everything's OK," Dicey whispered, curling down onto the cold seat to sleep. ❖

ACCENT ON...
SOCIAL SERVICES FOR TEENS

Dicey faced a terrible dilemma not knowing where her mother was, what was wrong with her, or when she might return. Where can adolescents go for help when they face such problems? Research local teen social service agencies. Then describe one that could help people like Dicey in circumstances like these. Explain the purpose, goals, and day-to-day functions of such a service, as well as how such an organization is financed and staffed. Show how teens could access such help without being embarrassed or afraid.

ON THE JOB
SECURITY GUARD

Security guards protect their employer's property from theft, illegal entry, and vandalism. Guards are often employed in urban or manufacturing centers, patrolling and inspecting business or government offices, stores, banks, hotels, schools, factories and warehouses, and other public or private concerns. Most security guards have at least a high school diploma and receive training in the use of firearms, first aid, and the handling of emergencies. Guards should have the ability to write well-organized reports, be in good physical health, be dependable, and have sound character.

UNDERSTANDING

1. Dicey thinks, "There was something odd about this whole trip." Bothered by the trip, she reasons carefully to figure out why. Find passages in the text that show Dicey's logical conclusions about what is wrong.

    Critical thinking is a way to search for truth by using logic, reason, and creativity. Dicey used critical thinking skills to figure out what was wrong. Do you know a good critical thinker? In two or three paragraphs describe a situation in which this person used critical thinking skills to solve a problem. ***Workshop 16***

2 Do you think Maybeth should be held back another year in second grade? Find support for your answer in the text.

    In any group, some people are quiet, while others are talkative. Being too talkative or too quiet can get a person into difficulty. Imagine you are supervising someone who is either *garrulous* (extremely talkative) or *taciturn* (untalkative). In a memo, tell the person the problems this trait is causing and offer suggestions for improving. ***Workshop 13***

3. Dicey is a complex character with not one, but many qualities. What are Dicey's qualities? Is she a realistic character? Do you believe she could do the things she did in the story? Find in the text evidence to support your view of Dicey's personality.

    Dicey has total responsibility for her family. Formulate five questions to use in interviewing adults, especially senior citizens, to find out what responsibilities they had when they were young. Be sure to ask if they think their responsibilities hurt or helped them in later life. Also develop questions about responsibilities to ask friends. Write down your questions and the data you collect.

4. When Dicey realizes that Momma has probably abandoned them, she wonders, "What could they [the children] do?" What possible courses of action does Dicey consider, and why does she reject these possibilities? Why does she decide to take the family to Bridgeport?

    Tough decisions are unavoidable. Think of a time when you or your friends had to make a difficult decision. What choice did you face, what things did you think about doing, what did you finally decide to do and why? Based on this experience, list the steps that would apply in any decision-making process.

5. Serious problems such as as mental health issues, homelessness, child abandonment, and other problems in the story do not have easy solutions. In groups, read local newspaper stories about serious problems such as violent crime, care for the elderly, and so on in your community. Select one problem for your group to investigate extensively. Develop specific interview questions to ask those who are involved in or understand the issue. For example, what do police do with abandoned children? Do additional research to develop your own ideas about the problem. Present your research and conclusions to an appropriate audience. ***Workshop 19***

A LAST WORD

How would you react if suddenly given a responsibility such as the one Dicey faced? What advice would you offer a friend in a similar situation?

CONNECTING

1. In *Homecoming*, hunger gnaws at the children. In most areas, food banks and missions help feed the hungry. Research community or national organizations that aid the hungry. Find out who runs these organizations, who works at them, who relies on them, and how great a need they fill. Present your findings in a detailed report to someone who can act on this information. This report should be accompanied by visual aids. Your report may take the form of a proposal for specific action. *Workshop 10*

2. Dicey is determined to get the children to Bridgeport. She faces a tremendous challenge and intends to triumph. Read local and national newspapers to find three or four stories about people who have overcome great adversity. Compare and contrast these stories to discover what these people have in common. What qualities and behavior do they share? Write a report telling about qualities and behavior that help people conquer adversity. Accompany the report with a poster or flyer listing the qualities and actions that help people overcome obstacles. *Workshop 9*

WRAP IT UP

UNIT 1

1. *The Declaration of Independence* and the poem "Freedom" offer views on freedom and advocate particular ways of obtaining it. Compare and contrast these two views of freedom. What events or circumstances do you believe helped shape each writer's definition of freedom? Is one definition more useful than the other? If so, why?

Write your own definition of freedom. Include a description of the conditions under which you would feel your freedom was being jeopardized and an explanation of what you would be prepared to do to maintain it.

2. "The Use of Force," the excerpt from *Narrative of the Life of Frederick Douglass*, and "Train Time" all depict one character deciding what is best for another character, who clearly disagrees. Compare the contest of wills in these three selections. In each case, which character do you think deserves to prevail? Why? Use details from the selections to explain whether you think the characters who make the decisions are justified in limiting the other characters' freedom.

In groups, discuss instances in which you would consider imposing your will on others. If you truly believed it was for their own good, would you force people to do something they did not want to do? Why?

UNIT
◇2◇
COMMUNITY AND RESPONSIBILITY

Community is more than just a set of boundaries on a map. To belong to a community is to interact with others and contribute to society. Belonging to a community provides many benefits— fellowship, security, a sense of purpose, personal satisfaction. It also includes certain responsibilities—to obey laws, to take care of oneself and one's property, and to help others. The selections in this unit show what it means for individuals to be part of a community.

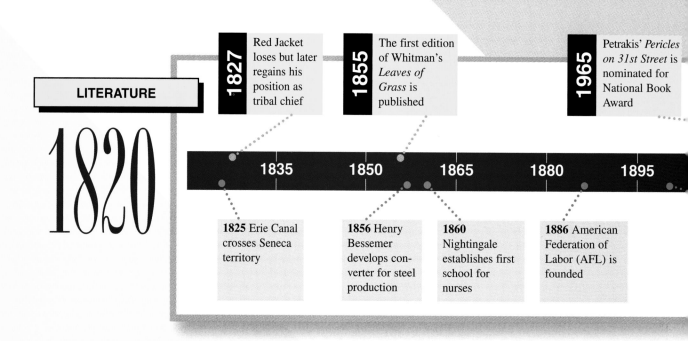

LITERATURE

1820

1827 Red Jacket loses but later regains his position as tribal chief

1855 The first edition of Whitman's *Leaves of Grass* is published

1965 Petrakis' *Pericles on 31st Street* is nominated for National Book Award

| | 1835 | | 1850 | | 1865 | | 1880 | | 1895 |

1825 Erie Canal crosses Seneca territory

1856 Henry Bessemer develops converter for steel production

1860 Nightingale establishes first school for nurses

1886 American Federation of Labor (AFL) is founded

from **The Speech of Chief Red-Jacket**
—Sagoyewatha

I Hear America Singing
—Walt Whitman

Geraldo No Last Name
—Sandra Cisneros

Steelworker
—Trudy Pax Farr

Lineage
—Margaret Walker

Barba Nikos
—Harry Mark Petrakis

from **The Youngest Science**
—Lewis Thomas

from **Exploring Careers: Health Occupations**

The First Seven Years
—Bernard Malamud

Remember
—Joy Harjo

| 1966 | Malamud's *The Fixer* wins National Book Award and Pulitzer Prize | 1971 | Margaret Walker awarded Fulbright scholarship | 1971 | Thomas starts writing a column for the *New England Journal of Medicine* | 1995 | Cisneros publishes "Only Daughter" |

2000

1925   1940   1955   1970   1985

1900 Greek immigration to the United States increases

1940 Aliens are required to register with the U.S. government

1970 Occupational Safety and Health Administration (OSHA) is established

1989 Fifty-seven percent of American women work outside of the home

LIFE and WORK

from *The Speech of Chief Red-Jacket*

EXPLORING

●●●●●●●●●●●●●●●●●●●●●●●●●●●●●

When people discuss religion and politics, calm conversations often turn into fierce arguments. Consider the times you have experienced or witnessed a shift from calm disagreement or debate to emotional argument. Discuss specific conduct that might help two people who hold opposing views express their different positions without becoming emotional and angry.

THEME CONNECTION... COMMUNITY FIRST

Sagoyewatha, chief of the Senecas, speaks for his community. The community has always been an essential component of many Native American philosophies. In the minds of Native Americans, community comes first, and individuals second. Their community includes animals and plants, which deserve the same respect accorded to human beings.

TIME & PLACE

This speech was delivered to a council in Buffalo in 1805. A missionary from Massachusetts named Mr. Cram had sought permission to convert the Native Americans in northern New York state who were members of the Iroquois League. The Iroquois League included Sagoyewatha's Seneca tribe. Sagoyewatha did not like the idea of learning the white people's religion and gave this speech to explain why.

THE WRITER'S CRAFT

REPETITION

Almost every sentence of Chief Red-Jacket's speech begins with the word *Brother*. Though he speaks at a time long before modern marketing techniques, he uses a strategy often implemented in today's advertisements—*repetition*. He repeats not only words but also the structure of phrases. This repetition of structure is a device called *parallelism*. Both types of repetition plant ideas in the minds of listeners. "The Gettysburg Address" also uses parallelism.

●●●●●●●●●●●●●●●●●●●●●●●●●●●●●●●●●●●●●●●

from The Speech of Chief Red-Jacket

Sagoyewatha

riend and brother, it was the will of the Great Spirit that we should meet together this day. He orders all things, and he has given us a fine day for our council. He has taken his garment from before the sun, and caused it to shine with brightness upon us; our eyes are opened, that we see clearly; our ears are unstopped, that we have been able to hear distinctly the words that you have spoken; for all these favors we thank the Great Spirit, and him only.

"*Brother*, this council fire was kindled by you; it was at your request that we came together at this time; we have listened with attention to what you have said; you requested us to speak our minds freely; this gives us great joy, for we now consider that we stand upright before you, and can speak what we think; all have heard your voice, and all speak to you as one man; our minds are agreed.

"*Brother*, you say you want an answer to your talk before you leave this place. It is right you should have one, as you are a great distance from home, and we do not wish to detain you; but we will first look back a little, and tell you what our fathers have told us, and what we have heard from the white people.

"*Brother, listen to what we say.* There was a time when our forefathers owned this great island [America]. Their **seats** extended from the rising to the setting sun. The Great Spirit had made it for the use of Indians. He had created the buffalo, the deer, and other animals for food. He made the bear, and the beaver, and their skins served us for clothing. He had scattered them over the country, and taught us how to take them. He had caused the earth to produce corn for bread. All this he had done for his red children because he loved them. If we had any disputes about hunting grounds, they were generally settled without the shedding of much blood: but an evil day came upon us; your forefathers crossed the great waters, and landed on this island. Their numbers were small; they found friends, and not enemies; they told us they had fled from their own country for fear of wicked men, and come here to enjoy their religion. They asked for a small seat; we took pity on them, granted their request, and they sat down amongst us; we gave them corn and meat; they gave us poison in return. The white people had now found our country, tidings were carried back, and more came amongst us; yet we did not fear them, we took them to be friends; they called us brothers; we believed them, and gave them a larger seat. At length, their numbers had greatly increased; they wanted more land; they wanted our country. Our eyes were opened, and our minds became uneasy. Wars took place; Indians were hired to fight against Indians, and many of our people were destroyed. They also brought strong liquors among us: it was strong and powerful, and has slain thousands.

"*Brother*, our seats were once large, and yours were very small; you have now

● ● ● ● ● ● ●
Our eyes were opened, . . .
● ● ● ● ● ● ●

About the Author

The name Sagoyewatha in the Iroquois language means "He Causes Them to Be Awake." Born in about 1756 at Canoga, New York, Sagoyewatha was a gifted speaker. His oratorical and political skills helped him become a Seneca chief. During the American Revolution, the Seneca sided with the British, who presented Sagoyewatha a red military coat, giving him the nickname "Red-Jacket." After the war, the Americans invited Iroquois leaders to meet with George Washington in 1792 to make peace. Sagoyewatha wanted peace but resisted attempts by whites to force their culture on the Seneca. In 1830, he died of cholera.

seat—property, ownership, position

FOCUS ON...
SOCIAL STUDIES

Many Christian missionaries sought to convert the Native Americans. Religious missionaries have worked in various countries and cultures over the last few centuries. Using reference books or on-line database resources, gather information on the work of missionaries in North America in the nineteenth or twentieth centuries. Write several paragraphs that describe the people, time, place, the purpose the missionaries had in coming to the area, and the effects the missionaries had on the indigenous peoples. You may also wish to prepare a map that illustrates the location of the areas you are writing about.

◆◆◆◆◆◆◆◆◆◆◆◆◆◆◆◆◆◆◆◆◆◆◆◆◆

become a great people, and we have scarcely a place left to spread our blankets; you have got our country, but are not satisfied; *you want to force your religion upon us.*

"*Brother, continue to listen.* You say that you are sent to instruct us how to worship the *Great Spirit* agreeably to his mind, and if we do not take hold of the religion which you white people teach, we shall be unhappy hereafter; you say that you are right, and we are lost; how do we know this to be true? We understand that your religion is written in a book; if it was intended for us as well as you, why has not the Great Spirit given it to us, and not only to us, but why did he not give to our forefathers the knowledge of that book, with the means of understanding it rightly? We only know what you tell us about it; how shall we know when to believe, being so often deceived by the white people?

"*Brother*, you say there is but one way to worship and serve the Great Spirit; if

• • • • • • •

...you want to force your religion upon us.

• • • • • • •

there is but one religion, why do you white people differ so much about it? Why not all agree, as you can all read the book?

"*Brother*, we do not understand these things; we are told that your religion was given to your forefathers, and has been handed down from father to son. We also have a religion which was given to our forefathers, and has been handed down to us their children. We worship that way. *It teacheth us to be thankful for all the favors we receive; to love each other, and to be united; we never quarrel about religion.*

"*Brother*, the Great Spirit has made us all; but he has made a great difference between his white and red children; he has given us a different complexion, and different customs; to you he has given the arts; to these he has not opened our eyes; we know these things to be true. Since he has made so great a difference between us in other things, why may we not conclude that he has given us a different religion

SPOTLIGHT ON...
MAKING OUTLINES

In his speech, Red-Jacket organized his ideas in a clear, orderly manner. In your own speeches and written communication, present your ideas in a clear, easy-to-follow order by using these guidelines:

- organize the main points of your speech or report into different categories
- cluster subtopics that elaborate on main points of each category
- arrange main topics and subtopics in a logical order (chronological, cause-and-effect, general to specific, and so on)
- revise your outline as needed

according to our understanding; the Great Spirit does right; he knows what is best for his children; we are satisfied.

"*Brother*, we do not wish to destroy your religion, or take it from you; we only want to enjoy our own.

"*Brother*, you say you have not come to get our land or our money, but to enlighten our minds. I will now tell you that I have been at your meetings, and saw you collecting money from the meeting. I cannot tell what this money was intended for, but suppose it was for your minister, and if we should conform to your way of thinking, perhaps you may want some from us.

"*Brother*, we are told that you have been preaching to white people in this place; these people are our neighbors; we are acquainted with them, we will wait a little while and see what effect your preaching has upon them. If we find it does them good, makes them honest, and less disposed to cheat Indians, we will then consider again what you have said.

"*Brother*, you have now heard our answer to your talk, and this is all we have to say at present. As we are going to part, we will come and take you by the hand, and hope the Great Spirit will protect you on your journey, and return you safe to your friends." ❖

ACCENT ON...
LAW

In his speech, Red Jacket talks about the Indians' loss of land to the white settlers. Land currently occupied by Native Americans is only a fraction of their original territory. Working with history or social studies students, discuss existing laws that now protect Native American lands. If possible, contact a local lawyer to find out what specific property rights the various tribes have.

UNDERSTANDING

1. Chief Red-Jacket's goal is to persuade the white members of his audience that the Indians neither need, nor want, the religion of white people. What elements make this speech so very persuasive?

   Develop your own persuasive speech or letter. For example, you may want to convince fellow club members to change a rule or take some action. State the issue, present evidence logically, anticipate and answer objections, and offer a conclusion. Keep the audience on your side by being fair, courteous, and objective. *Workshops 10 and 11*

2. Red-Jacket proposes an empirical study to decide if the white man's religion is worthy to be adopted. Empirical research is practical, not theoretical. It bases conclusions on real life observations and experimentation. Empirical research helps people make practical decisions. Discuss whether or not Chief Red-Jacket's empirical research will provide him with sufficient data to make an informed decision.

   Devise your own empirical research plan that states the issue, describes research methods and results, and recommends action. In your plan, you may want to determine whether your school needs to add a student lounge or study center.

A LAST WORD

Would you be willing to put your community's needs ahead of your individual needs? What causes would be worth such a sacrifice?

CONNECTING

1. As a class, plan and conduct a Native American Arts Day in your school. You might work with a social studies class and break into groups. Different groups could collect samples of artwork—painting, jewelry, clothing, pottery, and masks. Other groups could invite dancers, chanters, and drummers to perform. Display books and posters on Native Americans. Invite Native American performers, artists, writers, and speakers to visit the school.

2. Many films have been made about Native Americans, some notable ones in recent years. Most can be found on video. Discuss and select two films about Native Americans, one from the 1950s and another made recently. Analyze the treatment of Native Americans in each film. Do the films reinforce stereotypes or present an informed view? Write a paper comparing the treatment of Native Americans in early and recent movies. *Workshop 5*

3. If possible, visit a Native American Reservation. Write an article for the school newspaper describing what you saw, heard, and learned. *Workshop 8*

I Hear America Singing

EXPLORING

• •

Sometimes we experience moments that seem perfect. We wish for nothing else. The airplane pilot or teacher or nurse's aide enjoys work as it happens, longing neither for the future nor the past. When have you been content during a present moment? Think of conditions—such as winning the race or visiting an old friend—that cause you to experience absolute joy in the "now." Discuss these moments and what makes them so special.

THEME CONNECTION...
INDIVIDUALS AND COMMUNITIES

In "I Hear America Singing," men and women sing happily while they work, prizing the moment and expressing their individuality. Each unique individual is also part of the community. Whitman praises both individuals and their democratic society.

TIME & PLACE

Walt Whitman was born in New York in 1819 when people still vividly recalled the Revolutionary War, and he lived through the Civil War. These struggles for freedom inspired Whitman to cherish the individual and democracy. Whitman's heroes included George Washington and Abraham Lincoln. These two men epitomized the ideals that Whitman admired and celebrated in his poetry.

THE WRITER'S CRAFT

FREE VERSE

Free verse is verse without meter and without rhyme. It "frees" the poet from stanza patterns, measured lines, and the idea that only some words are suited to poetry. Free verse allows the poet to use unrhymed lines of any length. In "I Hear America Singing," repetition and descriptive lists help to unify the poem and give it rhythm.

I Hear America Singing

Walt Whitman

I hear America singing, the varied carols I hear:
Those of mechanics—each one singing his, as it should be,
        blithe and strong;
The carpenter singing his, as he measures his plank or
        beam,
The mason singing his, as he makes ready for work, or
        leaves off work;
The boatman singing what belongs to him in his boat—the
        deckhand singing on the steamboat deck;
The shoemaker singing as he sits on his bench—the hatter
        singing as he stands;
The wood cutter's song—the **ploughboy**'s on his way in the
        morning, or at noon intermission, or at sundown;
The delicious singing of the mother—or of the young wife
        at work—or of the girl sewing or washing—
Each singing what belongs to him or her and to none else;
The day what belongs to the day—at night, the party of
        young fellows, **robust**, friendly,
Singing, with open mouths, their strong melodious songs. ❖

About the Author

Walt Whitman (1819–1892) broke rules to give poetry new form and a new subject. The son of a farmer and carpenter, Whitman left school at age twelve to be a printer's apprentice. He held many jobs: teacher, carpenter, journalist, and, during the Civil War, a hospital aide. Whitman revolutionized American poetry by abandoning traditional poetic techniques and conventional subjects, replacing them with free verse. In his controversial volume of poetry, *Leaves of Grass* (1855), he celebrated democracy, equality, and ordinary people.

blithe—frivolous and lively

ploughboy—farmer

robust—strong, hearty

ACCENT ON...
ART & TECHNOLOGY

Whitman's use of language sculpts an image of his characters for his readers. Working with art students, discuss ways in which a modern sculpture of one of the characters could be created by using plastics technology or metallurgic technology. Use the information in the poem to choose a medium to create a sculpture of one of the characters.

SPOTLIGHT ON...
BUILDING SELF-ESTEEM

In the poem, Whitman celebrates each of the worker's roles. It is important for people to feel good about themselves and the jobs they perform. You, too, can take satisfaction in the work you do. Keep in mind the following:

* Working hard and doing your best builds self-esteem.
* All jobs are important, no matter how big or how small.
* Working effectively and productively makes you proud of your efforts.
* Working responsibly and honestly helps you feel good about yourself and your work.

UNDERSTANDING

1. Name the items catalogued in "I Hear America Singing," and define unfamiliar terms. Write a catalogue of ten modern occupations that were unknown in Whitman's time but are similar to the jobs Whitman listed. Choose a method of organization—for example, according to pay or education required—and arrange your catalogue accordingly.

2. Locate words and lines in "I Hear America Singing" that explain what America's workers are singing about. Using this information as the basis of your discussion, write one page comparing and contrasting the attitude of Whitman's workers with the attitudes of people you know toward their work. *Workshop 9*

3. Free verse contains unrhymed lines of various lengths. To be poetry, the lines must be tied together. Repetition helps connect lines and stress ideas. List examples of repetition of words, phrases, and vowel and consonant sounds.

   Write a paragraph about something you like to do, such as riding a motorcycle or acting in a play. Repeat words and phrases to unify and emphasize your description. *Workshop 2*

4. Poets choose words with care. Often a poem's words surprise readers or allow them to see or hear something. List five words in the poem that surprise you, or that appeal to sight or sound. List striking phrases.

   Write a paragraph about a job you have had, or a position you have held on a team or club. Use vivid, descriptive words so that your readers see and hear what you experienced. *Workshop 2*

FOCUS ON... MUSIC

Whitman's poetry is lyrical and rhythmic. In the poem, "I Hear America Singing," his words not only describe the songs of workers, but the words themselves take on a rhythm that is musical. What songs do you know that relate to a certain job? For example, what folk songs do you remember that celebrated miners, railroad workers, and so on? Seek out such a song or two and write down the lyrics. Then illustrate the song using your own drawing or using images from magazines and newspapers.

A LAST WORD

As citizens, we are part of many communities: we belong to neighborhoods, cities, companies, and businesses. What responsibilities do we have to the communities to which we belong? Why?

CONNECTING

1. Prepare a brief written or oral report that describes the modern equivalent of an occupation Whitman mentions. Your report should contain facts about how to prepare for this occupation, a description of the work involved in this occupation, and information on potential job opportunities.

2. Whitman praises work. Sometimes, however, work produces defective products or poor service. Brainstorm in groups about experiences you have had with faulty products or unsatisfactory service. Find a complaint that your group agrees is significant enough to pursue. Review the mechanics of writing business letters, specifically of complaints. Together write a letter of complaint to the person or agency you wish to take action. ***Workshop 12***

Geraldo No Last Name

EXPLORING

People the world over, regardless of race, culture, or nationality, are fundamentally the same. All people—from the Asanti tribes in Africa to the farmers in the midwestern United States—sing, dance, create art, work, and raise children. All are human beings first, Africans, Mexicans, or Americans second. Every individual's life is precious to family and friends; the loss of one life brings sorrow and perhaps hardship. Does society place equal value on each person, or does it assign less value to the lives of some people than to others? What evidence can you cite to support your answer?

THEME CONNECTION...
ON THE FRINGE OF COMMUNITY

The story focuses on Geraldo, one of the hundreds of anonymous souls in our community. In every community exist people on the fringe who don't quite fit in. Geraldo is one of these people. Marin's sincere concern about him identifies her as a responsible member of the human community.

TIME & PLACE

Today, about 14 million people of Mexican national origin are citizens of the United States. Many more are here temporarily, most working legally, some illegally. Mexican workers in California, Texas, Oregon, Idaho, and Washington are visible in fields and orchards, restaurants, hotels, and other places where their work is needed. Because of the large number of Mexicans and Mexican Americans, their food, music, and language have become part of the United States culture. Examinations, signs, and directions are often provided in both Spanish and English. In some cities—such as Los Angeles, California, and San Antonio, Texas—one will hear Spanish spoken almost as often as English.

THE WRITER'S CRAFT
POINT OF VIEW

Every story is told by someone. It may be told by a character in the story, the *I*. This is a first person narrator. It may be told by an all-knowing (omniscient) author who uses *he*, *she*, and *they* (third-person pronouns) while telling what happens to the characters. Point of view is the term used to indicate the teller of the tale. "Geraldo No Last Name" is told from the third person point of view.

Geraldo No Last Name

Sandra Cisneros

She met him at a dance. Pretty too, and young. Said he worked in a restaurant, but she can't remember which one. Geraldo. That's all. Green pants and Saturday shirt. Geraldo. That's what he told her.

And how was she to know she'd be the last one to see him alive. An accident, don't you know. Hit and run. Marin, she goes to all those dances. Uptown. Logan. Embassy. Palmer. Aragon. Fontana. The Manor. She likes to dance. She knows how to do **cumbias** and **salsas** and **rancheras** even. And he was just someone she danced with. Somebody she met that night. That's right.

That's the story. That's what she said again and again. Once to the hospital people and twice to the police. No address. No name. Nothing in his pockets. Ain't it a shame.

Only Marin can't explain why it mattered, the hours and hours, for somebody she didn't even know. The hospital emergency room. Nobody but an intern working all alone. And maybe if the surgeon would've come, maybe if he hadn't lost so much blood, if the surgeon had only come, they would know who to notify and where.

But what difference does it make? He wasn't anything to her. He wasn't her boyfriend or anything like that. Just another brazer who didn't speak English. Just another wetback. You know the kind. The ones who always look ashamed. And what was she doing out at three a.m. anyway? Marin who was sent home with her coat and some aspirin. How does she explain?

She met him at a dance. Geraldo in his shiny shirt and green pants. Geraldo going to a dance.

What does it matter?

They never saw the kitchenettes. They never knew about the two-room flats and sleeping rooms he rented, the weekly money orders sent home, the currency exchange. How could they?

His name was Geraldo. And his home is in another country. The ones he left behind are far away, will wonder, shrug, remember. Geraldo—he went north . . . we never heard from him again. ❖

About the Author

Sandra Cisneros (1954–) grew up in Chicago. Her Mexican-American family moved frequently when she was young, from one Hispanic neighborhood to another. She began writing at the age of ten. Cisneros attended Loyola University, majoring in English, then earned a Master of Fine Arts degree at the University of Iowa. Though she taught high school English for two years, most of her energies have been focused on her writing. She has earned numerous grants and fellowships, including a MacArthur grant in 1995.

cumbia—a dance

salsa—a dance

ranchera—a dance

ACCENT ON...
EMERGENCY HEALTH CARE

• •

Marin sat in the hospital emergency room with the dying Geraldo, waiting for additional staff to arrive. How is emergency health care provided in most hospitals? Discuss ways in which modern urban emergency rooms handle incoming cases. What types of new diagnostic technology could have helped Geraldo? How might Geraldo's case have been handled differently?

FOCUS ON...
MUSIC

The story mentions several different kinds of dances. Are you familiar with any of them? Find out how dances like cumbias, salsas, and rancheras are done. Using print or on-line data resources, gather information about these and other Latin dances. Tape examples of the music associated with each kind of dance.

UNDERSTANDING

1. What do you think the daily life of Geraldo was like based on the brief information the story provides?

    Using the details the story gives about Geraldo, elaborating with your own imagination, write a character sketch of Geraldo describing not only his appearance, but his inner qualities as well.

2. The hit and run driver was at fault, of course, for Geraldo's injuries. The story, however, suggests that others may have been responsible for his death. Who else played a role in Geraldo's fatal accident?

    A police report must provide all the precise details of an accident: date, time, location, victims, time police arrived on the scene, time ambulance arrived, and statements from witnesses. Attached to the report is a sketch showing the streets and the position of the automobiles and/or victims involved. Assume that you and a partner are the police officers called to the scene of Geraldo's accident. Write a police report. Manufacture necessary details.

3. Scan the story for statements that appeal to your emotions. In contrast to Cisnero's story, a news article about the event would be entirely objective, without opinions or feelings. Write a newspaper article about Geraldo's accident. Move from most important details to least important. Answer the questions who?, what?, where?, why?, and how? Make up missing details such as date, time, and Marin's last name. *Workshop 8*

CONNECTING

1. Some Americans would like to limit the rights of immigrants. A number of people seek legislation that would eliminate bilingual education (education in the student's native language) in public schools. Other bills would take away the rights of children of illegal immigrants to attend public school and receive free medical care. Choose one of these issues, research it, and write a letter to a state legislator stating and supporting your opinion. *Workshop 11*

2. With a partner or small group, develop a dramatization of the interviews between Marin and the police and/or Marin and the hospital personnel. A narrator could provide background information. Write a script, practice, and then present the play before an audience.

3. Using your own expertise or with some assistance from a teacher or another student, rewrite the story, or a portion of it, in Spanish. Read the story to the class in Spanish.

A LAST WORD

"All are human beings first, Africans, Mexicans, or Americans second." How does our quality of life suffer if we treat some people as less important than others? Why is it important to treat people as *human beings first*?

Women at Work

- *Steelworker*
- *Lineage*

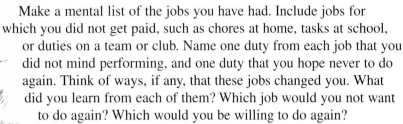

EXPLORING

Make a mental list of the jobs you have had. Include jobs for which you did not get paid, such as chores at home, tasks at school, or duties on a team or club. Name one duty from each job that you did not mind performing, and one duty that you hope never to do again. Think of ways, if any, that these jobs changed you. What did you learn from each of them? Which job would you not want to do again? Which would you be willing to do again?

THEME CONNECTION...
BELONGING

Work often allows people to share at least one common interest: their jobs. This shared interest creates a community. Frequently, employees working together establish close relationships based on the pride they take in performing their responsibilities, particularly when those responsibilities involve difficult skills or shared risks.

Such is the case in "Steelworkers." Margaret Walker's "Lineage" also portrays community—community united by family and ethnic ties.

TIME & PLACE

"Steelworker" occurs in Chicago, Illinois, the heart of the American Midwest. It takes place during the late 1970s or early 1980s, before hard economic times forced several steel mills to close permanently. Farr discusses the various jobs she performed as a mill worker, and she describes her feelings when she and many of her co-workers were permanently laid off and, finally, the factory closed entirely.

A poem by Margaret Walker offers another look at strong women who worked hard at another industry—farming and raising families.

THE WRITER'S CRAFT

IMAGERY

"Steelworker" offers vivid imagery: words and phrases that appeal to the senses. Imagery includes *the furnace tips*, pouring out a *soup of liquid fire*, making a *sunset glow*. Farr wears a *metallic-like coat* and *one-fingered mitts*, and *shakes the sparks* from her clothing. She cuts in half *bowl-shaped chunks of steel*, creating a *waterfall of fantastic colors*.

Walker's "Lineage" also uses imagery. The poem appeals to our sense of touch and smell when it says, for example, that the grandmothers have "veins rolling roughly over quick hands" and smell like "soap and onions and wet clay."

Steelworker

Trudy Pax Farr

About the Author

Trudy Pax Farr is originally from Celina, Ohio, where she grew up on a farm. She has held a variety of jobs, including teaching English as a second language. For many years she lived in Chicago. As a writer, she has had essays published in a number of periodicals. Farr presently lives in Minnesota.

My first day. The BOP (Basic Oxygen Process) Shop towers some six or seven stories. Everywhere there is equipment of gigantic proportions. Ladles, cranes, transfer cars. We workers are dwarfed beside them. Forklift trucks and bulldozers run around like beetles.

I stand mesmerized when the huge furnace tips and slowly pours out its liquid fire—what other name can I give that brilliant soup? "Don't look at it," another worker says, "you need these," and he gives me some small blue-lensed glasses that I can clip on my safety glasses and flip up or down as I need. As the steel flows from the tap hole of the furnace into the waiting ladle, a sunset glow sweeps over everything and, for a brief moment, there is color in this drab, **relentlessly** gray building.

Many feet above—I can barely make out the operator in the cab—runs the crane, its runway spanning the width of the building. It comes now, and with much creaking and straining, laboriously lifts the filled ladle. When it does, some steel sloshes over and a glowing puddle sits on the ground after the crane glides away.

I become a burner. I don a stiff metallic-like coat and leggings, strap leather gaiters over shoes. A welder-type shield over my face, leather one-fingered mitts for my hands. All to protect me from the "sparks" (in fact, small droplets of hot steel) that shower down when oxygen, flame, and air meet molten steel. Still, those sparks find their way down my shirt front, into my gloves. At first, I stop to inspect each small burn, but before long I do as the seasoned burners do: simply shake the spark out of my glove the best I can, hold my shirt away from my body and let it tumble down, and continue at the job. Under all that fireproof clothing, my T-shirt and bra are filled with small burn holes. My hands are pock-marked.

Steel: durable, **impregnable**, indestructible. I cut through it like butter. At a touch, the flame of my torch turns that sturdy mass of steel into flowing liquid. What power!

Sometimes I cut scrap—old rods from the stoppers that close the opening on the ladles. Sometimes I help prepare molds for the next batch of steel—I cut off the steel that has spilled over the edges and has hardened there. Sometimes I'm called to the ladle liners—steel has worked its way in between the bricks of the ladle lining and now they need to get those "frozen bricks" out. (This is tricky: Cut the spilled steel, but not the ladle that it's attached to.) Sometimes I work the mixers (large heated drums that hold the molten iron until the furnaces are ready for it)—then it's iron, not steel, that we cut away. It has sloshed around the opening, building up layer after layer until we need to clean away big chunks. Sometimes there are spills on the railroad tracks—a mold full of molten steel has toppled and the hardened metal has to be cleared. All these jobs are small and are done with a hand-held torch.

But more often than not, I work in the "strawberry patch." What a colorful name for yet another ugly spot: an area just outside the BOP Shop where they dump

relentlessly—harshly or persistently

impregnable—cannot be overcome

SPOTLIGHT ON...
FOLLOWING A SCHEDULE

In Farr's essay, the author describes how arbitrarily workers' schedules were assigned. Why would a schedule be so important in a steel mill? In your own life, establish a schedule by doing the following:

1. Invest in a monthly calendar, or make one from notebook paper.
2. Write down all project due dates and test dates in one ink color.
3. Incorporate your work schedule in the same calendar, but use a different color of ink.
4. Write down any social activities in yet another color.
5. Add any family or outside obligations in yet another color.
6. Note any conflicts in your schedule so that you can resolve them. Use your leisure time to work ahead on projects. Think of ways you can improve how you schedule your time to get the most out of each day.

the leftovers from ladles—big bowl-shaped chunks of steel and sediment that must be cut in half before a crane can lift them. Then I work with an unwieldy fifteen-foot rod that can reach far into the crevice I create as I burn. Out of that crevice comes a waterfall of fantastic colors. Through my blue-tinted glasses (now I use those glasses my fellow worker gave me on that first day), I watch it flow like candle wax: red, bright orange, **magenta**—snaking out, layer upon layer, each quickly fading to a paler shade. A thing of beauty. The only beauty in this gray and dusty place.

One day I meet a photographer—he's come to make an ad for Ford. It will show a spanking-new car springing effortlessly and ready-made from the molten steel. He is surprised to find women working in the mill and asks about burning. I proudly explain the process. Then, "Tell me," he says, "how do you breathe in here?" How indeed? I develop a chronic cough.

Little by little, I begin to feel like a real part of the mill crew. I know I have made it when I begin breaking in new workers. Occasionally the new worker is a woman. On those days, the mill seems different: less austere, more hospitable. We relax, work smoothly; we have to answer to no one, have nothing to prove.

I try to befriend some of the old-time women—those left from the days of World War II when women did so many of the mill jobs: welders, track gang, crane operators, observers. I am fascinated with their life stories: how they came to the mill during the war; how they managed to stay on after everyone told them that their patriotic duty of taking a job in the mill was over, that their patriotic duty *now* was to go home and be a full-time wife. But, for the most part, they seem to resent us newcomers. They complain because we have it easier than they did, because we don't work hard enough, because we demand too much. And sometimes because too many of us are black.

Women at work in an airplane fuel tank factory in Ohio during World War II.

magenta—
purplish red

FOCUS ON... SCIENCE

In her essay, Farr describes several steps in the process of steelmaking. Write two or three paragraphs that describe just how steel is made, including the chemical process. How has the process and/or the technology changed since the early 1980s, when this essay was written? You may also wish to prepare a three-dimensional model that illustrates the process.

◆◆◆◆◆◆◆◆◆◆◆◆◆◆◆◆◆◆◆◆◆◆

amiable—friendly

We—all of us in the mill—work around the clock. There are no weekends, no holidays. Steelmaking, they tell us, can take no rest. We come and go—at eight, at four, at midnight. We meet briefly, passing the baton, so to speak, of our particular job. If no relief shows up, we stay for an extra turn (shift).

For single mothers with small children, the schedule is pure hell. Some might call it irony; I call it injustice: Single mothers who so desperately need these relatively well-paying jobs have to face impossible conditions. And no exceptions can be made. (Although I've seen a man get a "special schedule" to accommodate his working wife.)

Each week, people cluster around the bulletin board to decipher their schedule for the coming week. Some read it and are silent: pleased or perhaps resigned. Others object. "Sunday, first turn! No way! Let me talk to that scheduler!" And off they stomp to Nurven's office—a small shanty next to the general foreman's. More often than not they soon come back, sit glumly and silently in the shanty. Nurven is not easily persuaded.

Accidents happen everywhere in the mill. But none so gruesome as those in the BOP Shop. I am on the midnight turn when the first fatality happens. I am working in another area, but hear the voice on the intercom. I don't suspect death— the voice is urgent, but not panicky: "Get a foreman down here. We have a problem." In the morning, I learn it was **amiable**, deliberate, soft-spoken Slow Joe, his fork-lift truck tipped over by a railroad transfer car. Not long after, there is the remote-control train operator, squashed by the very cars he is manipulating. Then the millwright caught in the huge cables of the crane he was working on. Another mill-wright crushed when the equipment he is repairing collapses on him. A man burned to death by steel that spills over the edge of the ladle. Each death wrenches me, twists my heart for days. But despite it all, I feel immune. Confident no such thing will happen to me.

Confident, until it happens to a burner.

They tell me about it when I come into the mill for my afternoon turn. A freak accident, they say. He was working on a strawberry, cutting it in half as usual, when the molten steel that had gathered in the crevice "backfired" and spewed out on him. He has third degree burns on most of his body. He is still alive, they say, but barely. Better to die, they say.

I go to the spot where it happened. I stand looking at the half-finished strawberry—a strawberry like any of the dozens I had worked on. I nudge a piece of something on the ground with my metal-tipped shoe. It is a portion of the burner's safety glasses, melted and contorted. And I think: The only reason I'm standing here and not lying in a burn unit somewhere in the city is a question of schedule. I decide I no longer want to be a burner.

I put aside the tools of the burner: torch and striker, rods and hoses. I put aside my fireproof clothing. I take up a trowel and hammer; I become a ladle liner.

The ladle liners' job: Build a floor and wall of firebrick inside the ladle, to keep the molten steel from burning right through the ladle. I heft the eighty-pound bags of cement, mixing it in big drums to make the "soup" that will seal the bricks together. I climb down into the huge container, big enough to hold two hundred tons of molten steel. I slap the bricks in place—clack, clack, clack—one layer, two layers. A wall to hold in all that heat and fire. Like a mason, I tap the brick with my hammer to make it break just so, the exact place, the exact size I need to fit this space, to snug this row.

Some of the ladles come to us direct from the **teeming** aisle, still hot from the recently poured steel. A pleasant thing on a cold night; not so in the summer.

Steelmaking—that's the heart of it. But the process, despite all our technological know-how, is still a surprisingly seat-of-the-pants operation. The final product is always iffy, and the furnace men are always nervous, often frantic. We try to have as little as possible to do with them, but all our work revolves around them. The ladles we line will carry the steel

they create, poured fresh and boiling hot from the furnaces.

A good day—things are perking along. One after another, the torpedo-shaped railroad cars come rolling in, bringing iron from the blast furnace. Iron, scrap, a few bags of this and that dumped into the furnaces. Then what wild rushing sounds: flame and fire, roar and grumble. Steel is being made. Frenzy everywhere. Prepare the molds. Are there enough? On what track shall they be put? Send for the crane: Take this ladle here, bring one from there. Workers pull on their metallic-like coats, ready to approach the heat and fire. On the platform, the steel pourers crook their arms over their faces, a futile attempt to shield themselves from the heat, the glare. They move in quickly, manipulate the flow, take a sample, and move away. Mold after mold is filled with the molten steel.

But not always—things do not always perk. . . .

Then there is time to sit. We gather in the shanty. (A name that reveals historical origins. Now it is no more than a room to the side of the foreman's office.) We talk about many things. (How Americans never live to be a hundred. "Speak for yourself!" says Love, **indignant**.) About the general foreman. (How he gives you days off, at the drop of a hat. "He don't know no number smaller than three," says Medicine Man.) Stories of the mill, perhaps already told too often, but part of our culture. There's always one newcomer who has not yet heard them. (How Beefco's dentures fell down through the opening in the ladle he was working on, landed in a bucket of mud and slush in front of Casper, who went running to the office, pale as the ghost for whom he is named. How Beefco went to retrieve them, wiped them on his

teeming—overflowing

indignant—angry over something that is not right

Steelmaking, they tell us, can take no rest.

furlough—official leave

metatarsal—having to do with the part of the foot that contains the five bones between the toes and the ankle

listlessly—without any energy

pants, put them back in his mouth . . . How they tied Potato's shoes together while he slept . . . How Richie the foreman got fired for stealing . . . How. . . .)

On those slow days, there's time for a leisurely lunch. We put packets of tacos, jars of soup, and foil-wrapped ears of corn on the salamanders, and stand around those drums of burning coke while the food heats. Once there was even a whole fish, wrapped and cooked, then spread open for everyone to feast on.

In summer, the heat is unbearable: In addition to nature's heat, we have the steelmaking heat and our heavy protective clothing. Everyone has their theory on how to combat it. Ice cubes in drinks, under hard hats, down shirts. The ice machine they installed in the shanty works overtime. But College Joe makes pot after pot of strong coffee on his little hot plate. "The hotter it gets," he insists, "the more coffee you hafta drink."

Seasons come and go in the mill. As far as I know, they will go on forever.

But one day, when the new schedule appears on the board, my name is on a separate list—the one entitled "**furlough.**" I don't mind. This has happened before, and it is a welcome break. A chance to forget about shift work, a chance to live a normal life for a week or two. There are rumors that this layoff is bigger, farther-reaching, but I dismiss those rumors. I have just invested in a pair of new **metatarsal** shoes—I am sure I will be using them for a long time. I walk to the locker room in my new shoes, put them and the rest of my work clothes in my locker, walk out the gate, and never set foot there again. The big layoff has hit.

Reporters begin trekking to this far southeast corner of Chicago—an area foreign to most of them. Nothing of consequence happens here. But now! Thousands laid off in one fell swoop. Mills closing with hardly a day's notice.

But what have they come to investigate? They nod **listlessly**, pencils suspended over their notebooks when we talk of women's hopes dashed, or returning to humdrum low-paying jobs. A Santa-less Christmas—that is what they want to hear. A starving child, foreclosures, suicides— these are stories they drool over. And there *are* those stories. When one surfaces, they perk up, smile. They begin scribbling in their notebooks.

Despite all the attention, we feel invisible to the nonsteelworker world. For some time, among ourselves, we keep our identity: We continue to meet at the union hall; government cheese, milk, and honey are distributed; a job training program is started. But there is not much hope. Other mills—and other industries, too—are closing. Even workers with training—machinists, plumbers, welders, electricians—find it hard to get a job. Workers are being shepherded through a funnel into the shrinking job pool. A few make it through. Most are left to flounder. There is a feeling of life having come to a halt; a feeling of depression: What will become of us, our community? A feeling of betrayal: So many loyal years given to the mill; now the company turns its back.

Little by little, our ties weaken, and we scatter.

What has happened to that small group of women who once called themselves steelworkers? I have lost track of all but a handful.

Some sought jobs similar to the mill—construction, apprenticeships. A few succeeded; most didn't. Some went back to previous jobs. Jobs that, when you came right down to it, they preferred all along. Jobs that pay less, but are less dirty, less dangerous, and, most importantly, have a decent work schedule—a schedule more compatible with raising kids. Some (like me) went back to school, seeking security and stability in nursing, computing, word

processing, teaching. A few fled the Rust Belt, along with the industries, looking for the much-touted jobs in the Sunbelt. I don't know what happened to them.

Sometimes, when I go past that deserted parking lot, now overgrown with weeds, the fences battered and falling, and I see the BOP Shop looming there just beyond, I recall the days at the mill. Then a part of me sighs with relief—the part of me that hated the midnight turns, the dirt, the danger, the harassment, the chaotic life. But another part of me is rather nostalgic—the part that felt the satisfaction of overcoming trepidation, that liked being a part of something BIG. The part of me that enjoyed so much the banter, the camaraderie, the oneness of the mill life. And if today, I were offered a chance to do it all over again, I'm not at all sure what my answer would be. ❖

ACCENT ON...
SAFETY TECHNOLOGY
• •
The author of the essay "Steelworker" was obviously concerned with safety on the job. What types of safety precautions do you take on the job, at school, or at home? Discuss with local firefighters ways in which modern technology is currently used to protect workers exposed to dangerous chemicals or extremely hot temperatures. Or, contact a local industry for information concerning its safety measures.

Lineage

Margaret Walker

My grandmothers were strong.
They followed plows and bent to toil.
They moved through fields sowing seed.
They touched earth and grain grew.
They were full of sturdiness and singing.
My grandmothers were strong.

My grandmothers are full of memories
Smelling of soap and onions and wet clay
With veins rolling roughly over quick hands
They have many clean words to say.
My grandmothers were strong.
Why am I not as they? ❖

About the Author

The daughter of a minister and a teacher, Margaret Walker grew up around books and learning. Born in 1915 in Birmingham, Alabama, Walker attended college and later worked as a social worker, newspaper reporter, and magazine editor. In 1942, she won the Yale Younger Poets Award for her first book of poetry, *For My People*. She was the first African American so honored. Walker also has taught English at Jackson State College, and eventually founded the college's Institute for the Study of History, Life, and Culture of Black People. Her most famous book is probably her historical novel, *Jubilee*.

UNDERSTANDING

1. Work is often difficult and dangerous. Find passages in "Steelworker" that show the difficulty and danger of working in the steel mill.

   Rewrite Farr's account of mill accidents, spark burns, raging heat, and other hardships of a mill worker. Create a newspaper feature intended to portray the dangers and difficulties of working in a steel mill. ***Workshop 9***

2. Both "Steelworker" and "Lineage" portray women with physical and spiritual strength. Write an essay in which you give your own definition of *strength*, supporting your definition with specific examples.

   Draw on the text, personal experience, and the dictionary for examples of different kinds of strength. Ask friends to explain their ideas of strength of character. ***Workshops 12 and 17***

3. Farr likes working in the steel mill above all for the camaraderie. Find examples in "Steelworker" to show that Farr enjoys feeling she is part of the mill community.

   Advertisers often appeal to our wish to belong. Commercials imply that owning brand X will give us friends, make us fit in, or make us popular. Watch your favorite one-hour television program, and analyze its commercials. Note the number of commercials and how they suggested that a product would help a person belong. Tell the class what you discovered.

A LAST WORD

Consider the communities of which you are a part—family, school, neighborhood, work. What is it about these groups of people that makes you feel as if you belong? Why is belonging important to us?

CONNECTING

1. With a partner, make arrangements to visit a business in your area that uses materials or heavy equipment that may pose some potential hazard. It might be a factory, a newspaper, or a farm. Ask the person in charge of the business about safety risks, precautions taken to avoid them, and statistics on work-related accidents. Create a chart or graph that shows these statistics. Write a report on safe working conditions in that business. ***Workshop 20***

2. "My grandmothers were strong," says Margaret Walker in "Lineage," for "they have many clean words to say." In groups, define "clean words." Then identify a cross-section of people in your school or community who might give "clean words." Develop interview questions to ask these people. The questions may range in topic from political viewpoints to how to entertain oneself on a rainy day. Compile the results of your interviews in a handbook offering advice to teenagers.

3. "Steelworker" helps you know what a mill worker does. Interview a worker to ask what she or he does all day and how she or he feels about the work. Then write a first-person account of a day on the job. ***Workshop 2***

Barba Nikos

EXPLORING

Culture is a complex term that incorporates everything about a people, including language, religion, music, dress, and even food. Enmeshed in history and tradition, the foods of a people can be a source of pride and pleasure. In the United States, where many different cultures exist side by side, it may be difficult to determine the foods that represent this country's cultural heritage. Consider your own experience. What foods hold a symbolic and significant place in your own family's traditions? What foods are part of American culture in general?

THEME CONNECTION...
COMMUNITIES WITHIN COMMUNITIES

Members of specific ethnic groups in the United States often live in the same part of a city, forming an ethnic community. Sharing the same culture, they feel connected and loyal to each other. In large cities, members of ethnic groups often stay together in neighborhoods such as Chinatown in San Francisco, Little Italy in New York City, and Little Havana in Miami. Like the Greek characters in this story, members of ethnic groups rely on and expect loyalty from members of their own communities.

TIME & PLACE

"Barba Nikos" by Harry Mark Petrakis, is part of Petrakis's autobiographical novel entitled *Stelmark: A Family Recollection* (1970). The event described takes place in Chicago, Illinois, sometime between 1934 and 1939, when the narrator was a teenager and before America's involvement in World War II. Petrakis explains that he and his teenage friends, boys from a variety of ethnic backgrounds, made it a practice to spend Saturdays trying to prove that they were really Americans. To make this point, they denounced their own cultures.

THE WRITER'S CRAFT
AUTOBIOGRAPHICAL NOVEL

This story is from the autobiographical novel of Harry Mark Petrakis. Autobiography, when written in the form of a novel, may stray from the truth at times, especially in providing names, dates, and places. It is loosely based on the author's own life and experiences, but the author is free to enhance events to make them more interesting.

Barba Nikos

Harry Mark Petrakis

here was one storekeeper I remember above all others in my youth. It was shortly before I became ill, spending a good portion of my time with a motley group of varied ethnic ancestry. We contended with one another to deride the customs of the old country. On our Saturday forays into neighborhoods beyond our own, to prove we were really Americans, we ate hot dogs and drank Cokes. If a boy didn't have ten cents for this repast he went hungry, for he dared not bring a sandwich from home made of the spiced meats our families ate.

One of our untamed games was to seek out the owner of a pushcart or a store, unmistakably an immigrant, and bedevil him with a chorus of insults and jeers. To prove allegiance to the gang it was necessary to reserve our fiercest **malevolence** for a storekeeper or peddler belonging to our own ethnic background.

For that reason I led a raid on the small, shabby grocery of old Barba Nikos, a short, sinewy Greek who walked with a slight limp and sported a flaring, handlebar mustache.

We stood outside his store and dared him to come out. When he emerged to do battle, we plucked a few plums and peaches from the baskets on the sidewalk and retreated across the street to eat them while he watched. He waved a fist and hurled epithets at us in ornamental Greek.

Aware that my mettle was being tested, I raised my arm and threw my half-eaten plum at the old man. My aim was accurate and the plum struck him on the cheek. He shuddered and put his hand to the stain. He stared at me across the street, and although I could not see his eyes, I felt them sear my flesh. He turned and walked silently back into the store. The boys slapped my shoulders in admiration, but it was a hollow victory that rested like a stone in the pit of my stomach.

At twilight when we disbanded, I passed the grocery alone on my way home. There was a small light burning in the store and the shadow of the old man's body outlined against the glass. Goaded by remorse, I walked to the door and entered.

The old man moved from behind the narrow wooden counter and stared at me. I wanted to turn and flee, but by then it was too late. As he motioned for me to come closer, I braced myself for a curse or a blow.

"You were the one," he said, finally, in a harsh voice.

I nodded mutely.

"Why did you come back?"

I stood there unable to answer.

"What's your name?"

"Haralambos," I said, speaking to him in Greek.

He looked at me in shock. "You are Greek!" he cried. "A Greek boy attacking a Greek grocer!" He stood appalled at the immensity of my crime. "All right," he said coldly. "You are here because you wish to make amends." His great mustache bristled

> ● ● ● ● ● ● ●
> …it was a hollow victory that rested like a stone in the pit of my stomach.
> ● ● ● ● ● ● ●

About the Author

Harry Mark Petrakis has worked as laborer, steelworker, real estate salesperson, speechwriter, free-lance writer, and lecturer. Born in St. Louis in 1923, he grew up in the Greek neighborhoods of Chicago. His writing is primarily about the immigrant experience in America. Critics have called him "a storyteller of immense exuberance." His first novel was published in 1959, and his collection of short stories *Pericles on 31st Street* was nominated for the National Book Award for fiction in 1965.

malevolence— ill will, spite

FOCUS ON... ECONOMICS

The narrator of the story works to pay for the fruit he and the others took. However, losses due to shoplifting or vandalism are seldom regained. To cover these losses, stores raise the prices of the merchandise they sell. Explore the cost of vandalism and theft to small merchants like the man in the story. Interview store owners to see what percentage of profits they lose each year, and what steps they have taken to minimize these losses.

in concentration. "Four plums, two peaches," he said. "That makes a total of 78 cents. Call it 75. Do you have 75 cents, boy?"

I shook my head.

"Then you will work it off," he said. "Fifteen cents an hour into 75 cents makes"—he paused—"five hours of work. Can you come here Saturday morning?"

"Yes," I said.

"Yes, Barba Nikos," he said sternly. "Show respect."

"Yes, Barba Nikos," I said.

"Saturday morning at eight o'clock," he said. "Now go home and say thanks in your prayers that I did not loosen your impudent head with a solid smack on the ear." I needed no further urging and fled.

Saturday morning, still apprehensive, I returned to the store. I began by sweeping, raising clouds of dust in dark and hidden corners. I washed the windows, whipping the squeegee swiftly up and down the glass in a fever of fear that some member of the gang would see me. When I finished I hurried back inside.

For the balance of the morning I stacked cans, washed the counter, and dusted

bottles of yellow wine. A few customers entered, and Barba Nikos served them. A little after twelve o'clock he locked the door so he could eat lunch. He cut himself a few slices of sausage, tore a large chunk from a loaf of crisp-crusted bread, and filled a small cup with a dozen black shiny olives floating in brine. He offered me the cup. I could not help myself and grimaced.

"You are a stupid boy," the old man said. "You are not really Greek, are you?"

"Yes, I am."

"You might be," he admitted grudgingly. "But you do not act Greek. Wrinkling your nose at these fine olives. Look around this store for a minute. What do you see?"

"Fruits and vegetables," I said. "Cheese and olives and things like that."

He stared at me with a massive scorn. "That's what I mean," he said. "You are a bonehead. You don't understand that a whole nation and a people are in this store."

I looked uneasily toward the storeroom in the rear, almost expecting someone to emerge.

"What about olives?" he cut the air with a sweep of his arm. "There are olives of many shapes and colors. Pointed black ones from Kalamata, oval ones from Amphissa, pickled green olives and sharp tangy yellow ones. **Achilles** carried black olives to Troy and after a day of savage battle leading his Myrmidons, he'd rest and eat cheese and ripe black olives such as these right here. You have heard of Achilles, boy, haven't you?"

"Yes," I said.

"Yes, Barba Nikos."

"Yes, Barba Nikos," I said.

He motioned at the row of jars filled with varied spices. "There is **origanon** there and **basilikon** and **daphne** and **sesame** and **miantanos**, all the marvelous flavorings that we have used in our food for thousands of years. The men of Marathon carried small packets of these spices into battle, and the scents reminded them of their homes, their families, and their children."

He rose and tugged his napkin free from around his throat. "Cheese, you said. Cheese! Come closer, boy, and I educate your **abysmal** ignorance." He motioned toward a wooden container on the counter. "That glistening white delight is feta, made from goat's milk, packed in wooden buckets to retain the flavor. Alexander the Great demanded it on his table with his casks of wine when he planned his campaigns."

He walked limping from the counter to the window where the piles of tomatoes, celery, and green peppers clustered. "I suppose all you see here are some random vegetables?" He did not wait for me to answer. "You are dumb again. These are some of the ingredients that go to make up a Greek salad. Do you know what a Greek salad really is? A meal in itself, an experience, an emotional involvement. It is created deftly and with grace. First, you place large lettuce leaves in a big, deep bowl." He spread his fingers and moved them slowly, carefully, as if he were arranging the leaves. "The remainder of the lettuce is shredded and piled in a small mound," he said. "Then comes celery, cucumbers, tomatoes sliced lengthwise, green peppers, origanon, green olives, feta, avocado, and anchovies. At the end you dress it with lemon, vinegar, and pure olive oil, glinting golden in the light."

He finished with a heartfelt sigh and for a moment closed his eyes. Then he opened one eye to mark me with a baleful intensity. "The story goes that **Zeus** himself created the recipe and assembled and mixed the ingredients on Mount Olympus one night when he had invited some of the other gods to dinner."

He turned his back on me and walked slowly again across the store, dragging one foot slightly behind him. I looked uneasily at the clock, which showed that it was a few minutes past one. He turned quickly and startled me. "And everything else in here," he said loudly. "White beans, lentils, garlic, crisp bread, **kokoretsi**, meat balls, mussels and clams." He paused and drew a deep, long breath. "And the wine," he went on, "wine from Samos, Santorini, and Crete, **retsina** and **mavrodaphne**, a taste almost as old as water . . . and then the fragrant melons, the pastries, yellow **diples** and golden **loukoumades**, the honey custard **galatobouriko**. Everything a part of our history, as much a part as the exquisite sculpture in marble, the bearded warriors, **Pan** and the **oracles at Delphi**, and the

> You don't understand that a whole nation and a people are in this store.

Achilles—a great warrior in Greek myths

origanon—a fragrant plant, especially oregano

basilikon—a plant of the mint family, basil

daphne—a shrub

sesame—an herb whose seeds are used as a flavoring

miantanos—a Greek flavoring

abysmal—extremely low or great

Zeus—the king of the gods in Greek mythology

kokoretsi—sheep entrails

retsina—a resin-flavored Greek wine

mavrodaphne—a sweet wine

diple—deep fried dough

loukoumades—sweet fried dough

galatobouriko—custard-filled filo

Pan—a Greek god of pastures, flocks, and shepherds

oracles at Delphi—a shrine through which a god reveals hidden knowledge or divine purpose

SPOTLIGHT ON... PAYING ATTENTION TO DETAILS

Barba Nikos describes Greek food to the narrator in careful detail. The details an author chooses to include alert you to what the author considers important. As you read, try to do the following:
- Note main characters' names and descriptions.
- Write down or underline unfamiliar words or phrases.
- Look for context clues to help you understand the plot and unfamiliar words or phrases.
- Pay particular attention to numbers and statistics.

You will learn more about what the author is trying to say and you will enjoy your reading more.

Homer—Greek epic poet

nymphs dancing in the shadowed groves under **Homer's** glittering moon." He paused, out of breath again, and coughed harshly. "Do you understand now, boy?"

He watched my face for some response and then grunted. We stood silent for a moment until he cocked his head and stared at the clock. "It is time for you to leave," he motioned brusquely toward the door. "We are square now. Keep it that way."

I decided the old man was crazy and reached behind the counter for my jacket and cap and started for the door. He called me back. From a box he drew out several soft, yellow figs that he placed in a piece of paper. "A bonus because you worked well," he said. "Take them. When you taste them, maybe you will understand what I have been talking about."

I took the figs and he unlocked the door and I hurried from the store. I looked back once and saw him standing in the doorway, watching me, the swirling tendrils of food curling like mist about his head.

I ate the figs late that night. I forgot about them until I was in bed, and then I

rose and took the package from my jacket. I nibbled at one, then ate them all. They broke apart between my teeth with a tangy nectar, a thick sweetness running like honey across my tongue and into the pockets of my cheeks. In the morning when I woke, I could still taste and inhale their fragrance.

I never again entered Barba Nikos's store. My spell of illness, which began some months later, lasted two years. When I returned to the streets I had forgotten the old man and the grocery. Shortly afterwards my family moved from the neighborhood.

Some twelve years later, after the war, I drove through the old neighborhood and passed the grocery. I stopped the car and for a moment stood before the store. The windows were stained with dust and grime, the interior bare and desolate, a store in a decrepit group of stores marked for razing so new structures could be built.

I have been in many Greek groceries since then and have often bought the feta and Kalamata olives. I have eaten countless

Greek salads and have indeed found them a meal for the gods. On the holidays in our house, my wife and sons and I sit down to a dinner of steaming, buttered **pilaf** like my mother used to make and lemon-egg **avgolemono** and roast lamb richly seasoned with cloves of garlic. I drink the red and yellow wines, and for dessert I have come to relish the delicate pastries coated with honey and powdered sugar. Old Barba Nikos would have been pleased.

But I have never been able to recapture the **halcyon** flavor of those figs he gave me on that day so long ago, although I have bought figs many times. I have found them pleasant to my tongue, but there is something missing. And to this day I am not sure whether it was the figs or the vision and passion of the old grocer that coated the fruit so sweetly I can still recall their savor and fragrance after almost thirty years. ❖

pilaf—a dish made of seasoned rice and often meat

avgolemono—a soup made of chicken stock, rice, egg yolks, and lemon sauce

halcyon—calming, pleasing

ACCENT ON...
AGRICULTURAL TECHNOLOGY

Grocers like Barba Nikos would have lost a certain percent of their fresh produce every day due to spoilage. Though supermarkets and other food stores still are concerned with loss because of spoilage, modern packaging and refrigeration methods have reduced those losses. What other techniques can reduce spoilage? Working with agriculture students, identify current approved and experimental processes or techniques that are helpful. If you like, contact the United States Department of Agriculture (USDA) to get more information.

ON THE JOB
SHOP MANAGER

In a small shop like Barba Nikos's the manager must juggle a variety of tasks to keep the operation running smoothly. To manage such a shop, a person needs to be extremely familiar with the product. Usually a high school diploma and a six-month apprenticeship are minimum requirements to become a shop manager. The shop manager's responsibilities include purchasing materials, maintaining equipment and supplies, keeping accurate records, and monitoring budget and schedule. In most shops, managers should know how to use computers, calculators, and automated equipment effectively. Being able to work with a variety of people and to manage one's time are also important skills.

UNDERSTANDING

1. Who was in the author's street gang? What things did the gang do, and why? Support your conclusions with passages from the story.

   Petrakis appreciated the "vision and passion of the old grocer." In your life, perhaps an adult's vision and passion have had a positive influence on you. Write a thank-you letter to someone who has positively influenced your life. In this letter, explain what the person did for you and why you are grateful. *Workshop 11*

2.  Why does the boy return to the shop? He does not know the shop-keeper, and there is no way he can be found out. Barba Nikos gives one reason, and you can infer others from the story.

   In a group, discuss times you may have done something you later regretted. Did you apologize? Why or why not? Why do you think the boy in the story should or should not have apologized? With your group, discuss times at school when an apology may or may not have made a difference. Then list the occasions when you think apologies are called for and would help.

3. Barba Nikos tells the young boy about the strong connection between Greek food and Greek mythology and history. He then asks, "Do you understand now, boy?" What should the boy have understood? Have you had to learn to understand and respect your own family's traditions, or perhaps those of a friend?

   In a brief oral presentation, share with the class information about customs unique to your family or your cultural background. For example, what holidays does your family observe? Do you do anything special on these holidays? Do you always have a family reunion on July 4 and serve hot dogs and baked beans, for instance? Does your family eat distinctive foods at certain times of year that have special meaning? *Workshop 19*

A LAST WORD

Imagine a city in which *all* of the people have the same background, the same culture. What would your own community be like without the richness of its diversity?

CONNECTING

1. Nikos is proud of his background and what he offers to his community. Interview an immigrant to this country. How does the person show pride in her or his background? How is this reflected in this person's daily life?

2. Locate an ethnic restaurant in your city or community. The telephone book will list all restaurants, often by type of food served. Call the restaurant ahead and arrange to meet with the manager or assistant manager. Then visit the restaurant and learn from the manager about service, prices, menu, and quality of food. Take careful note, too, of atmosphere. Afterwards write a restaurant review describing the restaurant to others so they know where it is and what makes it unique. *Workshop 2*

Nursing

• *from The Youngest Science*
• *from Exploring Careers*

EXPLORING

At one time or another, most people have needed a nurse's help. We rely on nurses, but how well do we understand their work or that of others in the health care professions? Imagine what a hospital nurse's daily routine is like. What different kinds of work do nurses perform? Which of a nurse's jobs would you find enjoyable? Which would you not enjoy? What characteristics must a person have in order to be a good nurse? Based on your thinking so far, would you make a good nurse? Why or why not?

THEME CONNECTION...
SERVING THE COMMUNITY

Lewis Thomas, a highly successful physician as well as a famous essayist, describes in detail what nurses did as professionals in 1903 and what they do today. Today, as in the past, close personal contact with the patient continues to be the most important and rewarding part of a nurse's work. The story of Kathy Wright, a nurse at Leeds Memorial Hospital, makes it clear that a registered nurse still attends closely to each patient's needs. The nursing profession, requiring selfless dedication to others, offers job satisfaction by enabling employees to serve their community.

TIME & PLACE

Nursing is a rapidly changing profession. At the beginning of the twentieth century, nurses were almost exclusively female. Once seen solely as assistants to male doctors, now they are treated as professionals. The roles of men and women in the medical workplace have come to overlap much more in the last hundred years. Women doctors and male nurses are now commonplace throughout the country.

THE WRITER'S CRAFT

CHRONOLOGICAL ORDER

Lewis Thomas organizes his essay chronologically and argues from personal experience. He begins by describing his mother's duties as a nurse at the turn of the century, gives his father's view, and describes his own experiences as a doctor and recent patient. He then reports changes occurring in modern nursing. Using chronological organization and personal experience helps Thomas persuade the reader that nurses hold hospitals together.

from *The Youngest Science*
Nurses

Lewis Thomas

About the Author

Lewis Thomas (1913–1993) was a highly successful physician, educator, hospital and medical school administrator, and author. He held a number of positions at prestigious institutions and wrote more than two hundred scientific and medical articles. In addition, Thomas wrote a popular column for the *New England Journal of Medicine*. Many of these philosophical, non-scientific writings focused on nature and humanity. *The Lives of a Cell: Notes of a Biology Watcher* (1974) received the National Book Award. Critics praised Thomas's writings for their wit and imagination.

entourage—group of attendants surrounding a person of high rank

frenetic—wildly excited

stipulated—specified as a condition of an agreement

meticulously—in an extremely careful manner

When my mother became a registered nurse at Roosevelt Hospital, in 1903, there was no question in anyone's mind about what nurses did as professionals. They did what the doctors ordered. The attending physician would arrive for his ward rounds in the early morning, and when he arrived at the ward office the head nurse would be waiting for him, ready to take his hat and coat, and his cane, and she would stand while he had his cup of tea before starting. Entering the ward, she would hold the door for him to go first, then his **entourage** of interns and medical students, then she followed. At each bedside, after he had conducted his examination and reviewed the patient's progress, he would tell the nurse what needed doing that day, and she would write it down on the part of the chart reserved for nursing notes. An hour or two later he would be gone from the ward, and the work of the rest of the day and the night to follow was the nurse's **frenetic** occupation. In addition to the **stipulated** orders, she had an endless list of routine things to do, all learned in her two years of nursing school: the beds had to be changed and made up with fresh sheets by an exact geometric design of folding and tucking impossible for anyone but a trained nurse; the patients had to be washed head to foot; bedpans had to be brought, used, emptied, and washed; temperatures had to be taken every four hours and **meticulously** recorded on the chart; enemas were to be given; urine and stool samples collected, labeled, and sent off to the laboratory; throughout the day and night, medications of all sorts, usually pills and various vegetable extracts and **tinctures**, had to be carried on trays from bed to bed. At most times of the year about half of the forty or so patients on the ward had **typhoid fever**, which meant that the nurse couldn't simply move from bed to bed in the performance of her duties; each typhoid case was screened from the other patients, and the nurse was required to put on a new gown and wash her hands in disinfectant before approaching the bedside. Patients with high fevers were sponged with cold alcohol at frequent intervals. The late-evening back rub was the rite of passage into sleep.

In addition to the routine, workaday schedule, the nurse was responsible for responding to all calls from the patients, and it was expected that she would do so on the run. Her rounds, scheduled as methodical progressions around the ward, were continually interrupted by these calls. It was up to her to evaluate each situation quickly: a sudden abdominal pain in a typhoid patient might signify intestinal **perforation**; the abrupt onset of weakness, thirst, and **pallor** meant intestinal **hemorrhage**; the coughing up of gross blood by a tuberculous patient was an emergency. Some of the calls came from neighboring patients on the way to recovery; patients on open wards always kept a close eye on each other: the man in the next bed might slip into a coma or seem

SPOTLIGHT ON... USING COMPUTERS

Lewis Thomas writes about the changes the nursing profession has undergone. One recent change is the increased use of computers in healthcare. Much of a patient's history and important medical information is kept on a computer database, for example. Whatever your profession, you, too, will probably use computers to do the following:

- acquire information from existing files, online systems, and so on
- organize data using spreadsheets or other basic programs
- analyze information, either onscreen or hard copy
- process reports or statistics
- communicate your findings in a clear, concise fashion

to be dying, or be indeed dead. For such emergencies the nurse had to get word immediately to the doctor on call, usually the intern assigned to the ward, who might be off in the outpatient department or working in the diagnostic laboratory (interns of that day did all the laboratory work themselves; technicians had not yet been invented) or in his room. Nurses were not allowed to give injections or to do such emergency procedures as spinal punctures or chest taps, but they were expected to know when such maneuvers were indicated and to be ready with appropriate trays of instruments when the intern arrived on the ward.

It was an exhausting business, but by my mother's accounts it was the most satisfying and rewarding kind of work. As a nurse she was a low person in the professional hierarchy, always running from place to place on orders from the doctors, subject as well to strict discipline from her own administrative superiors on the nursing staff, but none of this came through in her recollections. What she remembered was her usefulness.

Whenever my father talked to me about nurses and their work, he spoke with high regard for them as professionals. Although it was clear in his view that the task of the nurses was to do what the doctor told them to, it was also clear that he admired them for being able to do a lot of things he couldn't possibly do, had never been trained to do. On his own rounds later on, when he became an attending physician himself, he consulted the ward nurse for her opinion about problem cases and paid careful attention to her observations and chart notes. In his own days of intern training (perhaps partly under my mother's strong influence, I don't know) he developed a deep and lasting respect for the whole nursing profession.

tincture—solution of medicine in alcohol

typhoid fever—a communicable disease causing high fever, intestinal illness, and intense headaches

perforation—hole

pallor—paleness

hemorrhage—bleeding

FOCUS ON...
SCIENCE

Nurses need to study many areas of science to receive a degree. For instance, student nurses take courses in chemistry to learn how various elements interact with one another. This helps them to understand how medicines work and why certain types of medicines should not be taken together. What other science courses do nurses take? Write a paragraph explaining how a certain science helps nurses perform their jobs.

◆◆◆◆◆◆◆◆◆◆◆◆◆◆◆◆◆◆◆◆◆◆◆◆

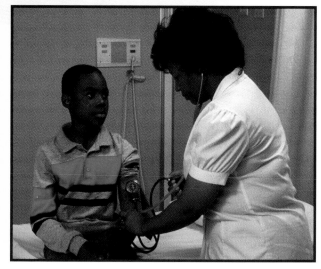

standoffish—not very friendly

adversarial—enemy

paraprofessional—a person trained to assist a doctor, lawyer, or other professional

contemplate—think about

I have spent all of my professional career in close association with, and close dependency on, nurses, and like many of my faculty colleagues, I've done a lot of worrying about the relationship between medicine and nursing. During most of this century the nursing profession has been having a hard time of it. It has been largely, although not entirely, an occupation for women, and sensitive issues of professional status, complicated by the special issue of the changing role of women in modern society, have led to a **standoffish**, often **adversarial** relationship between nurses and doctors. Already swamped by an increasing load of routine duties, nurses have been obliged to take on more and more purely administrative tasks: keeping the records in order; making sure the supplies are on hand for every sort of ward emergency; supervising the activities of the new **paraprofessional** group called LPNs (licensed practical nurses), who now perform much of the bedside work once done by RNs (registered nurses); overseeing ward maids, porters, and cleaners; seeing to it that patients scheduled for X rays are on their way to the X-ray department on time. Therefore, they have to spend more

of their time at desks in the ward office and less time at the bedsides. Too late maybe, the nurses have begun to realize that they are gradually being excluded from the one duty which had previously been their most important reward but which had been so taken for granted that nobody mentioned it in listing the duties of a nurse: close personal contact with patients. Along with everything else nurses did in the long day's work, making up for all the tough and sometimes demeaning jobs assigned to them, they had the matchless opportunity to be useful friends to great numbers of human beings in trouble. They listened to their patients all day long and through the night, they gave comfort and reassurance to the patients and their families, they got to know them as friends, they were depended on. To **contemplate** the loss of this part of their work has been the deepest worry for nurses at large, and for the faculties responsible for the curricula of the nation's new and expanding nursing schools. The issue lies at the center of the running argument between medical school and nursing school administrators, but it is never clearly stated. Nursing education has been upgraded in recent years. Almost all the former hospital schools, which took in high-school graduates and provided an RN certificate after two or three years, have been replaced by schools attached to colleges and universities, with a four-year curriculum leading simultaneously to a bachelor's degree and an RN certificate.

The doctors worry that nurses are trying to move away from their historical responsibilities to medicine (meaning, really, to the doctors' orders). The nurses assert that they are their own profession, responsible for their own standards, coequal colleagues with physicians, and they do not wish to become mere ward administrators or technicians (although some of them, carrying the new and prestigious title of "nurse practitioner," are being trained within nursing schools to perform some of the most complex technological responsibilities in hospital emergency rooms and intensive care units). The doctors claim that what the nurses really want is to become substitute psychiatrists. The nurses reply that they have unavoidable responsibilities for the mental health and well-being of their patients, and that these are different from the doctors' tasks. Eventually the arguments will work themselves out, and some sort of agreement will be reached, but if it is to be settled intelligently, some way will have to be found to preserve and strengthen the traditional and highly personal nurse-patient relationship.

I have had a fair amount of firsthand experience with the issue, having been an apprehensive patient myself off and on over a three-year period on the wards of the hospital for which I work. I am one up on most of my physician friends because of this experience. I know some things they do not know about what nurses do.

One thing the nurses do is to hold the place together. It is an astonishment, which every patient feels from time to time, observing the affairs of a large, complex hospital from the vantage point of his bed, that the whole institution doesn't fly to pieces. A hospital operates by the constant interplay of powerful forces pulling away at each other in different directions, each force essential for getting necessary things done, but always at odds with each other. The intern staff is an almost irresistible force in itself, learning medicine by doing medicine, assuming all the responsibility within reach, pushing against an immovable attending and administrative staff, and frequently at odds with the nurses. The attending physicians are individual entrepreneurs trying to run small **cottage industries** at each bedside. The diagnostic laboratories are **feudal fiefdoms**, prospering from the **insatiable** demands for their services from the interns and residents. The medical students are all over the place, learning as best they can and complaining that they are not, as they believe they should be, at the **epicenter** of everyone's concern. Each individual worker in the place, from the chiefs of surgery to the dieticians to the ward maids, porters, and elevator operators, lives and works in the conviction that the whole apparatus would come to a standstill without his or her individual contribution, and in one sense or another each of them is right.

My discovery, as a patient first on the medical service and later in surgery, is that the institution is held together, *glued* together, enabled to function as an organism, by the nurses and by nobody else.

> ...the nurse was responsible for responding to all calls from the patients, ...

cottage industries—businesses whose labor force usually consists of families working at home using their own equipment

feudal fiefdoms—estates from the political system of the Middle Ages

insatiable—never getting enough

epicenter—the center

The nurses, the good ones anyway (and all the ones on my floor were good), make it their business to know everything that is going on. They spot errors before errors can be launched. They know everything written on the chart. Most important of all, they know their patients as unique human beings, and they soon get to know the close relatives and friends. Because of this knowledge, they are quick to sense apprehensions and act on them. The average sick person in a large hospital feels at risk of getting lost, with no identity left beyond a name and a string of numbers on a plastic wristband, in danger always of being whisked off on a **litter** to the wrong place to have the wrong procedure done, or worse still, *not* being whisked off at the right time. The attending physician or the house officer, on rounds and usually in a hurry, can murmur a few reassuring words on his way out the door, but it takes a confident, competent, and cheerful nurse, there all day long and in and out of the room on one chore or another through the night, to bolster one's confidence that the situation is indeed manageable and not about to get out of hand.

Knowing what I know, I am all for the nurses. If they are to continue their professional feud with the doctors, if they want their professional status enhanced and their pay increased, if they infuriate the doctors by their claims to be equal professionals, if they ask for the moon, I am on their side. ❖

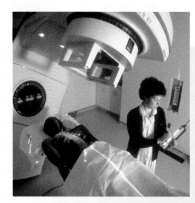

ON THE JOB
RADIOLOGIC TECHNICIAN

Besides doctors and nurses, many other medical staff help to make a hospital run smoothly. One such staff person is the radiologic technician, who operates modern medical imaging equipment such as MRI (magnetic resonance imaging), ultrasound devices, CT (computerized tomography), and other scanners. These machines are used in medical diagnosis. Such a technician must have a high school diploma, good oral and written communication skills, and a solid science background. Professional training is required, usually two years in length and leading to an associate's degree. Technicians must pass a certification exam and are held to a high standard of ethics and moral conduct.

ACCENT ON...
HEALTH CARE TECHNOLOGY

Nurses spend much of their time checking and updating patient records. Have students work with a data processing class or medical records professional to discuss ways in which current technology makes such record-keeping and information processing less time consuming and more beneficial to the patient than it was in the past.

from Exploring Careers
Health Occupations

athy Wright is a nurse at Leeds Memorial Hospital. She works in the surgical intensive care unit and takes care of patients who are in serious condition following surgery. Most patients go back to their rooms after an operation. But not all of them. Kathy's patients are in such critical condition that they are in a special unit where they can be watched every minute for changes that could mean life or death.

To provide the 24-hour care so necessary for these patients, the nurses at Leeds Memorial work day, evening, or night shifts of 8 hours each. The shifts rotate, so that Kathy and the other nurses in surgical intensive care take turns on each of the three shifts. This week Kathy is working from 7 A.M. to 3 P.M.

Kathy grew up in a household where medical research and hospital gossip were ordinary topics of dinner table conversation. Her father is a sales representative for a drug company, and her mother is a pediatrician. As a girl, she heard enough about the "real world" of medicine and nursing to dispel any romantic notions that she might have picked up from novels or from television. Listening to the adults talk about their work, Kathy soon came to realize that a professional health career means lots of work and responsibility.

To become a registered nurse (RN), Kathy completed a 5-year program at a university that led to a B.S. degree in nursing. As a student nurse, she had a heavy dose of science courses, including chemistry, anatomy, microbiology, physiology, nutrition, and public health. Clinical practice—working in the university hospital under the close supervision of the nursing instructor—was another important part of her training.

After graduation, Kathy took the state board examination for licensure. In New York, as in all states, nurses must have a license. Just as a driver's license is proof that you know how to drive, the license required to practice nursing, medicine, dentistry, dental hygiene, or pharmacy, for example, shows that you know enough about your profession to provide safe and proper care.

Kathy chose the B.S. program in nursing because she wanted to keep her options open. She knew, from her talks with her mother, that advancement opportunities for nurses were best for those with a bachelor's degree. And she felt that, after several years of bedside nursing, she might want to move into another kind of job.

At this point, just a few years out of nursing school, she thinks she'll probably stay in hospital nursing. Still, from time to time Kathy thinks seriously about making a change. She wonders what it would be like to fulfill her youthful dream of nursing needy people abroad as a Peace Corps volunteer or a Medico nurse. She also thinks about returning to nursing school for the master's degree or Ph.D. she would need to teach or do research.

The bachelor's degree program that Kathy completed isn't the only way to become a nurse. Hospitals offer 3-year diploma programs and community and junior colleges offer 2-year associate degree programs. However, the bachelor's degree program in nursing generally opens more doors than either of the other two. Some states now require a 4-year B.S. degree for all RNs and efforts are under way to require a bachelor's degree for all registered nurses. It's important to consider all of the different kinds of training programs before choosing one.

SPOTLIGHT ON...
DRAWING CONCLUSIONS

As nurses examine patients, they must draw conclusions about the patients health, based on the facts. As you read, you need to watch for stated facts, but you also need to figure out, or infer, ideas that have not been stated explicity. When you make inferences, you affect the way you draw conclusions.

1. Read the author's statements and facts.
2. Think about the implications of the statements you read.
3. Draw conclusions by combining stated facts with the inferences you make.

◆◆◆◆◆◆◆◆◆◆◆◆◆◆◆◆◆◆◆◆◆◆◆◆◆

Kathy gets off the elevator at the third floor, walks through the heavy double doors, and stops at the nurses' station. There she spends a few minutes with Mr. Cochrane and Ms. Wall, the two nurses who have been on duty to give a general report to the incoming nurses. The group is joined by Ms. Rubel, the nurse who will be on the day shift with Kathy this week.

Ms. Wall begins talking to Kathy about the patients they share. "Mr. Young needed medication for pain at 2 o'clock," she explains, "and Ms. Lance's temperature rose to 102 degrees around midnight, but went down shortly thereafter. Otherwise, their vital signs were normal. Ms. Vaughn slept very well. Ms. Lance is scheduled to be discharged from intensive care tomorrow."

"Fine," replies Kathy. "See you tomorrow."

The nurses in the surgical intensive care unit at Leeds Memorial practice primary nursing. This means that each nurse is responsible on a 24-hour-a-day basis for the continuity, planning, and evaluation of nursing care for one to three patients. Currently, Kathy is responsible for Mr. Young, Ms. Lance, and Ms. Vaughn, while Ms. Rubel is responsible for two other patients. Nurses may act as associate nurses to patients during the absence of their primary nurse. ❖

UNDERSTANDING

1.  If a student thinking of becoming a nurse had time to read only one piece, either "Nurses" or "Health Occupations," which one would you recommend and why? Working with several classmates, list points of similarity in each essay's discussion of the nursing profession. Then list differences. Cite specific passages to support your conclusions. ***Workshop 9***

2. According to Lewis Thomas, changes have taken place in the nurse-physician relationship in this century. How does he describe these changes, and why are they important?

    List other relationships that have changed: parents and children, men and women, teachers and students, employer and employee, coach and athlete. Consider how these changes influence your life or your community. Then write a newspaper editorial describing the significance for the community of changes in a relationship. ***Workshop 8***

3. Taken together, "Health Occupations" and "Nurses" give us a good idea of how one becomes a nurse and what nurses do. Drawing material from both pieces, write a brief memo to a fellow student who is interested in the nursing field. Explain what nurses do and how to become one. ***Workshop 13***

A LAST WORD

As the use of technology increases, many jobs are changing. Are those changes always good? Does "progress" always serve the community?

CONNECTING

1.  In groups, choose a television show or movie that depicts work in hospitals. List the ethical issues raised in the program and discuss those most likely to occur in actual hospitals or real medical practices. Your group should then gather information about the ethical issues it believes are of genuine concern to physicians, nurses, paramedics, and patients. Present your findings to the class in a collaborative oral report. ***Workshop 19***

2. Use the internet to e-mail a nursing school, hospital or nursing home. Ask a doctor or nurse to explain their views of what a nurse's job ought to be. Find out if they think the role of nurses is changing for the better or worse, and why. Report back to the class on your findings. ***Workshop 14***

3. Arrange to "shadow"—to follow around for part of a day—someone who works in a medical occupation. For example, you may arrange to shadow an orderly, an X-ray technician, or a nurse. You may spend part of a day in a hospital or an urgent care center. When you visit, observe and make notes about what the job you are shadowing seems to involve. Prepare a brief oral report to the class describing your observations. ***Workshop 19***

Community Ties

• *The First Seven Years*

• *Remember*

EXPLORING

● ● ● ● ● ● ● ● ● ● ● ● ● ● ● ● ● ● ●

Parenting is an inexact art at best. Parents generally raise their children as well as they can, given the fact that mistakes are inevitable. Whether you feel that you have been well or poorly parented, you have undoubtedly judged some parenting practices to be better than others, and perhaps you have even made some decisions about how (or whether) you will become a parent. Consider the effective and ineffective parenting practices that you have observed. What practices would you use if you were a parent?

THEME CONNECTION...
SELF AND COMMUNITY

A community is any group to which people belong, such as a family, team, school, or nation. In "The First Seven Years," Feld's family constitutes a community, and understandably as head of the family, Feld feels responsible for his daughter's future. Eventually Feld learns that he also has a responsibility to Sobel, his assistant for the past five years.

Joy Harjo's poem "Remember" urges readers to remember they are part of a larger whole. As members of any community, we are responsible for one another to some extent.

TIME & PLACE

"The First Seven Years" takes place in Brooklyn, New York, in a low-income neighborhood occupied mainly by Jewish immigrants from Poland. Feld has lived in New York long enough to have established his shoemaker's business. Sobel, however, arrived more recently. A Polish refugee from Hitler's German army, which invaded Poland in 1938, Sobel "had by the skin of his teeth escaped Hitler's incinerators."

Unlike Malamud, Harjo does not focus on a single location as she emphasizes relationships. Harjo's narrator mentions experiences in Iowa City and at the "corner of Fourth and Central." Writing today for a contemporary audience, Harjo asks us to value ties among all people.

THE WRITER'S CRAFT

PLOT STRUCTURE

Events in most short stories or novels usually have a conflict between one or more central characters. This conflict builds to a central **climax**, or turning point, which occurs when the conflict cannot worsen. This climax may change a character forever. The climactic meeting of Sobel and Feld that occurs in Sobel's room causes Feld to have a revelation. This revelation permanently changes Feld's attitude.

The First Seven Years

Bernard Malamud

eld, the shoemaker, was annoyed that his helper, Sobel, was so insensitive to his reverie that he wouldn't for a minute cease his fanatic pounding at the other bench. He gave him a look, but Sobel's bald head was bent over the **last** as he worked and he didn't notice. The shoemaker shrugged and continued to peer through the partly frosted window at the near-sighted haze of falling February snow. Neither the shifting white blur outside, nor the sudden deep remembrance of the snowy Polish village where he had wasted his youth could turn his thoughts from Max the college boy, (a constant visitor in the mind since early that morning when Feld saw him trudging through the snowdrifts on his way to school) whom he so much respected because of the sacrifices he had made throughout the years—in winter or direst heat—to further his education. An old wish returned to haunt the shoemaker: that he had a son instead of a daughter, but this blew away in the snow for Feld, if anything, was a practical man. Yet he could not help but contrast the diligence of the boy, who was a peddler's son, with Miriam's unconcern for an education. True, she was always with a book in her hand, yet when the opportunity arose for a college education, she had said no she would rather find a job. He had begged her to go, pointing out how many fathers could not afford to send their children to college, but she said she wanted to be independent. As for education, what was it, she asked, but books, which Sobel, who diligently read the classics, would as usual advise her on. Her answer greatly grieved her father.

A figure emerged from the snow and the door opened. At the counter the man withdrew from a wet paper bag a pair of battered shoes for repair. Who he was the shoemaker for a moment had no idea, then his heart trembled as he realized, before he had thoroughly discerned the face, that Max himself was standing there, embarrassedly explaining what he wanted done to his old shoes. Though Feld listened eagerly, he couldn't hear a word, for the opportunity that had burst upon him was deafening.

He couldn't exactly recall when the thought had occurred to him, because it was clear he had more than once considered suggesting to the boy that he go out with Miriam. But he had not dared speak, for if Max said no, how would he face him again? Or suppose Miriam, who harped so often on independence, blew up in anger and shouted at him for his meddling? Still, the chance was too good to let by: all it meant was an introduction. They might long ago have become friends had they happened to meet somewhere, therefore was it not his duty—an obligation—to bring them together, nothing more, a harmless **connivance** to replace an accidental encounter in the subway, let's say, or a mutual friend's introduction in the street? Just let him once see and talk to her and he would for sure be interested. As for Miriam, what possible harm for a working girl in an office, who met only loud-mouthed salesmen and illiterate shipping

About the Author

"People say I write so much about misery, but you write about what you write best," Bernard Malamud (1914–1986) once commented. He was born in Brooklyn, where his parents eked out a living as owners of a small grocery. After graduating from City College of New York, he took odd jobs during the day and wrote stories at night. Eventually Malamud became a college English professor and a successful writer of novels and stories about people struggling to create a better life in a world fraught with tragic pitfalls. His Russian-Jewish heritage and the Holocaust influenced his realistic, often tragic depiction of the human condition.

last—a block or form shaped like a human foot, used in repairing shoes

connivance—a secret understanding or act

clerks, to make the acquaintance of a fine scholarly boy? Maybe he would awaken in her a desire to go to college; if not—the shoemaker's mind at last came to grips with the truth—let her marry an educated man and live a better life.

When Max finished describing what he wanted done to his shoes, Feld marked them, both with enormous holes in the soles which he pretended not to notice, with large white-chalk x's, and the rubber heels, thinned to the nails, he marked with o's, though it troubled him he might have mixed up the letters. Max inquired the price, and the shoemaker cleared his throat and asked the boy, above Sobel's insistent hammering, would he please step through the side door there into the hall. Though surprised, Max did as the shoemaker requested, and Feld went in after him. For a minute they were both silent, because Sobel had stopped banging, and it seemed they understood neither was to say anything until the noise began again. When it did, loudly, the shoemaker quickly told Max why he had asked to talk to him.

"Ever since you went to high school," he said, in the dimly lit hallway, "I watched you in the morning go to the subway to school, and I said always to myself, this is a fine boy that he wants so much an education."

"Thanks," Max said, nervously alert. He was tall and grotesquely thin, with sharply cut features, particularly a beaklike nose. He was wearing a loose, long slushy overcoat that hung down to his ankles, looking like a rug draped over his bony shoulders, and a soggy, old brown hat, as battered as the shoes he had brought in.

● ● ● ● ● ● ●

Just let him once see and talk to her and he would for sure be interested.

● ● ● ● ● ● ●

"I am a business man," the shoemaker abruptly said to conceal his embarrassment, "so I will explain you right away why I talk to you. I have a girl, my daughter Miriam— she is nineteen—a very nice girl and also so pretty that everybody looks on her when she passes by in the street. She is smart, always with a book, and I thought to myself that a boy like you, an educated boy—I thought maybe you will be interested some-time to meet a girl like this." He laughed a bit when he had finished and was tempted to say more but had the good sense not to.

Max stared down like a hawk. For an uncomfortable second he was silent, then he asked, "Did you say nineteen?"

"Yes."

"Would it be all right to inquire if you have a picture of her?"

"Just a minute." The shoemaker went into the store and hastily returned with a snapshot that Max held up to the light.

"She's all right," he said.

Feld waited.

"And is she sensible—not the flighty kind?"

"She is very sensible."

After another short pause, Max said it was okay with him if he met her.

"Here is my telephone," said the shoe-maker, hurriedly handing him a slip of paper. "Call her up. She comes home from work six o'clock."

Max folded the paper and tucked it away into his worn leather wallet.

"About the shoes," he said. "How much did you say they will cost me?"

"Don't worry about the price.

"I just like to have an idea."

"A dollar—dollar fifty. A dollar fifty," the shoemaker said.

FOCUS ON...
SCIENCE

Though Feld was a shoemaker, much of his work was in *repairing* shoes. Since about 1900, shoes have been mass produced using automated equipment. For example, shoes can be designed using a computer. The leather or other materials can now be cut using laser technology and sewn with the help of computer-run stitching machines. Find out how several different kinds of shoes are designed and made. Create a diagram showing the various stages of production and the methods used.

◆ ◆ ◆ ◆ ◆ ◆ ◆ ◆ ◆ ◆ ◆ ◆ ◆ ◆ ◆ ◆ ◆ ◆ ◆ ◆

At once he felt bad, for he usually charged two twenty-five for this kind of job. Either he should have asked the regular price or done the work for nothing.

Later, as he entered the store, he was startled by a violent clanging and looked up to see Sobel pounding with all his might upon the naked last. It broke, the iron striking the floor and jumping with a thump against the wall, but before the enraged shoemaker could cry out, the assistant had torn his hat and coat from the hook and rushed out into the snow.

So Feld, who had looked forward to anticipating how it would go with his daughter and Max, instead had a great worry on his mind. Without his temperamental helper he was a lost man, especially since it was years now that he had carried the store alone. The shoemaker had for an age suffered from a heart condition that threatened collapse if he dared exert himself. Five years ago, after an attack, it had appeared as though he would have either to sacrifice his business upon the auction block and live on a pittance thereafter, or put himself at the mercy of some unscrupulous employee who would in the end probably ruin him. But just at the moment of this darkest despair, this Polish refugee, Sobel, appeared one night from the street and begged for work. He was a stocky man, poorly dressed, with a bald head that had once been blond, a severely plain face and soft blue eyes prone to tears over the sad books he read, a young man but old—no one would have guessed thirty. Though he confessed he knew nothing of shoemaking, he said he was apt and would work for a very little if Feld taught him the trade. Thinking that with, after all, a **landsman**, he would have less to fear than from a complete stranger, Feld took him on and within six weeks the refugee rebuilt as good a shoe as he, and not long thereafter expertly ran the business for the thoroughly relieved shoemaker.

Feld could trust him with anything and did, frequently going home after an hour or two at the store, leaving all the money in the till, knowing Sobel would guard every cent of it. The amazing thing was that he demanded so little. His wants were few; in money he wasn't interested

landsman—a person from the same country

SPOTLIGHT ON...
USING NONVERBAL CUES

In the story, Feld admits to himself that he had sensed all along that Sobel had deep feelings for Miriam. Sobel, too, believes that Miriam knows how he feels, though he has never told her in so many words. You also give and receive nonverbal cues in your communications with others. Look for the following nonverbal cues as others communicate with you:

1. facial expressions
2. body movements and posture
3. silences
4. actions

repugnant—
distasteful

—nothing but books, it seemed—which he one by one lent to Miriam, together with his profuse, queer written comments, manufactured during his lonely rooming house evenings, thick pads of commentary which the shoemaker peered at and twitched his shoulders over as his daughter, from her fourteenth year, read page by sanctified page, as if the word of God were inscribed on them. To protect Sobel, Feld himself had to see that he received more than he asked for. Yet his conscience bothered him for not insisting that the assistant accept a better wage than he was getting, though Feld had honestly told him he could earn a handsome salary if he worked elsewhere, or maybe opened a place of his own. But the assistant answered, somewhat ungraciously, that he was not interested in going elsewhere, and though Feld frequently asked himself what keeps him here? why does he stay? he finally answered it that the man, no doubt because of his terrible experiences as a refugee, was afraid of the world.

After the incident with the broken last, angered by Sobel's behavior, the shoemaker decided to let him stew for a week in the rooming house, although his own strength was taxed dangerously and the business suffered. However, after several sharp nagging warnings from both his wife and daughter, he went finally in search of Sobel, as he had once before, quite recently, when over some fancied slight— Feld had merely asked him not to give Miriam so many books to read because her eyes were strained and red—the assistant had left the place in a huff, an incident which, as usual, came to nothing for he had returned after the shoemaker had talked to him, and taken his seat at the bench. But this time, after Feld had plodded through the snow to Sobel's house—he had thought of sending Miriam but the idea became **repugnant** to him—the burly landlady at the door informed him in a nasal voice that Sobel was not at home, and though Feld knew this was a nasty lie, for where had the refugee to go? still for some reason he was not completely sure of—it may have been the cold and his fatigue—he decided not to insist on seeing him. Instead he went home and hired a new helper.

Having settled the matter, though not entirely to his satisfaction, for he had much more to do than before, and so, for example, could no longer lie late in bed mornings because he had to get up to open the store for the new assistant, a speechless, dark man with an irritating rasp as he worked, whom he would not trust with the key as he had Sobel. Furthermore, this one, though able to do a fair repair job, knew nothing of grades of leather or prices, so Feld had to make his own purchases; and every night at closing time it was necessary to count the money in the till and lock up. However, he was not dissatisfied, for he lived much in his thoughts of Max and Miriam. The college boy had called her, and they arranged a meeting for this coming Friday night. The shoemaker would personally have preferred Saturday, which he felt would make it a date of the first magnitude, but he learned Friday was Miriam's choice, so he said nothing. The day of the week did not matter. What mattered was the aftermath. Would they like each other and want to be friends? He sighed at all the time that would have to go by before he knew for sure. Often he was tempted to talk to Miriam about the boy, to ask whether she thought she would like his type—he had told her only that he considered Max a nice boy and had suggested he call her—but the one time he tried she snapped at him—justly—how should she know?

At last Friday came. Feld was not feeling particularly well so he stayed in bed, and Mrs. Feld thought it better to remain in the bedroom with him when Max called. Miriam received the boy, and her parents could hear their voices, his throaty one, as they talked. Just before leaving, Miriam brought Max to the bedroom door and he stood there a minute, a tall, slightly

hunched figure wearing a thick, droopy suit, and apparently at ease as he greeted the shoemaker and his wife, which was surely a good sign. And Miriam, although she had worked all day, looked fresh and pretty. She was a large-framed girl with a well-shaped body, and she had a fine open face and soft hair. They made, Feld thought, a first-class couple.

Miriam returned after 11:30. Her mother was already asleep, but the shoemaker got out of bed and after locating his bathrobe went into the kitchen, where Miriam, to his surprise, sat at the table, reading.

"So where did you go?" Feld asked pleasantly.

"For a walk," she said, not looking up.

"I advised him," Feld said, clearing his throat, "he shouldn't spend so much money."

"I didn't care."

The shoemaker boiled up some water for tea and sat down at the table with a cupful and a thick slice of lemon.

"So how," he sighed after a sip, "did you enjoy?"

"It was all right."

He was silent. She must have sensed his disappointment, for she added, "You can't really tell much the first time."

"You will see him again?"

Turning a page, she said that Max had asked for another date.

"For when?"

"Saturday."

"So what did you say?"

"What did I say?" she asked, delaying for a moment—"I said yes."

Afterwards she inquired about Sobel, and Feld, without exactly knowing why, said the assistant had got another job. Miriam said nothing more and began to

> ● ● ● ● ● ● ●
> # Would they like each other and want to be friends?
> ● ● ● ● ● ● ●

read. The shoemaker's conscience did not trouble him; he was satisfied with the Saturday date.

During the week, by placing here and there a deft question, he managed to get from Miriam some information about Max. It surprised him to learn that the boy was not studying to be either a doctor or lawyer but was taking a business course leading to a degree in accountancy. Feld was a little disappointed because he thought of accountants as bookkeepers and would have preferred "a higher profession." However, it was not long before he had investigated the subject and discovered that Certified Public Accountants were highly respected people, so he was thoroughly content as Saturday approached. But because Saturday was a busy day, he was much in the store and therefore did not see Max when he came to call for Miriam. From his wife he learned there had been nothing especially revealing about their meeting. Max had rung the bell and Miriam had got her coat and left with him—nothing more. Feld did not probe, for his wife was not particularly observant. Instead, he waited up for Miriam with a newspaper on his lap, which he scarcely looked at so lost was he in thinking of the future. He awoke to find her in the room with him, tiredly removing her hat. Greeting her, he was suddenly inexplicably afraid to ask anything about the evening. But since she volunteered nothing he was at last forced to inquire how she had enjoyed herself. Miriam began something noncommittal but apparently changed her mind, for she said after a minute, "I was bored."

When Feld had sufficiently recovered from his anguished disappointment to ask why, she answered without hesitation, "Because he's nothing more than a materialist."

"What means this word?"

"He has no soul. He's only interested in things."

He considered her statement for a long time but then asked, "Will you see him again?"

"He didn't ask."

"Suppose he will ask you?"

"I won't see him."

He did not argue; however, as the days went by he hoped increasingly she would change her mind. He wished the boy would telephone, because he was sure there was more to him than Miriam, with her inexperienced eye, could discern. But Max didn't call. As a matter of fact he took a different route to school, no longer passing the shoemaker's store, and Feld was deeply hurt.

Then one afternoon Max came in and asked for his shoes. The shoemaker took them down from the shelf where he had placed them, apart from the other pairs. He had done the work himself and the soles and heels were well built and firm. The shoes had been highly polished and somehow looked better than new. Max's Adam's apple went up once when he saw them, and his eyes had little lights in them.

Unit 2: Community and Responsibility

"How much?" he asked, without directly looking at the shoemaker.

"Like I told you before," Feld answered sadly. "One dollar fifty cents."

Max handed him two crumpled bills and received in return a newly minted silver half dollar.

He left. Miriam had not been mentioned. That night the shoemaker discovered that his new assistant had been all the while stealing from him, and he suffered a heart attack.

Though the attack was very mild, he lay in bed for three weeks. Miriam spoke of going for Sobel, but sick as he was Feld rose in wrath against the idea. Yet in his heart he knew there was no other way, and the first weary day back in the shop thoroughly convinced him, so that night after supper he dragged himself to Sobel's rooming house.

He toiled up the stairs, though he knew it was bad for him, and at the top knocked at the door. Sobel opened it and the shoemaker entered. The room was a small, poor one, with a single window facing the street. It contained a narrow cot, a low table and several stacks of books piled haphazardly around on the floor along the wall, which made him think how queer Sobel was, to be uneducated and read so much. He had once asked him, Sobel, why you read so much? and the assistant could not answer him. Did you ever study in a college someplace? he had asked, but Sobel shook his head. He read, he said, to know. But to know what, the shoemaker demanded, and to know, why? Sobel never explained, which proved he read much because he was queer.

Feld sat down to recover his breath. The assistant was resting on his bed with his heavy back to the wall. His shirt and trousers were clean, and his stubby fingers, away from the shoemaker's bench, were strangely pallid. His face was thin and pale, as if he had been shut in this room since the day he had bolted from the store.

"So when you will come back to work?" Feld asked him.

To his surprise, Sobel burst out, "Never." Jumping up, he strode over to the window that looked out upon the miserable street. "Why should I come back?" he cried.

"I will raise your wages."

"Who cares for your wages!"

The shoemaker, knowing he didn't care, was at a loss what else to say.

"What do you want from me, Sobel?"

"Nothing."

"I always treated you like you was my son."

Sobel vehemently denied it. "So why you look for strange boys in the street they should go out with Miriam? Why you don't think of me?"

The shoemaker's hands and feet turned freezing cold. His voice became so hoarse he couldn't speak. At last he cleared his throat and croaked, "So what has my daughter got to do with a shoemaker thirty-five years old who works for me?"

"Why do you think I worked so long for you?" Sobel cried out. "For the stingy wages I sacrificed five years of my life so you could have to eat and drink and where to sleep?"

"Then for what?" shouted the shoemaker.

"For Miriam," he blurted—"for her."

The shoemaker, after a time, managed to say, "I pay wages in cash, Sobel," and lapsed into silence. Though he was seething with excitement, his mind was coldly clear, and he had to admit to

> ●●●●●●●
> ## She knows who I am and what is in my heart.
> ●●●●●●●

himself he had sensed all along that Sobel felt this way. He had never so much as thought it consciously, but he had felt it and was afraid.

"Miriam knows?" he muttered hoarsely.

"She knows."

"You told her?"

"No."

"Then how does she know?"

"How does she know?" Sobel said. "Because she knows. She knows who I am and what is in my heart."

Feld had a sudden insight. In some devious way, with his books and commentary, Sobel had given Miriam to understand that he loved her. The shoemaker felt a terrible anger at him for his deceit.

"Sobel, you are crazy," he said bitterly. "She will never marry a man so old and ugly like you."

Sobel turned black with rage. He cursed the shoemaker, but then, though he trembled to hold it in, his eyes filled with tears and he broke into deep sobs. With his back to Feld, he stood at the window, fists clenched, and his shoulders shook with his choked sobbing.

Watching him, the shoemaker's anger diminished. His teeth were on edge with pity for the man, and his eyes grew moist. How strange and sad that a refugee, a grown man, bald and old with his miseries, who had by the skin of this teeth escaped Hitler's incinerators, should fall in love, when he had got to America, with a girl less than half his age. Day after day, for five years he had sat at his bench, cutting and hammering away, waiting for the girl to become a woman, unable to ease his heart with speech, knowing no protest but desperation.

"Ugly I didn't mean," he said half aloud.

Then he realized that what he had called ugly was not Sobel but Miriam's life if she married him. He felt for his daughter a strange and gripping sorrow, as if she were already Sobel's bride, the wife, after all, of a shoemaker, and had in her life no more than her mother had. And all his dreams for her—why he had slaved and destroyed his heart with anxiety and labor—all these dreams of a better life were dead.

The room was quiet. Sobel was standing by the window reading, and it was curious that when he read he looked young.

"She is only nineteen," Feld said brokenly. "This is too young yet to get married. Don't ask her for two years more, till she is twenty-one, then you can talk to her."

Sobel didn't answer. Feld rose and left. He went slowly down the stairs but once outside, though it was an icy night the crisp falling snow whitened the street, he walked with a stronger stride.

But the next morning, when the shoemaker arrived, heavy-hearted, to open the store, he saw he needn't have come, for his assistant was already seated at the last, pounding leather for his love. ❖

Remember

Joy Harjo

Remember the sky that you were born under,
know each of the star's stories.
Remember the moon, know who she is. I met her
in a bar once in Iowa City.
Remember the sun's birth at dawn, that is the
strongest point of time. Remember sundown
and the giving away to night.
Remember your birth, how your mother struggled
to give you form and breath. You are evidence of
her life, and her mother's, and hers.
Remember your father. He is your life, also.
Remember the earth whose skin you are:
red earth, black earth, yellow earth, white earth
brown earth, we are earth.
Remember the plants, trees, animal life who all have their
tribes, their families, their histories, too. Talk to them,
listen to them. They are alive poems.
Remember the wind. Remember her voice. She knows the
origin of this universe. I heard her singing Kiowa war
dance songs at the corner of Fourth and Central once.
Remember that you are all people and that all people
are you.
Remember that you are this universe and that this
universe is you.
Remember that all is in motion, is growing, is you.
Remember that language comes from this.
Remember the dance that language is, that life is.
Remember. ❖

About the Author

In her poetry, Joy Harjo weaves questions and answers about the struggle to achieve harmony and balance in life. Harjo was born in 1951 in Oklahoma, a member of the Creek tribe. Her Native American heritage gives her a dual perspective on what it means to be "American." Many of her poems explore the theme of survival as well as other concerns of universal significance.

Harjo is a professor of English at the University of New Mexico.

ON THE JOB

ACCOUNTANT

Max was going to school for a degree in accounting. Keeping tabs of financial records, recording credits and debits, paying bills on time, working with spreadsheets, managing tax records, and investing the company's money are some of the duties of an accountant. Generally, an accountant needs a two- or four-year degree in accounting. To become a Certified Public Accountant, a candidate must pass a rigorous four-part examination.

ACCENT ON...
ACCOUNTING PRACTICES

In "The First Seven Years," Feld did not have an accountant and did not know an employee was stealing from him. Today most cash registers are electronic and can run a tape at the end of the day to balance against what is in the till. A store manager can discover almost immediately any discrepancy. What other safeguards do store managers employ to ensure the books balance? Find out from talking to store managers what type of accounting system would work best for a small business like Feld's.

UNDERSTANDING

A LAST WORD

As community members, we are responsible for our own actions. To what extent are we responsible for others' actions?

1. What ideas about education does Malamud present in his short story? Base your conclusions on specific passages from the text. Interview a faculty member to find out what a practicing teacher thinks about education. Share the results of your interview with your class.

2. At the end of the story, Feld "had to admit to himself he had sensed all along that Sobel felt this way" about Miriam. Reread the story to find events that might have made Feld suspect that Sobel loved Miriam.

   Working with a group, make a case in one or two written paragraphs recommending either Max or Sobel as Miriam's husband. Use evidence from the text to form opinions about temperament (sensitivity or feelings), looks, goals, self-control, and age. Present your group's recommendation to the class.

3. Imagine that the conversation between Feld and Sobel at the end of the story had not taken place. Instead, suppose that Sobel wrote a letter to Feld resigning from his position at the shoe shop. Write this letter of resignation from Sobel to Feld. Be sure to include all the information that Sobel tells Feld during their final meeting, any details you think Sobel ought to have included. Write in the tone of voice you think Sobel might have used. *Workshop 11*

4. Joy Harjo's poem urges readers to remember, among other things, "the plants, trees, animal life who all have their / tribes, their families, their histories, too. Talk to them, / listen to them. They are alive poems." Discuss in your group what you think this advice asks you to do. Then develop a plan for following this advice. Describe your group's plan to the class. *Workshop 19*

CONNECTING

1. Feld, knowing that Sobel will not earn much repairing shoes, regrets that Miriam will probably marry Sobel. Feld knows from experience that small businesses are not always profitable. What small businesses in your community seem likely to provide a family with a comfortable living? Gather information about local small businesses in order to suggest whether or not starting a business might one day be a good career choice.

2. Harjo's poem says "Remember the earth whose skin you are: red earth, black earth, yellow earth, white earth / brown earth, we are earth . . . / Remember that you are all people and that all people are you." The lines remind us that we are all the same—people living on this planet Earth. Develop a written and visual presentation that expresses the idea that all people are valuable and all people are connected. *Workshop 20*

WRAP IT UP

UNIT 2

1. In "I Hear America Singing," Walt Whitman celebrates the working people of the United States. In "Steelworker," Trudy Pax Farr describes her job in a steel mill. Lewis Thomas admires the work of nurses in the excerpt from *The Youngest Science*. What aspects of the American worker does each selection highlight? How are the authors' views of work similar? Use details from the selections to support your opinions.

Survey members of the working community in your area. Ask for demographic information, such as level of education and current job. Include questions about workers' attitudes, and use the information you gather to write a description of the local work force.

2. "Geraldo No Last Name," and "The First Seven Years" each feature a character struggling with his or her responsibility to another member of the community. In "Geraldo No Last Name," Marin barely knows Geraldo, but she feels the need to stay at the hospital with him. In "The First Seven Years" Feld tries to balance his responsibility to his daughter Marin with his responsibility to his employee Sobel. Compare and contrast the attitudes of Marin, Nikos, and Feld toward community responsibility.

What responsibilities do you have to other members of your community? Write an essay explaining your view. Include examples to illustrate your main points.

UNIT 3

CHALLENGE AND SUCCESS

People often strive for success. Scoring the touchdown, earning the high grade, getting the job—to succeed is to "win," to accomplish one's goal. Some individuals become obsessed with success, pursuing a particular goal without considering anyone or anything else. Other individuals find success is not what they expected it to be and begin to question their goals. As the selections in this unit demonstrate, people have many different ideas about what constitutes success and how best to achieve it.

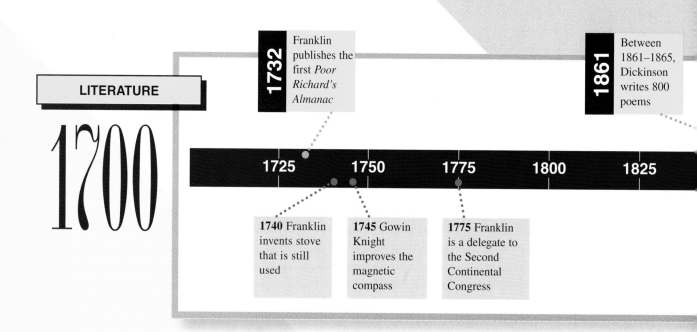

LITERATURE

1700

1725   1750   1775   1800   1825

1732 Franklin publishes the first *Poor Richard's Almanac*

1861 Between 1861–1865, Dickinson writes 800 poems

1740 Franklin invents stove that is still used

1745 Gowin Knight improves the magnetic compass

1775 Franklin is a delegate to the Second Continental Congress

Success is counted sweetest
—Emily Dickinson

from On the Pulse of Morning
—Maya Angelou

The Chrysanthemums
—John Steinbeck

from Polar Dream
—Helen Thayer

from A Snow Walker's Companion
—Garrett and Alexandra Conover

Martinez' Treasure
—Manuela Williams Crosno

Talent
—Annie Dillard

from The Autobiography
—Benjamin Franklin

from Instant American History
—Irwin Unger

1939 Steinbeck's *The Grapes of Wrath* is published

1975 Dillard receives Pulitzer Prize for *Pilgrim at Tinker Creek*

1988 Helen Thayer reaches the magnetic North Pole

1993 Angelou reads a poem at the Clinton inauguration

1875   1900   1925   1950   1975

2000

1865 The Civil War ends

1929 Stock market crashes, plunging the United States into an economic depression

1978 First man traveling alone by dogsled reaches the North Pole

1989 Treasure hunters find $1 billion in gold off the coast of South Carolina

LIFE and WORK

Longing and Hope

- *Success is counted sweetest*
- *from On the Pulse of Morning*

EXPLORING

Parents generally hope that their children will become successful, but parents do not often explain in specific terms what they mean by "successful." What are some indicators of "success" in our society? How do you measure success? Is a bestseller a successful book? What makes a supervisor successful? Do you think of yourself as successful? Consider these questions in your group. Working collaboratively, compose a definition of success and support it with specific examples from your group's discussion.

THEME CONNECTION...
TREASURING SUCCESS

Emily Dickinson expresses in this poem the fundamental idea that people value what they do not have. Those who never succeed attach great importance to success; only someone in "sorest need" of nectar is able "to comprehend" it fully; the defeated soldier can better define victory than the triumphant soldier. The poem captures the longing of those who have not fulfilled their desires.

Maya Angelou's poem proclaims everyone's chance to achieve his or her desires. Angelou declares that it is in your hands to shape the present moment and choose your future. Every day brings a new beginning and new hope.

TIME & PLACE

Both Emily Dickinson and Maya Angelou respond in their poetry to the immediate events of the day. Emily Dickinson's life (1830–1886) spanned the Civil War. In "Success is counted sweetest," she refers to the war when describing the dying soldier. Maya Angelou's "On the Pulse of Morning" was written to be read aloud in January, 1993, at the Presidential inauguration of President William Clinton. Angelou's poem offers encouragement and hope to a society suffering from homelessness, domestic violence, and crime. She says each day brings with it new possibilities for success and proclaims each person's ability to use the day well.

THE WRITER'S CRAFT

QUATRAIN

Most of Dickinson's poems are written in four line stanzas, called **quatrains**. To compose "Success is counted sweetest," Dickinson chose this ancient stanza form. To make her ideas fit into this form, Dickinson must rhyme the final sounds of the first and third lines and the final sounds of the second and fourth lines. Using this stanza form also requires the poet to stress three syllables in each line, so that when you read them, you feel you have to say them more strongly than you say other syllables.

Success is counted sweetest

Emily Dickinson

Success is counted sweetest
By those who ne'er succeed.
To comprehend a nectar
Requires sorest need.

Not one of all the purple Host
Who took the Flag today
Can tell the definition
So clear of Victory

As he defeated—dying—
On whose forbidden ear
The distant strains of triumph
Burst agonized and clear! ❖

About the Author

"Success is counted sweetest" is one of the few poems Emily Dickinson published in her lifetime, though 1,123 poems were found neatly packed in a box after her death. She had written many poems on grocery lists, old envelopes, bills, and recipes. Dickinson (1830–1886) lived and died in Amherst, Massachusetts. After an unsatisfying year of college, she returned home to live with her family. She never married and traveled little, her secluded, quiet life providing a stark contrast to her intense creativity. Dickinson produced some of America's greatest poetry.

SPOTLIGHT ON... RESPONDING TO CRITICISM

Failing to succeed at a task often causes a person to receive criticism. Even when one does succeed, others may criticize one's work or methods of accomplishing a goal. When you receive criticism, follow these guidelines to respond appropriately.

1. Ask yourself if the criticism is accurate.
2. If the criticism is accurate, identify ways to correct the situation.
3. If the criticism is incorrect, think of positive ways to correct the perception.
4. Try not to take the criticism personally; instead, use it as a means of self-evaluation.

from *On the Pulse of Morning*

Maya Angelou

About the Author

Maya Angelou (1928–) worked for a time as a street-car conductor, a cook and a waitress. She danced in nightclubs and eventually went to New York to study dance and perform in Broadway productions. Angelou spent several years in Africa as an editor and a teacher. Back in the United States, she began writing poetry, songs, screenplays, and a television series. She received an Emmy nomination for her role in the television miniseries *Roots* and wrote the acclaimed autobiography *I Know Why the Caged Bird Sings*. She wrote her poem "On the Pulse of Morning" for the 1993 inauguration of President William Clinton.

Lift up your eyes upon
This day breaking for you.
Give birth again
To the dream.

Women, children, men,
Take it into the palms of your hands,
Mold it into the shape of your most
Private need. Sculpt it into
The image of your most public self.
Lift up your hearts.
Each new hour holds new chances
For a new beginning.
Do not be wedded forever
To fear, yoked eternally
To **brutishness**.

The horizon leans forward,
Offering you space
To place new steps of change.
Here, on the pulse of this fine day,
You may have the courage
To look up and out and upon me,
The Rock, the River, the Tree, your country.
No less to **Midas** than the **mendicant**.
No less to you now than the **mastodon** then.

Here, on the pulse of this new day,
You may have the grace to look up and out
And into your sister's eyes,
And into your brother's face,
Your country,
And say simply
Very simply
With hope—
Good morning. ❖

brutishness—beast-like, showing little intelligence or sensibility

Midas—legendary king who turned everything he touched to gold

mendicant—beggar

mastodon—a large, extinct mammal similar to the elephant

FOCUS ON... ART

Angelou describes an image of taking the day and molding it to one's needs. In a medium of your choice, create your own image of the new day and what it represents to you. You may choose to make a collage or a watercolor painting, or to sculpt your image out of traditional or untraditional materials.

◆ ◆

UNDERSTANDING

1. Dickinson's poem "Success is counted sweetest" offers three examples that show how human beings best appreciate and understand what they do not have. Find these examples in the poem.

   Do you agree or disagree with the poem's idea that we appreciate best what we do not have or have not achieved? Test the soundness of your opinion by trying something new—applying for a job you really want or taking lessons to learn something you have always wanted to do (such as play the piano or ski). Write an essay describing the experience. Include the reasons why you wanted to obtain the particular job or skill and how you feel about your attempt to achieve it. ***Workshop 1***

2. Maya Angelou's poem is encouraging, positive, and reassuring. Find passages in the poem that show Angelou's optimism.

   To a friend or fellow employee who seems depressed, write a good news letter that offers reasons to feel optimistic and hopeful. ***Workshop 11***

3. Both "Success is counted sweetest" and "On the Pulse of Morning" portray life as involving difficult challenges. Examine both poems to identify the difficulties that challenge people.

   Angelou's poem strongly urges readers to act. She believes that people can take control of and change their lives. Working in groups, develop a list of instances when teenagers did take control of their lives to do something positive at school or work.

CONNECTING

1. Write a proposal to do volunteer work to benefit those people whom we tend to label "unsuccessful" or "unfortunate." To prepare a sound proposal, first brainstorm possibilities with your class. Once you identify some possibilities, investigate them carefully. You might discover, for example, that one person is needed to serve food in a shelter, while a group of four or five is needed to take pets to the elderly in a nursing home. Having discovered where volunteer work is called for, develop a proposal for carrying out such work. ***Workshop 10***

2. Conduct a poll in your school or community. Design a series of questions that determine whether your interviewees are generally optimistic or pessimistic about their lives and futures. Include questions of a specific nature. What do they appreciate about their lives? In what ways do they hope their children's lives will be similar or different? Compile your findings in a chart, graph, or other visual display. Draw some conclusions about the attitudes in your school or community. Share your findings with your school newspaper. ***Workshop 20***

> ## A LAST WORD
>
> Dickinson says one must experience failure to truly understand success. If you were unable to achieve a victory, would you have a greater comprehension of what that victory meant? Can victory be fully understood without ever experiencing defeat?

The Chrysanthemums

EXPLORING

Have you ever felt that given half a chance you could do a job as well or better than the person doing it? With your group, talk about occasions when you have seen employees perform well or badly. How do you define an excellent worker? What are the characteristics of a mediocre or poor worker? In your journal, list your positive qualities and abilities and the challenges and responsibilities that your abilities can help you handle.

THEME CONNECTION... THE NEED FOR CHALLENGES

Elisa Allen suffers from a life without significant challenges. A woman of exceptional ability, she needs a demanding outlet for her many gifts. Instead she must focus her energy and talent merely on growing chrysanthemums and cleaning house. Elisa longs to be able to choose new experiences and challenging adventures.

TIME & PLACE

This story takes place in the 1930s, on a ranch in the foothills around the Salinas Valley of California. Henry and Elisa Allen live and work close to nature during the Great Depression. At this time, jobs were difficult to find, and the stock market crash of 1929 had started an economic crisis that would last until World War II.

Throughout the Depression, traveling repairmen were common. Although to Elisa the man on the wagon seems free and independent, he is trapped by poverty.

THE WRITER'S CRAFT

SIMILE

The term *simile* is used to describe a statement that says two objects are similar. Such statements use *like* or *as.* A few of the similes in "The Chrysanthemums" include: the "fog of winter . . . sat *like* a lid"; "plows . . . left the . . . earth shining *like* metal"; and "the horse and the donkey drooped *like* unwatered flowers."

A simile always offers readers a new way to view something. Readers might ask how winter is like a lid or how shining earth is like metal. No single answer is right. Each person responds to the suggestions of similes in his or her unique way.

The Chrysanthemums

John Steinbeck

he high grey-flannel fog of winter closed off the Salinas Valley from the sky and from all the rest of the world. On every side it sat like a lid on the mountains and made of the great valley a closed pot. On the broad, level land floor the gang plows bit deep and left the black earth shining like metal where the shares had cut. On the foothill ranches across the Salinas River, the yellow stubble fields seemed to be bathed in pale cold sunshine, but there was no sunshine in the valley now in December. The thick willow scrub along the river flamed with sharp and positive yellow leaves.

It was a time of quiet and of waiting. The air was cold and tender. A light wind blew up from the southwest so that the farmers were mildly hopeful of a good rain before long; but fog and rain do not go together.

Across the river, on Henry Allen's foothill ranch there was little work to be done, for the hay was cut and stored and the orchards were plowed up to receive the rain deeply when it should come. The cattle on the higher slopes were becoming shaggy and rough-coated.

Elisa Allen, working in her flower garden, looked down across the yard and saw Henry, her husband, talking to two men in business suits. The three of them stood by the tractor shed, each man with one foot on the side of the little Fordson. They smoked cigarettes and studied the machine as they talked.

Elisa watched them for a moment and then went back to her work. She was thirty-five. Her face was lean and strong and her eyes were as clear as water. Her figure looked blocked and heavy in her gardening costume, a man's black hat pulled low down over her eyes, clod-hopper shoes, a figured print dress almost completely covered by a big corduroy apron with four big pockets to hold the snips, the trowel and scratcher, the seeds and the knife she worked with. She wore heavy leather gloves to protect her hands while she worked.

She was cutting down the old year's chrysanthemum stalks with a pair of short and powerful scissors. She looked down toward the men by the tractor shed now and then. Her face was eager and mature and handsome; even her work with the scissors was over-eager, over-powerful. The chrysanthemum stems seemed too small and easy for her energy.

She brushed a cloud of hair out of her eyes with the back of her glove, and left a smudge of earth on her cheek in doing it. Behind her stood the neat white farm house with red geraniums close-banked around it as high as the windows. It was a hard-swept looking little house with hard-polished windows, and a clean mud-mat on the front steps.

Elisa cast another glance toward the tractor shed. The strangers were getting into their Ford coupe. She took off a glove and put her strong fingers down into the forest of new green chrysanthemum sprouts that were growing around the old roots. She spread the leaves and looked down among the close-growing stems. No aphids were there, no sowbugs or snails or cutworms. Her terrier fingers destroyed such pests before they could get started.

About the Author

John Steinbeck (1902–1968) received the Nobel Prize for Literature in 1962. Born in Salinas, California, Steinbeck set many of his stories in this region. Steinbeck's writings reflect broad and varied experience. He attended Stanford University on and off for five years, leaving without a degree. He also worked in a sugar beet factory, on a road-building gang, and on ranches. When he married for the first time, Steinbeck asked for help from his father, who provided him with a small house and a $25.00 monthly allowance. Steinbeck became famous for the novels *Tortilla Flat* (1935) and *The Grapes of Wrath* (1939).

smugness—
self-satisfaction

prairie schooner—
covered wagon

mongrel—a cross
between different
breeds

Elisa started at the sound of her husband's voice. He had come near quietly, and he leaned over the wire fence that protected her flower garden from cattle and dogs and chickens.

"At it again," he said. "You've got a strong new crop coming."

Elisa straightened her back and pulled on the gardening glove again. "Yes. They'll be strong this coming year." In her tone and on her face there was a little **smugness**.

"You've got a gift with things," Henry observed. "Some of those yellow chrysanthemums you had this year were ten inches across. I wish you'd work out in the orchard and raise some apples that big."

Her eyes sharpened. "Maybe I could do it, too. I've a gift with things, all right. My mother had it. She could stick anything in the ground and make it grow. She said it was having planters' hands that knew how to do it."

"Well, it sure works with flowers," he said.

"Henry, who were those men you were talking to?"

"Why, sure, that's what I came to tell you. They were from the Western Meat Company. I sold those thirty head of three-year-old steers. Got nearly my own price, too."

"Good," she said. "Good for you."

"And I thought," he continued, "I thought how it's Saturday afternoon, and we might go into Salinas for dinner at a restaurant, and then to a picture show—to celebrate, you see."

"Good," she repeated. "Oh, yes. That will be good."

Henry put on his joking tone. "There's fights tonight. How'd you like to go to the fights?"

● ● ● ● ● ● ●
"You've got a gift with things,"...
● ● ● ● ● ● ●

"Oh, no," she said breathlessly. "No, I wouldn't like fights."

"Just fooling, Elisa. We'll go to a movie. Let's see. It's two now. I'm going to take Scotty and bring down those steers from the hill. It'll take us maybe two hours. We'll go in town about five and have dinner at the Cominos Hotel. Like that?"

"Of course I'll like it. It's good to eat away from home."

"All right, then. I'll go get up a couple of horses."

She said, "I'll have plenty of time to transplant some of these sets, I guess."

She heard her husband calling Scotty down by the barn. And a little later she saw the two men ride up the pale yellow hillside in search of the steers.

There was a little square sandy bed kept for rooting the chrysanthemums. With her trowel she turned the soil over and over, and smoothed it and patted it firm. Then she dug ten parallel trenches to receive the sets. Back at the chrysanthemum bed she pulled out the little crisp shoots, trimmed off the leaves of each one with her scissors and laid it on a small orderly pile.

A squeak of wheels and plod of hoofs came from the road. Elisa looked up. The country road ran along the dense bank of willows and cottonwoods that bordered the river, and up this road came a curious vehicle, curiously drawn. It was an old spring-wagon, with a round canvas top on it like the corner of a **prairie schooner**. It was drawn by an old bay horse and a little grey-and-white burro. A big stubble-bearded man sat between the cover flaps and drove the crawling team. Underneath the wagon, between the hind wheels, a lean and rangy **mongrel** dog walked sedately. Words were painted on the canvas, in clumsy, crooked

FOCUS ON...
BIOLOGY

Elisa apparently takes great pleasure and pride in her ability to grow chrysanthemums in her garden. She understands much about horticulture. Horticulture deals with the science and art of gardening. What kinds of plants might a gardener in your area grow? What are the soil and climate like where you live? What flowers can be cultivated and what flowers grow wild? Working with students in biology, create a diagram depicting the horticulture practiced in your area. Include a map showing the climate and annual precipitation.

letters. "Pots, pans, knives, sisors, lawn mores, Fixed." Two rows of articles, and the triumphantly definitive "Fixed" below. The black paint had run down in little sharp points beneath each letter.

Elisa, squatting on the ground, watched to see the crazy, loose-jointed wagon pass by. But it didn't pass. It turned into the farm road in front of her house, crooked old wheels skirling and squeaking. The rangy dog darted from between the wheels and ran ahead. Instantly the two ranch shepherds flew out at him. Then all three stopped, and with stiff and quivering tails, with taut straight legs, with ambassadorial dignity, they slowly circled, sniffing daintily. The caravan pulled up to Elisa's wire fence and stopped. Now the newcomer dog, feeling out-numbered, lowered his tail and retired under the wagon with raised hackles and bared teeth.

The man on the wagon seat called out, "That's a bad dog in a fight when he gets started."

Elisa laughed. "I see he is. How soon does he generally get started?"

The man caught up her laughter and echoed it heartily. "Sometimes not for weeks and weeks," he said. He climbed stiffly down, over the wheel. The horse and the donkey drooped like unwatered flowers.

Elisa saw that he was a very big man. Although his hair and beard were greying, he did not look old. His worn black suit was wrinkled and spotted with grease. The laughter had disappeared from his face and eyes the moment his laughing voice ceased. His eyes were dark, and they were full of the brooding that gets in the eyes of teamsters and of sailors. The calloused hands he rested on the wire fence were cracked, and every crack was a black line. He took off his battered hat.

"I'm off my general road, ma'am," he said. "Does this dirt road cut over across the river to the Los Angeles highway?"

Elisa stood up and shoved the thick scissors in her apron pocket. "Well, yes, it does, but it winds around and then **fords** the river. I don't think your team could pull through the sand."

fords—crosses

asperity—
harshness, rough-
ness of manner

He replied with some **asperity**, "It might surprise you what them beasts can pull through."

"When they get started?" she asked.

He smiled for a second. "Yes. When they get started."

"Well," said Elisa, "I think you'll save time if you go back to the Salinas road and pick up the highway there."

He drew a big finger down the chicken wire and made it sing. "I ain't in any hurry, ma'am. I go from Seattle to San Diego and back every year. Takes all my time. About six months each way. I aim to follow nice weather."

Elisa took off her gloves and stuffed them in the apron pocket with the scissors. She touched the under edge of her man's hat, searching for fugitive hairs. "That sounds like a nice kind of way to live," she said.

He leaned confidentially over the fence. "Maybe you noticed the writing on my wagon. I mend pots and sharpen knives and scissors. You got any of them things to do?"

"Oh, no," she said, quickly. "Nothing like that." Her eyes hardened with resistance.

"Scissors is the worst thing," he explained. "Most people just ruin scissors

trying to sharpen 'em, but I know how. I got a special tool. It's a little bobbit kind of thing, and patented. But it sure does the trick."

"No. My scissors are all sharp."

"All right, then. Take a pot," he continued earnestly, "a bent pot, or a pot with a hole. I can make it like new so you don't have to buy no new ones. That's a saving for you."

"No," she said shortly. "I tell you I have nothing like that for you to do."

His face fell to an exaggerated sadness. His voice took on a whining undertone. "I ain't had a thing to do today. Maybe I won't have no supper tonight. You see I'm off my regular road. I know folks on the highway clear from Seattle to San Diego. They save their things for me to sharpen up because they know I do it so good and save them money."

"I'm sorry," Elisa said irritably. "I haven't anything for you to do."

His eyes left her face and fell to searching the ground. They roamed about until they came to the chrysanthemum bed where she had been working. "What's them plants, ma'am?"

The irritation and resistance melted from Elisa's face. "Oh, those are chrysanthemums, giant whites and yellows. I raise them every year, bigger than anybody around here."

"Kind of a long-stemmed flower? Looks like a quick puff of colored smoke?" he asked.

"That's it. What a nice way to describe them."

"They smell kind of nasty till you get used to them," he said.

"It's a good bitter smell," she retorted, "not nasty at all."

He changed his tone quickly. "I like the smell myself."

"I had ten-inch blooms this year," she said.

The man leaned farther over the fence. "Look. I know a lady down the road a piece, has got the nicest garden you ever seen. Got nearly every kind of flower but no chrysanthemums. Last time I was mending a copper-bottom washtub for her (that's a hard job but I do it good), she said to me, 'If you ever run across some nice chrysanthemums I wish you'd try to get me a few seeds.' That's what she told me."

Elisa's eyes grew alert and eager. "She couldn't have known much about chrysanthemums. You can raise them from seed, but it's much easier to root the little sprouts you see there."

"Oh," he said. "I s'pose I can't take none to her, then."

"Why yes you can," Elisa cried. "I can put some in damp sand, and you can carry them right along with you. They'll take root in the pot if you keep them damp. And then she can transplant them."

"She'd sure like to have some, ma'am. You say they're nice ones?"

"Beautiful," she said. "Oh, beautiful." Her eyes shone. She tore off the battered hat and shook out her dark pretty hair. "I'll put them in a flower pot, and you can take them right with you. Come into the yard."

While the man came through the picket gate Elisa ran excitedly along the geranium-bordered path to the back of the house. And she returned carrying a big red flower pot. The gloves were forgotten now. She kneeled on the ground by the starting bed and dug up the sandy soil with her fingers and scooped it into the bright new flower pot. Then she picked up the little pile of shoots she had prepared. With her strong fingers she pressed them into the sand and tamped around them with her knuckles. The man stood over her. "I'll tell you what to do," she said. "You remember so you can tell the lady."

"Yes, I'll try to remember."

"Well, look. These will take root in about a month. Then she must set them out, about a foot apart in good rich earth like this, see?" She lifted a handful of dark soil for him to look at. "They'll grow fast and tall. Now remember this: In July tell her to cut them down, about eight inches from the ground."

"Before they bloom?" he asked.

"Yes, before they bloom." Her face was tight with eagerness. "They'll grow right up again. About the last of September the buds will start."

She stopped and seemed perplexed. "It's the budding that takes the most care," she said hesitantly. "I don't know how to tell you." She looked deep into his eyes, searchingly. Her mouth opened a little, and she seemed to be listening. "I'll try to tell you," she said. "Did you ever hear of planting hands?"

"Can't say I have, ma'am."

"Well, I can only tell you what it feels like. It's when you're picking off the buds you don't want. Everything goes right down into your fingertips. You watch your fingers work. They do it themselves. You can feel how it is. They pick and pick the buds. They never make a mistake. They're with the plant. Do you see? Your fingers and the plant. You can feel that, right up your arm. They know. They never make a mistake. You can feel it. When you're like that you can't do anything wrong. Do you see that? Can you understand that?"

She was kneeling on the ground looking up at him. Her breast swelled passionately.

The man's eyes narrowed. He looked away self-consciously. "Maybe I know,"

"...those are chrysanthemums, giant whites and yellows...."

SPOTLIGHT ON...
GIVING DIRECTIONS

In the story, Elisa attempted to give the fix-it man accurate directions to get to the main highway and directions on how to transplant the flowers. When you are giving someone directions, keep the following suggestions in mind:

1. Find out exactly what his or her destination is.
2. Keep your directions as short, simple, and clear as you can. Avoid including any unnecessary information.
3. Provide landmarks or visual clues to help the person follow the directions.
4. Draw a simple diagram or map, if possible.

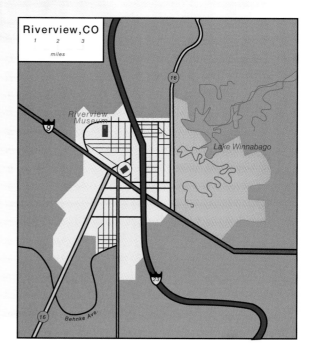

anvil—a heavy iron block on which metal is shaped

he said. "Sometimes in the night in the wagon there—"

Elisa's voice grew husky. She broke in on him, "I've never lived as you do, but I know what you mean. When the night is dark—why, the stars are sharp-pointed, and there's quiet. Why, you rise up and up! Every pointed star gets driven into your body. It's like that. Hot and sharp and—lovely."

Kneeling there, her hand went out toward his legs in the greasy black trousers. Her hesitant fingers almost touched the cloth. Then her hand dropped to the ground. She crouched low like a fawning dog.

He said, "It's nice, just like you say. Only when you don't have no dinner, it ain't."

She stood up then, very straight, and her face was ashamed. She held the flower pot out to him and placed it gently in his arms. "Here. Put it in your wagon, on the seat, where you can watch it. Maybe I can find something for you to do."

At the back of the house she dug in the can pile and found two old and battered aluminum saucepans. She carried them

back and gave them to him. "Here, maybe you can fix these."

His manner changed. He became professional. "Good as new I can fix them." At the back of his wagon he set a little **anvil**, and out of an oily tool box dug a small machine hammer. Elisa came through the gate to watch him while he pounded out the dents in the kettles. His mouth grew sure and knowing. At a difficult part of the work he sucked his under-lip.

"You sleep right in the wagon?" Elisa asked.

"Right in the wagon, ma'am. Rain or shine I'm dry as a cow in there."

"It must be nice," she said. "It must be very nice. I wish women could do such things."

"It ain't the right kind of a life for a woman."

Her upper lip raised a little, showing her teeth. "How do you know? How can you tell?" she said.

"I don't know, ma'am," he protested. "Of course I don't know. Now here's your kettles, done. You don't have to buy no new ones."

"How much?"

"Oh, fifty cents'll do. I keep my prices down and my work good. That's why I have all them satisfied customers up and down the highway."

Elisa brought him a fifty-cent piece from the house and dropped it in his hand. "You might be surprised to have a rival some time. I can sharpen scissors, too. And I can beat the dents out of little pots. I could show you what a woman might do."

He put his hammer back in the oily box and shoved the little anvil out of sight. "It would be a lonely life for a woman, ma'am, and a scary life, too, with animals creeping under the wagon all night." He climbed over the singletree, steadying himself with a hand on the burro's white rump. He settled himself in the seat, picked up the lines. "Thank you kindly, ma'am," he said. "I'll do like you told me; I'll go back and catch the Salinas road."

"Mind," she called, "if you're long in getting there, keep the sand damp."

"Sand, ma'am? . . . Sand? Oh, sure. You mean around the chrysanthemums. Sure I will." He clucked his tongue. The beasts leaned luxuriously into their collars. The mongrel dog took his place between the back wheels. The wagon turned and crawled out the entrance road and back the way it had come, along the river.

Elisa stood in front of her wire fence watching the slow progress of the caravan. Her shoulders were straight, her head thrown back, her eyes half-closed, so that the scene came vaguely into them. Her lips moved silently, forming the words "Good-bye—good-bye." Then she whispered, "That's a bright direction. There's a glowing there." The sound of her whisper startled her. She shook

● ● ● ● ● ● ●
"I wish women could do such things."
● ● ● ● ● ● ●

herself free and looked about to see whether anyone had been listening. Only the dogs had heard. They lifted their heads toward her from their sleeping in the dust, and then stretched out their chins and settled asleep again. Elisa turned and ran hurriedly into the house.

In the kitchen she reached behind the stove and felt the water tank. It was full of hot water from the noonday cooking. In the bathroom she tore off her soiled clothes and flung them into the corner. And then she scrubbed herself with a little block of pumice, legs and thighs, loins and chest and arms, until her skin was scratched and red. When she had dried herself she stood in front of a mirror in her bedroom and looked at her body. She tightened her stomach and threw out her chest. She turned and looked over her shoulder at her back.

After a while she began to dress, slowly. She put on her newest underclothing and her nicest stockings and the dress which was the symbol of her prettiness. She worked carefully on her hair, penciled her eyebrows and rouged her lips.

Before she was finished she heard the little thunder of hoofs and the shouts of Henry and his helper as they drove the red steers into the corral. She heard the gate bang shut and set herself for Henry's arrival.

His step sounded on the porch. He entered the house calling, "Elisa, where are you?"

"In my room, dressing. I'm not ready. There's hot water for your bath. Hurry up. It's getting late."

When she heard him splashing in the tub, Elisa laid his dark suit on the bed, and shirt and socks and tie beside it. She stood his polished shoes on the floor beside the bed. Then she went to the porch and sat primly and stiffly down. She looked toward

the river road where the willow-line was still yellow with frosted leaves so that under the high grey fog they seemed a thin band of sunshine. This was the only color in the grey afternoon. She sat unmoving for a long time. Her eyes blinked rarely.

Henry came banging out of the door, shoving his tie inside his vest as he came. Elisa stiffened and her face grew tight. Henry stopped short and looked at her. "Why— why, Elisa. You look so nice!"

"Nice? You think I look nice? What do you mean by 'nice'?"

Henry blundered on. "I don't know. I mean you look different, strong and happy."

"I am strong? Yes, strong. What do you mean 'strong'?"

He looked bewildered. "You're playing some kind of a game," he said helplessly. "It's a kind of a play. You look strong enough to break a calf over your knee, happy enough to eat it like a watermelon."

For a second she lost her rigidity. "Henry! Don't talk like that. You didn't know what you said." She grew complete again. "I'm strong," she boasted. "I never knew before how strong."

Henry looked down toward the tractor shed, and when he brought his eyes back to her, they were his own again. "I'll get

out the car. You can put on your coat while I'm starting."

Elisa went into the house. She heard him drive to the gate and idle down his motor, and then she took a long time to put on her hat. She pulled it here and pressed it there. When Henry turned the motor off she slipped into her coat and went out.

The little roadster bounced along on the dirt road by the river, raising the birds and driving the rabbits into the brush. Two cranes flapped heavily over the willow-line and dropped into the river-bed.

Far ahead on the road Elisa saw a dark speck. She knew.

She tried not to look as they passed it, but her eyes would not obey. She whispered to herself sadly, "He might have thrown them off the road. That wouldn't have been much trouble, not very much. But he kept the pot," she explained, "He had to keep the pot. That's why he couldn't get them off the road."

The roadster turned a bend and she saw the caravan ahead. She swung full around toward her husband so she could not see the little covered wagon and the mismatched team as the car passed them.

In a moment it was over. The thing was done. She did not look back.

She said loudly, to be heard above the motor, "It will be good, tonight, a good dinner."

"Now you're changed again," Henry complained. He took one hand from the wheel and patted her knee. "I ought to take you in to dinner oftener. It would be good for both of us. We get so heavy out on the ranch."

"Henry," she asked, "could we have wine at dinner?"

"Sure we could. Say! That will be fine."

● ● ● ● ● ● ●

"That's a bright direction. There's a glowing there."

● ● ● ● ● ● ●

She was silent for a while; then she said, "Henry, at those prize fights, do the men hurt each other very much?"

"Sometimes a little, not often. Why?"

"Well, I've read how they break noses, and blood runs down their chests. I've read how the fighting gloves get heavy and soggy with blood."

He looked around at her. "What's the matter, Elisa? I didn't know you read things like that." He brought the car to a stop, then turned to the right over the Salinas River bridge.

"Do any women ever go to the fights?" she asked.

"Oh, sure, some. What's the matter, Elisa? Do you want to go? I don't think you'd like it, but I'll take you if you really want to go."

She relaxed limply in the seat. "Oh, no. No. I don't want to go. I'm sure I don't." Her face was turned away from him. "It will be enough if we can have wine. It will be plenty." She turned up her coat collar so he could not see that she was crying weakly—like an old woman. ❖

ACCENT ON...
HORTICULTURE

Elisa's garden does well under her "planter's hands." If she had a greenhouse, she could grow a large variety of plants and flowers. Design a greenhouse where Elisa could grow any number of beautiful specimens. Keep in mind that a greenhouse is usually made of glass or plastic and has a slanted roof to admit as much sunlight as possible. Consider how much space your greenhouse would provide, and plan on the kinds of plants you would raise, when you would start them, and where you would place them in the greenhouse.

ON THE JOB
SMALL APPLIANCE REPAIR

Today traveling repair people have virtually disappeared from America. However, many persons continue to make their living repairing small appliances. Some persons who repair small appliances and tools may have little formal training in that field, but many have taken high school or college courses in electronics and industrial arts. Such repair work is often done in small storefront shops or home repair shops. A part-time job in such a shop usually offers opportunities for on-the-job training. Repair shop workers must be detail-minded, patient, and good with their hands. The work tends to be solitary. A knowledge of mechanics and basic physics or physical science is also helpful.

UNDERSTANDING

1. Even if Elisa Allen said nothing, the reader could tell a great deal about her from her physical appearance, clothing, and nonverbal messages. Examine Elisa's actions and appearance, and explain what they reveal about her.

   For at least 15 minutes, observe one person's nonverbal messages. Write a character sketch of that person based on your interpretation of his or her appearance and actions. *Workshop 2*

2. The perception Elisa has of the traveling repairman's life on the road may not correspond to the reader's perception. Find passages that show Elisa's view. Then find passages that influence your own view. Do you agree with Elisa?

   People's perceptions or interpretations of what they see and hear often differ. Bring a picture to class that has no explanatory caption. Ask classmates to write down what they think is happening in the picture. Compare various perceptions of the picture.

3. Everyone seeks to be understood. What does Elisa want others to understand? Find passages in the text to support your conclusions.

   In order to understand others, people must learn to listen well to one another. In a group, identify the skills of a good listener. Develop a chart that enables you to monitor and evaluate how skillfully an individual listens. *Workshop 15*

CONNECTING

1. Both Elisa Allen and the traveling repairman experience isolation. The repairman is physically isolated as he travels. Elisa's isolation is spiritual, not physical. A woman in a male-dominated world, she cannot confide in anyone, or join in work traditionally done by men. With a group, brainstorm to decide who might feel cut off from others. What are ways to help these people feel more like they belong to a community? What advice would you give, for example, to new students transferring to your school in their junior year? With your class, prepare an advice manual for making friends and feeling included at school.

2. Do you think Henry Allen is a good husband? Use passages in the story to explain why or why not.

   Evaluating characters in a story involves the same kind of thinking that goes into evaluation reports. One kind of evaluation report is the incident report, the written record of an unexpected problem. Recall an accident you witnessed on television or in person. In memo form, write a one page incident report concerning this accident. *Workshops 3 and 13*

A LAST WORD

Have you ever felt like Elisa Allen, unable to pursue meaningful challenges in your life? What prevented you from pursuing such challenges? How might a person combat this problem?

Blazing Trails in the Snow

• *from Polar Dream*
• *from A Snow Walker's Companion*

EXPLORING

Before the final achievement of a major goal, a person generally takes multiple small steps leading to the big one. For example, many of the skills and information you are learning in school today may very well be small steps in the direction of a major dream in your future. Think of your ultimate goal. Is there anything you are doing right now that is one of many steps leading to your goal? Describe a goal you recently achieved. Explain how you felt when you made it.

THEME CONNECTION...
CHALLENGE MEANS RISK

Challenging goals usually involve risk. In some cases, the risk may involve no more than embarrassment or wasted time. Sometimes, however, challenge means danger, the risk of life and limb or the risk of reputation and fortune. We look up to those who take reasonable risks because they are unafraid to do the things others only imagine. Unplanned, careless risk-takers, of course, prompt dismay, not admiration.

TIME & PLACE

In 1980, Helen Thayer walked on skis and on foot over the frozen arctic seas around a maze of islands until she reached the magnetic North Pole. She traveled alone, her only companion being a husky named Charlie. Beginning on Little Cornwallis Island in the Northwest Territories of Canada, Thayer traveled across the ice up the coast of Bathurst Island, up to King Christian Island, maneuvered around several other small islands, and came back down to Helena Island. Thayer's fascination with trekking in snow-covered terrain is not unique to her. The selection on methods of hauling a toboggan in "A Snow Walker's Companion" reminds us that others share her enthusiasm for exploring harsh territory.

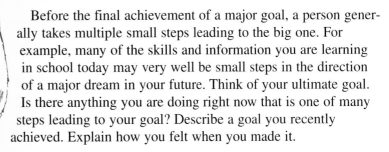

THE WRITER'S CRAFT
NOTHING BUT THE TRUTH

Nonfiction is factual information based on real people and real events. In the first selection, Helen Thayer gives the reader a first-hand personal account of her polar adventure, told exactly the way it happened. It is based on journals written at the time—no embellishments, no changes in names or locations. The second selection is an example of objective technical writing that explains how toboggans work and are hauled.

from *Polar Dream*
Polar Bear Pass

Helen Thayer

Day 5

Today from my camp at Black Point I hoped to travel fifteen miles across Goodsir Inlet to Rapid Point. Nine miles deep by fifteen miles wide, Goodsir Inlet cuts into the eastern shore of Bathurst Island. And to reach Rapid Point I had to cross the outlet of Polar Bear Pass, a wide, low-lying valley stretching about twenty miles between the western and eastern shores of Bathurst, dividing the island into unequal north and south sections. The floor of the long, sheltered valley averages only ninety feet above sea level. Many streams and rivers flow from the rolling hills on each side of the valley into the large Goodsir River, which, during the summer thaw, flows swiftly eastward into Goodsir Inlet. The sheltered valley is home to a variety of Arctic animals, including denning female polar bears and their cubs, musk-ox, Peary caribou, lemmings, Arctic hare, Arctic fox, and ermine. But in April, the river is frozen solid and the valley is used by polar bears crossing from the sea ice on one side of Bathurst to the sea ice on the opposite shore. Hence the name Polar Bear Pass.

During my observation of polar bear tracks during the first five days of my journey, I saw no tracks in areas of multi-year ice, such as the area of frozen mounds I had passed through on day three. However, I saw many tracks in areas of cracked and moderately rough ice and pressure ridges, especially around the minor ridges. No doubt the areas in which seals can maintain breathing holes dictate where the polar bears hunt in their never-ending quest for food.

The day started well. I decided to take advantage of the clear visibility and cut straight across the Inlet instead of following the coast. I found a series of ice pans, some several hundred feet wide, surrounded by rougher ice caused by the pressuring of the pan edges. When one pan ended I crossed over the rough edges to another smooth pan a few feet away. I was making good time, skirting some large mounds of ice over fifteen feet high sprinkled here and there. They were all different shapes, streaked with the now familiar tints of pale blue.

We crossed over several cracks in the ice, some only a hair's width and others perhaps six inches across. Charlie didn't like to cross the wider ones. He always hesitated but followed in response to a sharp tug on his leash. He was afraid of falling into the water. I wondered if an Arctic dog instinctively has respect for the cold, chilling waters, knowing that a dip can be fatal.

We were crossing Polar Bear Pass outlet and as I skied I remarked to Charlie, "I wish they had called this place Squirrel Pass. I could handle that." I had seen two sets of bear tracks as we set out at 7:30 in the morning. Now it was close to ten o'clock, almost time to eat. There was a larger **hummock** of ice ahead about twenty feet high. It looked like a small iceberg. I decided to stop to eat on the other side.

About twenty feet in front of the iceberg, Charlie stopped and began growling

hummock—a ridge

loudly, his back hair standing on end. I had no doubt that it was a bear. I tore my skis off, unclipped the sled ropes from my harness, grabbed the rifle and flare gun, and stood waiting with Charlie at my side still clipped to my harness. He was at the end of his chain, snarling, staring straight at the wall of ice. Every nerve in my body was tense.

Suddenly, a full-grown male bear stepped out from behind the ice, paused momentarily, then with unbelievable speed bounded straight as an arrow for my sled. He flipped the offending object to one side with a mighty swipe of a massive front paw as if it were a tiny toothpick. I stood terrified, rooted to the spot. Charlie's growls were deafening. Then the bear, only twenty feet away, apparently saw me for the first time and partly rose up on its hind legs, dwarfing me as I stood there. The bear began to charge and I was jolted into action. My right thumb on Charlie's collar clip pressed down and instantly released him. I dropped the flare gun and raised the rifle to fire point blank at the bear as Charlie raced to its right rear leg and hung on with all the strength in his powerful black body.

As I fired, the bear dropped onto all fours and the bullet zinged harmlessly over its head. Now, its mouth open, it desperately tried to reach Charlie, but he was hanging on, twisting away from those vicious teeth. Around and around they went until, finally, the more powerful bear tore away from Charlie's grip and raced off into the distant ice with Charlie in hot pursuit.

I stood there glad to be alive, watching Charlie and the bear disappear into the distance. But my relief was short-lived. Charlie was gone. Would he come back? How could I find him? It was useless to go after him. Would the bear turn and injure him? So many questions but no answers. I was frantic. I had never been so afraid in my life, but now I felt numb. I turned my sled right side up and, still holding the rifle, sat down, praying that Charlie would come back. I walked around to keep warm, looking into the distance, hoping to see Charlie. I had no idea how long I could wait. I couldn't bring myself to think of what I would do if he didn't return. I thought about the bear. It had expressed an anger I had not seen in the previous bear encounters. It had moved swiftly and silently except for a moment before he appeared ready to charge. At that moment I was sure I detected a slight hiss from its partly open mouth.

Suddenly I saw a black spot away in the distance. Could that be Charlie? It had to be. The black spot rapidly became larger. It *was* Charlie. He was flying over the ice with long graceful strides straight toward me. I dropped the rifle and ran to greet him. We met twenty yards away in a flurry of black fur, hugs, and kisses. He was panting hard. I buried my face in his thick neck fur and wanted to cry with joy, but didn't dare. I had learned my lesson on day two when I cried and my eyelids froze shut. Instead, we returned to my sled and had a short celebration party of crackers and peanut butter cups. On the way back I picked up the rifle where I had dropped it on the ice.

I sat on my sled feeding Charlie, thinking of my encounter with the bear. It seemed to have lasted a lifetime, but couldn't have been more than five minutes, perhaps less. When I fired at the bear I felt at the time I had to use my last line of defense, but now I was thankful the bear had dropped onto all fours and the bullet

> ● ● ● ● ● ● ●
> I stood
> there glad
> to be alive,...
> ● ● ● ● ● ●

FOCUS ON...
SCIENCE

Thayer experienced brutally cold weather in her travels. Write several paragraphs that describe what the weather would be like on such an expedition, the dangers associated with the weather, and how a person should be prepared to deal with it. Make a list of the equipment needed, clothing to wear, and other necessary supplies. Prepare a map that shows the location of Thayer's expedition.

◆ ◆ ◆ ◆ ◆ ◆ ◆ ◆ ◆ ◆ ◆ ◆ ◆ ◆ ◆ ◆ ◆ ◆

mettle—strength of spirit to do one's best

chaotic— unorganized or confused

missed. It was better that way. The bear was unhurt and Charlie had chased it away.

I wondered what would have happened if I had fired a single shot into the bear's chest. I knew now, beyond a doubt, that at close range it would be highly dangerous to wound a bear. This bear had demonstrated more power, anger, and speed than I could have imagined. I was surprised at the way it had reared on its hind legs. I shook my head when I thought of what little protection I had against a bear charging out from behind the ice at close range. Charlie had shown no fear. He was on his **mettle**. Now that he had stopped panting, he wore a big doggy smile. This was fun to him. Not for me. My hands were still shaking. The energy was drained from my body. I felt sick to my stomach.

Obviously I had chosen a bad place to stop and eat, so I gathered things up to leave. Later we went past the iceberg, where I was surprised to see a partly eaten seal lying not far from a breathing hole. The head was intact but looked crushed. The skin and fat along the back had been eaten. Apparently we had disturbed a feeding bear. No wonder he had been so angry.

Charlie chewed on the seal. I let him eat for a few minutes as a reward. Then it

occurred to me that the bear might come back to finish his meal. If so, I definitely didn't want to share the same space with him again. Once was enough. Much to Charlie's disgust I pulled him away. He tried to drag the seal with him and I imagined him thinking, "What a waste." But it was time for us to leave, as fast as possible and without Charlie's seal. We continued our journey through the pass outlet. It was almost noon and we were only halfway across. I kept looking nervously over my shoulder. I couldn't get that wild, violent scene out of my mind.

We ran out of smooth ice pans at about the middle of the inlet. During the short summer thaw, the full force of the river flows out into the center of the inlet, pushing the ice into a **chaotic** jumble. After another hour we were through the worst and back to the smoother pans. But the afternoon glare had settled over the ice, cutting visibility down to about a mile. Trying to see ahead to Rapid Point, I could only guess where it was. My map showed it to be a point of flat, sea-level land, about five miles ahead, that gained only one hundred feet in elevation three miles inland. There appeared to be a large river mouth there, so I could expect rough ice at the point.

I skied from one ice pan to another. In one place the ice became a smooth highway and I could see a tall, slender pillar of ice standing by itself in the far distance. It was in line with Rapid Point so I aimed for it and in no time we were alongside it. At least thirty feet high, it was white and gracefully slender. I stopped to eat and take a photo. I lined my sled and Charlie up in front of the pinnacle and set my camera on the tripod I carried with me. With the timer set I ran to stand at Charlie's side. I had my mask off and was smiling at the camera but there was no click. The camera had frozen again. The joys of Arctic photography. After a few more tries I gave up and with painful, cold fingers took Charlie's photo by himself.

At five o'clock, with the sun setting in the west, I could see Rapid Point. It was so flat I couldn't tell land ice from sea ice. I veered out around the point into a haunting, **desolate**, lonely moonscape. The strong sea currents swept around the point and were pulled into the inlet we had just passed. Huge plates of ice a hundred feet wide were lifted up onto each other. Some plates had ridden up over their neighbors, leaving their sharp edges pointing to the sky. As we worked our way around the point, I could only guess where the land began. The ice creaked and groaned as it protested the abuse it was being dealt from the sea currents. I kept to the less angled plates, but my skis still slid sideways to the bottom. Charlie didn't like it at all. There were too many cracks in the ice for his liking. But we kept going until the ice flattened. I didn't want to camp on the unstable ice near those swift currents and I was glad to get away from that strange, lonely, ghostly place.

It was six o'clock. It had been a long, emotionally exhausting day. More than anything, I wanted to get into my sleeping bag and go to sleep to give my mind some relief. Charlie was happy now that we had passed the broken ice of Rapid Point, but he was tired. As soon as we stopped he curled up and went to sleep even before eating his dinner.

He didn't wake up until I had set up camp, cooked dinner, and made the nightly eight o'clock base camp call. Then he was ready to eat. He enthusiastically crunched his dog food, ate three crackers for dessert, then curled up again. He, too, had had a long day. It was hard work chasing polar bears and protecting me. With a last pat and a "Good night, Charlie," I crawled into my tent, slid into my sleeping bag, and slept soundly without a single dream about bears. ❖

desolate—
deserted, lifeless

ACCENT ON...
METEOROLOGY

Thayer deals with incredibly cold conditions for over 345 miles, facing gale-force winds and ice storms and trekking on dangerous, unstable ice floes. Weather stations are located in various spots along the Arctic Circle; getting information from such stations is imperative when planning an adventure such as Helen Thayer's. Find out what kinds of technological requirements a meteorological center would have in such terrain and climate. Describe in two pages what an arctic weather station would be like, what its purpose would be, and how it would be staffed.

from A Snow Walker's Companion: Winter Trail Skills from the Far North

TECHNICAL WRITING

Garrett and Alexandra Conover

tumpline—a sling formed by a strap slung over the forehead or chest

HAULING METHODS

Toboggans are hauled using either soft lines or two poles affixed to the front of the toboggan. The poles run forward about seven feet and have a leather strap from one to the other about a foot from the ends. After years of traveling with both formats, we have seen no clear advantage of using one over the other.

Soft lines are versatile, can be coiled out of the way, and don't take up much space. When a hauler winds his or her arms through them, they can take up the small shocks and swaying and rolling of walking, and they soften the pitching of the toboggan on drift-covered lakes. They are easy for beginners to master and can be adjusted readily for length. If overtaken by a toboggan on a downgrade, the snowshoer can step out of the way and control the toboggan as with a brake line.

Poles are a fixed length and a bit harder to learn to handle effectively, but they allow you to back up if you wander into overflow or bad ice, and can slow a toboggan on a mild downgrade by applying reverse

pressure. Shocks are absorbed through the poles either by resting your forearms along the part that extends beyond the strap or by resting your hands over the ends. You can even wind your arms through the poles behind you so you can really lean into your pull, but this is accomplished by bending the wrists, whereas in a soft-line system the lines bend around your forearms. For some people, the position is not comfortable enough for long periods. Poles do take up some space, but they can be folded back over the load and even used as brake lines from the side or rear.

A separate short push pole can also be used in moving toboggans. This is used at the rear of the load, giving additional assistance in propelling and steering.

In both pole and soft-line hauling, the basics of wearing the strap are the same. Not surprisingly, the leather strap itself may be identical, whether it connects to loops in quarter-inch tow lines or is tied or tacked to spruce poles. In both cases, the leather is two or perhaps two-and-a-half inches wide and, like a **tumpline**, distributes the pressure of the load over a wide area.

There are three basic hauling positions. The first is used only for light or moderate

SPOTLIGHT ON...
SCANNING/SKIMMING

As you read for information, like that in the excerpt from *A Snow Walker's Companion*, you may find it helpful to scan or skim the material first to identify the key words or concepts that are most important. As you skim or scan an article, follow these steps:
1. Quickly look over the whole article to find headings or sub-headings that the writer has used to organize the material.
2. Jot down notes or phrases of main ideas as you read. Don't stop for all the details, though.
3. After you have skimmed the material once, go back to read in depth and absorb all the details the author included.

loads, and some people never use it at all. The center of the wide part of the strap rests over the back of the neck while the ends pass forward over the shoulders and then rearward to the load under the arms. In this way, neck and shoulders distribute the pressure over a wide area, and a good lean into the hauling keeps the body aligned. If your load exceeds 130 pounds or so, you will not favor this method for long periods.

The next most common harness config-uration has the strap passing over one shoulder and across the chest diagonally, then under the opposite arm. Again, the weight is distributed over a wide area, and the position of the strap allows for sus-tained heavy-duty hauling. By simply alternating high and low sides, you can equalize any **asymmetry** over the day and rest each side, much as paddlers do by switching sides.

The third method is to pass the strap around the outside of both arms and across the upper chest. This holds the most favor

with people who are short or short-waisted, although it works for anyone. It is a good method to keep in mind as a rest position to relieve strains brought on by other positions while still hauling. Experienced haulers shift through all the methods over a day, and this seems to provide enough variation to keep the body from tiring of any one position.

The diagonal over-one-shoulder and upper-chest methods are appropriate for heavy loads up to the limits of haulability. For anatomical reasons, women sometimes resist these methods, but, happily, the methods work well for both sexes.

For extreme situations such as steep hills or riverbank ascents, or simply moving a toboggan in marginal conditions, the towing strap can be worn tumpline-fashion with a determined lean into the strap. Such measures are often required to gain a river-bank or height of land or some other rela-tively short-term goal. You may also favor this method if you have to continue moving in difficult hauling conditions. ❖

asymmetry—
the state of being unbalanced or uneven

UNDERSTANDING

1. The black husky Charlie contributed in many ways to Thayer's well-being. Find passages that mention or imply Charlie's importance on this difficult journey.

   Animals are being used more to help people overcome difficulties. Research how agencies use animals to perform tasks or how pets enrich people's lives. Prepare a report and illustrate your presentation with visual aids such as photocopied handouts, enlarged photos, or posters. *Workshop 20*

2. *A Snow Walker's Companion* discusses the advantages of hauling a toboggan by using soft lines or two poles, and it also explains the three basic ways to use a leather strap. Discuss with your group the advantages and disadvantages of soft-line and pole hauling and the three uses of the leather strap. Which techniques do you think Thayer used?

   Choose something you know how to do well that could be done in front of the class such as iron a shirt, build a model car, or play a scale on a musical instrument. Write directions explaining how to do this task. Then ask a partner to follow your instructions in front of the class. *Workshop 4*

3. Thayer's trip was definitely an adventure few people have experienced. What challenges did she face? How did she meet them?

   Assume you own a company called Polar Adventure that arranges toboggan tours in the arctic region. Write the text of an advertisement to attract customers.

CONNECTING

1. In groups, investigate and plan a two-day adventure trip in a nearby recreation area. Consider weather, terrain, and wildlife. Itemize necessary food and equipment. Discuss transportation and hazards. You may want to consult experts for more information. Prepare a brochure that fully explains everything about this trip. *Workshop 21*

2. Thayer set a goal and met the challenges involved in attaining it. A goal is any objective you decide to accomplish. Achieving small daily goals can lead to larger successes. Set a large goal for yourself. Plan the separate steps you will take each day to achieve this goal. Your plan will record the goal and provide space to record each thing you do to reach this goal. *Workshop 4*

3. Survival becomes a problem for everyone in the event of an earthquake, hurricane, flood, or other natural disaster. Research the materials and equipment families should have on hand to prepare for natural disasters that might happen in your area. Develop a survival guide to help people be prepared for an emergency.

A LAST WORD

Thayer took a great risk in her journey to the North Pole, battling fiercely cold weather and encountering animals such as the polar bear. Do you value success more if it comes as the result of a great challenge? Are there certain challenges that are not worth the risk?

Martinez' Treasure

EXPLORING

The power of the human spirit can create joy in each day despite depressing circumstances. One's attitude toward life makes all the difference. In your own life or the lives of others, can you cite situations in which a positive attitude was the key to happiness or success? How does one develop and keep a positive attitude?

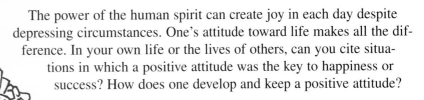

THEME CONNECTION...
SUCCESS AS HAPPINESS

Success means the achievement of something planned for and desired. When they are young, Rosa and Juan happily plan ahead. They are hopeful and expectant. The harshness of daily life, however, takes away their hope and happiness. When they become content with what they have achieved, desiring nothing more, they are once again happy.

TIME & PLACE

An interesting thing about stories reflecting the fairy tale tradition is that they have a universal quality. They could happen at any time and any place. This story takes place in the American Southwest "long ago." It could have happened last week or one hundred years ago. Furthermore, Juan and Rosa in the Southwest could have been David and Alice in Vermont. What matters more than setting or character is the lesson the story teaches.

THE WRITER'S CRAFT
THE MORAL OF THE STORY

"Martinez' Treasure" does not revolve around complex characters, exciting twists of action, or an elaborate setting. It exists instead to teach a moral lesson. Manuela Crosno's tale most resembles a fairy tale, where time is vague ("so long ago no one can remember"), the scene is merely sketched ("where the mountains meet the desert"), trouble challenges the main characters, and the supernatural has a place in natural experience.

Martinez' Treasure

Manuela Williams Crosno

There was once a man named Juan Martinez who lived near the mountains, but it was so long ago no one can remember just where he lived. He had a wife named Rosa, a burro whom he called Jose, and two goats. Rosa had a small flock of chickens. At one time Juan and Rosa had been young and carefree, but now they were quite old. A warm summer sun shining down many years had so wrinkled their faces, that they seemed as old as the wrinkled hills about them.

They lived where the mountains meet the desert and the forest begins. Each day Martinez walked among the trees and gathered small pieces of wood. He loaded these on Jose's back, which had become scarred and bent from many loads. At one time Jose had moved slowly because he was lazy, as are all burros, but now the burden of age had been added to his **indolence**, so that he barely moved along in the midday heat.

For many years, Juan and Rosa had lived in a small house, which Juan proudly called their *casa*. From time to time they had repaired the house with **adobe**, which they patted on with their bare hands, until now all its sides bulged like **buttresses**. The roof leaned badly, as if it were trying to shelter its owners for their few remaining years and found the task almost too great.

Juan and Rosa were very poor. In summer, they raised beans and corn to eat through the winter, and chili peppers to season the beans. The red strings of peppers hanging over the roof of their *casa* in the fall were the only colorful things about it. With the small amount of money Juan received for the firewood he sold, they were able to buy a bit of food—flour for the **tortillas** and, occasionally, cheese for the enchiladas. Their few items of clothing consisted of worn-out pieces their relatives no longer would wear.

Juan and Rosa had no children. Except when they went to the village, they seldom saw a living thing—just Jose, who was not good company, their two goats, the chickens, and a few lizards that darted from their path as they went about their work.

When they were young, they had made great plans for themselves. But trying to produce food from the dry soil had been difficult. Gradually they lost themselves in work and forgot how to laugh or play. Finally, they talked of nothing except their work and completely abandoned their early dreams. They forgot they had ever been happy, and they accepted their monotonous and meager living as a way of life. All they knew was work and more work.

The two people were busy all day long. Martinez would be gone for hours, loading old Jose's back with wood. The next day, Martinez would go to the village, several miles away, to sell the wood. Then he would gather another load of wood, and so on, day in and day out.

For poor Rosa, each day was the same. She would rise early and milk the two goats. Then, unless there were many rains, she would drive the goats out to eat the **grama grass** that grew meagerly on the desert. She worked hard in the fields, with the goats close by.

Sometimes she baked in the oven, which was like those built by Indians who

> **He saw the box sticking out of the side of the arroyo....**

FOCUS ON... LANGUAGE

Crosno's language clearly implies the Hispanic culture of the Southwest. Check out the meanings of the following words, then find four or five additional words that come from this culture. Make a miniature word booklet, giving definitions for each word, writing sample sentences, and adding illustrations or clip art to add meaning to the words in your word book. You could also include a section for native Spanish speakers. Give the meaning of the word in Spanish, and write a sentence in Spanish.

adobe	casa	metate
pueblo	tortilla	arroyo

lived in the **pueblos** along the river. The round adobe oven looked like a huge beehive sitting on the ground. At one side near the bottom was a small opening, and above it a smaller hole through which smoke escaped. Rosa heated the oven by burning wood in it. Then she removed the hot coals and put in small pieces of dough. When baked, the dough became dark brown and brittle, unlike the tortillas she sometimes baked for special days. When Rosa made tortillas, she used a **metate** to grind the corn, and then flattened and shaped the cakes with her hands. The cakes came out white, with some brown spots. Juan always told Rosa they were the best tortillas he had ever tasted.

One evening Juan came home much later than usual. It had been dark for several hours. Rosa had stood at the window, holding a candle, peering anxiously out into the darkness, looking for a sign of him. When he finally stood in the doorway, she noticed that his clothing was dusty and caked with mud. Jose stood behind him. Instead of the usual load of wood, a box or chest, about eighteen inches deep and wide and two feet long, was tied across the burro's sagging back. Together Juan and Rosa removed the box and dragged it inside, for it was very heavy and covered with hard-packed soil.

Juan told Rosa an interesting story. While Juan was gathering wood, Jose had wandered to the edge of a small arroyo. The burro's weight caused some soil on the side of the **arroyo** to give way, and Jose slid to the bottom of the ditch, a distance of a few feet. Juan walked down into the arroyo to get the burro. He saw the box sticking out of the side of the arroyo where the earth had crumbled. All day he dug about it with sticks, only to find it was too heavy for him to lift onto the burro's back. He dragged the chest along the top of the arroyo to a place where the ditch was deeper than Jose was tall, and there he lowered it onto the burro's back and brought it home.

Rosa's first concern was for Juan. She gave him dry clothing and a bowl of hot chili. Then, they could no longer contain their excitement, and they turned their attention to the box, wondering what it contained. But they could find no place where it might be opened; it had no lock, and its

pueblos—communal dwellings characteristic of several Native American peoples of the Southwest

metate—pronounced me-tah-tay; a slightly hollowed-out stone in which grain and corn were ground

arroyo—a dry stream bed

SPOTLIGHT ON... WORKING COOPERATIVELY

In the story, Rosa and Juan worked long, hard hours to make ends meet. Before they thought they were rich, and even after, they worked together to share the workload. In any working relationship, people must work as a team. As you establish such working relationships, keep the following guidelines in mind:

1. Discuss with your team members what your goals and tasks are.
2. Divide the tasks up evenly among the members of the team.
3. Discuss and resolve problems as they occur. Do not let feelings of resentment build.
4. Encourage each other and let your partners know you appreciate their efforts.

◆◆◆◆◆◆◆◆◆◆◆◆◆◆◆◆◆◆

top could not be pried off. The chest was rusty, so they scraped it with knives and even washed its sides in an effort to find a way to open it. They worked very late by the light of the crude candle that Rosa had carefully made. Still, they found no way to open the box, and so they decided to sleep and try again in the morning.

At daybreak, they again tried to open the box. Remembering stories of hidden gold, they were certain the chest was filled with old Spanish coins. Therefore, they did not want anyone to know of their discovery. They had to find a way to open it themselves.

But promises of riches could not keep them from their work. Soon after the first warm glow of sunlight came through their window, habit called them to their usual tasks. They hid the box away under some old blankets and baskets, and, all day, they thought about it and the treasure it contained.

Again they worked late into the night, trying to open the box. They could see small letters carved into the metallike

material, but neither of them had the opportunity to learn to read. Above the letters was a single ornament, standing out from the chest as if for emphasis as well as design.

Juan and Rosa were strangely content now that they thought they were rich. They spent many hours trying to open the chest, and while they were working, a great change came over them. They became happy, and they remained so! Now that they had gold, they did not mind that they appeared poor. They knew they could buy fine clothing! They did not mind that Jose was old. They could buy many burros with the gold in the chest! They worked uncomplainingly, and they ate their meager food as if it, too, contained great richness.

Finally, Martinez said to his wife, "We must tell no one about the box, and we must think hard how to open it. Some day I will find how to open it!"

"That is right," she agreed. "We must tell no one!"

"Even if we could open the box," added her husband, "we would be afraid to keep the gold about. We would want to store it someplace. Here it is safely hidden—and we will leave it here as if we had stored it away! We are rich people!"

They put the chest away, hiding it carefully, and walked in lively steps around the room—almost dancing.

"Look, my Juan," said Rosa, "we are not so old!"

Now they felt as they had when they were young, so they began to do many things that were new to them. They did not work so long each day, and yet they seemed to get as much done as before. Juan sang half-remembered phrases of old songs in a shaky treble as he gathered wood. Rosa planted morning glories all around the *casa*, covering its barrenness. Their blossoms were large and blue and made the old, brown adobe look beautiful! Juan and Rosa kept the goat corral and the chicken pen clean. They even tolerated Jose and brushed his tattered coat until it was almost shiny.

Happiness, it seemed, came to them in great amounts. Their relatives in the village noticed this change. There was a new freshness in Rosa's old, wrinkled cheeks, and Juan smiled so often that he seemed younger. Their eyes sparkled with gladness.

"Juan and Rosa are not so poor, after all," said their relatives, and, having more respect for them, they gave them better clothes to wear. One of Juan's brothers, Pancho, gave them a young burro to replace Jose. Pancho's wife scolded him for it later, but it brought much happiness to Juan. With the new burro, he could

gather wood faster than ever and hurry back to his *casa* and the box containing his treasure. Jose was left to wander about on the desert and spend his time in idleness. Finally, he was given to Rosa's nephew's son, Cruz, a gentle *niño*, who was kind to him.

So the days passed, and Juan and Rosa knew great joy. They had not learned yet how to open the chest, but they thought that some day they would. It seemed not to matter greatly how soon.

The years quickly came and quickly went, and finally *los viejos* died—first Rosa, and then Juan, who died at the home of his brother, Pancho.

> • • • • • • •
> …they never doubted that they would find the chest filled with gold pieces.
> • • • • • • •

After Juan's funeral, Pancho's wife said to her husband, "Go and get the burro you gave to Juan. He no longer needs it, and the beast will but die!"

So Pancho took his older brother Tomas with him, and together they went to Juan's house to get the burro. They found the little mouse-colored animal standing **disconsolately** near the corral where Juan had left him several days earlier. But before they took him with them, they entered Juan's house and found the chest. The two brothers tried in vain to open it.

"This," they agreed, "is why Juan and Rosa did not seem poor! The box is so heavy, it must be filled with gold!"

Together they loaded the chest onto the wagon, hid it in Pancho's house under cover of darkness, and told no one, except Pancho's wife, of their discovery. They reasoned at once that they had done more to help Juan and Rosa than had their other brothers or sisters, so the chest was rightly theirs. They knew happiness as they

niño—pronounced **neen**-yo; Spanish word for child

los viejos—Spanish for "the old people"

disconsolately— without hope

arca vieja—Spanish for "old chest"

dreamed of what they would do with the gold, because, like Juan and Rosa, they never doubted that they would find the chest filled with gold pieces. Pancho's wife made plans to be the richest, the most beautiful, and the finest-clothed woman in the village. She spoke of money in such hushed tones that the villagers thought her husband was going to receive an inheritance.

Even though the brothers finally attacked the chest with heavy tools, as Juan and Rosa never would have done, they could not split it apart! Finally they grew impatient and began to look for ways to get it open. Late one afternoon, Pancho stopped at the home of the village doctor, a learned man who could read well.

"Doctor Gardea," he said, "my wife has been complaining of a bad hurting in the head. I wish you would come to my *casa*." (This was not true, but Pancho's wife had agreed to pretend illness.)

It had already grown dark when Dr. Gardea came to Pancho's house. After talking with the wife, he prescribed two days of absolute quiet. He had lived in the village long enough to know that she was considered a gossip and troublemaker, so he told himself, whimsically, that this would stop her talking for a few days. The doctor was a busy man, and the woman's whisperings of wealth had not yet reached his ears.

He was about to take his leave when Pancho asked, "Have you ever seen this **arca vieja**? It has been in my family for years!" (Pancho was never one to be concerned with truth.) "It belonged to the father of my father, and to his father before him. It has been kept in the *casa* of Juan, my brother, and both Tomas and I have

forgotten how to open it. Will you read for us what the letters say?"

The doctor stepped over to the chest and knelt beside it. Tomas and Pancho and Pancho's wife stood beside him trying to hide their excitement; their hearts pounded rapidly! Silently reading the Latin script, the doctor asked, "Are you sure you want to open the chest? You do remember the message?"

"Oh, yes!" replied the brothers together. "We want to open it!"

The doctor seemed reluctant. "In addition to the message, the letters tell just how to open it," he remarked. With a quick jerk, he tore aside one corner of the ornament, and there unfastened the clasp that would allow the top to open. He was a discreet man, however, and did not lift the lid, but left the house.

Pancho closed the door and locked it carefully after the doctor had gone. Now the three people could not hide their excitement! Soon they would be rich! Already they could feel the gold pieces sliding through their fingers! They quickly opened the lid.

The firelight fell on the chest, which was filled with *santos*—wooden images of the saints! Hastily, in their anxiety to get at the treasure they thought was hidden away beneath the figures, they threw these out on the floor. They bruised and tore their hands, but soon the box was completely empty—except for a heavy cross roughly hewn from granite rock. There had been no worldly treasure in the chest.

The brothers argued with one another, and Pancho's wife became miserable. Now her neighbors would learn that Pancho was not to receive any wealth, that they were to remain poor, after all.

● ● ● ● ● ● ●
"Are you sure you want to open the chest?"
● ● ● ● ● ● ●

A thought came to her which she told to Pancho. "Perhaps the *santos* belonged to Rosa's family. Juan and Rosa buried the gold under their house and filled the box with Rosa's *santos* instead!"

So Pancho and Tomas set about digging for the gold, which, they convinced themselves, had been removed from the chest and buried or hidden away by Juan and Rosa. They dug up all the earth in and about the old *casa*, never finding any treasure. They spent several unhappy years digging, neglecting their crops and growing poorer and more miserable. Finally, the brothers quarreled and went their separate ways.

Sometime later, Pancho met Dr. Gardea in the village. Perhaps the message on the chest told where the treasure was hidden!

He demanded, "You will tell me what was carved into the *arca vieja*?" It was hardly a question.

The doctor, believing firmly in the power of the written word, hesitated. Then he repeated the curious message to Pancho. "Whoever possesses this chest will be happy so long as he opens it not!" ❖

ACCENT ON...
ANIMAL HUSBANDRY

Raising animals on a farm is hard work, as Juan and Rosa discovered over the course of their lives. Animal husbandry, or the science of raising livestock, has been practiced for thousands of years. Think about raising animals on a farm of your own. Write a 1–2 page proposal to raise your own livestock. What types of animals would you raise? How would you house, feed, breed, and care for these animals? In addition, figure out the cost of raising livestock. Then describe the purpose of raising these animals—will you raise them to provide food for your family, or will you sell the animals after they have matured? How will this affect the cost of raising the animals?

ON THE JOB
PHOTO-JOURNALIST

A photojournalist would have been eager to be present when the treasure chest was opened, in order to photograph its contents. A photojournalist needs to pay attention to details and tell a story with pictures. To pursue this career, a person should have an interest in current events and social issues as well as photography. He or she needs to know the variety of film technology available and be able to think creatively. This job also requires a strong sense of responsibility and integrity.

UNDERSTANDING

1. Juan and Rosa change after they find the chest. In what ways do they change and what do these changes bring about?

   Suppose you decide that you have changed in ways that would help you to be considered for a certain job. Therefore, you want to submit a personal letter along with the standard application form. In the letter, adopt a positive attitude as you explain the qualities and abilities you offer the company. ***Workshop 11***

2.  Martinez portrays the effect of a supposed treasure chest on two sets of relatives: Juan and Rosa, and Pancho, his wife, and his brother Tomas. Juan and Rosa believe from the day they find it until they die that the large box contains a treasure. Pancho and his allies eventually discover that the box holds no treasure. With a group, compare and contrast the attitudes and behavior of those in the story who think they are rich with the attitudes and behavior of those who think they are poor. Working collaboratively, develop a list of examples taken from daily life that illustrate Martinez' point that what we think influences our attitude and actions. Present you group's list to the class.

3. Had Pancho known what the writing on the chest said, do you think he would have opened it? What would most people do? What would you do? Discuss things people do today to try to get rich quick or to get something for nothing.

   Think about something expensive you would like to own such as a car, boat, or video camera. Collect print advertisements, including classified ads, of the product you wish to own. In what ways do these advertisements play on people's desires and fears? Explain to your class the techniques your advertisements use to sell the product.

A LAST WORD

Juan and Rosa's belief that they are rich changes their lives even though it is not true. How important is perception in your daily life? Is it more important to think of yourself as successful than to actually succeed?

CONNECTING

1.  Juan and Rosa's attitude toward everything in their lives changed once they believed they owned treasure, and "They worked uncomplainingly…" A positive attitude is one of the most important qualities an employee can possess. Working in groups, develop and distribute a survey for employees. Survey students with part-time jobs as well as individuals in the work force full time. Include questions that ask the workers how they feel about their jobs and if they enjoy going to work each day. Present your findings to the class using visual aids such as charts and graphs. ***Workshop 20***

2. Find a fairy tale, fable, or parable from your culture or ethnic background which teaches a moral lesson. Combine this story with those selected by others in the class. Publish your own volume of fairy tales, fables, and parables from many cultures, especially those represented in your school or community.

Talent

EXPLORING

Talent might be defined as one's "natural abilities." Using this definition, consider your natural abilities, and speculate on how you came by them. Remember that talents need not be related to school: you may have an ability to make others laugh, an ability to disassemble and reassemble items easily, an ability to make friends easily, an ability to make common sense decisions, or perhaps a number of different talents. Since all people have natural abilities, you should not feel that you are bragging when you identify yours; you are simply noting those characteristics that make you who you are.

THEME CONNECTION...
EVERYONE CAN SUCCEED

Success is often identified with people who have inborn gifts. Successful people seem to possess special abilities that give them an advantage over the rest of us. Annie Dillard dispels this theory in "Talent." She says that every individual is capable of succeeding. All that is needed is education and hard work.

TIME & PLACE

Annie Dillard, a contemporary writer, urges the reader, "Don't wait for anything. Learn something first," and says, "while you are getting to know it, you will get to love it, and that love will direct you in what to do." Eventually you will discover what you love, and having done so working at it will not be so hard. Her advice entails taking small steps and meeting small challenges to achieve an ultimate goal. Notice that Dillard's examples of famous people are men. Only in this century is Dillard right that everyone—women included—can achieve success.

THE WRITER'S CRAFT

ESSAY

Essays are usually very structured pieces of writing. The essayist puts a statement of the main idea of the essay, the thesis, at the beginning of the writing, and then supports it with examples and details in subsequent paragraphs. Each of these supporting paragraphs also includes its own main idea, or topic sentence. The examples and details of that paragraph will fit around the topic sentence. Dillard uses this traditional essay format in her definition essay, "Talent."

Talent

Annie Dillard

precocious—
exhibiting exceptional
qualities at an
unusually early age

There is no such thing as talent. If there are any inborn, God-given gifts, they are in the **precocious** fields of music, mathematics, and chess; if you have such a gift, you know it by now. All the rest of us, in all the other fields, are not talented. We all start out dull and weary and uninspired. Apart from a few like Mozart, there never have been any great and accomplished little children in the world. Genius is the product of education.

Perhaps it's a cruel thing to insist that there is no such thing as talent. We all want to believe—at least I do—that being selfless was "easy" for Albert Schweitzer, that Faulkner's novels just popped into his head, that Rembrandt painted because he "had to." We want to believe all these nonsensical things in order to get ourselves off the hook. For if these people had no talent, then might the rest of us have painting or writing or great thinking as an option? We, who have no talent? I think the answer is yes, absolutely.

So I maintain that the people who have made something of their lives—the Pasteurs and Cezannes and Melvilles—were neither more talented nor more disciplined nor more energetic nor more driven than the rest of us. They were simply better educated. Some of them did it the hard way, studying all the difficult works of their fields at home on their own. Others studied in school. But they all studied. You won't find a writer who hasn't studied the details of the works of other writers—although occasionally you find an American writer like Hemingway or Whitman who deliberately pretended to be spontaneous and unstudied, probably in order to mislead the competition. And occasionally you find a writer like Thoreau, a very well educated Harvard man whose reading was in the Greek classics and in whose work most readers overlook the evidences of scholarship and effort simply because they don't want to see them.

It's hard work, doing something with your life. The very thought of hard work makes me queasy. I'd rather die in peace. Here we are, all equal and alike and none of us much to write home about—and some people choose to make themselves into physicists or thinkers or major-league pitchers, knowing perfectly well that it will

About the Author

Annie Dillard (1945–) received the Pulitzer Prize in 1975 for her first book, *Pilgrim at Tinker Creek*, a collection of essays and observations written while Dillard lived in Virginia's Roanoke Valley. Dillard has been a contributing editor or columnist for several publications and is a professor of writing and writer in residence at Wesleyan University in Connecticut.

FOCUS ON... LITERATURE

Annie Dillard has often been praised for her insights on nature. Read an essay by Dillard that deals with nature. Identify its main ideas. Then explain why you do or do not agree with Dillard's views.

◆◆◆◆◆◆◆◆◆◆◆◆◆◆◆◆◆◆◆◆◆

be nothing but hard work. But I want to tell you that it's not as bad as it sounds. Doing something does not require discipline; it creates its own discipline.

People often ask me if I discipline myself to write, if I work a certain number of hours a day on a schedule. They ask this question with envy in their voices and awe on their faces and a sense of **alienation** all over them, as if they were addressing an armored tank or a talking giraffe or Niagara Falls. We all want to believe that other people are natural wonders; it gets us off the hook.

Now, it happens that when I wrote my first book of prose, I worked an hour or two a day for a while, and then in the last two months, I got excited and worked very hard, for many hours a day. People can lift cars when they want to. People can recite the **Koran**, too, and run in marathons. These things aren't ways of life; they are merely possibilities for everyone on certain occasions of life. You don't lift cars around the clock or write books every year. But when you do, it's not so hard. It's not superhuman. It's very human. You do it for love. You do it for love and respect for your own life; you do it for love and respect for the world; and you do it for love and respect for the task itself.

If I had a little baby, it would be hard for me to rise up and feed that little baby in the middle of the night. It would be hard; but it certainly wouldn't be a discipline. It wouldn't be a **regimen** I imposed on myself out of **masochism**, nor would it be the flowering of some extraordinary internal impulse. I would do it, grumbling, for love and because it has to be done.

Of course it has to be done. And something has to be done with your life too: something specific, something human. But don't wait around to be hit by love. Don't wait for anything. Learn something first. Then while you are getting to know it, you will get to love it, and that love will direct you in what to do. So many times when I was in college I used to say of a course like Seventeenth Century Poetry or European History, "I didn't like it at first, but now I like it." All of life is like that—a sort of dreary course which gradually gets interesting if you work at it.

I used to live in **perpetual** dread that I would one day read all the books that I would ever be interested in and have nothing more to read. I always figured that when that time came I would force myself to learn wildflowers, just to keep awake. I dreaded it, because I was not very interested in wildflowers but thought I should be. But things kept cropping up and one book has led to another and I haven't had to learn wildflowers yet. I don't think there's much danger of coming to the end of the line. The line is endless. I urge you to get in it, to get in line. It's a long line—but it's the only show in town. ❖

alienation— separation from someone or something

Koran—the book composed of sacred writings accepted by Muslims as revelations made to Muhammad by Allah through the angel Gabriel

regimen— a systematic plan

masochism—a taste for suffering

perpetual—continual

ON THE JOB

SOUND ENGINEER

A sound engineer is responsible for the technical aspects of recording music. The engineer decides on the placement of microphones and determines what equipment will be necessary to make a recording. Often each musician's part of a song will be recorded separately. The engineer's job is to mix the various parts together, including the vocalist's if there is one, to create a harmonious, complete song. Creativity as well as a thorough knowledge of current recording technique is necessary to be a successful sound engineer.

UNDERSTANDING

1. Identify the main idea in each of the nine paragraphs of Dillard's essay, and create an outline or diagram that shows her organizational pattern. Which sentence does she use as a thesis?

2. Good writers support general statements with specific examples. Find passages in which Dillard does this.

   Write an essay in which you use specific examples from your own experience to agree or disagree with the following statement: Life is like "a sort of dreary course which gradually gets interesting if you work at it." ***Workshop 5***

3. Dillard says that "Doing something does not require discipline; it creates its own discipline." How does Dillard define "discipline"? What does she mean by this statement? Find passages to support your conclusions.

   Using discipline as one of five qualities you praise, write a letter of recommendation for yourself. Imagine that this letter is intended to get you a summer job you would really like to have. ***Workshop 11***

CONNECTING

1. Write an essay of definition for your school newspaper's editorial page. Define a term like *snob*, *scapegoat*, *loner*, *busybody*, *optimist*, or *team player*. Use personal experiences to support your thesis. Be careful not to defame others. ***Workshop 12***

2. Read a variety of editorials and commentaries published in newspapers to find a writer you enjoy reading. Write a letter to this person. Explain the writing process that you've been taught, and ask the columnist to explain the process he or she follows to produce work. For instance, you might ask how she finds topics to write about. Include other questions that will help you understand how professional writers work.

   In your group, circulate the newspaper columns you favor. Explain why you enjoy them. Share your letter with those in your group. ***Workshops 1 and 11***

3. Dillard urges her audience to learn, to get an education, and to work hard. Is her view widespread at your school or community? Working in a group, interview businesspeople, educators, and friends. Do they agree or disagree with Dillard's views on education and talent? Research education using the Internet and library resources. ***Workshop 18***

A LAST WORD

Do you agree with Dillard that "There is no such thing as talent"? Are some individuals gifted with more natural skill in fields such as athletics or writing, or can people acquire these gifts?

ACCENT ON...
LIBRARY TECHNOLOGY

Annie Dillard says she used to fear that she would run out of books that she liked to read. Finding books that interest you can take some time and effort, but it's well worth it. Create your own personal reading list and bibliography. Start by making a list of three or more categories of subjects you like to read about. Then use the on-line card catalog at your local library to locate at least fifty titles of books, videos, CD-ROM's, periodicals, and so on that fit into each category. Compile your listings on a disk, then print out a mini-booklet of your personal bibliography.

Benjamin Franklin

• *from The Autobiography*

• *from Instant American History*

EXPLORING

• • • • • • • • • • • • • • • • • • • •

Everyone has habits. In fact, many people begin each new year by resolving to break bad habits and acquire good ones. The Greek philosopher Aristotle said that people become virtuous by *practicing* a virtue until they make it a habit. For example, a man who wishes to be honest practices saying and doing honest things until honesty becomes automatic. To what extent do good and bad habits influence your own behavior and that of friends and relatives? For what reasons would you, or would you not, recommend Aristotle's approach to gaining virtue to anyone you know?

THEME CONNECTION... CHALLENGING YOURSELF

Benjamin Franklin decided to improve his character. He challenged himself to behave virtuously all the time. To meet this challenge successfully, Franklin decided to overcome many bad habits and replace them with good ones. He invented a method to attain moral perfection. His clever plan challenged him to practice honest self-examination and self-discipline. Variations of this plan have been practiced over the years by those who seek a systematic way to consider and improve their personal behavior.

TIME & PLACE

Franklin began *The Autobiography* in 1771 at the age of 65. He worked on it four times during the next nineteen years, producing four distinct parts. The selection on moral perfection comes from part one, consisting of 86 pages Franklin addressed to his son, William, who was then governor of New Jersey. Franklin's life story ends at the year 1758 because illness kept him from going further. Franklin lived during a period scholars describe as "The Age of Reason," or "The Enlightenment." During this time, most people believed, as did Franklin, that reason alone could be depended upon to guide human beings to universal truths.

THE WRITER'S CRAFT

PROCESS: TELLING HOW

Franklin's description of working towards moral perfection consists of separate explanations of how to do things. For instance, he describes how he selected and arranged 13 moral virtues. He also sets forth how to make and improve a record book, and he tells how he pursued the virtue of "order." Franklin so clearly explains each of these processes that one can easily follow them. Explaining how something happens or how it is done is called "process analysis."

from *The Autobiography*
Moral Perfection

Benjamin Franklin

It was about this time that I conceived the bold and **arduous** project of arriving at moral perfection. I wished to live without committing any fault at any time; I would conquer all that either natural inclination, custom, or company might lead me into. As I knew, or thought I knew, what was right and wrong, I did not see why I might not always do the one and avoid the other. But I soon found I had undertaken a task of more difficulty than I had imagined. While my care was employed in guarding against one fault, I was often surprised by another; habit took the advantage of inattention; inclination was sometimes too strong for reason. I concluded, at length, that the mere **speculative** conviction that it was our interest to be completely virtuous was not sufficient to prevent our slipping; and that the contrary habits must be broken, and good ones acquired and established, before we can have any dependence on a steady, uniform **rectitude** of conduct. For this purpose I therefore contrived the following method.

In the various enumerations of the moral virtues I had met with in my reading, I found the catalogue more or less numerous, as different writers included more or fewer ideas under the same name. Temperance, for example, was by some confined to eating and drinking, while by others it was extended to mean the moderating of every other pleasure, appetite, inclination or passion, bodily or mental, even to our **avarice** and ambition. I proposed to myself, for the sake of clearness, to use rather more names with fewer ideas annexed to each, than a few names with more ideas; and I included under thirteen names of virtues all that at that time occurred to me as necessary or desirable, and annexed to each a short **precept**, which fully expressed the extent I gave to its meaning.

These names of virtues, with their precepts were:

1. TEMPERANCE. Eat not to dullness; drink not to elevation.

2. SILENCE. Speak not but what may benefit others or yourself; avoid trifling conversation.

3. ORDER. Let all your things have their places; let each part of your business have its time.

4. RESOLUTION. Resolve to perform what you ought; perform without fail what you resolve.

5. FRUGALITY. Make no expense but to do good to others or yourself; i.e., waste nothing.

6. INDUSTRY. Lose no time; be always employed in something useful; cut off all unnecessary actions.

7. SINCERITY. Use no hurtful deceit; think innocently and justly, and, if you speak, speak accordingly.

arduous—difficult to accomplish

speculative—relating to a theory rather than a fact

rectitude—righteousness

avarice—greediness

precept—a principle

FOCUS ON...
HISTORY

Benjamin Franklin was a man with great imagination and abilities. His accomplishments seem phenomenal to us today. What did Franklin's contemporaries think of him? Did they see value in his inventions and discoveries? Find three sources that describe Franklin in the words of people who knew him. Use the information you collect to write a feature article or develop a short video depicting his character.

8. JUSTICE. Wrong none by doing injuries or omitting the benefits that are your duty.

9. MODERATION. Avoid extremes; **forbear** resenting injuries so much as you think they deserve.

10. CLEANLINESS. Tolerate no uncleanness in body, clothes, or habitation.

11. TRANQUILITY. Be not disturbed at trifles, or accidents common or unavoidable.

12. CHASTITY. Rarely use venery but for health or offspring, never to dullness, weakness, or the injury of your own or another's peace or reputation.

13. HUMILITY. Imitate Jesus and Socrates.

My intention being to acquire the *habitude* of all these virtues. I judged it would be well not to distract my attention by attempting the whole at once, but to fix it on one of them at a time; and, when I should be master of that, then to proceed to another, and so on, till I should have gone through the thirteen; and, as the previous acquisition of some might facilitate the acquisition of certain others, I arranged them with that view, as they stand above.

Temperance first, as it tends to **procure** that coolness and clearness of head which is so necessary where constant **vigilance** was to be kept up, and guard maintained against the **unremitting** attraction of ancient habits and the force of perpetual temptations. This being acquired and established, *Silence* would be more easy; and my desire being to gain knowledge at the same time that I improved in virtue, and considering that in conversation it was obtained rather by the use of the ears than of the tongue, and therefore wishing to break a habit I was getting into of prattling, punning, and joking, which only made me acceptable to trifling company, I gave *Silence* the second place. This and the next, *Order*, I expected would allow me more time for attending to my project and my studies; *Resolution*, once become habitual, would keep me firm in my endeavours to obtain all the subsequent virtues; *Frugality* and *Industry* freeing me from my remaining debt, and producing affluence and independence, would make more easy the practice of *Sincerity* and *Justice*, etc., etc. Conceiving then, that, agreeably to the advice of Pythagoras in his Golden Verses, daily examination would be necessary, I contrived the following method for conducting that examination.

forbear—to hold back from

procure—acquire

vigilance—the quality or state of being watchful

unremitting—constant

eradicate—get rid of or remove

multiplicity—a large number

overbearing—bossy or arrogant

insolent—insulting or rude

I made a little book, in which I allotted a page for each of the virtues. I ruled each page with red ink, so as to have seven columns, one for each day of the week, marking each column with a letter for the day. I crossed these columns with thirteen red lines, marking the beginning of each line with the first letter of one of the virtues, on which line, and in its proper column, I might mark, by a little black spot, every fault I found upon examination to have been committed respecting that virtue upon that day.

I determined to give a week's strict attention to each of the virtues successively. Thus, in the first week, my great guard was to avoid even the least offence against *Temperance*, leaving the other virtues to their ordinary chance, only marking every evening the faults of the day. Thus, if in the first week I could keep my first line, marked *T*, clear of spots, I supposed the habit of that virtue so much strengthened, and its opposite weakened, that I might venture extending my attention to include the next, and for the following week keep both lines clear of spots. Proceeding thus to the last, I could go through a course complete in thirteen weeks, and four courses in a year. And like him who, having a garden to weed, does not attempt to **eradicate** all the bad herbs at once, which would exceed his reach and his strength, but works on one of the beds at a time, and, having accomplished the first, proceeds to a second, so I should have, I hoped, the encouraging pleasure of seeing on my pages the progress I made in virtue, by clearing successively my lines of their spots, till in the end, by a number of courses, I should be happy in viewing a clean book, after a thirteen weeks' daily examination. . . .

> ● ● ● ● ● ● ●
> I determined to give a week's strict attention to each of the virtues. . . .
> ● ● ● ● ● ● ●

The precept of *Order* requiring that *every part of my business should have its allotted time*, one page in my little book contained the following scheme of employment for the twenty-four hours of a natural day. . . .

I entered upon the execution of this plan for self-examination, and continued it with occasional intermissions for some time. I was surprised to find myself so much fuller of faults than I had imagined; but I had the satisfaction of seeing them diminish. To avoid the trouble of renewing now and then my little book, which, by scraping out the marks on the paper of old faults to make room for new ones in a new course, became full of holes, I transferred my tables and precepts to the ivory leaves of a memorandum book, on which the lines were drawn with red Ink, that made a durable stain, and on those lines I marked my faults with a black-lead pencil, which marks I could easily wipe out with a wet sponge. After a while I went through one course only in a year, and afterwards only one in several years, till at length I omitted them entirely, being employed in voyages and business abroad, with a **multiplicity** of affairs that interfered; but I always carried my little book with me. . . .

My list of virtues contained at first but twelve; but a Quaker friend having kindly informed me that I was generally thought proud; that my pride showed itself frequently in conversation; that I was not content with being in the right when discussing any point, but was **overbearing**, and rather **insolent**, of which he convinced me by mentioning several instances; I determined endeavoring to cure myself, if I could, of this vice or folly among the rest, and I added *Humility* to my list, giving an extensive meaning to the word. . . . ❖

from *Instant American History*

Benjamin Franklin: A Man Who Didn't Waste Any Time Watching TV

Irwin Unger

From the ages of 12 to 17, he published a newspaper with his brother, then ran an extremely successful printing business. When he was 22, he bought a poorly published newspaper and turned it into a lively and successful journal of news and ideas. By the time he was 26, he had published the first edition of *Poor Richard's Almanack*, the most widely read publication in the colonies for the next 25 years. He founded the American Philosophical Society. He reorganized the American postal system to make it profitable. He founded the University of Pennsylvania, formulated a theory of heat absorption, discovered electrical polarity, measured the Gulf Stream, designed ships, tracked storm paths, invented bifocal lenses, the lightning rod, and the Franklin stove, and studied French, Spanish, Italian, and Latin in his spare time. He coauthored the Declaration of Independence, and then finally, at the age of 81, even though he was so crippled by gout that he couldn't stand up, he attended the Constitutional Convention, making significant contributions to the final document. He was also a devoted husband (despite a reputation as a ladies' man) and the doting father of ten children. ❖

ACCENT ON...
DATA STORAGE

Franklin devised a little book with a page for each virtue and a system of recording his progress. What if he had had a computer to help him store information? With the help of a computer instructor or a software program with which you are familiar, design a computerized system for tracking your daily progress toward a goal such as becoming physically fit. After you have designed your program, try it out for a week or two to make sure it works, then demonstrate how it works to the class.

ON THE JOB
PRINTING PRESS TECHNICIAN

Working a web or sheet-fed press requires extensive training, available either on-the-job or at a recognized technical school. Most modern presses are run by computers, so additional technical training is required to learn the computerized technology involved. Press technicians need to have good skills in math, good analytical skills, and an ability to work well with others.

SPOTLIGHT ON...
KEEPING RECORDS

Keeping a precise record of your activities or progress is an excellent way of staying organized and focused. Franklin's daily chart helped him achieve some of his goals. You, too, may want to use such a technique to keep track of your progress. Here are some tips for keeping good records:

1. Decide exactly what kind of information you want to track.
2. Devise a simple chart or form that requires little time to complete. A calendar works well.
3. Maintain your record-keeping every day.
4. Review your process regularly. Are there improvements you could make in the system?
5. Label your records and keep them for future reference.

UNDERSTANDING

1. Why did Franklin decide that he could attain moral perfection only if he followed a method?

   Habits cause everyone to do and say many things. Consider the occasions when habits influenced your own or a friend's words and actions. Write an essay that classifies these habits. In your essay, try to reach conclusions. For example, which habits seem most common, most difficult to break, and most and least troublesome? *Workshop 1*

2. Carefully read Franklin's definitions of "justice" and "moderation." Paraphrase Franklin's two definitions, writing them in your own words. Then write your own brief responses to Franklin's two definitions. In each response, explain why you think Franklin's definitions hold true today, or why you think "justice" and "moderation" need new definitions for the modern world. *Workshops 7 and 12*

3. Why did Franklin add "humility" to his list? What kind of behavior does he seem to attach to humility? Develop your own formal definition of "humility" and support it with three examples from the lives of people you know. *Workshop 12*

A LAST WORD

Do you think it is possible to attain moral perfection? What steps would you take to replace bad habits with good ones?

CONNECTING

1. Develop in a group a list of rules accompanied by definitions or brief explanations that will help your own or any group function well. Compare your group's rules with those of other groups in the class. As a class, agree on a single comprehensive set of rules. Accept this set as the official statement of group rules to be followed by all class members when they work collaboratively.

2. In Franklin's day, everyone agreed on the meaning of right and wrong, that honesty and kindness were good qualities, and that theft and cruelty were not. Today, however, people do not entirely agree about right and wrong behavior. What virtues do people in your school or community value? With a group, gather information about the virtues honored most by those you know. Prepare a list to share with your class that explains these virtues.

3. Identify either five skills or five virtues you would like to achieve. Make a chart similar to Franklin's and use it for at least one week. Your chart should accurately record your success or failure. *Workshop 20*

UNIT 3

WRAP IT UP

1. In *Polar Dream*, Thayer describes her success in crossing Polar Bear Pass. Elisa in "The Chrysanthemums" enjoys great success cultivating her flowers, while Juan and Rosa in "Martinez' Treasure" believe they have found a treasure chest full of gold. According to Dickinson's poem, which character best comprehends success?

Think of a time in your life when you truly understood success. Did you achieve something important, or were you unable to reach your goal? Prepare a speech describing your experience and how it helped you to understand the meaning of success. How did you change as a result of this experience?

2. The excerpt from Angelou's poem states that each new day brings a fresh opportunity to succeed. Dilliard asserts in her essay "Talent," that anyone can succeed if he or she works hard enough. Franklin believes he may succeed in his quest for moral perfection by approaching the task systematically. Each author firmly believes that success is attainable. Compare the tools for success recommended in these three selections. What does each author suggest you need to do to be successful?

Write an inspirational poem or essay that lists the tools you believe are necessary for success. Encourage others to work toward achieving difficult goals.

UNIT
◆4◆
INNOCENCE AND EXPERIENCE

Innocence and experience are often opposites. Those in a state of innocence often naively believe that everyone is good-hearted and that every situation will work for the best. With experience comes first-hand knowledge of human strengths, weaknesses, and potential. Experience may shatter innocence, replacing it with wisdom. As the selections in this unit demonstrate, individuals learn and grow throughout life; the innocence of youth gradually gives way to the experience of maturity.

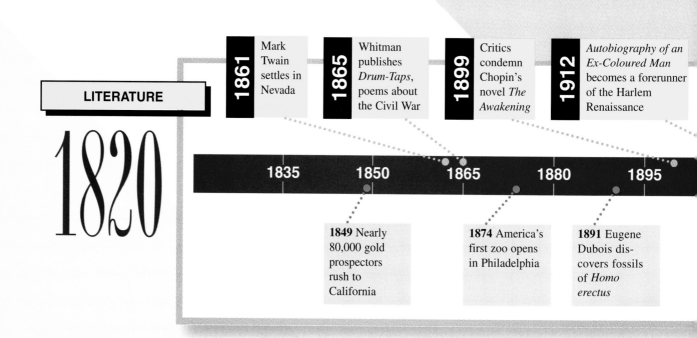

LITERATURE

1861 Mark Twain settles in Nevada

1865 Whitman publishes *Drum-Taps*, poems about the Civil War

1899 Critics condemn Chopin's novel *The Awakening*

1912 *Autobiography of an Ex-Coloured Man* becomes a forerunner of the Harlem Renaissance

1820

1835   1850   1865   1880   1895

1849 Nearly 80,000 gold prospectors rush to California

1874 America's first zoo opens in Philadelphia

1891 Eugene Dubois discovers fossils of *Homo erectus*

1926 Hughes publishes his first book

1966 Eiseley narrates TV series *Animal Secrets*

1976 Hayden appointed Consultant in Poetry to the Library of Congress

1978 E.B. White receives the Pulitzer Prize

1989 Tan's first novel, *The Joy Luck Club*, is published

1925   1940   1955   1970   1985

2000

1924 U.S. Congress passes Immigration Act

1925 Hughes, working as a busboy, is "discovered" by poet Vachel Lindsay

1963 Betty Friedan's *The Feminine Mystique* is published

LIFE and WORK

from *Roughing It*
I Find Fool Gold

EXPLORING

Imagine you are notified that you have inherited 20 million dollars from a distant relative, and a check for this amount will be delivered to you in a week's time. How will this news affect the next seven days of your life? Tell a partner how it will change your actions and your relationships at school. Compare your view with that of others in the class.

THEME CONNECTION...
DEALING WITH INEXPERIENCE

The inexperienced narrator of "I Find Fool Gold" knows nothing about prospecting. In his eagerness to strike it rich, however, he rushes out alone to search for precious metals, expecting to "find masses of silver lying all about the ground." Although the narrator senses that his inexperience might cause him to look ridiculous, still he fails to turn to his friends for expert advice. Rather than ask these seasoned prospectors what they think of his sample ore, he confidently presents it to them as genuine gold. He is humiliated, of course, when these experienced miners identify his discovery as worthless mica.

Because he mistakenly neglects to ask experienced people to share their knowledge, the narrator exposes his own folly and ignorance.

TIME & PLACE

This story takes place in 1848, when the discovery of gold in California led a wave of prospectors to descend on the American West. Spurred by dreams of riches, these men combed the mountains and streams of California, Nevada, and Oregon in hopes of finding gold and silver. Although thousands joined in the search, most came away empty-handed. Perhaps some, like Twain, who failed to strike it rich, nevertheless were enriched by the experience.

THE WRITER'S CRAFT

HYPERBOLE

"Hyperbole" means extreme exaggeration or overstatement. A writer uses hyperbole to make readers laugh. As this story begins, Twain uses hyperbole in comparing the size of the Humboldt River to that of the Mississippi. While the "monster" Mississippi is a mile wide, a person can "run and jump across the Humboldt River" and "drink it dry." Of course the Humboldt cannot be jumped, nor can it be drunk "dry," but using this hyperbole allows Twain to poke fun at the Western landscape.

from *Roughing It*
I Find Fool Gold

Mark Twain

fter leaving the Sink, we traveled along the Humboldt River a little way. People accustomed to the monster milewide Mississippi grow accustomed to associating the term *river* with a high degree of watery **grandeur**. Consequently, such people feel rather disappointed when they stand on the shores of the Humboldt or the Carson and find that a "river" in Nevada is a sickly **rivulet** which is just the counterpart of the Erie Canal in all respects save that the canal is twice as long and four times as deep. One of the pleasantest and most invigorating exercises one can contrive is to run and jump across the Humboldt River till he is overheated, and then drink it dry.

On the fifteenth day we completed our march of two hundred miles and entered Unionville, Humboldt County, in the midst of a driving snowstorm. Unionville consisted of eleven cabins and a **liberty pole**. Six of the cabins were strung along one side of a deep canyon, and the other five faced them. The rest of the landscape was made up of **bleak** mountain walls that rose so high into the sky from both sides of the canyon that the village was left, as it were, far down in the bottom of a **crevice**. It was always daylight on the mountaintops a long time before the darkness lifted and revealed Unionville.

We built a small, rude cabin in the side of the crevice and roofed it with canvas, leaving a corner open to serve as a chimney, through which the cattle used to tumble occasionally, at night, and mash our furniture and interrupt our sleep. It was very cold weather and fuel was scarce. Indians brought brush and bushes several miles on their backs; and when we could catch a **laden** Indian, it was well—and when we could not (which was the rule, not the exception), we shivered and bore it.

I confess, without shame, that I expected to find masses of silver lying all about the ground. I expected to see it glittering in the sun on the mountain summits. I said nothing about this, for some instinct told me that I might possibly have an exaggerated idea about it, and so, if I betrayed my thought, I might bring **derision** upon myself. Yet I was as perfectly satisfied in my own mind as I could be of anything that I was going to gather up, in a day or two, or at furthest a week or two, silver enough to make me satisfactorily wealthy—and so my fancy was already busy with plans for spending this money. The first opportunity that offered, I sauntered carelessly away from the cabin, keeping an eye on the other boys, and stopping and contemplating the sky when they seemed to be observing me; but as soon as the coast was manifestly clear, I fled away as guiltily as a thief might have done and never halted till I was far beyond sight and call. Then I began my search with a feverish excitement that was brimful of expectation—almost, of certainty.

I crawled about the ground, seizing and examining bits of stone, blowing the dust from them or rubbing them on my clothes, and then peering at them with anxious

grandeur—
magnificence

rivulet—a small
stream

liberty pole—flag
pole

bleak—exposed and
barren

crevice—a narrow
opening resulting
from a split or crack
in a rock

laden—loaded

derision—ridicule or
scorn

FOCUS ON...
HISTORY

The Gold Rush of 1849 had a monumental effect on the development and expansion of the West. For the next several decades, thousands migrated westward in search of riches. What was the success rate for these prospectors and adventurers? What insights can be gleaned from their experiences? With classmates, carry out research and then participate in a panel discussion about the effects of the Gold Rush, or write a report on a specific event having to do with the rush to find gold and other riches in the mid- to late 1800s in the West. For the report, prepare a map that illustrates the progression of western migration during the time period on which your report focuses.

◆ ◆

augmenting—becoming greater or more intense

forsook—abandoned

reconnoiter—to survey to gain information

privations—lack of what is needed for existence

hope. Presently I found a bright fragment and my heart bounded! I hid behind a boulder and polished it and scrutinized it with a nervous eagerness and a delight that was more pronounced than absolute certainty itself could have afforded. The more I examined the fragment the more I was convinced that I had found the door to fortune. I marked the spot and carried away my specimen. Up and down the rugged mountainside I searched, with always increasing interest and always **augmenting** gratitude that I had come to Humboldt and come in time. Of all the experiences of my life, this secret search among the hidden treasures of silverland was the nearest to unmarred ecstasy. It was a delirious revel. By and by, in the bed of a shallow rivulet, I found a deposit of shining yellow scales, and my breath almost **forsook** me! A gold mine, and in my simplicity I had been content with vulgar silver! I was so excited that I half believed my overwrought imagination was deceiving me. Then a fear came upon me that people might be observing me and would guess my secret. Moved by this thought, I made a circuit of the place, and ascended a knoll to **reconnoiter**.

Solitude. No creature was near. Then I returned to my mine, fortifying myself against possible disappointment, but my fears were groundless—the shining scales were still there. I set about scooping them out, and for an hour I toiled down the windings of the stream and robbed its bed. But at last the descending sun warned me to give up the quest, and I turned homeward laden with wealth. As I walked along I could not help smiling at the thought of my being so excited over my fragment of silver when a nobler metal was almost under my nose. In this little time the former had so fallen in my estimation that once or twice I was on the point of throwing it away.

The boys were as hungry as usual, but I could eat nothing. Neither could I talk. I was full of dreams and far away. Their conversation interrupted the flow of my fancy somewhat, and annoyed me a little, too. I despised the sordid and commonplace things they talked about. But as they proceeded, it began to amuse me. It grew to be rare fun to hear them planning their poor little economies and sighing over possible **privations** and distresses when a gold

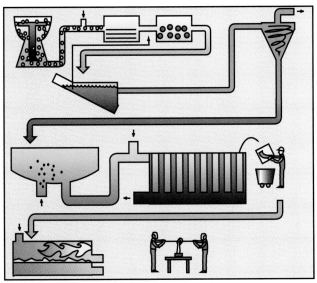

SPOTLIGHT ON...
UNDERSTANDING SYSTEMS

In the story, the narrator does not understand the system used to extract precious metals from the earth. Just as he needed to know and understand this system, so all of us need to comprehend how any system works:
1. Ask what the purpose of a system is.
2. Find out how the system works.
3. Investigate what happens when the system fails.
4. Explore what happened when part of a system is modified.

◆ ◆ ◆ ◆ ◆ ◆ ◆ ◆ ◆ ◆ ◆ ◆ ◆ ◆ ◆ ◆ ◆

mine, all our own, lay within sight of the cabin, and I could point it out at any moment. Smothered hilarity began to oppress me, presently. It was hard to resist the impulse to burst out with exultation and reveal everything; but I did resist. I said within myself that I would filter the great news through my lips calmly and be serene as a summer morning while I watched its effect in their faces. I said:

"Where have you all been?"

"Prospecting."

"What did you find?"

"Nothing."

"Nothing? What do you think of the country?"

"Can't tell, yet," said Mr. Ballou, who was an old gold miner, and had likewise had considerable experience among the silver mines.

"Well, haven't you formed any sort of opinion?"

"Yes, a sort of a one. It's fair enough here, maybe, but overrated. Seven-thousand-dollar ledges are scarce, though. That Sheba may be rich enough, but we don't own it; and, besides, the rock is so full of base metals that all the science in the world can't work it. We'll not starve here, but we'll not get rich, I'm afraid."

"So you think the prospect is pretty poor?"

"No name for it!"

"Well, we'd better go back, hadn't we?"

"Oh, not yet—of course not. We'll try it a riffle first."

"Suppose, now—this is merely a supposition, you know—suppose you could find a ledge that would yield, say, a hundred and fifty dollars a ton—would that satisfy you?"

"Try us once!" from the whole party.

"Or suppose—merely a supposition, of course—suppose you were to find a ledge that would yield two thousand dollars a ton—would *that* satisfy you?"

"Here—what do you mean? What are you coming at? Is there some mystery behind all this?"

"Never mind. I am not saying anything. You know perfectly well there are no rich mines here—of course you do. Because you have been around and examined for yourselves. Anybody would know that, that had been around. But just for the sake of argument, suppose—in a kind of general way—suppose some person were to tell

contemptible—
worthy of scorn

ostentatious—
showy, conspicuous
display

you that two-thousand-dollar ledges were simply contemptible—**contemptible**, understand—and that right yonder, in sight of this very cabin, there were piles of pure gold and pure silver—oceans of it—enough to make you all rich in twenty-four hours! Come!"

"I should say he was as crazy as a loon!" said old Ballou, but wild with excitement, nevertheless.

"Gentlemen," said I, "I don't say anything—I haven't been around, you know, and of course don't know anything—but all I ask of you is to cast your eye on *that*, for instance, and tell me what you think of it!" and I tossed my treasure before them.

There was an eager scrabble for it, and a closing of heads together over it under the candlelight. Then old Ballou said:

"Think of it? I think it is nothing but a lot of granite rubbish and nasty glittering mica that isn't worth ten cents an acre!"

So vanished my dreams. So melted my wealth away. So toppled my airy castle to the earth and left me stricken and forlorn.

Moralizing, I observed, then, that "all that glitters is not gold."

Mr. Ballou said I could go further than that, and lay it up among my treasures of knowledge that *nothing* that glitters is gold. So I learned then, once for all, that gold in its native state is but dull, unornamental stuff, and that only lowborn metals excite the admiration of the ignorant with an **ostentatious** glitter. However, like the rest of the world, I still go on underrating men of gold and glorifying men of mica. Commonplace human nature cannot rise above that. ❖

ON THE JOB
MINING EQUIPMENT OPERATOR

To operate much of the equipment used in mining today requires at least a high school diploma and two years of college or technical school training in mining techniques and equipment and/or metallurgy. A background in earth and physical science is also helpful. Some operators are graduates of four year college programs. They major in engineering or metallurgy and study systems technology and environmental issues as well.

ACCENT ON...
METALLURGY

Metallurgy is the science of extracting metals from ores and preparing the metals for commercial use. Had Twain's narrator really found gold, eventually a metallurgist would have had to separate the gold from the ore. How do metallurgists today separate valuable metals from their ores? Research the methods used to obtain a valuable metal in its pure form. Write a two-page summary of the process used and share the information with your classmates in an oral presentation.

UNDERSTANDING

1. What clues does Twain give to indicate that he is not particularly impressed with the town of Unionville? Arrange these clues in an outline for a paragraph by order of importance, from least damaging details to most damaging. Create a topic sentence that reflects Twain's overall opinion of Unionville.

2. What impression of Unionville does Twain's description convey? Cite specific details that contribute to this impression.

    Details are especially important in technical documents such as instruction manuals for electronic equipment. Practice presenting details clearly by writing a one-page summary of part, or all, of an instruction manual. ***Workshop 7***

3. Sometimes we inadvertently expose our own character flaws. Certainly Twain's narrator does when he is a young man. Find places in the text where the narrator remembers unintentionally disclosing his own weaknesses.

    Since the words people use reveal a great deal about them, choosing exactly the right words to express meaning is important. Keep a list of the words you hear spoken around you in the course of a single day and write down the impression each word gives of the person using it. Compare your list with those of several of your classmates. Do certain words seem always to give a specific impression? Does the impact of some words differ depending on the situation or tone of voice?

4.  Working with several classmates, re-read the end of the story. The experienced prospectors call the narrator's treasure "granite rubbish" and "nasty glittering mica." Although glitter excites only the ignorant, says the narrator, "I still go on underrating men of gold and glorifying men of mica. Commonplace human nature cannot rise above that." In your group, decide what this remark means.

CONNECTING

1. When he arrives in Unionville, the narrator has grand dreams of becoming wealthy. Eventually his dreams vanish. Disappointment is, of course, part of life. Interview teenagers and adults who have experienced disappointment, and ask them how they handled it. Then share your findings with several group members. Do certain patterns emerge? Does your research suggest some common causes of disappointment? Are there common ways to guard against it or deal with it?

2. Advertising is a field that sells images of "glitter." Working with a partner, examine magazine and newspaper advertising techniques. Using these, create a display that shows the inflated promises advertisers offer—promises that can seldom be met. ***Workshop 20***

from *The Joy Luck Club*

Two Kinds

EXPLORING

Most parents want their children's lives to be better than their own. With the best of intentions, they may push their children to excel in school and other activities, hoping that this prodding will lead to the child's happy, successful life. Sometimes, however, parents' wishes for their children contradict what the children want for themselves, and conflict results. What responsibilities do parents have to help their children prepare for the future? When should parents allow children to find their own way?

THEME CONNECTION... RESISTING EXPERIENCE

The mother in "Two Kinds" has experienced and triumphed over great hardship and suffering. Her own experiences cause her to believe that "you could be anything you wanted to be." When she encourages her daughter to discover and develop her potential, however, the child rebels, saying, "I won't be what I'm not." The story explores the clash between the experienced mother's point of view and that of the child.

TIME & PLACE

This fictitious story is based loosely on actual experience. Amy Tan's parents came to the United States from China in 1949, just two and a half years before Tan's birth. Between 1941 and 1950, more than 16,000 Chinese immigrants entered this country, fleeing the rise of Mao Tse-tung's Communist regime. Their cultural traditions of hard work and family unity enabled the Chinese immigrants to create strong, prosperous communities in America.

THE WRITER'S CRAFT

USING DIALECT

Amy Tan tells the story of a child with immigrant parents. The immigrant mother speaks a *dialect*, a special version of any language. Special versions are usually spoken in particular regions of a country. To create dialect, Tan uses many techniques, such as leaving out the articles *a* and *an*: "You can be prodigy, too."

from *The Joy Luck Club*
Two Kinds

Amy Tan

y mother believed you could be anything you wanted to be in America. You could open a restaurant. You could work for the government and get good retirement. You could buy a house with almost no money down. You could become rich. You could become instantly famous.

"Of course you can be **prodigy**, too," my mother told me when I was nine. "You can be best anything. What does Auntie Lindo know? Her daughter, she is only best tricky."

America was where all my mother's hopes lay. She had come here in 1949 after losing everything in China: her mother and father, her family home, her first husband, and two daughters, twin baby girls. But she never looked back with regret. There were so many ways for things to get better.

We didn't immediately pick the right kind of prodigy. At first my mother thought I could be a Chinese Shirley Temple. We'd watch Shirley's old movies on TV as though they were training films. My mother would poke my arm and say, "*Ni kan*"—You watch. And I would see Shirley tapping her feet, or singing a sailor song, or pursing her lips into a very round O while saying, "Oh my goodness."

"*Ni kan*," said my mother as Shirley's eyes flooded with tears. "You already know how. Don't need talent for crying!"

Soon after my mother got this idea about Shirley Temple, she took me to a beauty training school in the Mission district and put me in the hands of a student who could barely hold the scissors without shaking. Instead of getting big fat curls, I emerged with an uneven mass of crinkly black fuzz. My mother dragged me off to the bathroom and tried to wet down my hair.

"You look like Negro Chinese," she lamented, as if I had done this on purpose.

The instructor of the beauty training school had to lop off these soggy clumps to make my hair even again. "Peter Pan is very popular these days," the instructor assured my mother. I now had hair the length of a boy's, with straight-across bangs that hung at a slant two inches above my eyebrows. I liked the haircut and it made me actually look forward to my future fame.

In fact, in the beginning, I was just as excited as my mother, maybe even more so. I pictured this prodigy part of me as many different images, trying each one on for size. I was a dainty ballerina girl standing by the curtains, waiting to hear the right music that would send me floating on my tiptoes. I was like the Christ child lifted out of the straw manger, crying with holy indignity. I was Cinderella stepping from her pumpkin carriage with sparkly cartoon music filling the air.

In all of my imaginings, I was filled with a sense that I would soon become *perfect*. My mother and father would adore me. I would be beyond reproach. I would never feel the need to sulk for anything.

But sometimes the prodigy in me became impatient. "If you don't hurry up and get me out of here, I'm disappearing for good," it warned. "And then you'll always be nothing."

prodigy—a highly talented child

Every night after dinner, my mother and I would sit at the Formica kitchen table. She would present new tests, taking her examples from stories of amazing children she had read in *Ripley's Believe It or Not*, or *Good Housekeeping, Reader's Digest*, and a dozen other magazines she kept in a pile in our bathroom. My mother got these magazines from people whose houses she cleaned. And since she cleaned many houses each week, we had a great assortment. She would look through them all, searching for stories about remarkable children.

The first night she brought out a story about a three-year-old boy who knew the capitals of all the states and even most of the European countries. A teacher was quoted as saying the little boy could also pronounce the names of the foreign cities correctly.

"What's the capital of Finland?" my mother asked me, looking at the magazine story.

All I knew was the capital of California, because Sacramento was the name of the street we lived on in Chinatown. "Nairobi!" I guessed, saying the most foreign word I could think of. She checked to see if that was possibly one way to pronounce "Helsinki" before showing me the answer.

The tests got harder—multiplying numbers in my head, finding the queen of hearts in a deck of cards, trying to stand on my head without using my hands, predicting the daily temperatures in Los Angeles, New York, and London.

One night I had to look at a page from the Bible for three minutes and then report everything I could remember. "Now Jehoshaphat had riches and honor in abundance and . . . that's all I remember, Ma," I said.

● ● ● ● ● ● ●

I was filled with a sense that I would soon become perfect.

● ● ● ● ● ● ●

And after seeing my mother's disappointed face once again, something inside of me began to die. I hated the tests, the raised hopes and failed expectations. Before going to bed that night, I looked in the mirror above the bathroom sink and when I saw only my face staring back—and that it would always be this ordinary face—I began to cry. Such a sad, ugly girl! I made high-pitched noises like a crazed animal, trying to scratch out the face in the mirror.

And then I saw what seemed to be the prodigy side of me—because I had never seen that face before. I looked at my reflection, blinking so I could see more clearly. The girl staring back at me was angry, powerful. This girl and I were the same. I had new thoughts, willful thoughts, or rather thoughts filled with lots of won'ts. I won't let her change me, I promised myself. I won't be what I'm not.

So now on nights when my mother presented her tests, I performed listlessly, my head propped on one arm. I pretended to be bored. And I was. I got so bored I started counting the bellows of the foghorns out on the bay while my mother drilled me in other areas. The sound was comforting and reminded me of the cow jumping over the moon. And the next day, I played a game with myself, seeing if my mother would give up on me before eight bellows. After a while I usually counted only one, maybe two bellows at most. At last she was beginning to give up hope.

Two or three months had gone by without any mention of my being a prodigy again. And then one day my mother was watching *The Ed Sullivan Show* on TV. The TV was old and the sound kept shorting out. Every time my mother got halfway up from the

FOCUS ON...
MUSIC

The narrator's mother hoped that her daughter was a prodigy—a genius. A number of people have been musical prodigies. Research biographical dictionaries of musicians and other reference sources to identify a classical musician or composer who became famous at a young age. Write a brief report describing the person's talent and telling how fame and success affected the person. Share your report orally with the class.

sofa to adjust the set, the sound would go back on and Ed would be talking. As soon as she sat down, Ed would go silent again. She got up, the TV broke into loud piano music. She sat down. Silence. Up and down, back and forth, quiet and loud. It was like a stiff embraceless dance between her and the TV set. Finally she stood by the set with her hand on the sound dial.

She seemed entranced by the music, a little frenzied piano piece with this mesmerizing quality, sort of quick passages and then teasing lilting ones before it returned to the quick playful parts.

"*Ni kan*," my mother said, calling me over with hurried hand gestures. "Look here."

I could see why my mother was fascinated by the music. It was being pounded out by a little Chinese girl, about nine years old, with a Peter Pan haircut. The girl had the sauciness of a Shirley Temple. She was proudly modest like a proper Chinese child. And she also did this fancy sweep of a curtsy, so that the fluffy skirt of her white dress cascaded slowly to the floor like the petals of a large carnation.

In spite of these warning signs, I wasn't worried. Our family had no piano and we couldn't afford to buy one, let alone reams of sheet music and piano lessons. So I could be generous in my comments when my mother bad-mouthed the little girl on TV.

"Play note right, but doesn't sound good! No singing sound," complained my mother.

"What are you picking on her for?" I said carelessly. "She's pretty good. Maybe she's not the best, but she's trying hard." I knew almost immediately I would be sorry I said that.

"Just like you," she said. "Not the best. Because you not trying." She gave a little huff as she let go of the sound dial and sat down on the sofa.

The little Chinese girl sat down also to play an encore of "Anitra's Dance" by Grieg. I remember the song, because later on I had to learn how to play it.

Three days after watching *The Ed Sullivan Show*, my mother told me what my schedule would be for piano lessons and piano practice. She had talked to Mr. Chong, who lived on the first floor of our apartment building. Mr. Chong was a retired piano teacher and my mother had traded housecleaning services for weekly lessons and a piano for me to practice on every day, two hours a day, from four until six.

When my mother told me this, I felt as though I had been sent to hell. I whined and then kicked my foot a little when I couldn't stand it anymore.

"Why don't you like me the way I am? I'm *not* a genius! I can't play the piano. And even if I could, I wouldn't go on TV if you paid me a million dollars!" I cried.

My mother slapped me. "Who ask you be genius?" she shouted. "Only ask you be your best. For you sake. You think I want you be genius? Hnnh! What for! Who ask you!"

"So ungrateful," I heard her mutter in Chinese. "If she had as much talent as she has temper, she would be famous now."

Mr. Chong, whom I secretly nicknamed Old Chong, was very strange, always tapping his fingers to the silent music of an invisible orchestra. He looked ancient in my eyes. He had lost most of the hair on top of his head and he wore thick glasses and had eyes that always looked tired and sleepy. But he must have been younger than I thought, since he lived with his mother and was not yet married.

I met Old Lady Chong once and that was enough. She had this peculiar smell like a baby that had done something in its pants. And her fingers felt like a dead person's, like an old peach I once found in the back of the refrigerator; the skin just slid off the meat when I picked it up.

I soon found out why Old Chong had retired from teaching piano. He was deaf. "Like Beethoven!" he shouted to me. "We're both listening only in our head!" And he would start to conduct his frantic silent **sonatas**.

Our lessons went like this. He would open the book and point to different things, explaining their purpose: "Key! Treble! Bass! No sharps or flats! So this is C major! Listen now and play after me!"

● ● ● ● ● ● ●
"Why don't you like me the way I am?"
● ● ● ● ● ● ●

And then he would play the C scale a few times, a simple chord, and then, as if inspired by an old, unreachable itch, he gradually added more notes and running trills and a pounding bass until the music was really something quite grand.

I would play after him, the simple scale, the simple chord, and then I just played some nonsense that sounded like a cat running up and down on top of garbage cans. Old Chong smiled and applauded and then said, "Very good! But now you must learn to keep time!"

So that's how I discovered that Old Chong's eyes were too slow to keep up with the wrong notes I was playing. He went through the motions in half-time. To help me keep rhythm, he stood behind me, pushing down on my right shoulder for every beat. He balanced pennies on top of my wrists so I would keep them still as I slowly played scales and **arpeggios**. He had me curve my hand around an apple and keep that shape when playing chords. He marched stiffly to show me how to make each finger dance up and down, **staccato** like an obedient little soldier.

He taught me all these things, and that was how I also learned I could be lazy and get away with mistakes, lots of mistakes. If I hit the wrong notes because I hadn't practiced enough, I never corrected myself. I just kept playing in rhythm. And Old Chong kept conducting his own private **reverie**.

So maybe I never really gave myself a fair chance. I did pick up the basics pretty quickly, and I might have become a good pianist at that young age. But I was so determined not to try, not to be anybody different that I learned to play only the most ear-splitting preludes, the most **discordant** hymns.

Over the next year, I practiced like this, dutifully in my own way. And then one day I heard my mother and her friend Lindo Jong both talking in a loud bragging tone of voice so others could hear. It was after church, and I was leaning against the brick wall wearing a dress with stiff white petticoats. Auntie Lindo's daughter, Waverly, who was about my age, was standing farther down the wall about five feet away. We had grown up together and shared all the closeness of two sisters squabbling over crayons and dolls. In other words, for the most part, we hated each other. I thought she was snotty. Waverly Jong had gained a certain amount of fame as "Chinatown's Littlest Chinese Chess Champion."

"She bring home too many trophy," lamented Auntie Lindo that Sunday. "All day she play chess. All day I have no time do nothing but dust off her winnings." She threw a scolding look at Waverly, who pretended not to see her.

"You lucky you don't have this problem," said Auntie Lindo with a sigh to my mother.

And my mother squared her shoulders and bragged: "Our problem worser than yours. If we ask Jing-mei wash dish, she hear nothing but music. It's like you can't stop this natural talent."

And right then, I was determined to put a stop to her foolish pride.

A few weeks later, Old Chong and my mother conspired to have me play in a talent show which would be held in the church hall. By then, my parents had saved up enough to buy me a secondhand piano, a black Wurlitzer spinet with a scarred bench. It was the showpiece of our living room.

For the talent show, I was to play a piece called "Pleading Child" from Schumann's *Scenes from Childhood*. It was a simple, moody piece that sounded more difficult than it was. I was supposed to memorize the whole thing, playing the repeat parts twice to make the piece sound longer. But I dawdled over it, playing a few bars and then cheating, looking up to see what notes followed. I never really listened to what I was playing. I daydreamed about being somewhere else, about being someone else.

The part I liked to practice best was the fancy curtsy: right foot out, touch the rose on the carpet with a pointed foot, sweep to the side, left leg bends, look up and smile.

My parents invited all the couples from the Joy Luck Club to witness my debut. Auntie Lindo and Uncle Tin were there. Waverly and her two older brothers had also come. The first two rows were filled with children both younger and older than I was. The littlest ones got to go first. They recited simple nursery rhymes, squawked out tunes on miniature violins, twirled Hula Hoops, pranced in pink ballet tutus, and when they bowed or curtsied, the audience would sigh in unison, "Awww," and then clap enthusiastically.

When my turn came, I was very confident. I remember my childish excitement. It was as if I knew, without a doubt, that the prodigy side of me really did exist. I had no fear whatsoever, no nervousness. I remember thinking to myself, This is it! This is it! I looked out over the audience, at my mother's blank face, my father's yawn, Auntie Lindo's stiff-lipped smile, Waverly's sulky expression. I had on a white dress layered with sheets of lace, and a pink bow in my Peter Pan haircut. As I sat

SPOTLIGHT ON...
IDENTIFYING FAULTY REASONING

The narrator's mother was greatly influenced by popular culture, especially through television and magazines. You, too, are bombarded every day with a variety of statements and claims. It takes careful reasoning to evaluate such media messages. Learn to identify the following kinds of faulty reasoning that may exist in media messages.

1. Cause and effect fallacies: effects do *not* arise logically from causes
   "If you use this product, you will be smart."
2. Circular reasoning: the same words or ideas are merely repeated to describe both cause and effect
   "He is a good writer because he uses words well."
3. Misleading sample: "statistics" that are not explained or qualified
   "Four out of five doctors surveyed endorsed this product." (How many doctors were surveyed? What kinds of doctors?)
4. Loaded words: broad, vague words and statements that allow people to interpret them subjectively
   "The candidate is typical in her rejection of accepted, traditional roles." (Typical of what? What roles does she "reject?")

down I envisioned people jumping to their feet and Ed Sullivan rushing up to introduce me to everyone on TV.

And I started to play. It was so beautiful. I was so caught up in how lovely I looked that at first I didn't worry how I would sound. So it was a surprise to me when I hit the first wrong note and I realized something didn't sound quite right. And then I hit another and another followed that. A chill started at the top of my head and began to trickle down. Yet I couldn't stop playing, as though my hands were bewitched. I kept thinking my fingers would adjust themselves back, like a train switching to the right track. I played this strange jumble through two repeats, the sour notes staying with me all the way to the end.

When I stood up, I discovered my legs were shaking. Maybe I had just been nervous and the audience, like Old Chong, had seen me go through the right motions and had not heard anything wrong at all. I swept my right foot out, went down on my knee, looked up and smiled. The room was quiet, except for Old Chong, who was beaming and shouting, "Bravo! Bravo! Well done!" But then I saw my mother's face, her stricken face. The audience clapped weakly, and as I walked back to my chair, with my whole face quivering as I tried not to cry, I heard a little boy whisper loudly to his mother, "That was awful," and the mother whispered back, "Well, she certainly tried."

And now I realized how many people were in the audience, the whole world it seemed. I was aware of eyes burning into my back. I felt the shame of my mother and father as they sat stiffly throughout the rest of the show.

We could have escaped during intermission. Pride and some strange sense of honor must have anchored my parents to their chairs. And so we watched it all: the eighteen-year-old boy with a fake mustache who did a magic show and juggled flaming hoops while riding a unicycle. The breasted girl with white makeup who sang from *Madama Butterfly* and got honorable mention. And the eleven-year-old boy who won first prize playing a tricky violin song that sounded like a busy bee.

After the show, the Hsus, the Jongs, and the St. Clairs from the Joy Luck Club came up to my mother and father.

"Lots of talented kids," Auntie Lindo said vaguely, smiling broadly.

"That was somethin' else," said my father, and I wondered if he was referring to me in a humorous way, or whether he even remembered what I had done.

Waverly looked at me and shrugged her shoulders. "You aren't a genius like me," she said matter-of-factly. And if I hadn't felt so bad, I would have pulled her braids and punched her stomach.

But my mother's expression was what devastated me: a quiet, blank look that said she had lost everything. I felt the same way, and it seemed as if everybody were now coming up, like gawkers at the scene of an accident, to see what parts were actually missing. When we got on the bus to go home, my father was humming the busy-bee tune and my mother was silent. I kept thinking she wanted to wait until we got home before shouting at me. But when my father unlocked the door to our apartment, my mother walked in and then went to the back, into the bedroom. No accusations. No blame. And in a way, I felt disappointed. I had been waiting for her to start shouting, so I could shout back and cry and blame her for all my misery.

I assumed my talent-show **fiasco** meant I never had to play the piano again. But two days later, after school, my mother came out of the kitchen and saw me watching TV.

"Four clock," she reminded me as if it were any other day. I was stunned, as though she were asking me to go through the talent-show torture again. I wedged myself more tightly in front of the TV.

"Turn off TV," she called from the kitchen five minutes later.

I didn't budge. And then I decided. I didn't have to do what my mother said anymore. I wasn't her slave. This wasn't China. I had listened to her before and look what happened. She was the stupid one.

She came out from the kitchen and stood in the arched entryway of the living room. "Four clock," she said once again, louder.

"I'm not going to play anymore," I said nonchalantly. "Why should I? I'm not a genius."

She walked over and stood in front of the TV. I saw her chest was heaving up and down in an angry way.

"No!" I said, and I now felt stronger, as if my true self had finally emerged. So this was what had been inside me all along.

"No! I won't!" I screamed.

She yanked me by the arm, pulled me off the floor, snapped off the TV. She was frighteningly strong, half pulling, half carrying me toward the piano as I kicked the throw rugs under my feet. She lifted me up and onto the hard bench. I was sobbing by now, looking at her bitterly. Her chest was heaving even more and her mouth was open, smiling crazily as if she were pleased I was crying.

"You want me to be someone that I'm not!" I sobbed. "I'll never be the kind of daughter you want me to be!"

"Only two kinds of daughters," she shouted in Chinese. "Those who are obedient and those who follow their own mind! Only one kind of daughter can live in this house. Obedient daughter!"

"Then I wish I wasn't your daughter. I wish you weren't my mother," I shouted.

fiasco—complete failure

As I said these things I got scared. It felt like worms and toads and slimy things crawling out of my chest, but it also felt good, as if this awful side of me had surfaced, at last.

"Too late change this," said my mother shrilly.

And I could sense her anger rising to its breaking point. I wanted to see it spill over. And that's when I remembered the babies she had lost in China, the ones we never talked about. "Then I wish I'd never been born!" I shouted. "I wish I were dead! Like them."

It was as if I had said the magic words. Alakazam!—and her face went blank, her mouth closed, her arms went slack, and she backed out of the room, stunned, as if she were blowing away like a small brown leaf, thin, brittle, lifeless.

It was not the only disappointment my mother felt in me. In the years that followed, I failed her so many times, each time asserting my own will, my right to fall short of expectations. I didn't get straight As. I didn't become class president. I didn't get into Stanford. I dropped out of college.

For unlike my mother, I did not believe I could be anything I wanted to be. I could only be me.

And for all those years, we never talked about the disaster at the recital or my terrible accusations afterward at the piano bench. All that remained unchecked, like a betrayal that was now unspeakable. So I never found a way to ask her why she had hoped for something so large that failure was inevitable.

And even worse, I never asked her what frightened me the most: Why had she given up hope?

For after our struggle at the piano, she never mentioned my playing again. The lessons stopped. The lid to the piano was closed, shutting out the dust, my misery, and her dreams.

So she surprised me. A few years ago, she offered to give me the piano, for my thirtieth birthday. I had not played in all those years. I saw the offer as a sign of forgiveness, a tremendous burden removed.

"Are you sure?" I asked shyly. "I mean, won't you and Dad miss it?"

"No, this your piano," she said firmly. "Always your piano. You only one can play."

"Well, I probably can't play anymore," I said. "It's been years."

"You pick up fast," said my mother, as if she knew this was certain. "You have natural talent. You could been genius if you want to."

"No I couldn't."

"You just not trying," said my mother. And she was neither angry nor sad. She said it as if to announce a fact that could never be disproved. "Take it," she said.

But I didn't at first. It was enough that she had offered it to me. And after that, every time I saw it in my parents' living room, standing in front of the bay windows, it made me feel proud, as if it were a shiny trophy I had won back.

Last week I sent a tuner over to my parents' apartment and had the piano reconditioned, for purely sentimental reasons. My mother had died a few months before and I had been getting things in order for my father, a little bit at a time. I put the jewelry in special silk pouches. The sweaters she had knitted in yellow, pink, bright orange—all the colors I hated—I put those in moth-proof boxes. I found some old Chinese silk dresses, the kind with little slits up the sides. I rubbed the old silk against my skin, then wrapped them in tissue and decided to take them home with me.

After I had the piano tuned, I opened the lid and touched the keys. It sounded even richer than I remembered. Really, it was a very good piano. Inside the bench were the same exercise notes with handwritten scales, the same secondhand music books with their covers held together with yellow tape.

I opened up the Schumann book to the dark little piece I had played at the recital. It was on the left-hand side of the page, "Pleading Child." It looked more difficult than I remembered. I played a few bars, surprised at how easily the notes came back to me.

And for the first time, or so it seemed, I noticed the piece on the right-hand side. It was called "Perfectly Contented." I tried to play this one as well. It had a lighter melody but the same flowing rhythm and turned out to be quite easy. "Pleading Child" was shorter but slower; "Perfectly Contented" was longer, but faster. And after I played them both a few times, I realized they were two halves of the same song. ❖

UNDERSTANDING

1. What does the mother wish for her child? What reasons can you find in the text for the mother's attempts to mold her daughter? How is this mother different from most mothers, yet how is she the same?

   Imagine yourself as the parent of a teenager. In an essay, write how you would help your son or daughter move toward a bright future. What do you wish for your child, and how will you help your child achieve success? *Workshops 1 and 2*

2. "Two Kinds" presents a contest between two wills. Find evidence in the text of the daughter's position in this contest. Does her position change when she becomes an adult recalling the conflict? Consider the meaning of the title and the significance of the final paragraph.

   Fold a piece of notebook paper in half. On one side list your goals for the future. Opposite each one on the other side of the paper, indicate whether that goal is self-selected, parent-selected, or a combination of both. Compare your findings with those of others in your class.

3. This story is not a bitter tale told by an angry adult. On the contrary, the narrator looks back with humor and acceptance. Identify passages that make the story funny and friendly rather than bitter.

Ask at least five adults how they selected their careers. Did parents steer them in this direction, was their entrance into this occupation self-directed, or was it purely accidental? Were their parents a help or a hindrance in determining their future? Report your findings to the class.

4.  Tan's use of dialogue adds life to her characters. What does the conversation among the parents reveal about them?

Write a one-page dialogue between two people who disagree. Attempt to convey their personalities strictly from what they say to each other. Exchange papers with a partner and ask for his or her reaction to the personalities of your two characters. Did they come across the way you intended?

CONNECTING

1. In the excerpt from *The Joy Luck Club*, neither the child nor the mother tries to imagine how the other person feels. To resolve conflict, however, one must try to see with the other person's eyes. Write an informative speech about the treatment of conflict on your favorite television situation comedy. What kinds of conflicts occur? How are they settled? Do they correspond to real life? Base your speech on at least two different programs. **Workshop 19**

2. Often people are so impressed with the skills of others that they ignore or minimize their own. Today, however, it is necessary to know your strengths, especially if you are looking for a job. Some companies expect applicants to make a videotape in which they discuss their skills and goals. Working with others, prepare a sample videotape that illustrates how job hunters should present themselves to potential employers.

3. David Bohm, a renowned physicist, says that thought is able both to create and bridge chasms between human beings. Thought—ideas and the assumptions underlying them—may divide or unite people. A good example of how ideas create conflict is available in "Today's Debate," a regular feature in the newspaper *USA Today*. Working with several classmates, read "Today's Debate" or its equivalent in a local newspaper. Your goal is to try to solve the conflict between the two opponents. If solving it is impossible, be able to explain why.

To solve the conflict, first it is necessary to understand it. Read and discuss each side of the argument. Locate the assumptions, the basic propositions, held by each opponent. Once you understand the debators' fundamental convictions, then locate any common ground both may already share. Finally, discuss the shifts in thought each person must make if opponents are to reach agreement or compromise. With a group, compose and mail an article to *USA Today* or the appropriate local newspaper explaining how the two debators could reach agreement. **Workshop 5**

A LAST WORD

It is important for us to acknowledge the individuality of each of our friends, family members, and acquaintances. Why do you think it might be particularly difficult to see family members as individuals? How can parents and children avoid conflict that arises from having different goals and expectations?

Saying Thank You

- *Those Winter Sundays*
- *Thank You, M'am*

EXPLORING

• •

If someone tried to steal from you, how would you react? Are there any circumstances that might cause you to help the person who tried to rob you? Have you ever thought you had someone figured out, only to later change your mind? For instance, maybe you resented or disliked someone and then later discovered that the person had done something to benefit you.

THEME CONNECTION... GAINING EXPERIENCE

In "Those Winter Sundays," the experienced adult speaker acknowledges his failure as a young boy to appreciate his father's selfless help. In Langston Hughes' "Thank You, M'am," a boy experiences a stranger's kindness and learns new ways to behave. Both Hayden and Hughes contrast youth and experience to suggest that knowledge comes with experience.

TIME & PLACE

Robert Hayden, who probes into black history and records the evils of slavery, also speaks for modern blacks who have no voice of their own. "Those Winter Sundays" shows Hayden's interest in recording various scenes from daily life.

Langston Hughes portrays in his stories the daily struggles of ordinary black people. He depicts in "Thank You, M'am" the poverty, desperation, and resourcefulness of average people. Both of these twentieth century writers show people coping with hardship, deprivation, and loneliness.

THE WRITER'S CRAFT

CONVERSATIONAL TONE

Both Hayden and Hughes recreate the sounds of natural conversation. Hayden's everyday words, contractions, repetition, and simple sentences make his poem sound informal. Like Hayden, Hughes also relies on simple words and sentences to create the speech of ordinary people.

Those Winter Sundays

Robert Hayden

Sundays too my father got up early
and put his clothes on in the blueblack cold,
then with cracked hands that ached
from labor in the weekday weather made
banked fires blaze. No one ever thanked him.

I'd wake and hear the cold splintering, breaking.
When the rooms were warm, he'd call,
and slowly I would rise and dress,
fearing the chronic angers of that house,

Speaking indifferently to him,
who had driven out the cold
and polished my good shoes as well.
What did I know, what did I know
of love's austere and lonely **offices**? ❖

About the Author

Robert Hayden (1913–1980) was born in a Detroit slum known as Paradise Valley. With the help of a scholarship, Hayden attended college and graduate school, then taught English for more than two decades at Fisk University in Nashville and later at the University of Michigan. Hayden's poetry often uses simple, direct language to convey universal truths and questions. One critic described Hayden as having a "remarkable capacity for compassion."

offices—duties, jobs

Thank You, M'am

Langston Hughes

She was a large woman with a large purse that had everything in it but hammer and nails. It had a long strap and she carried it slung across her shoulder. It was about eleven o'clock at night, and she was walking alone, when a boy ran up behind her and tried to snatch her purse. The strap broke with the single tug the boy gave it from behind. But the boy's weight, and the weight of the purse combined caused him to lose his balance so, instead of taking off full blast as he had hoped, the boy fell on his back on the sidewalk, and his legs flew up. The large woman simply turned around and kicked him right square in his blue-jeaned sitter. Then she reached down, picked the boy up by his shirt front, and shook him until his teeth rattled.

After that the woman said, "Pick up my pocketbook boy, and give it here."

She still held him. But she bent down enough to permit him to stoop and pick up her purse. Then she said, "Now ain't you ashamed of yourself."

Firmly gripped by his shirt front, the boy said "Yes'm."

The woman said, "What did you want to do it for?"

The boy said, "I didn't aim to."

She said, "You a lie!"

By that time two or three people passed, stopped, turned to look, and some stood watching.

"If I turn you loose, will you run?" asked the woman.

"Yes'm," said the boy.

"Then I won't turn you loose," said the woman. She did not release him.

"I'm very sorry, lady, I'm sorry," whispered the boy.

"Um-hum! And your face is dirty. I got a great mind to wash your face for you. Ain't you got nobody home to tell you to wash your face?"

"No'm," said the boy.

"Then it will get washed this evening," said the large woman starting up the street, dragging the frightened boy behind her.

He looked as if he were fourteen or fifteen, frail and willow-wild, in tennis shoes and blue jeans.

The woman said, "You ought to be my son. I would teach you right from wrong. Least I can do right now is to wash your face. Are you hungry?"

"No'm," said the being-dragged boy. "I just want you to turn me loose."

"Was I bothering *you* when I turned that corner?" asked the woman.

"No'm."

"But you put yourself in contact with *me*," said the woman. "If you think that that contact is not going to last awhile, you got another thought coming. When I get through with you, sir, you are going to remember Mrs. Luella Bates Washington Jones."

Sweat popped out on the boy's face and he began to struggle. Mrs. Jones stopped, jerked him around in front of her, put a half nelson about his neck, and continued to drag him up the street. When she got to her door, she dragged the boy inside, down a hall, and into a large kitchenette-furnished room at the rear of the house. She switched on the light and left the door open. The boy could hear other roomers laughing and talking in the large house. Some of their doors were

About the Author

Throughout his life, Langston Hughes (1902–1967) traveled, working as a seaman on a cargo ship, a waiter in a Paris nightclub, and a busboy in Washington, D.C. He wrote poems on the side and published his first collection in 1926. Hughes finished college while contributing poems to several popular magazines. Though known primarily for his sensitive and rhythmic poetry, Hughes also wrote short stories, novels, plays, essays, articles, and an autobiography. Considered the cornerstone of African-American literature, he articulated the struggles and triumphs inherent in the black experience.

FOCUS ON...
PSYCHOLOGY

Though Roger has several chances to run away from Mrs. Jones, he chooses to remain. He also has a chance to steal her unattended purse, but he decides against this as well. Although Mrs. Jones gives him the freedom to act irresponsibly, Roger chooses to act honestly. He does not want Mrs. Jones to distrust him.

Think of a time in your life when you were given a choice like this. What were the choices available to you, and how did you decide to behave? Write about this incident in your journal.

◆ ◆

William H. Johnson, *Man in a Vest,* ca. 1939 (National Museum of American Art)

open, too, so he knew he and the woman were not alone. The woman still had him by the neck in the middle of her room.

She said, "What is your name?"

"Roger," answered the boy.

"Then, Roger, you go to that sink and wash your face," said the woman, where-upon she turned him loose—at last. Roger looked at the door—looked at the woman—looked at the door—*and went to the sink.*

"Let the water run until it gets warm," she said. "Here's a clean towel."

"You gonna take me to jail?" asked the boy, bending over the sink.

"Not with that face, I would not take you nowhere," said the woman. "Here I am trying to get home to cook me a bite to eat and you snatch my pocketbook! Maybe you ain't been to your supper either, late as it be. Have you?"

"There's nobody home at my house," said the boy.

"Then we'll eat," said the woman. "I believe you're hungry—or been hungry—to try to snatch my pocketbook."

"I wanted a pair of blue suede shoes," said the boy.

"Well, you didn't have to snatch *my* pocketbook to get some suede shoes," said Mrs. Luella Bates Washington Jones. "You could of asked me."

"M'am?"

The water dripping from his face, the boy looked at her. There was a long pause. A very long pause. After he had dried his face and not knowing what else to do dried it again, the boy turned around, wondering what next. The door was open. He could make a dash for it down the hall. He could run, run, run, run, *run!*

The woman was sitting on the day bed. After awhile she said, "I were young once and I wanted things I could not get."

There was another long pause. The boy's mouth opened. Then he frowned, but not knowing he frowned.

The woman said, "Um-hum! You thought I was going to say *but, didn't you? You thought I was going to say, but I didn't snatch people's pocketbooks.* Well, I wasn't going to say that." Pause. Silence. "I have done things, too, which I would not tell you, son—neither tell God, if He didn't already know. So you set down while I fix us something to eat. You might run that comb through your hair so you will look presentable."

In another corner of the room behind a screen was a gas plate and an icebox. Mrs. Jones got up and went behind the screen. The woman did not watch the boy to see if he was going to run now, nor did she watch her purse which she left behind her on the day bed. But the boy took care to sit on the far side of the room where he thought she could easily see him out of the corner of her eye, if she wanted to. He did not trust the woman not to trust him. And he did not want to be mistrusted now.

"Do you need somebody to go to the store," asked the boy. "Maybe to get some milk or something."

"Don't believe I do," said the woman, "unless you just want sweet milk yourself. I was going to make cocoa out of this canned milk I got here."

"That will be fine," said the boy.

She heated some lima beans and ham she had in the icebox, made the cocoa, and set the table. The woman did not ask the boy anything about where he lived, or his folks, or anything else that would embarrass him. Instead, as they ate, she told him about her job in a hotel beauty shop that stayed open late, what the work was like, and how all kinds of women came in and out, blondes, redheads, and brunettes. Then she cut him a half of her ten-cent cake.

"Eat some more, son," she said.

When they were finished eating she got up and said, "Now, here, take this ten dollars and buy yourself some blue suede shoes. And next time, do not make the mistake of latching onto *my* pocketbook *nor nobody else's*—because shoes come by devilish like that will burn your feet. I got to get my rest now. But I wish you would behave yourself, son, from here on in."

She led him down the hall to the front door and opened it. "Goodnight! Behave yourself, boy!" she said, looking out into the street.

The boy wanted to say something else other than, "Thank you, m'am," to Mrs. Luella Bates Washington Jones, but he couldn't do so as he turned at the barren stoop and looked back at the large woman in the door. He barely managed to say, "Thank you," before she shut the door. And he never saw her again. ❖

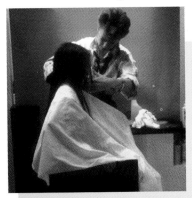

ACCENT ON...
CRIMINOLOGY

Roger not only received a face washing and a free meal, but he also received a lesson in life from Mrs. Jones. Not all would-be victims can help young teens in trouble. What kind of crime prevention program could you design to help kids on the street stay out of trouble? Consult local outreach or teen support programs to get ideas for your own proposal.

ON THE JOB

HAIRSTYLIST

To become a licensed hairstylist, a person must enroll in an accredited school. Most training programs can be completed in a year or less. Working in such a personal service industry requires knowledge and experience in issues of hygiene, current styles and trends, and changing technology. A background in chemistry and physiology is also helpful. Hairstylists should be patient, adept at working with a diverse clientele, and interested in pleasing the customer. Jobs in hairstyling establishments usually require long hours standing, though some jobs offer flexible hours.

UNDERSTANDING

1. We learn about people from noticing what they say and do, from observing their appearance, and from studying their surroundings and circumstances. Locate in "Those Winter Sundays" and in "Thank You, M'am" comments, actions, living conditions, and physical appearances that reveal the qualities of Hayden's father and of Luella Bates Washington Jones. In an essay, compare and contrast the two characters. *Workshop 9*

2. What is meant by the comment that Roger "did not trust the woman *not* to trust him. And he did not want to be mistrusted now"?

   Working with several classmates, consider the kinds of behavior that cause you to trust a supervisor at work, a parent, or someone else in a position of authority. Collaborate with others to design a strategy for building trust. Write a proposal that explains your strategy and proposes a test for it. *Workshop 10*

3. In the poem "Those Winter Sundays," several words have powerful connotations. They move the reader's emotions. List words in the poem that seem not only to have a dictionary definition (denotation), but which also have the power to touch the reader's feelings (connotation). Next to each word, list the feeling or feelings it arouses.

   Write a memo telling a colleague you are disappointed in his or her work, and ask the colleague to improve. In the memo, underline words that soften the message. Then write a paragraph that explains the emotional impact of the underlined words. *Workshop 13*

CONNECTING

1. If a young person in your community were wandering the streets late at night, had no parents, no money, and no place to go, what help could your community provide for the person? What would happen, for example, to the young person who stole a purse and got caught?

   Research your community's system for dealing with juveniles. Prepare a lecture or visual presentation in which you explain exactly what resources your community provides for troubled youths. *Workshop 19*

2. A mentor is an adult to whom a young person can turn to for good advice, trust, and genuine concern. Virtually every teenager would benefit from having a mentor. If there is a mentor program at your school, find out how it works, and analyze its strengths and weaknesses. Present your findings in a report. If a mentor program does not exist, work with your classmates to set up a program. *Workshop 5*

A LAST WORD

Everyone has heard of the generation gap. How can people bridge this gap and learn from one another? Consider particular communication skills that might help young people share ideas and feelings with older people.

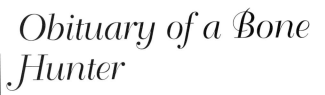

Obituary of a Bone Hunter

EXPLORING

What is courage? Is it the total absence of fear? Or can one simultaneously be afraid and brave? Perhaps a truly brave person is one who faces danger even while experiencing terrible fear. Think of situations in which you or a friend stood up to danger or pain even though you were frightened. Consider, too, occasions when you faced danger with absolute courage, feeling no fear. Do you think there are times when it might be wise to be ruled by fear and to back off from a conflict or dangerous situation?

THEME CONNECTION...
THE VOICE OF EXPERIENCE

In this selection, Eiseley looks back over his long career as an anthropologist to explain why he "didn't find the skull." Writing from the perspective of long experience, Eiseley identifies some of the hopes, fears, and values that interfered with his goals as an anthropologist. As a young, relatively inexperienced man, fear proved an obstacle. As an established professor, pride got in the way. And on one occasion reverence for life stopped his explorations.

TIME & PLACE

Loren Eiseley writes about searching for the fossil remains of the earliest prehistoric man and hoping by his discovering them to become famous. Eiseley continued his search for decades, starting in the southwestern part of the United States in the 1920s. Writing near the end of his career, he speculates about why he did not discover a "significant" fossil. Eiseley recalls three major chances to find that significant fossil. Each time, either through fear or a desire to have "done well by life" or through disbelief, he lets the chance go.

THE WRITER'S CRAFT
BUILDING SUSPENSE

Eiseley excels at creating suspense. In each part of his essay, the reader is kept in suspense, in a state of uncertainty. The reader must wait for additional information. Suspense is the element in fiction or nonfiction that keeps the reader turning pages to find out what will happen next. Clever writers offer clues to prepare readers for the outcome.

Obituary of a Bone Hunter

Loren Eiseley

I

The papers and the magazines reprint the stories endlessly these days—of Sybaris the sin city, or, even further back, that skull at Tepexpan. One's ears are filled with chatter about assorted magnetometers and how they are used to pick up the traces of buried objects and no one has to guess at all. They unearth the city, or find the buried skull and bring it home. Then everyone concerned is famous overnight.

I'm the man who didn't find the skull. I'm the man who'd just been looking twenty years for something like it. This isn't sour grapes. It's their skull and welcome to it. What made me sigh was the **geophysics** equipment. The greatest gambling game in the world—the greatest wit-sharpener—and now they do it with amplifiers and electronically mapped grids. An **effete** age, gentlemen, and the fun gone out of it.

There are really two kinds of bone hunters—the big bone hunters and the little bone hunters. The little bone hunters may hunt big bones, but they're little bone hunters just the same. They are the consistent losers in the most difficult game of chance that men can play: the search for human origins. Eugene Dubois, the discoverer of **Pithecanthropus**, hit the jackpot in a gamble with such stupendous odds that the most devoted numbers enthusiast would have had better sense than to stake his life on them.

I am a little bone hunter. I've played this game for a twenty-year losing streak. I used to think it all lay in the odds—that it was luck that made the difference between the big and little bone hunters. Now I'm not so sure any longer. Maybe it's something else.

Maybe sometimes an uncanny **clairvoyance** is involved, and if it comes you must act or the time goes by. Anyhow I've thought about it a lot in these later years. You think that way as you begin to get grayer and you see pretty plainly that the game is not going to end as you planned.

With me I think now that there were three chances: the cave of spiders, the matter of the owl's egg, and the old man out of the Golden Age. I muffed them all. And maybe the old man just came to show me I'd sat in the big game for the last time.

II

In that first incident of the spiders, I was playing a hunch, a long one, but a good one still. I wanted to find Neanderthal man, or any kind of ice-age man, in America. One or two important authorities were willing to admit he *might* have got in before the last ice sheet; that he *might* have crossed Bering Strait with the mammoth. He might have, they said, but it wasn't likely. And if he had, it would be like looking for humming birds in the Bronx to find him.

Well, the odds were only a hundred to one against me, so I figured I'd look. That was how I landed in the cave of spiders. It was somewhere west out of Carlsbad, New Mexico, in the Guadalupe country. Dry. With sunlight that would blister cactus. We were cavehunting with a dynamiter and a young Harvard assistant. The

About the Author

As a boy, Loren Eiseley (1907–1977) loved to collect natural artifacts and archaeological specimens in his native Nebraska. In college, he studied anthropology and English, working part-time as editor of the school literary magazine. He became a respected and honored professor of anthropology, but more than that, he was able to bring his love of science and nature alive through his writings. He wrote books as well as essays, articles, and poems that were included in both science journals and literary anthologies.

geophysics—the physics of the earth

effete—marked by weakness or decadence

Pithecanthropus—an ancient human

clairvoyance—ability to perceive matters beyond the range of ordinary perception

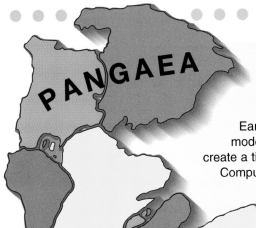

PANGAEA

dynamiter was to blow boulders away from fallen entrances so we could dig what lay underneath.

We found the cave up a side canyon, the entrance blocked with fallen boulders. Even to my youthful eyes it looked old, incredibly old. The waters and the frosts of centuries had eaten at the boulders and gnawed the cave roof. Down by the vanished stream bed a little gleam of worked flints caught our eye.

We stayed there for days, digging where we could and leaving the blasting till the last. We got the Basket Maker remains we had come to get—the earliest people that the scientists of that time would concede had lived in the Southwest. Was there anything more? We tamped a charge under one huge stone that blocked the wall of the cave and scrambled for the outside. A dull boom echoed down the canyon and the smoke and dust slowly blew away.

Inside the cave mouth the shattered boulder revealed a crack behind it. An opening that ran off beyond our spot lights. The hackles on my neck crawled. This might be the road to—something earlier? There was room for only one man to worm his way in. The dynamiter was busy with his tools. "It's probably nothing," I said to the assistant. "I'll just take a quick look."

As I crawled down that passage on my belly, I thought once or twice about rattlesnakes and what it might be like to meet one on its own level where it could look you in the eye. But after all I had met snakes before in this country, and besides I had the feeling that there was something worth getting to beyond.

I had it strong—too strong to turn back. I twisted on and suddenly dropped into a little chamber. My light shot across it. It was too low and close, and this was the end of the cave. But there was earth on the floor beneath me, the soft earth that must be dug, that might hold something more ancient than the cave entrance. I couldn't stand up; the roof was too low. I would have to dig on hands and knees. I set the light beside me and started to probe the floor with a trench shovel. It was just then that the fear got me.

The light lay beside me shining on the ceiling—a dull, velvety-looking ceiling, different from the stone around. I don't know when I first sensed that something was wrong, that the ceiling was moving, that waves were passing over it like the wind in a stand of wheat. But suddenly I

Pangaea (from Greek *pangaia*, or "all earth") is German meteorologist Alfred Wegener's hypothetical continent from which all continents formed.

primal—primitive, basic

fecund—fruitful, fertile

did; suddenly I dropped the shovel and thrust the light closer against the roof. Things began to detach themselves and drop wherever the light touched them. Things with legs. I could hear them plop on the soft earth around me.

I shut off the light. The plopping ceased. I sat on my knees in the darkness, listening. My mind was centered on just one thing—escape. I knew what that wavering velvet wall was. Millions upon millions of daddy-long-legs—packed in until they hung in layers. Daddy-long-legs, the most innocent and familiar of all the spider family. I wish I could say I had seen black widows there among them. It would help now, in telling this.

But I didn't. I didn't really see anything. If I turned on the light that hideous dropping and stirring would commence again. The light woke them. They disliked it.

If I could have stood up it would have been different. If they had not been overhead it would have been different. But they had me on my knees and they were above and all around. Millions upon millions. How they got there I don't know. All I know is that up out of the instinctive well of my being flowed some ancient, **primal** fear of the crawler, the walker by night. One clambered over my hand. And above they dangled, dangled. . . . What if they all began to drop at once?

I did not light the light. I had seen enough. I buttoned my jacket close, and my sleeves. I plunged blindly back up the passage down which I had wriggled and which, luckily, was free of them.

Outside the crew looked at me. I was sweating, and a little queer. "Close air," I gasped; "a small hole, nothing there."

We went away then in our trucks. I suppose in due time the dust settled, and the fox found his way in. Probably all that horrible **fecund** mass eventually crept, in its single individualities, back into the desert where it frightened no one. What it was doing there, what evil unknown to mankind it was plotting, I do not know to this day. The evil and the horror, I think now, welled out of my own mind, but somehow that multitude of ancient life in a little low dark chamber touched it off. It did not pass away until I could stand upright again. It was a fear out of the old, four-footed world that sleeps within us still.

Neanderthal man? He might have been there. But I was young and that was only a first chance gone. Yes, there were things I might have done, but I didn't do them. You don't tell your chief dynamiter that you ran from a daddy-long-legs. Not in that country. But do you see, it wasn't *one* daddy-long-legs. That's what I can't seem to make clear to anyone. It wasn't just one daddy-long-legs. It was millions of them. Enough to bury you. And have you ever thought of being buried under spiders? I thought not. You begin to get the idea?

III

I had a second chance and again it was in a cave I found. This time I was alone, tramping up a canyon watching for bones, and I just happened to glance upward in the one place where the cave could be seen. I studied it a long time—until I could feel the chill crawling down my back. This might be it; this might be the place. . . . This time I would know. This time there would be no spiders.

Through the glasses I could make out a fire blackened roof, a projecting ledge

> ● ● ● ● ● ● ●
> # What if they all began to drop at once?
> ● ● ● ● ● ● ●

above the cave mouth, and another one below. It was a small, strange hide-out, difficult to reach, but it commanded the valley on which the canyon opened. And there was the ancient soot-impregnated cave roof. Ancient man had been there.

I made that climb. Don't ask me how I did it. Probably there had been an easier route ages ago. But I came up a naked chimney of rock down which I lost my knapsack and finally the geologist's pick that had helped me hack out a foothold in the softening rock.

When I flung myself over the ledge where the cave mouth opened, I was shaking from the exhausting muscle tension and fear. No one, I was sure, had come that way for a thousand years, and no one after me would come again. I did not know how I would get down. It was enough momentarily to be safe. In front of me the cave mouth ran away darkly into the mountain.

I took the flashlight from my belt and loosened my sheath knife. I began to crawl downward and forward, wedging myself over sticks and fallen boulders. It was a clean cave and something was there, I was sure of it. Only, the walls were small and tight. . . .

They were tighter when the voice and the eyes came. I remember the eyes best. I caught them in my flashlight the same instant that I rammed my nose into the dirt and covered my head. They were big eyes and coming my way.

I never thought at all. I just lay there dazed while a great roaring **buffeting** thing beat its way out over my body and went away.

It went out into the silence beyond the cave mouth. A half minute afterward, I

peered through my fingers and rolled weakly over. Enough is enough. But this time I wasn't going back empty-handed. Not I. Not on account of a mere bird. Not if I *had* thought it was a mountain lion, which it could just as well have been. No owl was going to stop me, not even if it was the biggest owl in the Rocky Mountains.

I twitched my ripped shirt into my pants and crawled on. It wasn't much farther. Over the heap of debris down which the great owl had charged at me, I found the last low chamber, the place I was seeking. And there in a pile of sticks lay an egg, an impressive egg, glimmering palely in the cavernous gloom, full of potentialities, and **fraught**, if I may say so, with destiny.

I affected at first to ignore it. I was after the buried treasures that lay beneath its nest in the cave floor. The egg was simply going to have to look after itself. Its parent had gone, and in a pretty rude fashion, too. I was no vandal, but I was going to be firm. If an owl's egg stood in the path of science—But suddenly the

buffeting—driving, moving

fraught—full of

> No owl was going to stop me, not even if it was the biggest owl in the Rocky Mountains.

SPOTLIGHT ON...
PUBLIC SPEAKING

Though Eiseley's essay is presented in printed form, the famous naturalist and writer was an accomplished speaker. For years he lectured at universities all over the country. In your own work and endeavors, you may be called upon to speak in front of groups. Whether communicating on the job or before an audience, here are some pointers to keep in mind:

1. Keep your specific purpose for speaking in mind at all times.
2. Don't ramble or go off on a tangent. Stick to your main points or ideas.
3. Try to speak in a pleasant voice, not too softly and not too loudly. Enunciate clearly.
4. Avoid slang and informal language.
5. Speak with confidence and authority. Don't get emotional or out of control.

◆◆◆◆◆◆◆◆◆◆◆◆◆◆◆◆◆◆

primatologist—a scientist who studies primates

precipice—a steep or overhanging place

chasm—a deep cleft in the earth, gorge

egg seemed very helpless, very much alone. I probed in the earth around the nest. The nest got in the way. This was a time for decision.

I know a **primatologist** who will lift a rifle and shoot a baby monkey out of its mother's arms for the sake of science. He is a good man, too, and goes home nights to his wife. I tried to focus on this thought as I faced the egg.

I knew it was a rare egg. The race of its great and lonely mother was growing scant in these mountains and would soon be gone. Under it might lie a treasure that would make me famed in the capitals of science, but suppose there was nothing under the nest after all and I destroyed it? Suppose . . .

Here in this high, sterile silence with the wind crying over frightful **precipices**, myself and that egg were the only living things. That seemed to me to mean something.

At last and quietly I backed out of the cave and slipped down into the **chasm** out of which I had come. By luck I did not fall.

Sometimes in these later years I think perhaps the skull was there, the skull that could have made me famous. It is not so bad, however, when I think that the egg became an owl. I had charge of it in the universe's sight for a single hour, and I had done well by life.

It is not the loss of the skull that torments me sometimes on winter evenings. Suppose the big, unutterably frightened bird never came back to its egg? A feeling of vast loss and desolation sweeps over me then. I begin to perceive what it is to doubt.

IV

It was years later that I met the old man. He was waiting in my office when I came

in. It was obvious from the timid glances of my secretary that he had been passed from hand to hand and that he had outwitted everybody. Someone in the background made a twisting motion at his forehead.

The old man sat, a colossal ruin, in the reception chair. The squirrel-like twitterings of the office people did not disturb him.

As I came forward he fished in a ragged wallet and produced a clipping. "You made this speech?" he asked.

"Why, yes," I said.

"You said men came here late? A few thousand years ago?"

"Yes, you see—"

"Young man," he interrupted, "you are frightfully wrong."

I was aware that his eyes were contracted to pin points and seemed in some danger of protruding on stalks.

"You have ignored," he rumbled, "the matter of the **Miocene** period—the Golden Age. A great civilization existed then, far more splendid than this— degenerate time." He struck the floor fiercely with his cane.

"But," I protested, "that period is twenty million years ago. Man wasn't even in existence. Geology shows—"

"Nothing!" said the massive **relic**. "Geology has nothing to do with it. Sit down. I know all about the Golden Age. I will prove to you that you are wrong."

I collapsed doubtfully into a chair. He told me that he was from some little town in Missouri, but I never believed it for a moment. He smelled bad, and it was obvious that if he brought news of the Golden Age, as he claimed, he had come by devious and dreadful ways from that far era.

"I have here," he said, thrusting his head forward and breathing heavily into my face, "a human jaw. I will unwrap it a little and you can see. It is from a cave I found."

"It is embedded in **stalactite** drippings," I murmured, hypnotized against my will. "That might represent considerable age. Where did you find it?"

He raised a protesting hand. "Later, son, later. You admit then—?"

I strained forward. "Those teeth," I said, "they are large—they look primitive." The feeling I had had at the mouth of the owl's cave came to me again overpoweringly. "Let me see a little more of the jaw. If the mental **eminence** should be lacking, you may have something important. Just let me handle it a moment."

With the scuttling **alacrity** of a crab, the old man drew back and popped the papers over his find. "You admit, then, that it is important? That it proves the Golden Age was real?"

Baffled, I looked at him. He eyed me with an equal wariness.

"Where did you find it?" I asked. "In this light it seemed—it might be—a fossil man. We have been looking a long time. If you would only let me see—"

"I found it in a cave in Missouri," he droned in a rote fashion. "You can never find the cave alone. If you will make a statement to the papers that the Golden Age is true, I will go with you. You have seen the evidence."

Once more I started to protest. "But this has nothing to do with the Golden Age. You may have a rare human fossil there. You are denying science—"

"Science," said the old man with frightening dignity, "is illusion." He arose. "I will not come back. You must make a choice."

For one long moment we looked at each other across the fantastic barriers of our

• • • • • • •

"Science… is illusion."

• • • • • • •

individual minds. Then, on his heavy oakwood cane, he hobbled to the door and was gone. I watched through the window as he crossed the street in a patch of autumn sunlight as **phantasmal** and unreal as he. Leaves fell raggedly around him until, a tatter among tatters, he passed from sight.

I rubbed a hand over my eyes, and it seemed the secretary looked at me strangely. How was it that I had failed this time? By unbelief? But the man was mad. I could not possibly have made such a statement as he wanted.

Was it pride that cost me that strange jaw bone? Was it academic dignity? Should I have followed him? Found where he lived? Importuned his relatives? Stolen if necessary, that remarkable fragment?

Of course I should! I know that now. Of course I should.

Thirty years have passed since the old man came to see me. I have crawled in many caverns, stooped with infinite aching patience over the bones of many men. I have made no great discoveries.

I think now that in some strange way that old man out of the autumn leaf-fall was the last test of the **inscrutable** gods. There will be no further chances. The egg and the spiders and the madman—in them is the obituary of a life dedicated to the folly of doubt, the life of a small bone hunter. ❖

ON THE JOB
ARCHAEOLOGICAL EXCAVATOR

An archaeological excavator assists archaeologists and anthropologists in removing upper layers of earth and debris to unearth artifacts and other anthropological evidence. These excavators work closely with archaeologists to determine the method of excavation to be used. To do this kind of work, a person should have extensive experience with a variety of excavation equipment, such as tractors, bulldozers, and other heavy equipment. They must also understand small, precise tools like the magnetometer. Such work also requires the ability to use appropriate measuring instruments, to follow directions, to work alone or with different kinds of people, and to work for long periods of time without rewards or findings. Jobs in excavating for archaeologists may be found through the government.

ACCENT ON...
ARCHAEOLOGY

How do archaeologists know how old a bone is? What sorts of tests do archaeologists run to determine the age of bones or artifacts? They can date an object by using archaeometry. Research one method of archaeometry, and report your findings to the class. Include information on how computers can contribute to the process, as well as any visuals that may help clarify your presentation.

UNDERSTANDING

1. In Part I, Eiseley says he is a "little bone hunter." What does he mean? How does Eiseley want the reader to feel about his decision to run from the spiders in the chamber? Cite passages that support your interpretation.

   Work with several classmates to identify occasions when fear is acceptable and other occasions when it is not. Provide concrete examples to support your conclusions. Write a letter either to console someone who understandably gave in to fear, or to congratulate someone who acted courageously despite fear. *Workshop 11*

2. What details in Part III make it clear that climbing the chimney of rock was extremely difficult and required courage?

   President Franklin D. Roosevelt said in his First Inaugural Address in 1933: "Let me assert my firm belief that the only thing we have to fear is fear itself." In a persuasive speech, use concrete examples to explain why you agree or disagree with Roosevelt. *Workshops 10 and 19*

3. In Part IV, locate references to the old man that might cause Eiseley to think him strange and perhaps mad. In what ways did Eiseley fail in his encounter with the old man?

   Role play the encounter between Eiseley and the old man, either basing your script on Eiseley's account or making up your own ending to the encounter.

CONNECTING

1. Loren Eiseley is courteous when the old man visits him in his office. His conduct reminds us that at work and at school, people with all kinds of attitudes and qualities meet and need to work together.

   Gather information about the personal characteristics that people value in colleagues. Identify, too, the qualities that you and others admire in teammates and co-workers. Having gathered information about the qualities colleagues should possess, prepare a list of guidelines that describe characteristics that people should try to develop if they are to work well with others.

2. Just as Eiseley had experiences that others find interesting, you have had experiences that would make a good story. Write a story about one of your experiences. Collaborate with your classmates to produce a book. Design a book jacket complete with a blurb from a known authority, a graphic design, a synopsis of the contents, and a photograph of the authors. Prepare a poster to be displayed in the school library and in bookstores. *Workshop 20*

The Story of an Hour

EXPLORING

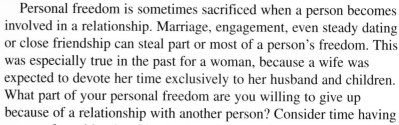

Personal freedom is sometimes sacrificed when a person becomes involved in a relationship. Marriage, engagement, even steady dating or close friendship can steal part or most of a person's freedom. This was especially true in the past for a woman, because a wife was expected to devote her time exclusively to her husband and children. What part of your personal freedom are you willing to give up because of a relationship with another person? Consider time having fun with other friends, time doing crafts and hobbies, or time just lying around reading or daydreaming. Can relationships exist in which neither party has to give up personal freedom? Or is that what a relationship is about?

THEME CONNECTION... WHEN INNOCENCE PASSES

Men and women enter marriage for the first time in a state of innocence; neither knows exactly how life will be forever after. Innocent expectations may be disappointed. When Kate Chopin wrote, couples could rarely give up when marriages went bad. Instead, they learned to adjust and compromise. Kate Chopin's story portrays a young woman's longing for independence because her marriage means loss of freedom.

TIME & PLACE

In September 1855, Kate Chopin's father was killed in a train accident when a bridge suddenly collapsed in St. Louis. This experience undoubtedly influenced Chopin's "The Story of an Hour." Chopin's tale offers social criticism. In the 1800s, women were little more than shadows of their husbands, and Kate Chopin was one of the first women to make the unfairness of this situation clear.

THE WRITER'S CRAFT
OMNISCIENT POINT OF VIEW

To decide on a story's point of view, figure out who is telling the story. How much does the storyteller, or narrator, know about the feelings and thoughts of characters? This story is told in the omniscient point of view. The omniscient, or "all knowing," author uses the third person and freely enters characters' minds. The author tells us how the main character, Louise, feels. The reader witnesses what no one else in the story knows—the ecstatic joy Louise feels on learning of her newly acquired freedom.

The Story of an Hour

Kate Chopin

nowing that Mrs. Mallard was afflicted with a heart trouble, great care was taken to break to her as gently as possible the news of her husband's death.

It was her sister Josephine who told her, in broken sentences; veiled hints that revealed in half concealing. Her husband's friend Richards was there, too, near her. It was he who had been in the newspaper office when intelligence of the railroad disaster was received, with Brently Mallard's name leading the list of "killed." He had only taken the time to assure himself of its truth by a second telegram, and had hastened to forestall any less careful, less tender friend in bearing the sad message.

She did not hear the story as many women have heard the same, with a paralyzed inability to accept its significance. She wept at once, with sudden, wild abandonment, in her sister's arms. When the storm of grief had spent itself she went away to her room alone. She would have no one follow her.

There stood, facing the open window, a comfortable, roomy armchair. Into this she sank, pressed down by a physical exhaustion that haunted her body and seemed to reach into her soul.

She could see in the open square before her house the tops of trees that were all aquiver with the new spring life. The delicious breath of rain was in the air. In the street below a peddler was crying his wares. The notes of a distant song which some one was singing reached her faintly, and countless sparrows were twittering in the eaves.

There were patches of blue sky showing here and there through the clouds that had met and piled one above the other in the west facing her window.

She sat with her head thrown back upon the cushion of the chair, quite motionless, except when a sob came up into her throat and shook her, as a child who has cried itself to sleep continues to sob in its dreams.

She was young, with a fair, calm face, whose lines bespoke repression and even a certain strength. But now there was a dull stare in her eyes, whose gaze was fixed away off yonder on one of those patches of blue sky. It was not a glance of reflection, but rather indicated a suspension of intelligent thought.

There was something coming to her and she was waiting for it, fearfully. What was it? She did not know; it was too subtle and elusive to name. But she felt it, creeping out of the sky, reaching toward her through the sounds, the scents, the color that filled the air.

Now her bosom rose and fell **tumultuously**. She was beginning to recognize this thing that was approaching to possess her, and she was striving to beat it back with her will—as powerless as her two white slender hands would have been.

When she abandoned herself a little whispered word escaped her slightly parted lips. She said it over and over under her breath: "free, free, free!" The vacant stare and the look of terror that had followed it went from her eyes. They stayed keen and bright. Her pulses beat fast, and the coursing blood warmed and relaxed every inch of her body.

About the Author

Kate Chopin (1851–1904) grew up in St. Louis, but at nineteen married and moved to New Orleans. Thirteen years later, she returned to her hometown as a widow with six children to support. She began writing and selling poems, stories, and sketches, drawing on her early days as a St. Louis debutante and on her life in Louisiana, which was full of mixed cultures, lifestyles, and dialects. Most of Chopin's works were quite popular and acclaimed by critics. The works that deal with women's and racial issues remain widely read and highly regarded.

tumultuously— violently

FOCUS ON... HEALTH

The doctors claimed that Mrs. Mallard died of heart disease, of "joy that kills." Find out more about heart disease and shocks to the cardiac system that can cause death. In particular, research statistics on the frequency and likelihood of such a manner of death. Write a summary of your findings to present to the class.

Childe Hassam,
The South Ledges,
Appledore 1913
(National Museum
of American Art)

elixir—potion that prolongs life

importunities—repeated urgent pleas or requests

She did not stop to ask if it were or were not a monstrous joy that held her. A clear and exalted perception enabled her to dismiss the suggestion as trivial.

She knew that she would weep again when she saw the kind, tender hands folded in death; the face that had never looked save with love upon her, fixed and gray and dead. But she saw beyond that bitter moment a long procession of years to come that would belong to her absolutely. And she opened and spread her arms out to them in welcome.

There would be no one to live for her during those coming years; she would live for herself. There would be no powerful will bending hers in that blind persistence with which men and women believe they have a right to impose a private will upon a fellow-creature. A kind intention or a cruel intention made the act seem no less a crime as she looked upon it in that brief moment of illumination.

And yet she had loved him—sometimes. Often she had not. What did it matter! What could love, the unsolved mystery, count for in face of this possession of self-assertion which she suddenly recognized as the strongest impulse of her being!

"Free! Body and soul free!" she kept whispering.

Josephine was kneeling before the closed door with her lips to the keyhole, imploring for admission. "Louise, open the door! I beg; open the door—you will make yourself ill. What are you doing, Louise? For heaven's sake open the door."

"Go away. I am not making myself ill." No; she was drinking in a very **elixir** of life through that open window.

Her fancy was running riot along those days ahead of her. Spring days, and summer days, and all sorts of days that would be her own. She breathed a quick prayer that life might be long. It was only yesterday she had thought with a shudder that life might be long.

She rose at length and opened the door to her sister's **importunities**. There was a feverish triumph in her eyes, and she carried herself unwittingly like a goddess of Victory. She clasped her sister's waist, and together they descended the stairs. Richards stood waiting for them at the bottom.

Some one was opening the front door with a latchkey. It was Brently Mallard who entered, a little travel-stained, composedly carrying his grip-sack and umbrella. He had been far from the scene of the accident, and did not even know there had been one. He stood amazed at Josephine's piercing cry; at Richards' quick motion to screen him from the view of his wife.

But Richards was too late.

When the doctors came they said she had died of heart disease—of joy that kills. ❖

UNDERSTANDING

1. What was Louise's immediate reaction to news of her husband's death? Does her behavior seem reasonable to you? How do you think most people respond to this kind of message? What thoughts did she have as she sat alone in her room?

   Assume that in addition to thinking, Louise was writing in a journal. Write the journal entry Louise might have written as she sat alone after taking in the news of her husband's death.

2. Explain the meaning of the passage: "There would be no powerful will bending hers in that blind persistence with which men and women believe they have a right to impose a private will upon a fellow-creature."

   Traditional wedding vows sometimes incorporate phrases such as "honor and obey." Many couples today write their own wedding vows and omit that phrase. Taking into consideration the rights of both husband and wife, write a new set of wedding vows. Try to define the freedoms and responsibilities of both marriage partners without using words that sound like legal jargon. ***Workshop 1***

3. Irony frequently occurs in "The Story of an Hour." Find examples of irony in the story. Remember, an ironic event or situation is one that turns out opposite from what might have been expected. Write a brief essay defining "irony" and desribe a time when verbal irony or irony of situation affected you. Offer a conclusion about how irony can make people feel. ***Workshop 12***

A LAST WORD

Does compromising with a friend or spouse have to mean losing your freedom? When should we be willing to compromise?

CONNECTING

1. Brently Mallard imposed his will on Louise, restricting her freedom to do as she wished. Attitudes and actions make any relationship strong. What attitudes and actions create mutual respect and strong bonds between two people? Work with several classmates to develop a list of five *attitudes* (ways of thinking) that help build positive feelings. Then develop a second list of five *actions* that help two people become and remain good friends.

   Use these lists as your basis for judging a popular television program that emphasizes friendships. Decide whether or not the show depicts friendship in a manner that corresponds with real life. Collaborate with group members to write a review of the television show for the school newspaper. Explain why the show is or is not an accurate, reliable presentation of friendship.

2. Doctors said Mrs. Louise Mallard died "of joy that kills." How is this ironic?

   Consult the newspaper to discover the format for obituaries. Write Louise Mallard's obituary as you think it would appear in your local newspaper. Some information missing in the story will have to be made up, as will a headline. ***Workshop 8***

Experiencing Nature

- *When I Heard the Learn'd Astronomer*
- *Twins*

EXPLORING

In a natural environment unaffected by cities and people, infinite varieties of creatures live out the patterns of their lives. Have you ever seen a bird building a nest, an egg hatching, the building of a beehive, or a bear capturing dinner? Describe how you felt as you observed a creature living naturally in its own environment. It has been said that cities deprive nature's creatures of places to live and also cut people off from nature's lessons and benefits. What do you think?

THEME CONNECTION...
EXPERIENCE AND NATURE

Human beings know how to build telescopes, travel in space, and create complex cities. Their experience and skill, however, may deprive humans of contact with nature. Whitman's astronomer does not succeed with his charts in showing the student the stars. Instead, his charts drive the student away. Similarly in White's essay, the zoo does not awaken most visitors to appreciate what they see.

TIME & PLACE

In 1948, while visiting the Bronx Zoo in New York City, E. B. White and his wife saw a doe that had just finished giving birth to twins. White notes that no other sightseers in the zoo who saw the doe and her fawns realized that something extraordinary had happened. Their failure to grasp the significance of the incident reveals the increasing separation of modern city dwellers from nature.

Writing approximately one hundred years before White, the poet Walt Whitman also indicates that a gulf sometimes separates human beings from nature. The learned astronomer lecturing in a hall misses the experience of seeing the stars brilliant in the "moist night air."

THE WRITER'S CRAFT

WORD CHOICE

E. B. White was an essayist and editorial writer for *The New Yorker* magazine for more than thirty years. As a major writer for a popular magazine, White had to be not only clever and interesting, but also clear. To achieve clarity, he put simple, plain words into sentences that are easy to follow. White, like Whitman, valued the language of ordinary people. In his poetry, Whitman used words from everyday life. He ordered these words into phrases and sentences that obey familiar grammatical rules.

When I Heard the Learn'd Astronomer

Walt Whitman

When I heard the learn'd astronomer,
When the proofs, the figures, were ranged in columns before me,
When I was shown the charts and diagrams, to add, divide, and
  measure them,
When I sitting heard the astronomer where he lectured with much
  applause in the lecture room,
How soon unaccountable I became tired and sick,
Till rising and gliding out I wandered off by myself,
In the mystical moist night air, and from time to time,
Looked up in perfect silence at the stars. ❖

FOCUS ON... ENVIRONMENTAL SCIENCE

Both Whitman and White appreciated the beauty of the world around them. The field of environmental science seeks to preserve this natural environment. Working with environmental science or biology students, study the area immediately adjacent to your school building. Think of ways in which your school could preserve or protect any natural areas around it. If your school is surrounded by other buildings, come up with ways that your school could provide a small section of natural habitat. Write your findings in a one- to two-page report.

◆ ◆ ◆ ◆ ◆ ◆ ◆ ◆ ◆ ◆ ◆ ◆ ◆ ◆ ◆

Twins

E. B. White

On a warm, miserable morning last week we went up to the Bronx Zoo to see the moose calf and to break in a new pair of black shoes. We encountered better luck than we had bargained for. The cow moose and her young one were standing near the wall of the deer park below the monkey house, and in order to get a better view we strolled down to the lower end of the park, by the brook. The path there is not much travelled. As we approached the corner where the brook trickles under the wire fence, we noticed a red deer getting to her feet. Beside her, on legs that were just learning their business, was a spotted fawn, as small and perfect as a trinket seen through a reducing glass. They stood there, mother and child, under a gray beech whose trunk was engraved with dozens of hearts and initials. Stretched on the ground was another fawn, and we realized that the doe had just finished twinning. The second fawn was still wet, still unrisen. Here was a scene of rare **sylvan** splendor, in one of our five favorite **boroughs**, and we couldn't have asked for more. Even our new shoes seemed to be working out all right and weren't hurting much.

The doe was only a couple of feet from the wire, and we sat down on a rock at the edge of the footpath to see what sort of start young fawns get in the deep fastnesses of Mittel Bronx. The mother, mildly resentful of our presence and dazed from her labor, raised one forefoot and stamped primly. Then she lowered her head, picked up the **afterbirth**, and began dutifully to eat it, allowing it to swing crazily from her mouth, as though it were a bunch of withered beet greens. From the monkey house came the loud, insane hooting of some **captious** primate, filling the whole woodland with a wild hooroar. As we watched, the sun broke weakly through, brightened the rich red of the fawns, and kindled their white spots. Occasionally a sightseer would appear and wander aimlessly by, but of all who passed none was aware that anything extraordinary had occurred. "Looka the kangaroos!" a child cried. And he and his mother stared sullenly at the deer and then walked on.

In a few moments the second twin gathered all his legs and all his ingenuity and arose, to stand for the first time sniffing the mysteries of a park for captive deer. The doe, in recognition of his achievement, quit her other work and began to dry him, running her tongue against the grain and paying particular attention to the key points.

About the Author

Elwyn Brooks White (1899-1985) is considered one of the finest essayists in American literature. He was born in New York, served in the army, went to college, then headed west to work on a newspaper. White returned to the East Coast to work on the new magazine, *The New Yorker*. In addition to his essays, magazine articles, and newspaper columns, E.B. White is beloved for his contribution to children's literature as the author of *Stuart Little*, *Charlotte's Web*, and *The Trumpet of the Swan*.

sylvan—characteristic of the woods or forest

borough—one of the five administrative divisions of New York City

afterbirth—the placenta and fetal membranes that are expelled after delivery

captious—ill-natured

Unit 4: Innocence and Experience

Meanwhile the first fawn tiptoed toward the shallow brook, in little stops and goes, and started across. He paused midstream to make a slight contribution, as a child does in bathing. Then, while his mother watched, he continued across, gained the other side, selected a hiding place, and lay down under a skunk-cabbage leaf next to the fence, in perfect concealment, his legs folded neatly under him. Without actually going out of sight, he had

● ● ● ● ● ● ●

…none was aware anything extraordinary had occurred.

● ● ● ● ● ● ●

managed to disappear completely in the shifting light and shade. From somewhere a long way off a twelve-o'clock whistle sounded. We hung around awhile, but he never budged. Before we left, we crossed the brook ourself, just outside the fence, knelt, reached through the wire, and tested the truth of what we had once heard: that you can scratch a new fawn between the ears without starting him. You can indeed. ❖

UNDERSTANDING

● ●

1. Neither White nor Whitman bluntly declares that people should appreciate and experience nature. Instead they make this point indirectly by giving the reader certain details. What observations do Whitman and White make that cause the reader to conclude that human beings are sometimes unaware of nature?

   Sometimes it is useful to present details and then let the reader draw conclusions. The following exercise offers a chance to practice letting well-chosen details influence the reader's ideas. Choose a busy place such as a gym, restaurant, subway, or shopping mall. Observe and take notes on people's behavior. What do they do and say? What do they wear? How do they move? Draw conclusions about the people you watch.

   In a brief essay, report the details you have witnessed. Present these details in such a way that by themselves they convey a message to the reader. Your goal is to influence the reader's thinking by means of your use of details. ***Workshops 2 and 10***

2. Using passages in the text as evidence, carefully explain how a mother deer who has just given birth behaves, especially toward her offspring.

   When White describes the mother deer's behavior, he is telling the reader how something is done. He explains a process. Like White, you know how many things are done, and like White, you are able to explain the process. Tell a partner how to do something that could be attempted at school, such as using a particular computer program, changing a bicycle tire, or juggling. Ask the partner to perform the process you describe. ***Workshop 4***

3. Walt Whitman's poem presents two ways to respond to a lecture on astronomy. With your group, identify these two ways and discuss the strengths and weaknesses of each. Write a brief essay explaining which response to the lecture you favor and why, or pointing out why neither response is satisfactory and offering a third possibility. ***Workshop 5***

CONNECTING

● ●

1. Reading about astronomers and zoos raises the question: What exactly is the work done by astronomers or the work done at zoos? Perhaps you would like to know more about other occupations. Begin by writing a letter to a person in a position of responsibility in the occupation of your choosing. For example, you might write to the head of the astronomy department at a university and ask for information about that field and an opportunity to meet and spend time with an expert in the field. ***Workshop 11***

2. ![icon] Walt Whitman's poem and E.B. White's essay both pose debatable questions. "I Heard the Learn'd Astronomer" causes us to wonder when experience in a field should replace learning fundamental principles in that subject area. "Twins" raises the issue of whether or not modern man is becoming insensitive to nature.

Most questions have two sides, and both sides usually have at least some merit. With a partner, identify an interesting controversial question—some local or national issue, for example, that is being reported in the media. Impartially gather information to support both sides of the issue. Assess the evidence your research uncovers. On the basis of this evidence, arrive at your own position on the question. With your partner, make a presentation explaining the issue, the merits of both sides, and the reasons for choosing one side over the other.

Workshops 10, 18, and 19

UNIT 4

WRAP IT UP

1. The narrators of "I Find Fool Gold" and "Obituary of a Bone Hunter" describe failed quests to find something in nature. In both cases, the hunters failed because they were distracted by other things. How did their innocence make them unprepared for their quests? What knowledge could have helped each of them? Use details from the selections to support your opinions.

2. In "Two Kinds" and "The Story of an Hour," a character who believes he or she has more experience—and therefore better judgment—dominates a less experienced character. Compare and contrast the situations of Jing-mei and Louise Mallard. In what ways are they innocent? Why do Jing-mei's mother

and Louise's husband exert such a strong influence over them? How does experience change the two "innocents"? Use details from the selections to support your conclusions.

Growing up is a continual process of gaining life experience and learning to make important decisions. Make a list of decisions you are now responsible for that used to be made by someone else. Looking back on the time when other people made these decisions for you, do you think you benefited from their experience? Does the guidance they once provided continue to influence you today?

UNIT

⑤

CHOICES AND POSSIBILITIES

Life is full of possibilities—places to live, people to know, careers to pursue. These abundant possibilities mean that we often must make difficult choices. Making a choice can be challenging, especially if the decision will have far-reaching consequences. Information and emotions limit the acceptable possibilities. Regardless of these limits, the choices we make have a great impact on the quality of our lives.

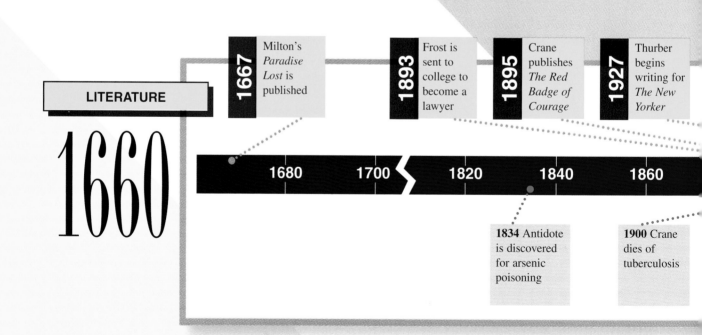

LITERATURE

1660

1667 Milton's *Paradise Lost* is published

1893 Frost is sent to college to become a lawyer

1895 Crane publishes *The Red Badge of Courage*

1927 Thurber begins writing for *The New Yorker*

1680　　1700　　1820　　1840　　1860

1834 Antidote is discovered for arsenic poisoning

1900 Crane dies of tuberculosis

A Rose for Emily
—William Faulkner

miss rosie
—Lucille Clifton

A Paradise Lost
—Roussel Sargent

The Scotty Who Knew Too Much
—James Thurber

The Wife's Story
—Ursula K. Le Guin

Trifles
—Susan Glaspell

The Road Not Taken
—Robert Frost

The Wayfarer
—Stephen Crane

from *I Can't Accept Not Trying*
—Michael Jordan

1931 Glaspell receives Pulitzer Prize for *Alison's House*

1940 Thurber's *Fables for Our Time* is published

1949 Faulkner wins Nobel Prize for Literature

1951 Le Guin is told to develop a money-making skill

1900   1920   1940   1960   1980

2000

1917 Four women are imprisoned for picketing for right to vote

1925 Sherwood Anderson encourages Faulkner to publish *Soldier's Pay*

1944 Cure for tuberculosis is discovered

1964 California's population tops the nation

1995 Jordan returns to professional basketball

LIFE and WORK

Life's Choices and Limits

- *A Rose for Emily*
- *miss rosie*

EXPLORING

You make choices all day long, but why do you choose the way you do? Do you think necessity—that is, external forces beyond your control such as environment and heredity—shape your decisions? Or do you think you are free to make your own choices? Sometimes choices are free, but not always. Consider your own decisions. Which ones seem free? Which ones do not?

THEME CONNECTION...
CHOICES AND CONSEQUENCES

In Faulkner's "A Rose for Emily" and Clifton's "miss rosie," the central characters fail to enjoy in old age the companionship, security, and success that most human beings seek. Instead, Emily Grierson changes from an attractive young woman into a hideous recluse because her father limits her choices, she herself makes bad choices, and circumstances beyond her control influence her.

Unlike Faulkner, who explores how choices impede an individual's possibilities, Clifton looks only at the consequences of lost possibilities.

TIME & PLACE

"A Rose for Emily" takes place in Jefferson, Mississippi, the fictional name Faulkner gave to Oxford, Mississippi, his home. The story, set in the late 1920s, is narrated by a citizen of Jefferson who interprets the views of the townspeople. This narrator describes episodes in Emily's life dating mainly from 1894, the year her father died, until her own death at age 74.

Emily's life unfolds at a time when the influence of old families, traditions, and economic enterprises is fading away. Miss rosie, however, is not presented in a historical context. She is a familiar part of today's landscape—the homeless elderly "bag lady" with no place to go.

THE WRITER'S CRAFT

JUMBLED TIME

In "A Rose for Emily," as in many of his novels, Faulkner jumbles the time sequence. Instead of beginning with the earliest event and proceeding in chronological order, the narrator weaves back and forth in time, leaping from the present to events ten and thirty years in the past and then to the present again. Faulkner jumbles time to involve the reader; the reader must pay close attention to what happens. Just as Faulkner uses a narrator, so in "miss rosie" Lucille Clifton presents things through a narrator's eyes and, in so doing, touches both past and present.

A Rose for Emily

William Faulkner

1

hen Miss Emily Grierson died, our whole town went to her funeral: the men through a sort of respectful affection for a fallen monument, the women mostly out of curiosity to see the inside of her house, which no one save an old manservant—a combined gardener and cook—had seen in at least ten years.

It was a big, squarish frame house that had once been white, decorated with **cupolas** and spires and scrolled balconies in the heavily lightsome style of the seventies, set on what had once been our most select street. But garages and cotton gins had encroached and **obliterated** even the **august** names of that neighborhood; only Miss Emily's house was left, lifting its stubborn and **coquettish** decay above the cotton wagons and the gasoline pumps—an eyesore among eyesores. And now Miss Emily had gone to join the representatives of those august names where they lay in the cedar-bemused cemetery among the ranked and anonymous graves of Union and Confederate soldiers who fell at the battle of Jefferson.

Alive, Miss Emily had been a tradition, a duty, and a care; a sort of hereditary obligation upon the town, dating from that day in 1894 when Colonel Sartoris, the mayor—he who fathered the edict that no Negro woman should appear on the streets without an apron—remitted her taxes, the dispensation dating from the death of her father on into **perpetuity**. Not that Miss Emily would have accepted charity. Colonel Sartoris invented an involved tale to the effect that Miss Emily's father had loaned money to the town, which the town, as a matter of business, preferred this way of repaying. Only a man of Colonel Sartoris' generation and thought could have invented it, and only a woman could have believed it.

When the next generation, with its more modern ideas, became mayors and aldermen, this arrangement created some little dissatisfaction. On the first of the year they mailed her a tax notice. February came, and there was no reply. They wrote her a formal letter, asking her to call at the sheriff's office at her convenience. A week later the mayor wrote her himself, offering to call or to send his car for her, and received in reply a note on paper of an **archaic** shape, in a thin, flowing calligraphy in faded ink, to the effect that she no longer went out at all. The tax notice was also enclosed, without comment.

They called a special meeting of the Board of Aldermen. A **deputation** waited upon her, knocked at the door through which no visitor had passed since she ceased giving china-painting lessons eight or ten years earlier. They were admitted by the old Negro into a dim hall from which a stairway mounted into still more shadow. It smelled of dust and disuse—a close, dank smell. The Negro led them into the parlor. It was furnished in heavy, leather-covered furniture. When the Negro opened the blinds of one window, they could see that the leather was cracked; and when they sat down, a faint dust rose sluggishly about their thighs, spinning with slow motions in the single sunray. On a tarnished gilt easel before the fireplace stood a crayon portrait of Miss Emily's father.

cupola—a small structure built on top of a roof

obliterated—removed from existence

august—marked by majestic dignity

coquettish—seeking attention

perpetuity—eternity

archaic—surviving from an earlier period

deputation—a group of people appointed to represent others

FOCUS ON...
LAW

Miss Emily was granted an exemption from paying her taxes from the date of her father's death on into perpetuity. Property taxes are collected in most areas of the United States. Find out how property taxes are computed, collected, and used in your region. Create a pie chart to show how the funds are used and present your findings orally to the class.

◆◆◆◆◆◆◆◆◆◆◆◆◆◆◆◆◆◆

pallid—lacking color

temerity—boldness, rashness

They rose when she entered—a small, fat woman in black, with a thin gold chain descending to her waist and vanishing into her belt, leaning on an ebony cane with a tarnished gold head. Her skeleton was small and spare; perhaps that was why what would have been merely plumpness in another was obesity in her. She looked bloated, like a body long submerged in motionless water, and of that **pallid** hue. Her eyes, lost in the fatty ridges of her face, looked like two small pieces of coal pressed into a lump of dough as they moved from one face to another while the visitors stated their errand.

She did not ask them to sit. She just stood in the door and listened quietly until the spokesman came to a stumbling halt. Then they could hear the invisible watch ticking at the end of the gold chain.

Her voice was dry and cold. "I have no taxes in Jefferson. Colonel Sartoris explained it to me. Perhaps one of you can gain access to the city records and satisfy yourselves."

"But we have. We are the city authorities, Miss Emily. Didn't you get a notice from the sheriff, signed by him?"

"I received a paper, yes," Miss Emily said. "Perhaps he considers himself the sheriff . . . I have no taxes in Jefferson."

"But there is nothing on the books to show that, you see. We must go by the—"

"See Colonel Sartoris." (Colonel Sartoris had been dead almost ten years.) "I have no taxes in Jefferson. Tobe!" The Negro appeared. "Show these gentlemen out."

2

So she vanquished them, horse and foot, just as she had vanquished their fathers thirty years before about the smell. That was two years after her father's death and a short time after her sweetheart—the one we believed would marry her—had deserted her. After her father's death she went out very little; after her sweetheart went away, people hardly saw her at all. A few of the ladies had the **temerity** to call, but were not received, and the only sign of life about the place was the Negro man—a young man then—going in and out with a market basket.

"Just as if a man—any man—could keep a kitchen properly," the ladies said; so they were not surprised when the smell developed. It was another link between the gross, teeming world and the high and mighty Griersons.

A neighbor, a woman, complained to the mayor, Judge Stevens, eighty years old.

"But what will you have me do about it, madam?" he said.

"Why, send her word to stop it," the woman said. "Isn't there a law?"

"I'm sure that won't be necessary," Judge Stevens said. "It's probably just a snake or a rat that nigger of hers killed in the yard. I'll speak to him about it."

The next day he received two more complaints, one from a man who came in diffident **deprecation**. "We really must do something about it, Judge. I'd be the last one in the world to bother Miss Emily, but we've got to do something." That night the Board of Aldermen met— three graybeards and one younger man, a member of the rising generation.

"It's simple enough," he said. "Send her word to have her place cleaned up. Give her a certain time to do it in, and if she don't . . ."

"Dammit, sir," Judge Stevens said, "will you accuse a lady to her face of smelling bad?"

So the next night, after midnight, four men crossed Miss Emily's lawn and slunk about the house like burglars, sniffing along the base of the brickwork and at the cellar openings while one of them performed a regular sowing motion with his hand out of a sack slung from his shoulder. They broke open the cellar door and sprinkled lime there, and in all the outbuildings. As they recrossed the lawn, a window that had been dark was lighted and Miss Emily sat in it, the light behind her, and her upright torso motionless as that of an idol. They crept quietly across the lawn and into the shadow of the locusts that lined the street. After a week or two the smell went away.

That was when people had begun to feel really sorry for her. People in our town, remembering how old lady Wyatt, her great-aunt, had gone completely crazy at last, believed that the Griersons held themselves a little too high for what they really were. None of the young men were quite good enough for Miss Emily and such. We had long thought of them as a **tableau**, Miss Emily a slender figure in white in the background, her father a spraddled silhouette in the foreground, his back to her and clutching a horsewhip, the two of them framed by the back-flung front door. So when she got to be thirty and was still single, we were not pleased exactly, but **vindicated**; even with insanity in the family she wouldn't have turned down all of her chances if they had really materialized.

deprecation— disapproval

tableau—picture

vindicated—justified, proven correct

> ● ● ● ● ● ● ●
> **Being left alone, and a pauper, she had become humanized.**
> ● ● ● ● ● ● ●

When her father died, it got about that the house was all that was left to her; and in a way, people were glad. At last they could pity Miss Emily. Being left alone, and a pauper, she had become humanized. Now she too would know the old thrill and the old despair of a penny more or less.

The day after his death all the ladies prepared to call at the house and offer condolence and aid, as is our custom. Miss Emily met them at the door, dressed as usual and with no trace of grief on her face. She told them that her father was not dead. She did that for three days, with the ministers calling on her, and the doctors, trying to persuade her to let them dispose of the body. Just as they were about to resort to law and force, she broke down, and they buried her father quickly.

We did not say she was crazy then. We believed she had to do that. We remembered all the young men her father had driven away, and we knew that with nothing left, she would have to cling to that which had robbed her, as people will.

3

She was sick for a long time. When we saw her again, her hair was cut short, making her look like a girl, with a vague resemblance to those angels in colored church windows—sort of tragic and serene.

The town had just let the contracts for paving the sidewalks, and in the summer after her father's death they began the work. The construction company came with niggers and mules and machinery, and a foreman named Homer Barron, a Yankee—a big, dark, ready man, with a big voice and eyes lighter than his face. The little boys would follow in groups to hear him cuss the niggers, and the niggers singing in time to the rise and fall of picks. Pretty soon he knew everybody in town. Whenever you heard a lot of laughing anywhere about the square, Homer Barron would be in the center of the group. Presently we began to see him and Miss Emily on Sunday afternoons driving in the yellow-wheeled buggy and the matched team of bays from the livery stable.

At first we were glad that Miss Emily would have an interest, because the ladies all said, "Of course a Grierson would not think seriously of a Northerner, a day laborer." But there were still others, older people, who said that even grief could not cause a real lady to forget *noblesse oblige*—without calling it noblesse oblige. They just said, "Poor Emily. Her kinsfolk should come to her." She had some kin in Alabama; but years ago her father had fallen out with them over the estate of old lady Wyatt, the crazy woman, and there was no communication between the two families. They had not even been represented at the funeral.

And as soon as the old people said, "Poor Emily," the whispering began.

● ● ● ● ● ● ●
"I want some poison," she said to the druggist.
● ● ● ● ● ● ●

"Do you suppose it's really so?" they said to one another. "Of course it is. What else could . . ." This behind their hands; rustling of craned silk and satin behind **jalousies** closed upon the sun of Sunday afternoon as the thin, swift clop-clop-clop of the matched team passed: "Poor Emily."

She carried her head high enough—even when we believed that she was fallen. It was as if she demanded more than ever the recognition of her dignity as the last Grierson; as if it had wanted that touch of earthiness to reaffirm her **imperviousness**. Like when she bought the rat poison, the arsenic. That was over a year after they had begun to say "Poor Emily," and while the two female cousins were visiting her.

"I want some poison," she said to the druggist. She was over thirty then, still a slight woman, though thinner than usual, with cold, haughty black eyes in a face the flesh of which was strained across the temples and about the eye-sockets as you imagine a lighthouse-keeper's face ought to look. "I want some poison," she said.

"Yes, Miss Emily. What kind? For rats and such? I'd recom—"

"I want the best you have. I don't care what kind."

The druggist named several. "They'll kill anything up to an elephant. But what you want is—"

"Arsenic," Miss Emily said. "Is that a good one?"

"Is . . . arsenic? Yes, ma'am. But what you want—"

"I want arsenic."

The druggist looked down at her. She looked back at him, erect, her face like a strained flag. "Why, of course," the druggist said. "If that's what you want. But the

Faulkner's story does not follow a clear, orderly time sequence, but rather switches back and forth between various times in the present and the past. Such a rich, sometimes complex writing style often requires careful, in-depth reading, or the reader may become confused or lost. To read more complex materials, follow these guidelines:

1. Before you read, scan the story or article to see how and whether the piece is divided or organized.
2. Read each section slowly and carefully.
3. As you read, make notes, an outline, or a time line to help you understand the story's time frame.
4. Reread any sections you did not thoroughly understand and note confusing passages.

law requires you to tell what you are going to use it for."

Miss Emily just stared at him, her head tilted back in order to look him eye for eye, until he looked away and went and got the arsenic and wrapped it up. The Negro delivery boy brought her the package; the druggist didn't come back. When she opened the package at home there was written on the box, under the skull and bones: "For rats."

4

So the next day we all said, "She will kill herself"; and we said it would be the best thing. When she had first begun to be seen with Homer Barron, we had said "She will marry him." Then we said, "She will persuade him yet," because Homer himself had remarked—he liked men, and it was known that he drank with the younger men in the Elks' Club—that he was not a marrying man. Later we said, "Poor Emily" behind the jalousies as they passed on Sunday afternoon in the glittering buggy, Miss Emily with her head high and Homer Barron with his hat cocked and a cigar in his teeth, reins and whip in a yellow glove.

Then some of the ladies began to say that it was a disgrace to the town and a bad example to the young people. The men did not want to interfere, but at last the ladies forced the Baptist minister—Miss Emily's people were Episcopal—to call upon her. He would never divulge what happened during that interview, but he refused to go back again. The next Sunday they again drove about the streets, and the following day the minister's wife wrote to Miss Emily's relations in Alabama.

So she had blood-kin under her roof again and we sat back to watch developments. At first nothing happened. Then we were sure that they were to be married. We learned that Miss Emily had been to the jeweler's and ordered a man's toilet set in silver, with the letters H. B. on each piece. Two days later we learned that she had bought a complete outfit of men's clothing, including a nightshirt, and we said, "They are married." We were really glad. We were glad because the two female cousins were even more Grierson than Miss Emily had ever been.

So we were not surprised when Homer Barron—the streets had been finished some time since—was gone. We were a little disappointed that there was not a public blowing-off, but we believed that he had gone on to prepare for Miss Emily's coming, or to give her a chance to get rid of the cousins. (By that time it was a **cabal**, and we were all Miss Emily's allies to help circumvent the cousins.) Sure enough, after another week they departed. And, as we had expected all along, within three days Homer Barron was back in town. A neighbor saw the Negro man admit him at the kitchen door at dusk one evening.

And that was the last we saw of Homer Barron. And of Miss Emily for some time. The Negro man went in and out with the market basket, but the front door remained closed. Now and then we would see her at a window for a moment, as the men did that night when they sprinkled the lime, but for almost six months she did not appear on the streets. Then we knew that this was to be expected too; as if that quality of her father which had thwarted her woman's life so many times had been too **virulent** and too furious to die.

When we next saw Miss Emily, she had grown fat and her hair was turning gray. During the next few years it grew grayer and grayer until it attained an even pepper-and-salt iron-gray, when it ceased turning. Up to the day of her death at seventy-four it was still that vigorous iron-gray, like the hair of an active man.

From that time on her front door remained closed, save for a period of six or seven years, when she was about forty, during which she gave lessons in china-painting. She fitted up a studio in one of the downstairs rooms, where the daughters and granddaughters of Colonel Sartoris' contemporaries were sent to her with the same regularity and in the same spirit that they were sent to church on Sundays with a twenty-five-cent piece for the collection plate. Meanwhile her taxes had been remitted.

Then the newer generation became the backbone and the spirit of the town, and the painting pupils grew up and fell away and did not send their children to her with boxes of color and tedious brushes and pictures cut from the ladies' magazines. The front door closed upon the last one and remained closed for good. When the town got free postal delivery, Miss Emily alone refused to let them fasten the metal numbers above her door and attach a mailbox to it. She would not listen to them.

Daily, monthly, yearly we watched the Negro grow grayer and more stooped, going in and out with the market basket.

Each December we sent her a tax notice, which would be returned by the post office a week later, unclaimed. Now and then we would see her in one of the downstairs windows—she had evidently shut up the top floor of the house—like the carven torso of an idol in a niche, looking or not looking at us, we could never tell which. Thus she passed from generation to generation—dear, inescapable, impervious, tranquil, and **perverse**.

And so she died. Fell ill in the house filled with dust and shadows, with only a doddering Negro man to wait on her. We did not even know she was sick; we had long since given up trying to get any information from the Negro. He talked to no one, probably not even to her, for his voice had grown harsh and rusty, as if from disuse.

She died in one of the downstairs rooms, in a heavy walnut bed with a curtain, her gray head propped on a pillow yellow and moldy with age and lack of sunlight.

5

The Negro met the first of the ladies at the front door and let them in, with their hushed, **sibilant** voices and their quick, curious glances, and then he disappeared. He walked right through the house and out the back and was not seen again.

The two female cousins came at once. They held the funeral on the second day, with the town coming to look at Miss Emily beneath a mass of bought flowers, with the crayon face of her father musing profoundly above the **bier** and the ladies sibilant and **macabre**; and the very old men—some in their brushed Confederate uniforms—on the porch and the lawn,

talking of Miss Emily as if she had been a contemporary of theirs, believing that they had danced with her and courted her perhaps, confusing time with its mathematical progression, as the old do, to whom all the past is not a diminishing road but, instead, a huge meadow which no winter ever quite touches, divided from them now by the narrow bottle-neck of the most recent decade of years.

Already we knew that there was one room in that region above stairs which no one had seen in forty years, and which would have to be forced. They waited until Miss Emily was decently in the ground before they opened it.

The violence of breaking down the door seemed to fill this room with pervading dust. A thin, **acrid** pall as of the tomb seemed to lie everywhere upon this room decked and furnished as for a bridal: upon the valance curtains of faded rose color, upon the rose-shaded lights, upon the dressing table, upon the delicate array of crystal and the man's toilet things backed with tarnished silver, silver so tarnished that the monogram was obscured. Among them lay a collar and tie, as if they had just been removed, which, lifted, left upon the surface a pale crescent in the dust. Upon a chair hung the suit, carefully folded; beneath it the two mute shoes and the discarded socks.

The man himself lay in the bed.

For a long while we just stood there, looking down at the profound and fleshless grin. The body had apparently once lain in the attitude of an embrace, but now the long sleep that outlasts love, that conquers even the grimace of love, had **cuckolded** him. What was left of

> ● ● ● ● ● ● ●
> Thus she passed from generation to generation— dear, inescapable, impervious, tranquil, and perverse.
> ● ● ● ● ● ● ●

perverse—stubbornly cranky

sibilant—a sound resembling that of the *s* or *sh* in *sash*

bier—a coffin and its stand

macabre—having death as a subject

acrid—sharp, harsh, irritating

cuckolded—betrayed

him, rotted beneath what was left of the nightshirt, had become **inextricable** from the bed in which he lay; and upon him and upon the pillow beside him lay that even coating of the patient and biding dust.

Then we noticed that in the second pillow was the indentation of a head. One of us lifted something from it, and leaning forward, that faint and invisible dust dry and acrid in the nostrils, we saw a long strand of iron-gray hair. ❖

ON THE JOB
· · · · · · · · · · · · · · · · ·
TAX COLLECTOR
· · · · · · · · · · · · · · · · ·

Tax collectors must know how to obtain data from a number of sources, how to organize data, and how to use computers to process and communicate important tax information. Consequently, they study college-level mathematics and accounting for at least two years. Collectors must also be familiar with appropriate procedures and laws pertinent to their area. They must understand the technical and political systems that form the framework of the taxes they are to collect.

ACCENT ON...
ARCHITECTURE RENOVATION
· ·

When stately old frame houses such as Miss Emily's with their cupolas, spires, and scrolled balconies fall into disrepair, renovating them requires careful attention to detail. Plan a detailed renovation of the building in Faulkner's story. Begin with plans for the exterior and interior. Then write a description of the work you would do inside and out to bring the home back to its former glory.

miss rosie

Lucille Clifton

About the Author

Lucille Clifton's prose and poetry have brought her many awards and honors, including grants from the National Endowment for the Arts. As co-author of the television program *Free to Be You and Me*, she won an Emmy Award in 1974. Clifton writes compassionately about ordinary humans and their daily struggles. Her books for children have been particularly popular. In 1979, Clifton was named poet laureate of Maryland, where she is poet-in-residence at Coppin State College.

When I watch you
wrapped up like garbage
sitting, surrounded by the smell
of too old potato peels
or
when I watch you
in your old man's shoes
with the little toe cut out
sitting, waiting for your mind
like next week's grocery
I say
When I watch you
you wet brown bag of a woman
who used to be the best looking gal in Georgia
used to be called the Georgia Rose
I stand up
through your destruction
I stand up ❖

UNDERSTANDING

1. A common response to suffering or crime is the question: "Why?" We ask "Why is this person poor and alone?" or "Why did the guilty person commit the crime?" Although Lucille Clifton does not tell us why Miss Rosie ends up destitute, Faulkner does tell us why Miss Emily turns into a killer. Find passages to show the many causes that contributed to the murder she committed.

   Create a life for Lucille Clifton's character Miss Rosie. Write a cause-effect essay in which you imagine and explain the factors that led to her present terrible situation. Imagine, for instance, possibilities available to her when she was young, circumstances that might have limited her options, and choices that helped bring her to her present situation. ***Workshop 6***

2. People belonging to different generations often hold differing attitudes and values, as in "A Rose for Emily." Where in this story does Faulkner indicate the differing outlook and values of the older and younger generations?

   Have you noticed a conflict between your values and those of members of an older generation? Orally or in writing, explain differences and similarities that exist between your values and those of another generation. Provide specific examples. Consider values such as courtesy, responsibility, duty, loyalty, and integrity.

A LAST WORD

To what extent did the choices made by Emily affect her later years? What kinds of choices have you made or will you make soon that have long-lasting effects?

CONNECTING

1. Neither Emily nor Miss Rosie make an effort to learn what others think. Friendless and isolated, they have no one to advise or comfort them. Their situations illustrate the crucial importance of being good communicators not only on the job and at school, but in daily life. Working collaboratively, develop an informative handbook or brochure that explains the various uses of communication, the skills of a good communicator, and examples of the kinds of communication expected in an array of occupations. ***Workshop 19***

2. Miss Emily and Miss Rosie might have ended differently had they chosen differently. Sound choices often depend on having complete information. To make an informed choice of a summer or part-time job, investigate a place you think you would like to work. Select a particular fast-food restaurant, bookstore, car wash, supermarket, clothing store, or other potential place of employment. Visit the site as a careful observer. Before your visit, brainstorm with a group to make a list of questions students want answered about any position. When you visit, ask a supervisor if she or a front-line worker would be willing to answer these questions. Use the information gained on site to develop a thorough report about what it would be like to work for this firm. Collaborate to put your own and your classmates' reports into a collection on summer and part-time occupations.

A Paradise Lost

EXPLORING

A hero is customarily defined as a courageous, strong, and moral warrior whose spectacular adventures influence the fate of a country or the world. Some believe that a true hero need not be involved in physical challenges and grand events. Instead the true hero possesses virtue, inner strength, and love. Consider your heroes, the people you look up to as role models. Which of their acts or qualities do you admire? Why? What motives do you think cause people to behave heroically, even to the point of sacrificing themselves for others?

THEME CONNECTION...
HEROIC POSSIBILITIES

Seventy-five-year-old Sarah lives alone in a violent world of looting, poverty, and homelessness where most think "the elderly would be better dead." Principled and resolute, she decides to rescue a stranger even though this choice involves enormous self-sacrifice.

TIME & PLACE

The action takes place in Oakland, California, in an imaginary future. How far in the future it takes place is for each reader to decide. The story was written in 1980, and so far history has not yet caught up with it. It is possible that environmental misuse, overpopulation, natural disasters, the greed of the "haves" and the despair and anger of the "have-nots" might produce Sarah's world very quickly. In her world, California state soldiers guard a California supply depot, where meager amounts of soap and food are dispensed to long lines of impoverished citizens. Law and order do not regulate daily life. Instead, violence and looting happen so regularly that even an ambulance needs an armed escort.

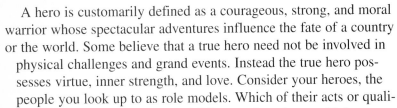

THE WRITER'S CRAFT

SCIENCE FICTION

Science fiction is the term given to short stories and novels that draw upon real science and technology and actual social institutions and problems to portray an imaginary future. These real elements raise the slight possibility that science fiction stories could happen. Chiefly a product of the twentieth century, science fiction has flourished primarily in the United States.

A Paradise Lost

Roussel Sargent

About the Author

Born in 1917 in the industrial Midlands of England, Roussel Sargent spent much of her childhood in a small fishing village of Devonshire. While an undergraduate at the University of London, she met and made friends with Americans. A visit to the United States followed, and in 1958 she immigrated to California, where she taught English Literature at Mills College for nearly thirty years. An avid reader, Sargent eventually became addicted to science fiction, an important influence being the works of Ursula K. Le Guin.

 here had been only a few people in Sarah's life who counted; now there was no one. There had been many books, once she had owned four or five thousand; now there were five. She was going back to them, and her own space in the tiny attic, as fast as she could. As usual, she felt apprehension; one day she would surely find the lock broken and a family moved in. The luxury of a whole ten by twelve foot room to herself was something she dared not hope would continue.

It had been a good day: a day of **apathy** when there was no sight or sound of violence, no looting or burning. After only two hours in line at the California State Supply Depot, where tired soldiers stood idly by, she had been given a small piece of soap, a carton of powdered milk, and a box of oatmeal. At the last minute the woman behind the counter had suddenly produced a two-ounce packet of butter and slipped it in the sack. Even now some people had kindly impulses. Most, however, felt that the elderly would be better dead. She agreed with them; *most* people would be better off dead. It was not that easy though. "The long habit of living indisposeth us for dying," she thought. Her brow furrowed; how long was it since she had bartered her copy of Thomas Browne? Who would want it these days?

She made her way steadily along the road between the sidewalks clogged with loungers, paupers, and beggars. She swerved automatically to avoid a man lying in the gutter: asleep? unconscious? dead? The nearer she got to her own place, the more thronged the crowded streets became, and the more **menacing** the almost silent figures on the sidewalks. With her goods stowed away in her **capacious** pockets, her ragged clothes, and her steady gait— "Thank God, I still have good feet and the use of my legs," thought Sarah—she did not give the impression of being too easy or too profitable a victim. She might be seventy-five, with a wild mop of white hair, and a wild, fierce expression, but she melted into a crowd reasonably well.

As she paused outside the peeling stucco house with its gaping-tiled roof, gathering her energy for the long pull up the three flights of stairs, she saw that the boy was still there.

He was a small, black boy, his back propped against the wall of the house, his head on his knees, and a filthy bandage round one leg. He raised his head and looked at her. There was no hope, no fear, and no interest in his large eyes, clouded with fever. The look was a reflex from a past which included people who cared and who belonged. She stopped; he looked; that was all.

Sarah spent the rest of the day thankfully in her still **inviolate** room, lost in *Persuasion*, savoring subtle moral niceties that no longer made sense in her world.

Late that evening, she went out, as she did most nights, to breathe some fresher air and look up at the unchanged sky. The stars, if pale, still held their accustomed places, and the moon was up. The boy was still there. He looked at her and disturbed her fragile peace.

apathy—lack of feeling or emotion

menacing—posing a threat

capacious—capable of containing a great deal

inviolate—pure, untouched

"Go off," she said sharply to him, "get back to your family. It's late."

The child's filmed eyes stared at her and gradually focussed, as a spark of intelligence came up from some **unfathomable** distance. "Got no folks," he said, and put his head back on his knees.

The next morning he was still there. He was lying against the wall now, gleaming with sweat. He had pulled off his shirt to cool himself, and his ribcage showed sharp against his skin. The sight roused Sarah to anger, as at an obscenity.

"Oh, come upstairs," she snapped. "Let's make you decent."

Her own strength was not sufficient to carry the child upstairs; she had to break her cardinal rule and ask for help. A good-natured **slattern** called Lena picked the boy up for her, wrinkling her nose as she did so. In an evil-smelling slum, he was nonetheless noticeably odorous.

"What d'you want him for?" she asked.

"I don't want him," said Sarah, "but he's sick and he's here."

"Where do you want him then?" as Sarah grudgingly unlocked the door and stood aside.

"On the floorboards there."

Lena put him down, and, straightening up, looked **brazenly** around the room. She took in the mattress by one wall, the upright kitchen chair, the two battered suitcases, and the rickety table with the bowl, mug, and other useful articles on it. She even stared boldly at the bucket that enabled Sarah to use the latrine infrequently.

FOCUS ON... MATH

The estimates for the number of homeless in this country have risen steadily in the last decade. What is the current estimate for the number of homeless in the United States? Who are the homeless? How are the figures determined? Research the numbers of homeless people over the past five to ten years. Include statistics about homeless children. Then, using a computer program, create a graph showing the results of your research.

"Nice place; roomy," she commented.

"Yes. Thank you for your kindness. I must look after the boy now."

Lena went reluctantly, but came back a few minutes later and knocked on the door. She was carrying some rags—nearly clean—and half a loaf. "Here," she said, "you'll need fresh bandages. Do you want some help?"

"I can manage, thank you." Sarah longed to slam the door in her face, but achieved an unwilling smile. Lena nodded and, with another look round the room, departed.

Sarah stripped the boy and unwrapped the bandage. There was a ragged gash on his leg; red, angry streaks radiated from it; the smell was revolting. Gagging but ruthless, Sarah washed him all over, cleaning the wound as well as she could with her precious soap. She rebandaged his leg, dragged him on to her mattress between the blankets, and wondered what to do next. She filled her mug with water, and the child drank eagerly, seeming to come back to consciousness for a moment. Later, she squeezed an orange, added a spoonful of sugar to the juice, and coaxed most of it down him.

It was a long day. She finished *Persuasion*, but the boy disturbed her concentration. He tossed and moaned, and all

unfathomable—impossible to comprehend

slattern—an untidy woman

brazenly—in a manner of contemptuous boldness

protracted—
prolonged, continued

Persuasion—
Jane Austen's last
completed novel,
published after her
death

**Antony and
Cleopatra**—William
Shakespeare's play
*Antony and
Cleopatra* about the
ill-fated love of Marc
Antony and
Cleopatra of Egypt

**Selected Poems of
Yeats**—poems by
the Irish author
William Butler Yeats

Oxford Blake—Sir
Geoffrey Keynes'
compilation of *The
Complete Writings
of William Blake*, an
English Romantic
writer

Paradise Lost—
epic poem by John
Milton that tells of
the fall of Adam
and Eve

she could do was replace the blankets when he pushed them off, or get him to take more liquid.

Throughout the restless, unendurably **protracted** hours of dark, Sarah sat upright on the chair, except when she had to go to the boy. Once, when she sponged his face, he said dreamily, "Mom?" and once, as she bent over him, his hand caught hers and held it tightly. She unclasped his and put it back under the blanket.

She made oatmeal for breakfast the next day; she only persuaded her patient to eat two spoonfuls, but she finished the rest herself. She had to keep her strength up, and she could not spend another day without searching for food. After she had changed the bandages, she locked the boy into her room and went out to a store which had not yet been looted, and which sometimes had food to exchange for her coupons. She came home early with a can of stew and some more oranges—at least in California, even in the towns, it was often possible to get fruit—to find that the boy had crawled to the door and was battering on it feebly.

He looked at her with frightened eyes, muttering in semi-delirium. "Why you lock me up, ol' witch? You aiming to eat me? I'll tell my Mom. I'll kill you."

"Get back into bed at once, you naughty boy," she said with a calm authority she did not feel, and to her surprise he obeyed her, and fell at once into a feverish sleep.

That night tiredness drove her to share the mattress with the boy. She lay down wincingly; she had always hated casual contact. Even with her husband, after they had shared love she had always wanted her own bed to herself. Yet she slept well. When she awoke, she found the boy lying against her, his head on her shoulder, one arm round her neck. She pushed him away—but gently—and got stiffly out of bed, though it was early.

The boy seemed a little stronger, but the red streaks on his leg were spreading upwards. "He needs drugs," thought Sarah. She had been washing him, and they were both sitting on the mattress, he propped up against her. His head was once more on her shoulder. The weight felt familiar and right. "He needs a doctor and proper treatment; he needs a hospital." She bit her lip and pondered.

"It's all there is to do," she thought at last. Getting painfully to her feet, she went and undid a suitcase and pulled out her books: **Persuasion**, **Antony and Cleopatra**, **Selected Poems of Yeats**, in paperback, a battered copy of the **Oxford Blake**, and a leatherbound edition of **Paradise Lost**. Her hands with their upstanding veins and their age blemishes moved gently and sensitively on the covers. Each volume was treated with equal respect and love, but the first four she replaced in the case. Then she sat down in her chair and opened up *Paradise Lost*.

"Of Man's First Disobedience, and the Fruit . . ." she began. She read rapidly through the first book until Pandemonium had been built, turning each page with tender decisiveness, holding the book firmly and warmly, as one might a baby. Then she broke her reading and began to skim. She stopped and read the description of Eden as Milton first presents it, next she turned to Adam's talk with Raphael. "Right Reason," she murmured to herself, and shut the book.

She dressed herself with care, putting on her better pair of shoes, those with holes only in the soles. She chose her dark cotton dress that looked almost respectable, and, though it was chilly, she left off her battered coat with its several pockets. Wrapping *Paradise Lost* in an old scarf, she went out and shut the door. For a moment she hesitated, key in hand. Then, "They'd have to break the lock to get him," she thought, and turned away, leaving the door unlocked as she began her long walk to the "good" part of the town with its adequate security.

Despite the care she had taken with her appearance, the proprietor of the Antiquarian Bookstore looked at her with suspicion and **hauteur** when she came in to his shop. He raised an eyebrow instead of speaking.

She put *Paradise Lost* on the counter and looked at him silently. The man picked it up and examined it; she caught the flicker of **cupidity** in his eyes.

"It's a very old copy," he said, as if this were a damning quality, "and no one reads Milton these days."

Putting back her head and speaking with all the **resonance** and all the aristocratic **insolence** of which she had once been so capable, she fixed him with her fierce eyes. "It is unfortunately true," she said, "that no one reads these days. But I did not think that book collectors were so ignorant that a man who pretends to be a specialist catering to them would not recognize a first edition. You are not the man I want. You had better give me back the book. I will find someone with some knowledge of his trade."

Half an hour later she came out of the shop victorious; he had known the right people, made the right phone calls, and each was satisfied. Long before she had finished her fatiguing walk home, her street would be electrified by the arrival of an ambulance with its usual escort of two armored cars of soldiers, and the child would have been taken off to hospital. All that was left for her to do was to force her weary legs to carry her back to her unlocked room. "I am content," she told herself, refusing to acknowledge the pain inside her chest that struggled to escape through her eyes, up her throat, like some bird of sorrow wishing to sing of loss. Erect and fierce, she set out on the long trek to discover if she still had a **sanctuary**. She had done the only right, the only reasonable, thing to do, but she did not therefore consider that this entitled her to find her room still empty when she got home.

There had been only a few people in Sarah's life; now there was no one. There had been many books; now there were four. ❖

hauteur—arrogance, haughtiness

cupidity—greed, desire for wealth

resonance—rich sound

insolence—boldness, overbearing contemptuousness

sanctuary— a place of refuge and protection

ACCENT ON...
INSTITUTIONAL DESIGN

• •

The homeless shelters found in urban areas are often crowded and makeshift. Design a halfway house for the homeless. Find out what facilities and services such an institution requires. If possible, visit one or two shelters that are presently in operation to gain firsthand knowledge of what features a shelter needs. Interview some shelter workers to get their opinions about features of a workable, practical shelter. Prepare a feasibility report for a shelter in your town.

ON THE JOB
• • • • • • • • • • • • • • •
EMERGENCY MEDICAL WORKER
• • • • • • • • • • • • • • •

To work on an emergency medical team requires at least two years of special training. Such workers need to have a desire to help people and an ability to work with all kinds of people under stressful and challenging conditions. Emergency workers must be able to deal with and relate to all age groups and be sensitive to special needs. Understanding and following important regulations, being able to think clearly and react quickly, and following directions are also essential skills in emergency medical work.

UNDERSTANDING

1. Why does Sargent call her story "A Paradise Lost"? Find evidence in the story that helps explain the meaning of the title.

   Most of us remember places, and perhaps even people, whom the years have treated badly. Write an essay in which you compare the condition of a place or person in the past with the present condition of that place or person. ***Workshop 9***

2. Does Sarah's behavior deserve to be called heroic? Define "heroic," and then find passages in the text to justify or discourage calling Sarah a hero.

   In a short speech, define "heroism." Then describe a friend or public figure you think fits this definition. Give examples of the person's behavior to support your definition. ***Workshops 12 and 19***

CONNECTING

A LAST WORD

Can you envision living in a world like that described in "A Paradise Lost"? Would you have the courage to help someone as Sarah did?

1. The boy in "A Paradise Lost" is alone and ill. Fortunately, Sarah knows how to go about getting help for him. If you discovered a 10-year-old who was homeless and ill, what community agencies would you contact to get help for the child? What hospital would admit him? Would free ambulance service be available? In groups, gather information on the various services your community provides for needy children and their families. Do these services seem adequate? Present your findings in a collaborative written report accompanied by appropriate visual aids. ***Workshops 1 and 20***

2. Two minor but significant points made in "A Paradise Lost" are that it is important to know your own abilities and it is important to have work. Sarah realizes that her abilities include a steady walk and the power, when need be, to assume an intimidating manner. What are your abilities? What job might these direct you towards?

   List the kinds of jobs you have done, both paid and unpaid. What skills did these jobs require? What knowledge? What personal qualities? Whether babysitting, raking leaves, mowing lawns, playing on a basketball team, or cleaning your room, you have demonstrated strengths that will help you perform paid work. Having figured out your strong points, identify a job you would like to hold either next summer or in the distant future.

   To find a job, examine the classified ads, talk to friends and parents, or call the unemployment office for information on available jobs. Write a letter of application for the position of your choice. In your letter, state your qualifications: the skills, knowledge, and personal qualities that make you a viable candidate for employment. ***Workshop 11***

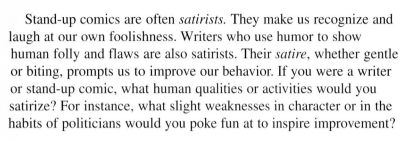

The Scotty Who Knew Too Much

EXPLORING

Stand-up comics are often *satirists*. They make us recognize and laugh at our own foolishness. Writers who use humor to show human folly and flaws are also satirists. Their *satire*, whether gentle or biting, prompts us to improve our behavior. If you were a writer or stand-up comic, what human qualities or activities would you satirize? For instance, what slight weaknesses in character or in the habits of politicians would you poke fun at to inspire improvement?

THEME CONNECTION...
SELF-DECEPTION AND POOR CHOICES

In "The Scotty Who Knew Too Much," the Scotty does not know the extent of his own limitations. One of his limitations is his willingness to judge things on the basis of appearances. These superficial judgments result in bad choices. Things are not always what they seem, the Scotty discovers.

TIME & PLACE

"The Scotty Who Knew Too Much" was written at a time when a nation of rural people who primarily made their living off the land was changing into an urbanized culture. With this change came the attitude that "the city" offered a superior life to that of "the country." This was not, of course, an attitude shared by those who grew up in the small towns of early twentieth century America. Born and raised in Columbus, Ohio, Thurber delighted in exposing the silliness and folly of both city and country dwellers, immortalizing especially the behavior of his own fantastic Ohio relatives.

THE WRITER'S CRAFT

THE FABLE

A fable is a short tale told in poetry or prose to teach a moral lesson. When the main characters in fables are animals, these tales are called beast fables. In *beast fables*, the animals behave like human beings to make a point about human behavior. Perhaps the most famous fables were written about 600 B.C. by a Greek slave named Aesop. Since Aesop, fables have been a popular form of literature.

The Scotty Who Knew Too Much

James Thurber

vitriol—in this case, sulfuric acid

Several summers ago there was a Scotty who went to the country for a visit. He decided that all the farm dogs were cowards, because they were afraid of a certain animal that had a white stripe down its back. "You are a pussycat and I can lick you," the Scotty said to the farm dog who lived in the house where the Scotty was visiting. "I can lick the little animal with the white stripe, too. Show him to me."

"Don't you want to ask any questions about him?" said the farm dog.

"Nah," said the Scotty. "You ask the questions."

So the farm dog took the Scotty into the woods and showed him the white-striped animal and the Scotty closed in on him, growling and slashing. It was all over in a moment and the Scotty lay on his back. When he came to, the farm dog said, "What happened?"

"He threw **vitriol**," said the Scotty, "but he never laid a glove on me."

A few days later the farm dog told the Scotty there was another animal all the farm dogs were afraid of. "Lead me to him," said the Scotty. "I can lick anything that doesn't wear horseshoes."

"Don't you want to ask any questions about him?" said the farm dog.

"Nah," said the Scotty. "Just show me where he hangs out." So the farm dog led him to a place in the woods and pointed out the little animal when he came along. "A clown," said the Scotty, "a pushover," and he closed in, leading with his left and exhibiting some mighty fancy footwork. In less than a second the Scotty was flat on his back, and when he woke up the farm dog was pulling quills out of him.

"What happened?" said the farm dog.

"He pulled a knife on me," said the Scotty, "but at least I have learned how you fight out here in the country, and now I am going to beat you up." So he closed in on the farm dog, holding his nose with one front paw to ward off the vitriol and covering his eyes with the other front paw to keep out the knives. The Scotty couldn't see his opponent and he couldn't smell his opponent and he was so badly beaten that he had to be taken back to the city and put in a nursing home.

Moral: It is better to ask some of the questions than to know all the answers. ❖

About the Author

American humorist and writer James Thurber (1894–1961) delighted America with his stories and cartoons. As a young man, Thurber wrote plays for college productions. Then he went to work for the U.S. State Department as a code clerk. Eventually he turned to journalism. In his twenties, he began to work for newspapers in Paris, Columbus, and New York. He became the managing editor of a new magazine in 1925—*The New Yorker*. As his writings and drawings became increasingly popular, he demoted himself to staff writer, then contributor, so that he would have more time to devote to his books, essays, children's books, short stories, and plays.

FOCUS ON... ART

Thurber was as well known for his cartoons as for his writings. Locate some of his cartoons and doodle-drawings and photocopy the one you like best. Then, imitating Thurber's style, create your own cartoon or comic strip to illustrate the selection "The Scotty Who Knew Too Much."

◆◆◆◆◆◆◆◆◆◆◆◆◆◆◆◆◆◆◆◆◆◆◆◆◆◆◆◆

UNDERSTANDING

1.  The humor in Thurber's story accounts for its widespread popularity. Find examples in the text of humorous elements. Using similar elements, work with your group to write a script for a comic encounter between two people who have personalities similar to the Scotty and the farm dog.

2. A beast fable assigns human qualities to animals for the purpose of satirizing human faults. What undesirable human characteristics does the Scotty possess? Discuss which of these qualities you dislike most and why.

   Identify a public figure whom you think resembles the Scotty. Write an essay that compares and contrasts the qualities of this public personality with those of the Scotty. **Workshop 9**

3. Blinded by conceit, the Scotty entirely lacks self-knowledge. Unaware of his limitations, he grossly overestimates his abilities and therefore fails. Locate passages that show the Scotty deceiving himself. Make a list of the questions you would have asked had you been in the Scotty's place. How would these questions and answers have prepared you to meet the enemies?

   On the job, it is important to have an accurate perception of one's abilities and knowledge. Write a memo from a supervisor to her or his employees explaining why the employees are expected to ask questions and investigate before starting a new project. **Workshop 13**

A LAST WORD

Have you ever allowed over-confidence to get the best of you? What steps can you take to avoid being misled and believing a difficult task will require no preparation?

CONNECTING

1. In a business consisting of more than one employee, differences in personal style are likely to create tension. Imagine you own a business and employ four people. One of them, your top salesperson, has a very strong personality. She never admits errors and blames others for her mistakes. She treats her coworkers as inferiors, loudly giving orders, always interrupting, and never listening. But she sells more of your product than anyone else does. It is time to prepare personnel evaluations. Write an evaluation of this salesperson in which you give her enough self-knowledge to see the truth about how her behavior affects others. If you succeed and she changes, the office will be harmonious. Unless you are tactful, however, your best salesperson will resign. **Workshop 5**

2.  The moral of Thurber's story is: "It is better to ask some of the questions than to know all the answers." People who think they "know all the answers" have closed minds and fail to grow in their life and work. Asking good questions, however, enriches life. Conduct research to learn how to become a skilled questioner. With your classmates, create a brochure explaining why asking sound questions is an essential life skill and how to develop this skill. You may wish to target this brochure to middle-schoolers. **Workshop 21**

The Scotty Who Knew Too Much

205

The Wife's Story

EXPLORING

"Metamorphosis" means complete transformation into a wholly different form. Just as metamorphosis tales have long been popular in literature (the fairy tale frog turns into a prince), so metamorphosis movies such as those about werewolves draw large audiences today. Usually metamorphosis involves a supernatural change in appearance; sometimes it involves a change only in character. People undergo this kind of metamorphosis. An honest person suddenly behaves dishonestly, or a calm person acts violently. Discuss cases of metamorphosis mentioned in the press or by your acquaintances. Is a person entirely responsible for his or her changed behavior? If a person's behavior transforms unexpectedly from being rude and inconsiderate to kind, do you give that person or outside influences credit for the metamorphosis?

THEME CONNECTION...
LOST POSSIBILITIES

Sometimes the choices we make do not turn out as we expected. The wife describes falling in love, choosing a mate, and living happily for a time. She implies the possibility that she and her husband will share a long, joyful union. The wife then tells of watching her mate transform completely into an ominous and destructive creature. Faced with the reality of her husband's transformation, the wife responds courageously to it.

TIME & PLACE

"The Wife's Story" takes place at an unspecified time in an imaginary past and covers an uncertain period of perhaps one year. The setting is an imaginary forest somewhere. The forest contains hills, shadowy woods, bright sunshine mornings, and moonlight. In this forest a family keeps its home. The action centers on the family at home, where the wife cares for the children.

THE WRITER'S CRAFT

FANTASY

Writing fantasy involves fashioning an entirely original world of imaginary times and places that are filled with magic and the supernatural. Readers willingly accept the world of fantasy, in part because it includes details from real life such as sunshine and hills. These details make the setting familiar. We also go along with fantasy because everything in it fits together: it has inner logic. By agreeing to enter the wholly improbable world of fantasy, the reader discovers truths about human experience.

The Wife's Story

Ursula K. Le Guin

e was a good husband, a good father. I don't understand it. I don't believe in it. I don't believe that it happened. I saw it happen but it isn't true. It can't be. He was always gentle. If you'd have seen him playing with the children, anybody who saw him with the children would have known that there wasn't any bad in him, not one mean bone. When I first met him he was still living with his mother over near Spring Lake, and I used to see them together, the mother and the sons, and think that any young fellow that was that nice with his family must be one worth knowing. Then one time when I was walking in the woods I met him by himself coming back from a hunting trip. He hadn't got any game at all, not so much as a field mouse, but he wasn't cast down about it. He was just larking along enjoying the morning air. That's one of the things I first loved about him. He didn't take things hard, he didn't grouch and whine when things didn't go his way. So we got to talking that day. And I guess things moved right along after that, because pretty soon he was over here pretty near all the time. And my sister said—see, my parents had moved out the year before and gone South, leaving us the place—my sister said, kind of teasing but serious, "Well! If he's going to be here every day and half the night, I guess there isn't room for me!" And she moved out— just down the way. We've always been real close, her and me. That's the sort of thing doesn't ever change. I couldn't ever have got through this bad time without my sis.

Well, so he came to live here. And all I can say is, it was the happy year of my life. He was just purely good to me. A hard worker and never lazy, and so big and fine-looking. Everybody looked up to him, you know, young as he was. Lodge Meeting nights, more and more often they had him to lead the singing. He had such a beautiful voice, and he'd lead off strong and the others following and joining in, high voices and low. It brings the shivers on me now to think of it, hearing it, nights when I'd stayed home from meeting when the children was babies—the singing coming up through the trees there, and the moonlight, summer nights, the full moon shining. I'll never hear anything so beautiful. I'll never know a joy like that again.

It was the moon, that's what they say. It's the moon's fault, and the blood. It was in his father's blood. I never knew his father, and now I wonder what become of him. He was from up Whitewater way, and had no kin around here. I always thought he went back there, but now I don't know. There was some talk about him, tales, that come out after what happened to my husband. It's something runs in the blood, they say, and it may never come out, but if it does, it's the change of the moon that does it. Always it happens in the dark of the moon. When everybody's home asleep. Something comes over the one that's got the curse in his blood, they say, and he gets up because he can't sleep, and goes out into the glaring sun, and goes off all alone—drawn to find those like him. And it may be so, because my husband would do that. I'd half rouse and say, "Where you going to?" and he'd say, "Oh, hunting, be back this evening," and it wasn't like him, even his voice was different. But I'd be so

About the Author

After studying foreign languages in college, Ursula K. Le Guin (1929–) began to teach French at the college level, then quickly turned to writing— especially science fiction. Her first several books won her acclaim in that field, including several Hugo awards and the National Book Award. Since the mid-1970s, her work has moved toward fantasy, historical fiction, poetry, plays, and nonfiction. Le Guin has taught and lectured on writing and the creative process in several states, in Australia and in England. She presently lives in Portland, Oregon.

sleepy, and not wanting to wake the kids, and he was so good and responsible, it was no call of mine to go asking "Why?" and "Where?" and all like that.

So it happened that way maybe three times or four. He'd come back late, and worn out, and pretty near cross for one so sweet-tempered—not wanting to talk about it. I figured everybody got to bust out now and then, and nagging never helped anything. But it did begin to worry me. Not so much that he went, but that he come back so tired and strange. Even, he smelled strange. It made my hair stand up on end. I could not endure it and I said, "What is that—those smells on you? All over you!" And he said, "I don't know," real short, and made like he was sleeping. But he went down when he thought I wasn't noticing, and washed and washed himself. But those smells stayed in his hair, and in our bed, for days.

And then the awful thing. I don't find it easy to tell about this. I want to cry when I have to bring it to my mind. Our youngest, the little one, my baby, she turned from her father. Just overnight. He come in and she got scared-looking stiff, with her eyes wide, and then she begun to cry and try to hide behind me. She didn't yet talk plain but she was saying over and over, "Make it go away! Make it go away!"

The look in his eyes, just for one moment, when he heard that. That's what I don't want ever to remember. That's what I can't forget. The look in his eyes looking at his own child.

I said to the child, "Shame on you, what's got into you?"—scolding but keeping her right up close to me at the same time, because I was frightened too. Frightened to shaking.

He looked away then and said something like, "Guess she just waked up dreaming," and passed it off that way. Or tried to. And so did I. And I got real mad

with my baby when she kept on acting crazy scared of her own dad. But she couldn't help it and I couldn't change it.

He kept away that whole day. Because he knew, I guess. It was just beginning dark of the moon.

It was hot and close inside, and dark, and we'd all been asleep some while, when something woke me up. He wasn't there beside me. I heard a little stir in the passage, when I listened. So I got up, because I could bear it no longer. I went out into the passage, and it was light there, hard sunlight coming in from the door. And I saw him standing just outside, in the tall grass by the entrance. His head was hanging. Presently he sat down, like he felt weary, and looked down at his feet. I held still, inside, and watched—I didn't know what for.

And I saw what he saw. I saw the changing. In his feet, it was, first. They got long, each foot got longer, stretching out, the toes stretching out and the foot getting long, and fleshy, and white. And no hair on them.

The hair begun to come away all over his body. It was like his hair fried away in the sunlight and was gone. He was white

ACCENT ON...
GRAPHIC DESIGN
• •

Metamorphosis tales come to life on movie and television screens thanks to morphing software. This software transforms one image into another. Working in groups, find out what types of morphing software are available, the costs of such software, their user-friendly value, the additional equipment needed to run the software, and the types of occupations that might have a use for it. Graphic design houses, advertising agencies, or larger libraries may have this information. If possible, visit a company that uses morphing technology.

all over, then, like a worm's skin. And he turned his face. It was changing while I looked. It got flatter and flatter, the mouth flat and wide, and the teeth grinning flat and dull, and the nose just a knob of flesh with nostril holes, and the ears gone, and the eyes gone blue—blue, with white rims around the blue—staring at me out of that flat, soft, white face.

SPOTLIGHT ON... CREATIVE THINKING

Le Guin's story takes an established story line—that of a human turning into a beast—and turns it around. Reversing an established pattern is one way to be creative in your own writing and thinking. As you approach a problem:

- look at it from unconventional angles
- use free association to explore options and solutions.

He stood up then on two legs.

I saw him, I had to see him, my own dear love, turned into the hateful one.

I couldn't move, but as I crouched there in the passage staring out into the day I was trembling and shaking with a growl that burst out into a crazy, awful howling. A grief howl and a terror howl and a calling howl. And the others heard it, even sleeping, and woke up.

It stared and peered, that thing my husband had turned into, and shoved its face up to the entrance of our house. I was still bound by mortal fear, but behind me the children had waked up, and the baby was whimpering. The mother anger come into me then, and I snarled and crept forward.

The man thing looked around. It had no gun, like the ones from the man places do. But it picked up a heavy fallen tree-branch in its long white foot, and shoved the end of that down into our house, at me. I snapped the end of it in my teeth and started to force my way out, because I knew the man would kill our children if it could. But my sister was already coming. I saw her running at the man with her head low and her mane high and her eyes yellow as the winter sun. It turned on her and raised up that branch to hit her. But I come out of the doorway, mad with the mother anger, and the others all were coming answering my call, the whole pack gathering, there in that blind glare and heat of the sun at noon.

The man looked round at us and yelled out loud, and brandished the branch it held. Then it broke and ran, heading for the cleared fields and plowlands, down the mountainside. It ran, on two legs, leaping and weaving, and we followed it.

I was last, because love still bound the anger and the fear in me. I was running when I saw them pull it down. My sister's teeth were in its throat. I got there and it was dead. The others were drawing back from the kill, because of the taste of the blood, and the smell. The younger ones were cowering and some crying, and my sister rubbed her mouth against her forelegs over and over to get rid of the taste. I went up close because I thought if the thing was dead the spell, the curse must be done, and my husband could come back—alive, or even dead, if I could only see him, my true love, in his true form, beautiful. But only the dead man lay there white and bloody. We drew back and back from it, and turned and ran, back up into the hills, back to the woods of the shadows and the twilight and the blessed dark. ❖

UNDERSTANDING

1. What details imply that the husband was once a truly good father and companion?

   Just as wives expect husbands to have good qualities, so employers expect certain qualities of their staff. How do employers define "good" when they apply this word to employees? In your group, brainstorm specific qualities employers expect good employees to possess. On your own, write a memo to an imaginary employer to recommend a classmate for promotion. Offer examples to demonstrate that he or she possesses the qualities employers value in employees. *Workshop 13*

2. Prior to the husband's physical transformation, what passages indicate that his *character* is altering? Basing your answer on evidence from the text, list reasons for the husband's changed behavior. With a group of classmates, discuss how these reasons relate to the behavior of real individuals.

   Do you know a friend or relative who, in a short period of time (one month to two years), changed in a significant and surprising way? Write a brief scene that depicts one change that took place.

3.  With a group, develop a convincing explanation of what the story means. What is its central theme and what minor ideas does it raise? Working collaboratively, write down your group's interpretation of "The Wife's Story." Present this interpretation to the class. *Workshop 5*

CONNECTING

1.  The couple's relationship in "The Wife's Story" begins in harmony and ends in hostility. This movement from harmony to discord raises the question: What causes conflict? How might conflict be resolved? Studies on conflict resolution deal with these issues. With a group, read material on the topic of conflict. From this reading develop a list of steps to take to settle conflicts. Apply these principles to a movie or television show. Compare and contrast how screenwriters handle conflict with the steps theorists recommend. *Workshop 9*

2. The transformed husband made his wife suffer. Because he changed, she had to endure tragedy. Today, victims of tragic events appear every day in newspapers and magazines. Editors and photographers often print vivid pictures of victims. They may show, for example, a woman kneeling over her son's body, or the weeping parents of a missing teenager. What should be the policy of newspapers about publishing photographs of victims? Investigate the policies of various newspapers about printing "grief photographs," sensational pictures of victims of tragedy. Then develop your own policy. Present it in a proposal to your school and local newspapers. *Workshop 10*

A LAST WORD

Imagine the shock of learning that someone you love has turned into a being you find impossible to love. How would you face such a life-altering event? What choices would you have?

Trifles

EXPLORING

Not many years ago a newspaper's classified advertisements listed two categories: "Help Wanted Men" and "Help Wanted Women." What kinds of jobs do you think were listed under each category? Remember that until relatively recently, society virtually denied women the opportunity to become doctors, lawyers, engineers, or architects. Entering trades such as plumbing, carpentry, or electrical repair was unheard of. "Women's Work," the term given to describe homemakers, child-care workers, housekeepers, nurses, and teachers, was deemed unimportant and trivial. Is a child-care worker less important than the mechanic you trust with your car? Is the person who keeps the house, prepares the meals, and watches the children less valuable than the one who brings home the paycheck? Suggest specific ways to increase awareness in your school or community of the importance of so-called "women's work."

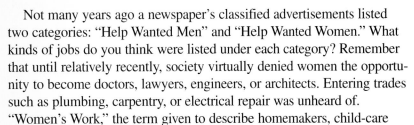

THEME CONNECTION...
CHOOSING TO PROTECT

In *Trifles,* Mrs. Peters and Mrs. Hale must make a serious decision. They must choose to protect their friend Mrs. Wright or report evidence against her to the Sheriff and the County Attorney. Mrs. Peters and Mrs. Hale decide to help Mrs. Wright. They judge her and find her innocent due to mitigating circumstances. When they choose to stand by Mrs. Wright, the two women silently defy the men.

TIME & PLACE

The story takes place in the rather harsh farmlands of Iowa in the early 1900s. Farm work was hard and a good deal of it fell to the farmer's wife, who was responsible for putting food on the table, providing clean clothes, and keeping a tidy home. She had no supermarket to help, so baking bread, preserving fruits and vegetables, sewing and quilting were important tasks.

THE WRITER'S CRAFT

IRONY

This play is filled with verbal irony, irony of situation, and dramatic irony. Verbal irony occurs when the speaker means the opposite of, or far more than, he or she actually says. Irony of situation takes place when some characters in a story or play know more than others do or when an event turns out in a manner contrary to expectation. Dramatic irony happens when the audience knows more about what is going on than do the characters involved in events.

Trifles

Susan Glaspell

About the Author

Susan Glaspell (1882–1948) was a cofounder and leader of the Provincetown Players and the Playwrights' Theatre in Massachusetts. She wrote dozens of one-act plays as well as longer works, among them *Alison's House*, which won the Pulitzer Prize for drama in 1931. Glaspell also wrote a book of short stories and nearly a dozen popular novels. Having lived the first thirty-two years of her life in Iowa, Susan Glaspell knew the country well, the cruel cold in the winter, stifling heat in the summer, and miles and miles of corn and wheat fields. This helped her as she wrote *Trifles* in 1920.

Characters

George Henderson, *county attorney*

Henry Peters, *sheriff*

Lewis Hale, *a neighboring farmer*

Mrs. Peters

Mrs. Hale

Scene *The kitchen in the now abandoned farmhouse of John Wright, a gloomy kitchen, and left without having been put in order—unwashed pans under the sink, a loaf of bread outside the breadbox, a dish towel on the table—other signs of incompleted work. At the rear the outer door opens and the* SHERIFF *comes in followed by the* COUNTY ATTORNEY *and* HALE. *The* SHERIFF *and* HALE *are men in middle life, the* COUNTY ATTORNEY *is a young man; all are much bundled up and go at once to the stove. They are followed by two women—the Sheriff's wife first; she is a slight wiry woman, a thin nervous face.* MRS. HALE *is larger and would ordinarily be called more comfortable looking, but she is disturbed now and looks fearfully about as she enters. The women have come in slowly, and stand close together near the door.*

COUNTY ATTORNEY: (*rubbing his hands*): This feels good. Come up to the fire, ladies.

MRS. PETERS (*after taking a step forward*): I'm not—cold.

SHERIFF (*unbuttoning his overcoat and stepping away from the stove as if to mark the beginning of official business*): Now, Mr. Hale, before we move things about, you explain to Mr. Henderson just what you saw when you came here yesterday morning.

COUNTY ATTORNEY: By the way, has anything been moved? Are things just as you left them yesterday?

SHERIFF (*looking about*): It's just the same. When it dropped below zero last night I thought I'd better send Frank out this morning to make a fire for us—no use getting pneumonia with a big case on, but I told him not to touch anything except the stove—and you know Frank.

COUNTY ATTORNEY: Somebody should have been left here yesterday.

SHERIFF: Oh—yesterday. When I had to send Frank to Morris Center for that man who went crazy—I want you to know I had my hands full yesterday, I knew you could get back from Omaha by today and as long as I went over everything here myself—

COUNTY ATTORNEY: Well, Mr. Hale, tell just what happened when you came here yesterday morning.

HALE: Harry and I had started to town with a load of potatoes. We came along the road from my place and as I got here I said, "I'm going to see if I can't get John Wright to go in with me on a party telephone." I spoke to Wright about it once before and he put me off, saying folks talked too much anyway, and all he asked was peace and quiet—I guess you know about how much he talked himself; but I thought maybe if I went to the house and talked about it before his wife, though I said to Harry that I didn't know as what his wife wanted made such difference to John—

COUNTY ATTORNEY: Let's talk about that later, Mr. Hale. I do want to talk about that, but tell now just what happened when you got to the house.

HALE: I didn't hear or see anything; I knocked at the door, and still it was all quiet inside. I knew they must be up, it was past eight o'clock. So I knocked again, and thought I heard somebody say, "Come in." I wasn't sure, I'm not sure yet, but I opened the door—this door (*indicating the door by which the two women are still*

standing*) and there in that rocker— (*pointing to it*) sat Mrs. Wright.

They all look at the rocker.

COUNTY ATTORNEY: What—was she doing?

HALE: She was rockin' back and forth. She had her apron in her hand and was kind of—pleating it.

COUNTY ATTORNEY: And how did she—look?

HALE: Well, she looked queer.

COUNTY ATTORNEY: How do you mean—queer?

HALE: Well, as if she didn't know what she was going to do next. And kind of done up.

COUNTY ATTORNEY: How did she seem to feel about your coming?

HALE: Why, I don't think she minded— one way or other. She didn't pay much attention. I said, "How do, Mrs. Wright, it's cold, ain't it?" And she said, "Is it?"— and went on kind of pleating at her apron. Well, I was surprised; she didn't ask me to come up to the stove, or to set down, but just sat there, not even looking at me, so I said, "I want to see John." And then she— laughed. I guess you would call it a laugh. I thought of Harry and the team outside, so I said a little sharp. "Can't I see John?" "No," she says, kind o' dull like. "Ain't he home?" says I. "Yes," says she, "he's home." "Then why can't I see him?" I asked her, out of patience. "'Cause he's dead," says she. "*Dead?*" says I. She just nodded her head, not getting a bit excited, but rockin' back and forth. "Why—where is he?" says I, not knowing what to say. She just

> ● ● ● ● ● ● ●
> ### "He died of a rope around his neck."
> ● ● ● ● ● ● ●

Trifles

pointed upstairs—like that *(himself pointing to the room above)*. I got up, with the idea of going up there. I walked from there to here—then I says, "Why, what did he die of?" "He died of a rope around his neck," says she, and just went on pleatin' at her apron. Well, I went out and called Harry. I thought I might—need help. We went upstairs and there he was lyin'—

COUNTY ATTORNEY: I think I'd rather have you go into that upstairs, where you can point it all out. Just go on now with the rest of the story.

HALE: Well, my first thought was to get that rope off. It looked . . . *(stops, his face twitches)* . . . but Harry, he went up to him, and he said, "No, he's dead all right, and we'd better not touch anything." So we went back down stairs. She was still sitting that same way. "Has anybody been notified?" I asked. "No," says she, unconcerned. "Who did this, Mrs. Wright?" said Harry. He said it businesslike—and she stopped pleatin' of her apron. "I don't know," she says. "You don't *know?*" says Harry. "No," says she. "Weren't you sleepin' in the bed with him?" says Harry. "Yes," says she, "but I was on the inside." "Somebody slipped a rope around his neck and strangled him and you didn't wake up?" says Harry. "I didn't wake up," she said after him. We must 'a looked as if we didn't see how that could be, for after a minute she said, "I sleep sound." Harry was going to ask her more questions but I said maybe we ought to let her tell her story first to the **coroner**, or the sheriff, so

Harry went fast as he could to Rivers' place, where there's a telephone.

COUNTY ATTORNEY: And what did Mrs. Wright do when she knew that you had gone for the coroner?

HALE: She moved from that chair to this one over here *(pointing to a small chair in the corner)* and just sat there with her hands held together and looking down. I got a feeling that I ought to make some conversation, so I said I had come in to see if John wanted to put in a telephone, and at that she started to laugh, and then she stopped and looked at me—scared. *(The COUNTY ATTORNEY, who has had his notebook out, makes a note.)* I dunno, maybe it wasn't scared. I wouldn't like to say it was. Soon Harry got back, and then Dr. Lloyd came, and you, Mr. Peters, and so I guess that's all I know that you don't.

COUNTY ATTORNEY *(looking around)*: I guess we'll go upstairs first—and then out to the barn and around there. *(to the SHERIFF)* You're convinced that there

was nothing important here—nothing that would point to any motive.

SHERIFF: Nothing here but kitchen things.

The COUNTY ATTORNEY, *after again looking around the kitchen, opens the door of a cupboard closet. He gets up on a chair and looks on a shelf. Pulls his hand away, sticky.*

COUNTY ATTORNEY: Here's a nice mess.

The women draw nearer.

MRS. PETERS *(to the other woman)*: Oh, her fruit; it did freeze. *(to the* COUNTY ATTORNEY*)* She worried about that when it turned so cold. She said the fire'd go out and her jars would break.

SHERIFF: Well, can you beat the women! Held for murder and worryin' about her preserves.

COUNTY ATTORNEY: I guess before we're through she may have something more serious than preserves to worry about.

HALE: Well, women are used to worrying over **trifles**.

The two women move a little closer together.

COUNTY ATTORNEY: *(with the* **gallantry** *of a young politician)*. And yet, for all their worries, what would we do without the ladies? *(The women do not unbend. He goes to the sink, takes a dipperful of water from the pail and pouring it into a basin, washes his hands. Starts to wipe them on the roller towel, turns it for a cleaner place.)* Dirty towels! *(kicks his foot against the pans under the sink)* Not much of a house-keeper, would you say ladies?

MRS. HALE *(stiffly)*: There's a great deal of work to be done on a farm.

COUNTY ATTORNEY: To be sure. And yet *(with a little bow to her)* I know there are some Dickson county farmhouses which do not have such roller towels.

He gives it a pull to expose its full length again.

MRS. HALE: Those towels get dirty awful quick. Men's hands aren't always as clean as they might be.

● ● ● ● ● ● ● ●
"Well, women are used to worrying over trifles."
● ● ● ● ● ● ● ●

COUNTY ATTORNEY: Ah, loyal to your sex, I see. But you and Mrs. Wright were neighbors. I suppose you were friends, too.

MRS. HALE *(shaking her head)*: I've not seen much of her of late years. I've not been in this house—it's more than a year.

COUNTY ATTORNEY: And why was that? You didn't like her?

MRS. HALE: I like her all well enough. Farmers' wives have their hands full, Mr. Henderson. And then—

COUNTY ATTORNEY: Yes—?

MRS. HALE *(looking about)*: It never seemed a very cheerful place.

COUNTY ATTORNEY: No—it's not cheerful. I shouldn't say she had the homemaking instinct.

MRS. HALE: Well, I don't know as Wright had, either.

COUNTY ATTORNEY: You mean that they didn't get on very well?

MRS. HALE: No, I don't mean anything. But I don't think a place'd be any cheer-fuller for John Wright's being in it.

COUNTY ATTORNEY: I'd like to talk more of that a little later. I want to get the lay of things upstairs now.

trifle—something of little value or importance

gallantry—an act of marked courtesy

Trifles 215

FOCUS ON...
LANGUAGE

Glaspell uses dialogue and stage directions to convey much of the information about the characters and what happens in the play. There is not much action. Make a chart listing five facts that surface in the play. Then next to your list, make two columns, one labeled *Stage Directions* and one labeled *Dialogue*. Write the actual dialogue or stage directions in the correct column to show which device the author uses to communicate each event or fact to the reader.

Stage Directions   Dialogue
1.   1.
2.   2.
3.   3.
4.   4.
5.   5.

◆ ◆ ◆ ◆ ◆ ◆ ◆ ◆ ◆ ◆ ◆ ◆ ◆ ◆ ◆ ◆ ◆ ◆

He goes to the left, where three steps lead to a stair door.

SHERIFF: I suppose anything Mrs. Peters does'll be all right. She was to take in some clothes for her, you know, and a few little things. We left in such a hurry yesterday.

COUNTY ATTORNEY: Yes, but I would like to see what you take, Mrs. Peters, and keep an eye out for anything that might be of use to us.

MRS. PETERS: Yes, Mr. Henderson.

The women listen to the men's steps on the stairs, then look about the kitchen.

MRS. HALE: I'd hate to have men coming into my kitchen, snooping around and criticising.

She arranges the pans under the sink which the COUNTY ATTORNEY *had shoved out of place.*

MRS. PETERS: Of course it's no more than their duty.

MRS. HALE: Duty's all right, but I guess that deputy sheriff that came out to make the fire might have got a little of this on. *(gives the roller towel a pull)* Wish I'd thought of that sooner. Seems mean to talk about her for not having things slicked up when she had to come away in such a hurry.

MRS. PETERS *(who has gone to a small table in the left rear corner of the room, and lifted one end of a towel that covers a pan)*: She had bread set.

Stands still.

MRS. HALE *(eyes fixed on a loaf of bread beside the breadbox, which is on a low shelf at the other side of the room. Moves slowly toward it.)*: She was going to put this in there. *(Picks up loaf, then abruptly drops it. In a manner of returning to familiar things.)* It's a shame about her fruit. I wonder if it's all gone. *(Gets up on the chair and looks.)* I think there's some here that's all right, Mrs. Peters. Yes—here; *(holding it toward the window)* this is cherries, too. *(looking again)* I declare I believe that's the only one. *(Gets down, bottle in her hand. Goes to the sink and wipes it off on the outside.)* She'll feel awful bad after all her hard work in the hot weather. I remember the afternoon I put up my cherries last summer.

She puts the bottle on the big kitchen table, center of the room. With a sigh, is about to sit down in the rocking-chair. Before she is seated realizes what chair it is; with a slow look at it, steps back. The chair which she has touched rocks back and forth.

MRS. PETERS: Well, I must get those things from the front room closet. *(She goes to the door at the right, but after looking into the other room, steps back.)* You coming with me, Mrs. Hale? You could help me carry them.

They go in the other room; reappear, MRS. PETERS carrying a dress and skirt, MRS. HALE following with a pair of shoes.

MRS. PETERS: My, it's cold in there.

She puts the clothes on the big table, and hurries to the stove.

MRS. HALE *(examining her skirt)*: Wright was close. I think maybe that's why she kept so much to herself. She didn't even belong to the Ladies Aid. I suppose she felt she couldn't do her part, and then you don't enjoy things when you feel shabby. She used to wear pretty clothes and be lively, when she was Minnie Foster, one of the town girls singing in the choir. But that—oh, that was thirty years ago. This all you was to take in?

MRS. PETERS: She said she wanted an apron. Funny thing to want, for there isn't much to get you dirty in jail,

> ● ● ● ● ● ● ●
>
> "She used to wear pretty clothes and be lively."
>
> ● ● ● ● ● ● ●

goodness knows. But I suppose just to make her feel more natural. She said they was in the top drawer in this cupboard. Yes, here. And then her little shawl that always hung behind the door. *(opens stair door and looks)* Yes, here it is.

Quickly shuts door leading upstairs.

MRS. HALE *(abruptly moving toward her)*: Mrs. Peters?

MRS. PETERS: Yes, Mrs. Hale?

MRS. HALE: Do you think she did it?

MRS. PETERS: *(in a frightened voice)*. Oh, I don't know.

MRS. HALE: Well, I don't think she did. Asking for an apron and her little shawl. Worrying about her fruit.

MRS. PETERS *(Starts to speak, glances up, where footsteps are heard in the room above. In a low voice.)*: Mr. Peters says it looks bad for her. Mr. Henderson is awful sarcastic in a speech and he'll make fun of her sayin' she didn't wake up.

MRS. HALE: Well, I guess John Wright didn't wake when they was slipping that rope under his neck.

MRS. PETERS: No, it's strange. It must have been done awful crafty and still. They say it was such a—funny way to kill a man, rigging it all up like that.

MRS. HALE: That's just what Mr. Hale said. There was a gun in the house. He says that's what he can't understand.

MRS. PETERS: Mr. Henderson said coming out that what was needed for the case was a motive; something to show anger, or—sudden feeling.

MRS. HALE *(who is standing by the table)*: Well, I don't see any signs of tippet—a cape

anger around here. (*She puts her hand on the dish towel which lies on the table, stands looking down at table one half of which is clean, the other half messy.*) It's wiped to here. (*Makes a move as if to finish work, then turns and looks at loaf of bread outside the breadbox. Drops towel. In that voice of coming back to familiar things.*) Wonder how they are finding things upstairs. I hope she had it a little more red-up up there. You know, it seems kind of *sneaking*. Locking her up in town and then coming out here and trying to get her own house to turn against her!

MRS. PETERS: But Mrs. Hale, the law is the law.

MRS. HALE: I s'pose 'tis. (*unbuttoning her coat*) Better loosen up your things, Mrs. Peters. You won't feel them when you go out.

*Mrs. Peters takes off her fur **tippet**, goes to hang it on hook at back of room, stands looking at the under part of the small corner table.*

MRS. PETERS: She was piecing a quilt.

She brings the large sewing basket and they look at the bright pieces.

MRS. HALE: It's log cabin pattern. Pretty, isn't it? I wonder if she was goin' to quilt it or just knot it?

Footsteps have been heard coming down the stairs. The SHERIFF enters followed by HALE and the COUNTY ATTORNEY.

SHERIFF: They wonder if she was going to quilt it or just knot it!

The men laugh; the women look abashed.

COUNTY ATTORNEY (*rubbing his hands over the stove*): Frank's fire didn't do

● ● ● ● ● ● ●

"I wonder if she was goin' to quilt it or just knot it?"

● ● ● ● ● ● ●

much up there, did it? Well, let's go out to the barn and get that cleared up.

The men go outside.

MRS. HALE (*resentfully*): I don't know as there's anything so strange, our takin' up our time with little things while we're waiting for them to get the evidence. (*She sits down at the big table smoothing out a block with decision.*) I don't see as it's anything to laugh about.

MRS. PETERS (*apologetically*): Of course they've got awful important things on their minds.

Pulls up a chair and joins Mrs. Hale at the table.

MRS. HALE (*examining another block*): Mrs. Peters, look at this one. Here, this is the one she was working on, and look at the sewing! All the rest of it has been so nice and even. And look at this! It's all over the place! Why, it looks as if she didn't know what she was about!

After she has said this they look at each other, then start to glance back at the door. After an instant MRS. HALE has pulled at a knot and ripped the sewing.

MRS. PETERS: Oh, what are you doing, Mrs. Hale?

MRS. HALE (*mildly*): Just pulling out a stitch or two that's not sewed very good. (*threading a needle*) Bad sewing always made me fidgety.

MRS. PETERS (*nervously*): I don't think we ought to touch things.

MRS. HALE: I'll just finish up this end. (*suddenly stopping and leaning forward*) Mrs. Peters?

MRS. PETERS: Yes, Mrs. Hale?

MRS. HALE: What do you suppose she was so nervous about?

MRS. PETERS: Oh—I don't know. I don't know as she was nervous. I sometimes sew awful queer when I'm just tired. *(MRS. HALE starts to say something, looks at MRS. PETERS, then goes on sewing.)* Well, I must get these things wrapped up. They may be through sooner than we think. *(putting apron and other things together)* I wonder where I can find a piece of paper, and string.

MRS. HALE: In that cupboard, maybe.

MRS. PETERS *(looking in cupboard)*: Why, here's a birdcage. *(holds it up)* Did she have a bird, Mrs. Hale?

MRS. HALE: Why, I don't know whether she did or not—I've not been here for so long. There was a man around last year selling canaries cheap, but I don't know as she took one; maybe she did. She used to sing real pretty herself.

MRS. PETERS *(glancing around)*: Seems funny to think of a bird here. But she must have had one, or why would she have a cage? I wonder what happened to it.

MRS. HALE: I s'pose maybe the cat got it.

MRS. PETERS: No, she didn't have a cat. She's got that feeling some people have about cats—being afraid of them. My cat got in her room and she was real upset and asked me to take it out.

MRS. HALE: My sister Bessie was like that. Queer, ain't it?

MRS. PETERS *(examining the cage)*: Why, look at this door. It's broke. One hinge is pulled apart.

MRS. HALE *(looking too)*: Looks as if someone must have been rough with it.

MRS. PETERS: Why, yes.

She brings the cage forward and puts it on the table.

MRS. HALE: I wish if they're going to find any evidence they'd be about it. I don't like this place.

MRS. PETERS: But I'm awful glad you came with me, Mrs. Hale. It would be lonesome for me sitting here alone.

MRS. HALE: It would, wouldn't it? *(dropping her sewing)* But I tell you what I do wish, Mrs. Peters. I wish I had come over sometimes when she was here. I—*(looking around the room)*—wish I had.

MRS. PETERS: But of course you were awful busy, Mrs. Hale—your house and your children.

MRS. HALE: I could've come. I stayed away because it weren't cheerful—and that's why I ought to have come. I—I've never liked this place. Maybe because it's down in a hollow and you don't see the road. I dunno what it is but it's a lonesome place and always was. I wish I had come over to see Minnie Foster some-times. I can see now—

Shakes her head.

MRS. PETERS: Well, you mustn't reproach yourself, Mrs. Hale. Somehow we just don't see how it is with other folks until—something comes up.

MRS. HALE: Not having children makes less work—but it makes a quiet house, and Wright out to work all day, and no company when he did come in. Did you know John Wright, Mrs. Peters?

MRS. PETERS: Not to know him; I've seen him in town. They say he was a good man.

MRS. HALE: Yes—good; he didn't drink, and kept his word as well as most, I guess, and paid his debts. But he was a hard man, Mrs. Peters. Just to pass the time of day with him—*(shivers)* Like a raw wind that gets to the bone. *(pauses, her eye falling on the cage)* I should think she would 'a wanted a bird. But what do you suppose went with it?

MRS. PETERS: I don't know, unless it got sick and died.

She reaches over and swings the broken door, swings it again. Both women watch it.

MRS. HALE: You weren't raised round here, were you? *(Mrs. Peters shakes her head.)* You didn't know—her?

MRS. PETERS: Not till they brought her yesterday.

MRS. HALE: She—come to think of it, she was kind of like a bird herself—real sweet and pretty, but kind of timid and—fluttery. How—she—did—change. *(silence; then as if struck by a happy thought and relieved to get back to everyday things)* Tell you what, Mrs. Peters, why don't you take the quilt in with you? It might take up her mind.

MRS. PETERS: Why, I think that's a real nice idea, Mrs. Hale. There couldn't possibly be any objection to it, could there? Now, just what would I take? I wonder if her patches are in here—and her things.

They look in the sewing basket.

MRS. HALE: Here's some red. I expect this has got sewing things in it. *(brings out a fancy box.)* What a pretty box.

● ● ● ● ● ● ● ●
"She was kind of like a bird herself."
● ● ● ● ● ● ● ●

Looks like something somebody would give you. Maybe her scissors are in here. *(Opens box. Suddenly puts her hand to her nose.)* Why— *(MRS. PETERS bends nearer, then turns her face away.)* There's something wrapped up in this piece of silk.

MRS. PETERS: Why, this isn't her scissors.

MRS. HALE *(lifting the silk)*: Oh, Mrs. Peters—it's—

MRS. PETERS *bends closer.*

MRS. PETERS: It's the bird.

MRS. HALE *(jumping up)*: But, Mrs. Peters—look at it! Its neck! Look at its neck! It's all—other side to.

MRS. PETERS: Somebody—wrung—its—neck.

Their eyes meet. A look of growing comprehension, of horror. Steps are heard outside. MRS. HALE slips box under quilt pieces, and sinks into her chair. Enter SHERIFF *and* COUNTY ATTORNEY. MRS. PETERS *rises.*

COUNTY ATTORNEY *(as one turning from serious things to little pleasantries)*: Well, ladies, have you decided whether she was going to quilt it or knot it?

MRS. PETERS: We think she was going to—knot it.

COUNTY ATTORNEY: Well, that's interesting, I'm sure. *(seeing the birdcage)* Has the bird flown?

MRS. HALE *(putting more quilt pieces over the box)*: We think the—cat got it.

COUNTY ATTORNEY *(preoccupied)*: Is there a cat? *(MRS. HALE glances in a quick covert way at MRS. PETERS).*

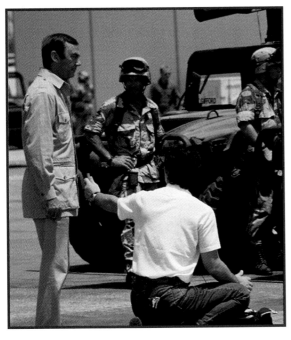

SPOTLIGHT ON...
ACQUIRING INFORMATION

In the play, the sheriff and the county prosecutor are looking for information that might point to a motive for the murder. In your school work and on the job, you may also be called upon to acquire specific information. As you prepare to collect data, ask yourself these questions:

1. What are some likely sources where I can find this information?
2. How can I confirm or verify the information I find?
3. How is this information pertinent to the question or problem I am trying to solve?
4. How can I store this information in a way that I can easily retrieve it?

MRS. PETERS: Well, not *now*. They're superstitious, you know. They leave.

COUNTY ATTORNEY *(to* SHERIFF PETERS, *continuing an interrupted conversation):* No sign at all of anyone having come from the outside. Their own rope. Now let's go up again and go over it piece by piece. *(They start upstairs.)* It would have to have been someone who knew just the—

MRS. PETERS *sits down. The two women sit there not looking at one another, but as if peering into something and at the same time holding back. When they talk now it is in the manner of feeling their way over strange ground, as if afraid of what they are saying, but as if they can not help saying it.*

MRS. HALE: She liked the bird. She was going to bury it in that pretty box.

MRS. PETERS *(in a whisper):* When I was a girl—my kitten—there was a boy took a hatchet, and before my eyes—and before I could get there—*(covers her face an instant)* If they hadn't held me back I would have—*(catches herself, looks upstairs where steps are heard, falters weakly)*—hurt him.

MRS. HALE *(with a slow look around her):* I wonder how it would seem never to have had any children around. *(pause)* No, Wright wouldn't like the bird—a thing that sang. She used to sing. He killed that, too.

MRS. PETERS *(moving uneasily):* We don't know who killed the bird.

MRS. HALE: I knew John Wright.

MRS. PETERS: It was an awful thing was done in this house that night, Mrs. Hale. Killing a man while he slept, slipping a rope around his neck that choked the life out of him.

MRS. HALE: His neck. Choked the life out of him.

Her hand goes out and rests on the birdcage.

MRS. PETERS *(with rising voice):* We don't know who killed him. We don't know.

MRS. HALE *(her own feeling not interrupted):* If there'd been years and years

Trifles

of nothing, then a bird to sing to you, it would be awful—still, after the bird was still.

MRS. PETERS (*something within her speaking*): I know what stillness is. When we homesteaded in Dakota, and my first baby died—after he was two years old, and me with no other then—

MRS. HALE (*moving*): How soon do you suppose they'll be through, looking for the evidence?

MRS. PETERS: I know what stillness is. (*pulling herself back*) The law has got to punish crime, Mrs. Hale.

MRS. HALE (*not as if answering that*): I wish you'd seen Minnie Foster when she wore a white dress with blue ribbons and stood up there in the choir and sang. (*a look around the room*) Oh, I wish I'd come over here once in a while! That was a crime! That was a crime! Who's going to punish that?

MRS. PETERS (*looking upstairs*): We mustn't—take on.

MRS. HALE: I might have known she needed help! I know how things can

be—for women. I tell you, it's queer, Mrs. Peters. We live close together and we live far apart. We all go through the same things—it's all just a different kind of the same thing. (*brushes her eyes; noticing the bottle of fruit, reaches out for it*) If I was you I wouldn't tell her her fruit was gone. Tell her it ain't. Tell her it's all right. Take this in to prove it to her. She—she may never know whether it was broke or not.

MRS. PETERS (*Takes the bottle, looks about for something to wrap it in; takes petticoat from the clothes brought from the other room, very nervously begins winding this around the bottle. In a false voice*): My, it's a good thing the men couldn't hear us. Wouldn't they just laugh! Getting all stirred up over a little thing like a—dead canary. As if that could have anything to do with—with—wouldn't they *laugh*!

The men are heard coming down stairs.

MRS. HALE (*under her breath*): Maybe they would—maybe they wouldn't.

COUNTY ATTORNEY: No, Peters, it's all perfectly clear except a reason for doing it. But you know juries when it comes to women. If there was some definite thing. Something to show—something to make a story about—a thing that would connect up with this strange way of doing it—

The women's eyes meet for an instant. Enter HALE from outer door.

HALE: Well, I've got the team around. Pretty cold out there.

COUNTY ATTORNEY: I'm going to stay here a while by myself. (*to the Sheriff*) You can send Frank out for me, can't you? I want to go over everything. I'm not satisfied that we can't do better.

SHERIFF: Do you want to see what Mrs. Peters is going to take in?

The COUNTY ATTORNEY goes to the table, picks up the apron, laughs.

COUNTY ATTORNEY: Oh, I guess they're not very dangerous things the ladies have picked out. *(Moves a few things about, disturbing the quilt pieces which cover the box. Steps back.)* No, Mrs. Peters doesn't need supervising. For that matter, a sheriff's wife is married to the law. Ever think of it that way, Mrs. Peters?

MRS. PETERS: Not—just that way.

SHERIFF *(chuckling)*: Married to the law. *(moves toward the other room)* I just want you to come in here a minute, George. We ought to take a look at these windows.

COUNTY ATTORNEY *(scoffingly)*: Oh, windows!

SHERIFF: We'll be right out, Mr. Hale.

> "The law has got to punish crime, Mrs. Hale."

HALE *goes outside. The SHERIFF follows the COUNTY ATTORNEY into the other room. Then MRS. HALE rises, hands tight together, looking intensely at MRS. PETERS, whose eyes make a slow turn, finally meeting MRS. HALE's. A moment MRS. HALE holds her, then her own eyes point the way to where the box is concealed. Suddenly MRS. PETERS throws back quilt pieces and tries to put the box in the bag she is wearing. It is too big. She opens box, starts to take bird out, cannot touch it, goes to pieces, stands there helpless. Sound of a knob turning in the other room. MRS. HALE snatches the box and puts it in the pocket of her big coat. Enter COUNTY ATTORNEY and SHERIFF.*

COUNTY ATTORNEY *(facetiously)*: Well, Henry, at least we found out that she was not going to quilt it. She was going to—what is it you call it, ladies?

MRS. HALE *(her hand against her pocket)*: We call it—knot it, Mr. Henderson. ❖

facetiously—joking in an appropriate manner

UNDERSTANDING

1. What evidence in the play can you find to show the kind of husband John Wright was? In what ways did he make the Wright home a pleasant or unpleasant place for Mrs. Wright to live and work?

   The attitudes and behavior of people at home, in a classroom, or on the job help make a place pleasant or cheerless. Physical surroundings, of course, also influence how much people enjoy being in a particular place. Assume you are responsible for making an office or work area pleasant and inviting. Prepare a design for this area. Accompany the design with a written explanation of why your plan includes the features it does. *Workshop 2*

2. The characters in *Trifles* frequently communicate nonverbally, using facial expressions, gestures, and body movement, conscious or not, to get across a message. Find examples of this in the play.

   Keep a record for a day of the nonverbal messages you receive from the people you encounter. Discuss your day's recording of nonverbal messages in a small group. Do your group's records cause you to accept or reject the widespread belief that people often place more trust in the nonverbal messages a person sends than in his or her words? Chart the views of your group and report this to the class.

3. Prepare a time line showing what you believe happened in the Wright residence between the time John Wright came home for dinner and the next day when Lewis Hale stopped by.

   Businesses often use time lines to display how a project will proceed over a certain period. Construct a time line for a project you would like to complete. Perhaps you want to remodel your bedroom or accomplish another task that is long and takes more than a few steps. Break the large task down into smaller tasks and estimate the time you will need to complete each. Use these estimates when planning your time line.

4. The two women, Mrs. Hale and Mrs. Peters, stand up for Mrs. Wright. They choose as women to protect another woman, even though Mrs. Wright is a murderer. What do you think compels them to do this?

   Think about a time when you tried on your own or as a member of a group to solve a problem. Write a description of this event. In your description, explain the problem, various ways it might have been handled, and the solution you finally chose. *Workshop 2*

CONNECTING

1. Some women still feel discriminated against in the workplace. They point at evidence of the "glass ceiling," an invisible barrier of discrimination that keeps them from positions of authority and prestige. Interview three to five working women. Ask for their views on the "glass ceiling." Have they felt discriminated against? If so, how did they handle it? Prepare an oral report based on your findings and present it to your class. *Workshop 19*

2. Working in groups, gather information about the agencies and resources available to or specializing in helping women in your community. Your group may wish to write, for example, to organizations such as the National Organization of Women (NOW) to gain information concerning help and opportunities for women in the United States. Collaboratively research this topic, and then present your findings in the form of a resource booklet to be distributed to women in the school. *Workshops 7 and 11*

3. Working in groups, research the legal implications in the play. Will Mrs. Wright be tried for her husband's death? What might her defense be? Write a script for the court scene Mrs. Wright will have to face. Write parts for the prosecution, defense lawyers, judge, Mrs. Wright, and witnesses who testify about her character and the character of her husband. Perform the skit for your class.

A LAST WORD

No matter how firmly you believe a person's action was wrong, you may not want to see that individual punished if you believe his or her action was justified. Are there any circumstances that you feel would justify a criminal act such as the one Mrs. Wright committed? Would you have turned her in?

ACCENT ON...
FORENSIC SCIENCE

While the men were searching various rooms looking for evidence, the women pieced together the crime and located key evidence right in the kitchen as they discussed the suspect and what they knew about her. In real investigations, criminalists, or forensic scientists, gather evidence at the scene of a crime, analyze it, and present it in court. Many games are now available that allow people to solve a mystery. Find such a game and play it with classmates to solve the mystery.

ON THE JOB
LAW ENFORCEMENT OFFICER

A law enforcement officer or police officer administers the law within a city or township. Like the sheriff in *Trifles*, a police officer has duties that include investigating cases, diffusing potentially dangerous situations, making arrests, and taking charge of prisoners. Police officers need analytical as well as interpersonal skills, problem-solving skills, and the ability to communicate effectively and take action when necessary. In order to become a police officer, a person needs some college coursework and also needs to pass both entrance and physical examinations.

Choosing a Path

- *The Road Not Taken*
- *The Wayfarer*
- *from I Can't Accept Not Trying*

EXPLORING

Each day you make many decisions. Some are small, and some may have serious consequences. What important decisions have influenced your own or your family's life? How would your life or your family's life be changed had a decision been different? Why do you think people decide as they do? For example, how much does luck contribute to choices? How are some decisions shaped by a person's underlying ethical code or religious beliefs? How important is careful thought or deliberation before making important decisions?

THEME CONNECTION... REASONS FOR CHOICES

In "The Wayfarer," "The Road Not Taken," and the excerpt from *I Can't Accept Not Trying*, people make choices. Notice the reasons for these choices. Crane's wayfarer rejects the pathway to truth because its weeds are dangerous knives; it is a difficult path. Frost's traveller prefers the path that "wanted [lacked] wear" and is "less traveled by." Michael Jordan could "have taken the easy path" but selects the difficult path because "if you put in the work, the results will come."

TIME & PLACE

Stephen Crane (1871–1900) and Robert Frost (1874–1963) grew up when the United States was developing inventions that would rapidly transform this country from a nation of farms to a nation of industries. As industries came into existence, so did opportunities for personal success. Many people, among them thousands of immigrants, optimistically strove to achieve their dreams. These three works all emphasize choices to be made in daily life. "The Road Not Taken" captures a quiet, isolated moment as the narrator chooses a path. "The Wayfarer" describes a moral choice; Jordan explains his choice to succeed.

THE WRITER'S CRAFT

SYMBOL

When one thing is itself, and at the same time stands for something entirely different from itself, we say it is a symbol. A national flag is a piece of cloth with a distinctive design. At the same time it stands for, or symbolizes, a nation. A husky is literally a dog; it is also the mascot that symbolizes the University of Washington in Seattle. In all three selections, the pathway or road is itself, and at the same time it stands for, or symbolizes, human life. For centuries literature has used the pathway or road to symbolize life.

The Road Not Taken

Robert Frost

About the Author

Robert Frost (1874–1963) wrote verse that seemed simple and direct, yet dealt with issues of personal integrity, relationships, and courage needed in an often bleak world. Frost spent much of his life in New England, where he attended college and then worked as a mill worker, a teacher, and a farmer for several years. His poetry, first published in England, later found success in the United States. As he became more successful as a writer, he taught and lectured at a number of colleges. Frost's thoughtfully crafted poetry appeals to a variety of readers, and he remains one of America's foremost poets.

Two roads **diverged** in a yellow wood,
And sorry I could not travel both
And be one traveler, long I stood
And looked down one as far as I could
To where it bent in the undergrowth;

Then took the other, as just as fair,
And having perhaps the better claim,
Because it was grassy and wanted wear;
Though as for that, the passing there
Had worn them really about the same,

And both that morning equally lay
In leaves no step had trodden black.
Oh, I kept the first for another day!
Yet knowing how way leads on to way,
I doubted if I should ever come back.

I shall be telling this with a sigh
Somewhere ages and ages hence:
Two roads diverged in a wood, and I—
I took the one less traveled by,
And that has made all the difference. ❖

diverged—
moved in different
directions from a
common point

Choosing a Path

The Wayfarer

Stephen Crane

About the Author

Stephen Crane (1871–1900) distinguished himself in college through his prowess as a baseball player, but he decided on a career in writing, becoming a news reporter and roving correspondent. He is best known for his short stories like "The Open Boat" and "The Bride Comes to Yellow Sky" and his realistic novels *Maggie: A Girl of the Streets* and *The Red Badge of Courage*. Crane's career was cut short when he contracted tuberculosis. He died at the age of thirty.

The wayfarer,
Perceiving the pathway to truth,
Was struck with astonishment.
It was thickly grown with weeds.
"Ha," he said,
"I see that none has passed here
In a long time."
Later he saw that each weed was a singular knife.
"Well," he mumbled at last,
"Doubtless there are other roads." ❖

SPOTLIGHT ON... MAKING DECISIONS

"The Road Not Taken," "The Wayfarer," and *I Can't Accept Not Trying* are about making choices, making decisions. How do you know if you are making a sound decision? Here are some guidelines:
- Define your goal.
- Articulate the problem or situation.
- Itemize the options.
- Analyze the possible outcomes of each alternative.
- Consider your goals and your values.
- Make your decision.
- Evaluate your decision.

from *I Can't Accept Not Trying*
Commitment

Michael Jordan

oming out of high school, if I had been any less committed or had any less desire to achieve, I would have taken the easy path and gone to another school. But I went to North Carolina because I realized that a lot of Dean Smith's players got drafted by NBA teams. People were telling me I should go around the difficult route, but I wasn't about to do that. I had locked in, committed to my goals. I wanted to find out. I wanted to know where I stood.

I've always believed that if you put in the work, the results will come. I don't do things halfheartedly. Because I know if I do, then I can expect halfhearted results. That's why I approached practices the same way I approached games. You can't turn it on and off like a faucet. I couldn't dog it during practice and then, when I needed that extra push late in the game, expect it to be there.

But that's how a lot of people approach things. And that's why a lot of people fail. They sound like they're committed to being the best they can be. They say all the right things, make all the proper appearances. But when it comes right down to it, they're looking for reasons instead of answers.

You see it all the time in professional sports. You can even see it in your friends or business associates. There are a million excuses for not paying the price. "If I was only given a particular opportunity" or "if only the coach, teacher or boss liked me better, I could have accomplished this or that." Nothing but excuses.

Part of this commitment is taking responsibility. That's not to say there aren't obstacles or distractions. If you're trying to achieve, there will be roadblocks. I've had them; everybody has had them. But obstacles don't have to stop you. If you run into a wall, don't turn around and give up. Figure out how to climb it, go through it, or work around it.

I got a very good lesson about distractions my junior year at North Carolina. My sophomore season turned out to be my best in college. Because of that, there were all kinds of expectations during my junior year. What I tried to do was come out and live up to those expectations.

I was trying to live up to everyone else's expectations for me instead of following my own road. I found myself standing around looking for the spectacular dunk, cheating out on the defensive end to get that breakaway situation.

Coach Smith called me in one day and showed me two films, one from the beginning of my sophomore season, the other from the beginning of my junior year. They were totally the opposite. I was looking for shortcuts and that wasn't how I got there. I still had the desire, but I had lost my focus.

You have to stick to your plan. A lot of people try to pull you down to their level because they can't achieve certain things. But very few people get anywhere by taking shortcuts. Very few people win the lottery to gain their wealth. It happens, but the odds certainly aren't with them. More people get it the honest way, by setting goals and committing themselves to achieving those goals.

That's the only way I'd want it anyway. ❖

FOCUS ON...
HEALTH

Among the important decisions you make every day are decisions affecting your health. If you want to make sound decisions about your health, keep a "Fitness and Nutrition" diary. In the diary, set up two sections, one on what you eat, another on physical exercise. Each day, fill out each section in detail. At the end of each day, compare your diet and exercise with the recommendations of doctors and nutritionists. How do you measure up? What should you do to conform to the advice of experts? To know what experts say about diet and exercise, seek out the various newsletters, magazines, and pamphlets which deal with health and fitness.

◆ ◆ ◆ ◆ ◆ ◆ ◆ ◆ ◆ ◆ ◆ ◆ ◆ ◆ ◆ ◆ ◆ ◆ ◆

UNDERSTANDING

● ●

1. In each of the three selections, a speaker explains reasons for making a decision. Find the decision to be made in each and the reason given for that choice.

   All day long you make decisions. Keep track of these decisions for a day, from the time you wake up in the morning until you finish eating lunch. Group these decisions according to how much serious thought or deliberation they require. Write a three-paragraph process essay. In the essay, describe the kinds of decisions you make and explain the characteristics of a serious decision. Also in your essay, give advice on how to consider an important issue carefully so that a good decision results. *Workshop 4*

2. A sense of regret or loss often follows hard decisions. Which lines in "The Road Not Taken" might be interpreted as revealing feelings of loss or regret?

   Develop five questions about decisions and use them to interview adults, especially those your parents' or grandparents' age. Write down their responses. Present the information you gather in a brief oral report. *Workshop 19*

3. The narrator in "The Wayfarer" says the path to truth is like "walking on knives." What does he mean? What choice does he make? What is he saying about how most people handle truth?

   Write an essay in which you define truth, and then explain whether people value truth today. Draw examples from television, movies, modern fiction, newspaper articles, and the behavior of friends or acquaintances. *Workshop 12*

A LAST WORD

If a career path seems difficult to you, will that prevent you from trying it? Do you believe a rewarding career would be worth the difficult choices you might have to make to pursue it? How do you decide if something is worth the necessary commitment?

CONNECTING

1. In high school, you make certain choices about elective classes, activities, and friends. With a group, list the kinds of choices you have faced in school in order to become a better student, athlete, musician, and so on. Prepare a brochure that explains decisions high school students make and gives advice on how to choose well. Share the brochure with eighth grade students who will be attending your school next year. *Workshop 21*

2. People in the workplace are faced with difficult choices every day, from whom to hire to what products and services the company will provide. Identify managers at three local businesses. Send each person a letter in which you inquire about the kinds of decisions made and the decision-making strategies used in that job. Share the responses with the class. *Workshop 11*

WRAP IT UP

UNIT 5

1. The Scotty in "The Scotty Who Knew Too Much" clearly chooses to fight other animals. The narrator of "The Road Not Taken" deliberately chooses the road "less traveled by," while the wayfarer in Stephen Crane's poem avoids the weedy path. What do the choices these characters made say about them? If each of them continues on the path he has chosen, how are their lives likely to turn out?

You have also made choices that will affect your future. With a group, list the kinds of choices you have faced their effects. Prepare a brochure that gives advice on how to choose well.

2. Emily Grierson ("A Rose for Emily") and Mrs. Wright (*Trifles*) both take another person's life. Do you think these characters purposely chose to kill? Use details from the selections to support your opinion.

Think of a time when you found yourself faced with difficult choices. Did you find a positive action to take to help the situation? If so, how? If not, why were you unable to do so? Write an action plan for making tough decisions. Include a list of your priorities in life. Knowing your priorities will make it easier to decide what to do when faced with two options of equal merit. Include reasons for avoiding destructive options.

UNIT
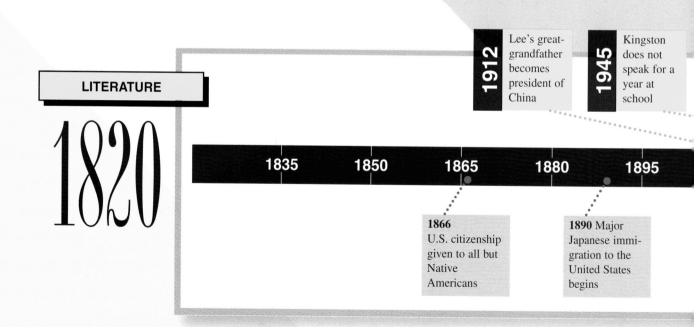

6

FRIENDSHIP AND FAMILY

When something wonderful happens, with whom do you share the good news? Whether it's a close friend, a sibling, or a parent, someone will be eager to hear of your success. This person listens to your concerns and offers support. Ties to friends and family members are among the strongest bonds we form in life, and the inspiration they provide can make a noticeable difference in our professional and personal lives. In addition, the traditions families pass from generation to generation can become a foundation on which to build a rewarding life. The selections in this unit probe the influence of family and friendships on personal growth, development, and adult life.

LITERATURE

1820

1912 Lee's great-grandfather becomes president of China

1945 Kingston does not speak for a year at school

1835   1850   1865   1880   1895

1866 U.S. citizenship given to all but Native Americans

1890 Major Japanese immigration to the United States begins

| 1969 | Momaday's *The Way to Rainy Mountain* is published | 1983 | Walker receives Pulitzer Prize for *The Color Purple* | 1985 | Poet Gary Soto begins writing prose | 1989 | Baker's *The Good Times* is published |

2000

1925   1940   1955   1970   1985

1933 Great Depression closes thousands of schools

1940 Chinese American population moves into second generation

1954 U.S. Supreme Court rules on *Brown v. Board of Education*

1957 *Leave It to Beaver* T.V. show airs

1995 United States, Mexico and others sign the NAFTA treaty

LIFE and WORK

Everyday Use

EXPLORING

Family relationships are complicated enough to keep advice columnists such as Ann Landers very busy. Parents and their children often fail to understand one another, and siblings frequently disagree. Describe the kinds of family relationships you have read about or observed. Does it seem that certain qualities make brothers and sisters friends? What attitudes or actions cause parents and their children to be close? For what reasons do you dislike or enjoy family get-togethers on holidays or vacations? Discuss the get-togethers you have experienced or heard about. What made these succeed or fail?

THEME CONNECTION...
FAMILY TIES

"Everyday Use" portrays connections among family members. Walker carefully explores a mother's relationship with her daughters, the interaction of two sisters, and the regard people have for their ancestors. In the story Walker suggests that a family has the potential to become either a community whose members share experiences and a common past, or a group of separate individuals alienated from one another. Ironically, Dee, who seeks her heritage, overlooks the importance of connecting with living family members.

TIME & PLACE

"Everyday Use" takes place in the late 1960s or early 1970s, when voices everywhere called for civil rights. Martin Luther King, Jr. inspired a nation to demand genuine equality; civil rights activists worked in the South to register black voters; Stokely Carmichael coined the phrase "black power"; and the Black Muslims, a radical political organization, became influential. The story's action takes place in the Southern countryside, where Maggie and her mother live together in a tin-roofed, three-room shack with roughly cut holes for windows and hard clay for a yard.

THE WRITER'S CRAFT
FREE ASSOCIATION

Walker wishes to reveal the mother's inner thoughts and to describe action. Therefore, Walker makes the mother the narrator, and she uses free association to interrupt the mother's story. Free association occurs when something, anything—an idea, word, object, person, musical phrase, or incident—suddenly interrupts a train of thought and sends the mind in a different direction. Because of free association, the mother's narrative does not follow an unbroken line from past to present. Instead, chronological order is interrupted, and the story ranges over various times and topics.

Everyday Use

Alice Walker

I will wait for her in the yard that Maggie and I made so clean and wavy yesterday afternoon. A yard like this is more comfortable than most people know. It is not just a yard. It is like an extended living room. When the hard clay is swept clean as a floor and the fine sand around the edges lined with tiny, irregular grooves, anyone can come and sit and look up into the elm tree and wait for the breezes that never come inside the house.

Maggie will be nervous until after her sister goes: she will stand hopelessly in corners, homely and ashamed of the burn scars down her arms and legs, eyeing her sister with a mixture of envy and awe. She thinks her sister has held life always in the palm of one hand, that "no" is a word the world never learned to say to her.

You've no doubt seen those TV shows where the child who has "made it" is confronted, as a surprise, by her own mother and father, tottering in weakly from backstage. (A pleasant surprise, of course: What would they do if parent and child came on the show only to curse out and insult each other?) On TV, mother and child embrace and smile into each other's faces. Sometimes, the mother and father weep; the child wraps them in her arms and leans across the table to tell how she would not have made it without their help. I have seen these programs.

Sometimes I dream a dream in which Dee and I are suddenly brought together on a TV program of this sort. Out of a dark and soft-seated limousine I am ushered into a bright room filled with many people. There I meet a smiling, gray, sporty man like Johnny Carson who shakes my hand and tells me what a fine girl I have. Then we are on the stage, and Dee is embracing me with tears in her eyes. She pins on my dress a large orchid, even though she has told me once that she thinks orchids are tacky flowers.

In real life I am a large, big-boned woman with rough, man-working hands. In the winter I wear flannel nightgowns to bed and overalls during the day. I can kill and clean a hog as mercilessly as a man. My fat keeps me hot in zero weather. I can work outside all day, breaking ice to get water for washing; I can eat pork liver cooked over the open fire minutes after it comes steaming from the hog. One winter I knocked a bull calf straight in the brain between the eyes with a sledgehammer and had the meat hung up to chill before nightfall. But of course all this does not show on television. I am the way my daughter would want me to be: a hundred pounds lighter, my skin like an uncooked barley pancake. My hair glistens in the hot, bright lights. Johnny Carson has much to do to keep up with my quick and witty tongue.

But that is a mistake. I know even before I wake up. Who ever knew a Johnson with a quick tongue? Who can even imagine me looking a strange white man in the eye? It seems to me I have talked to them always with one foot raised in flight, and with my head turned in whichever way is farthest from them. Dee, though. She would always look anyone in the eye. Hesitation was no part of her nature.

sidle—to walk with one side slightly to the front, instead of facing straight forward

"How do I look, Mama?" Maggie says, showing just enough of her thin body enveloped in pink skirt and red blouse for me to know she's there, almost hidden by the door.

"Come out into the yard," I say.

Have you ever seen a lame animal, perhaps a dog run over by some careless person rich enough to own a car, **sidle** up to someone who is ignorant enough to be kind to him? That is the way my Maggie walks. She has been like this, chin on chest, eyes on ground, feet in shuffle, ever since the fire that burned the other house to the ground.

Dee is lighter than Maggie, with nicer hair and a fuller figure. She's a woman now, though sometimes I forget. How long ago was it that the other house burned? Ten, twelve years? Sometimes I can still hear the flames and feel Maggie's arms sticking to me, her hair smoking and her dress falling off her in little black papery flakes. Her eyes seemed stretched open, blazed open by the flames reflected in them. And Dee. I see her standing off under the sweet gum tree she used to dig gum out of; a look of concentration on her face as she watched the last dingy gray board of the house fall in toward the red-hot brick chimney. Why don't you dance around the ashes? I'd wanted to ask her. She had hated the house that much.

I used to think she hated Maggie, too. But that was before we raised the money, the church and me, to send her to Augusta to school. She used to read to us without pity; forcing words, lies, other folks' habits, whole lives upon us two, sitting trapped and ignorant underneath her voice. She washed us in a river of make-believe, burned us with a lot of knowledge we didn't necessarily need to know. Pressed

● ● ● ● ● ● ●
She washed us in a river of make-believe…
● ● ● ● ● ●

us to her with the serious way she read, to shove us away at just the moment, like dimwits, we seemed about to understand.

Dee wanted nice things. A yellow organdy dress to wear to her graduation from high school; black pumps to match a green suit she'd made from an old suit somebody gave me. She was determined to stare down any disaster in her efforts. Her eyelids would not flicker for minutes at a time. Often I fought off the temptation to shake her. At sixteen she had a style of her own—and knew what style was.

I never had an education myself. After second grade the school was closed down. Don't ask me why: in 1927 colored asked fewer questions than they do now. Sometimes Maggie reads to me. She stumbles along good-naturedly but can't see well. She knows she is not bright. Like good looks and money, quickness passed her by. She will marry John Thomas (who has mossy teeth in an earnest face), and then I'll be free to sit here and I guess just sing church songs to myself. Although I never was a good singer. Never could carry a tune. I was always better at a man's job. I used to love to milk till I was hooked in the side in '49. Cows are soothing and slow and don't bother you, unless you try to milk them the wrong way.

I have deliberately turned my back on the house. It is three rooms, just like the one that burned, except the roof is tin; they don't make shingle roofs any more. There are no real windows, just some holes cut in the sides, like the portholes in a ship, but not round and not square, with rawhide holding the shutters up on the outside. This house is in a pasture, too, like the other one.

No doubt when Dee sees it she will want to tear it down. She wrote me once that no matter where we "choose" to live, she will manage to come see us. But she will never bring her friends. Maggie and I thought about this, and Maggie asked me, "Mama, when did Dee ever *have* any friends?"

She had a few. **Furtive** boys in pink shirts hanging about on washday after school. Nervous girls who never laughed. Impressed with her they worshiped the well-turned phrase, the cute shape, the scalding humor that erupted like bubbles in lye. She read to them.

When she was courting Jimmy T, she didn't have much time to pay to us, but turned all her faultfinding power on him. He *flew* to marry a cheap gal from a family of ignorant flashy people. She hardly had time to **recompose** herself.

When she comes I will meet—but there they are!

Maggie attempts to make a dash for the house, in her shuffling way, but I stay her with my hand. "Come back here," I say. And she stops and tries to dig a well in the sand with her toe.

It is hard to see them clearly through the strong sun. But even the first glimpse of leg out of the car tells me it is Dee. Her feet were always neat-looking, as if God himself had shaped them with a certain style. From the other side of the car comes a short, stocky man. Hair is all over his head a foot long and hanging from his chin like a kinky mule tail. I hear Maggie suck in her breath. "Uhnnnh" is what it sounds like. Like when you see the wriggling end of a snake just in front of your foot on the road. "Uhnnnh."

Dee next. A dress down to the ground, in this hot weather. A dress so loud it hurts my eyes. There are yellows and oranges enough to throw back the light of the sun. I feel my whole face warming from the heat waves it throws out. Earrings gold, too, and hanging

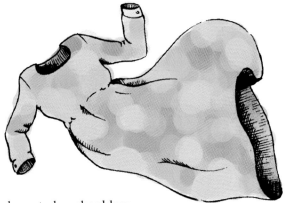

down to her shoulders. Bracelets dangling and making noises when she moves her arm up to shake the folds of the dress out of her armpits. The dress is loose and flows, and as she walks closer, I like it. I hear Maggie go "Uhnnnh" again. It is her sister's hair. It stands straight up like the wool on a sheep. It is black as night, and around the edges are two long pigtails that rope about like small lizards disappearing behind her ears.

"Wa-su-zo-Tean-o!" she says, coming on in that gliding way the dress makes her move. The short, stocky fellow, with the hair to his navel is all grinning, and he follows up with "Asalamalakim, my mother and sister!" He moves to hug Maggie, but she falls back, right up against the back of my chair. I feel her trembling there, and when I look up I see the perspiration falling off her chin.

"Don't get up," says Dee. Since I am stout it takes something of a push. You can see me trying to move a second or two before I make it. She turns, showing white heels through her sandals, and goes back to the car. Out she peeks next with a Polaroid. She stoops down quickly and lines up picture after picture of me sitting there in front of the house with Maggie cowering behind me. She never takes a shot without making sure the house is included. When a cow comes nibbling around the edge of the yard, she snaps it and me and Maggie and

furtive—sly

recompose— to restore to composure, calm

In the story, the narrator and Maggie are unfamiliar with the Black Muslim greeting "Asalamalakim" and handshake that Dee's companion offers. You, too, may be unfamiliar with the practices and traditions of various ethnic groups. To work successfully with people from culturally diverse backgrounds, always seek to understand them.

- Recognize the value of the ethnic, social, and educational backgrounds of the people who work with you.
- Understand and tolerate different views and unfamiliar approaches to situations.
- Learn about and understand the beliefs and values of others.

the house. Then she puts the Polaroid in the back seat of the car and comes up and kisses me on the forehead.

Meanwhile Asalamalakim is going through the motions with Maggie's hand. Maggie's hand is as limp as a fish, and probably as cold, despite the sweat, and she keeps trying to pull it back. It looks like Asalamalakim wants to shake hands but wants to do it fancy. Or maybe he don't know how people shake hands. Anyhow, he soon gives up on Maggie.

"Well," I say. "Dee."

"No, Mama," she says. "Not 'Dee,' Wangero Leewanika Kemanjo!"

"What happened to 'Dee'?" I wanted to know.

"She's dead," Wangero said. "I couldn't bear it any longer, being named after the people who oppress me."

"You know as well as me you was named after your Aunt Dicie," I said. Dicie is my sister. She named Dee. We called her "Big Dee" after Dee was born.

"But who was she named after?" asked Wangero.

"I guess after Grandma Dee," I said.

"And who was she named after?" asked Wangero.

"Her mother," I said, and saw Wangero was getting tired. "That's about as far back as I can trace it," I said. Though, in fact, I probably could have carried it back beyond the Civil War through the branches.

"Well," said Asalamalakim, "there you are."

"Uhnnnh," I heard Maggie say.

"There I was not," I said, "before 'Dicie' cropped up in our family, so why should I try to trace it that far back?"

He just stood there grinning, looking down on me like somebody inspecting a Model A car. Every once in a while he and Wangero sent eye signals over my head.

"How do you pronounce this name?" I asked.

"You don't have to call me by it if you don't want to," said Wangero.

"Why shouldn't I?" I asked. "If that's what you want us call you, we'll call you."

"I know it might sound awkward at first," said Wangero.

"I'll get used to it," I said. "Ream it out again."

Well, soon we got the name out of the way. Asalamalakim had a name twice as long and three times as hard. After I tripped over it two or three times he told me to just call him Hakim-a-barber. I wanted to ask him was he a barber, but I didn't really think he was, so I didn't ask.

"You must belong to those beef-cattle peoples down the road," I said. They said "Asalamalakim" when they met you, too, but they didn't shake hands. Always too busy: feeding the cattle, fixing the fences, putting up salt-lick shelters, throwing down hay. When the white folks poisoned some of the herd, the men stayed up all night with rifles in their hands. I walked a mile and a half just to see the sight.

Hakim-a-barber said, "I accept some of their doc-trines, but farming and raising cattle is not my style." (They didn't tell me, and I didn't ask, whether Wangero [Dee] had really gone and married him.)

We sat down to eat, and right away he said he didn't eat collards, and pork was unclean. Wangero, though, went on through the chitlins and corn bread, the greens and everything else. She talked a blue streak over the sweet potatoes. Everything delighted her. Even the fact that we still used the benches her daddy made for the table when we couldn't afford to buy chairs.

"Oh, Mama!" she cried. Then turned to Hakim-a-barber. "I never knew how lovely these benches are. You can feel the rump prints," she said, running her hands under-neath her and along the bench. Then she gave a sigh, and her hand closed over Grandma Dee's butter dish. "That's it!" she said. "I knew there was something I wanted to ask you if I could have." She jumped up from the table and went over in the corner where the churn stood, the milk in it **clabber** by now. She looked at the churn and looked at it.

"This churn top is what I need," she said. "Didn't Uncle Buddy whittle it out of a tree you all used to have?"

"Yes," I said.

"Uh huh," she said happily. "And I want the **dasher**, too."

"Uncle Buddy whittle that, too?" asked the barber.

Dee (Wangero) looked up at me.

"Aunt Dee's first husband whittled the dash," said Maggie so low you almost couldn't hear her. "His name was Henry, but they called him Stash."

"Maggie's brain is like an elephant's," Wangero said, laughing. "I can use the churn top as a centerpiece for the alcove table," she said, sliding a plate over the churn, "and I'll think of something artistic to do with the dasher."

When she finished wrap-ping the dasher, the handle stuck out. I took it for a moment in my hands. You didn't even have to look close to see where hands pushing the dasher up and down to make butter had left a kind of sink in the wood. In fact, there were a lot of small sinks; you could see where thumbs and fingers had sunk into the wood. It was beautiful light yellow wood, from a tree that grew in the yard where Big Dee and Stash had lived.

After dinner Dee (Wangero) went to the trunk at the foot of my bed and started rifling through it. Maggie hung back in the kitchen over the dishpan. Out came Wangero with two quilts. They had been pieced by Grandma Dee, and then Big Dee and me had hung them on the quilt frames on the front porch and quilted them. One was in the Lone Star pattern. The other was Walk Around the Mountain. In both of them were scraps of dresses Grandma Dee had worn fifty and more years ago. Bits

> ● ● ● ● ● ● ●
> ## She'd probably be backward enough to put them to everyday use.
> ● ● ● ● ● ● ●

clabber—sour milk that has thickened or curdled

dasher—a device with blades for agitating a liquid, as milk in a churn

FOCUS ON...
HOME ECONOMICS

The narrator in the story refers to quilt patterns such as Lone Star and Walk Around the Mountain. What do such patterns look like? How many pieces are needed for each pattern, how many pieces can be cut from a yard, and how many yards of different fabrics would be needed for the quilt? Research these two quilt patterns and find out how each quilt is designed. Write a short explanation of each process, and draw a diagram to show how each design is pieced to complete the pattern.

◆ ◆ ◆ ◆ ◆ ◆ ◆ ◆ ◆ ◆ ◆ ◆ ◆ ◆ ◆ ◆ ◆

and pieces of Grandpa Jarrell's Paisley shirts. And one teeny faded blue piece, about the size of a penny matchbox, that was from Great Grandpa Ezra's uniform that he wore in the Civil War.

"Mama," Wangero said sweet as a bird. "Can I have these old quilts?"

I heard something fall in the kitchen, and a minute later the kitchen door slammed.

"Why don't you take one or two of the others?" I asked. "These old things was just done by me and Big Dee from some tops your grandma pieced before she died."

"No," said Wangero. "I don't want those. They are stitched around the borders by machine."

"That'll make them last better," I said.

"That's not the point," said Wangero. "These are all pieces of dresses Grandma used to wear. She did all this stitching by hand. Imagine!" She held the quilts securely in her arms, stroking them.

"Some of the pieces, like those lavender ones, come from old clothes her mother handed down to her," I said, moving to touch the quilts. Dee (Wangero) moved back just enough so that I couldn't reach the quilts. They already belonged to her.

"Imagine!" she breathed again, clutching them closely to her bosom.

"The truth is," I said, "I promised to give them quilts to Maggie, for when she marries John Thomas."

She gasped like a bee had stung her.

"Maggie can't appreciate these quilts!" she said. "She'd probably be backward enough to put them to everyday use."

"I reckon she would," I said. "God knows I been saving 'em for long enough with nobody using 'em. I hope she will!" I didn't want to bring up how I had offered Dee (Wangero) a quilt when she went away to college. Then she had told me they were old-fashioned, out of style.

"But they're *priceless*!" she was saying now, furiously; for she has a temper. "Maggie would put them on the bed, and in five years they'd be in rags. Less than that!"

"She can always make some more," I said. "Maggie knows how to quilt."

Dee (Wangero) looked at me with hatred. "You just will not understand. The point is these quilts, *these* quilts!"

"Well," I said, stumped. "What would *you* do with them?"

"Hang them," she said. As if that was the only thing you *could* do with quilts.

Maggie by now was standing in the door. I could almost hear the sound her feet made as they scraped over each other.

"She can have them, Mama," she said, like somebody used to never winning anything or having anything reserved for her. "I can 'member Grandma Dee without the quilts."

I looked at her hard. She had filled her bottom lip with checkerberry snuff, and it gave her face a kind of dopey, hangdog look. It was Grandma Dee and Big Dee who taught her how to quilt herself. She stood there with her scarred hands hidden in the folds of her skirt. She looked at her sister with something like fear, but she wasn't mad at her. This was Maggie's portion. This was the way she knew God to work.

When I looked at her like that something hit me in the top of my head and ran down to the soles of my feet. Just like when I'm in church and the spirit of God touches me and I get happy and shout. I did something I never had done before: hugged Maggie to me, then dragged her on into the room, snatched the quilts out of Miss Wangero's hands and dumped them into Maggie's lap. Maggie just sat there on my bed with her mouth open.

"Take one or two of the others," I said to Dee.

But she turned without a word and went out to Hakim-a-barber.

"You just don't understand," she said, as Maggie and I came out to the car.

"What don't I understand?" I wanted to know.

"Your heritage," she said. And then she turned to Maggie, kissed her, and said, "You ought to try to make something of yourself, too, Maggie. It's really a new day for us. But from the way you and Mama still live, you'd never know it."

She put on some sunglasses that hid everything above the tip of her nose and her chin.

Maggie smiled; maybe at the sunglasses. But a real smile, not scared. After we watched the car dust settle, I asked Maggie to bring me a dip of snuff. And then the two of us sat there just enjoying, until it was time to go in the house and go to bed. ❖

ACCENT ON...
CLOTHING CONSTRUCTION
• •

In the story, the narrator comments on Dee's brightly colored print dress, "a dress so loud it hurts my eyes." The narrator likes it for its loose, flowing style. Design clothing for yourself in a style that reflects your own taste. Determine what kind of apparel it will be. Then create a design board that provides detailed instructions for how the outfit will look. Note design, color, fabric, and assembly directions.

ON THE JOB
• • • • • • • • • • • • • •
LITERACY PARA-PROFESSIONAL
• • • • • • • • • • • • • •

To work in adult education, most people need a college degree. However, a paraprofessional job teaching literacy requires little more than a desire to teach, an aptitude for working with people, and several months of on-the-job training. Teaching literacy entails helping adult non-readers learn to read. To teach adults the alphabet and how to recognize words, paraprofessionals need certain skills. They should follow instructions carefully, communicate well orally and in writing, and have good interpersonal skills. Familiarity with computer-aided instruction programs is also helpful.

UNDERSTANDING

1. When Maggie's mother hugs her for the first time, the mother is experiencing an epiphany—a sudden flash of recognition. Locate information in the text that indicates that the mother sees Maggie's essence, her real nature. Tell in writing about a time when you had an epiphany, a moment when you suddenly understood something. ***Workshops 1 and 2***

2.  In telling the story, the mother reveals a great deal about herself. For example, she comments on her own appearance, things she knows how to do, her longings, and attitudes. Gather from the text a complete list of the mother's various characteristics.

   Working collaboratively, create a job description for the ideal parent. In your description, include some of the mother's traits in "Everyday Use," such as physical strength, special skills, and commitment to family. ***Workshop 3***

3. Alice Walker's story shows readers two ways to define "heritage." The mother and Maggie think of "heritage" very differently than Dee does. In fact, Dee accuses her mother of not understanding her own heritage. Explain the two ways of viewing heritage that emerge from "Everyday Use."

   Think of something from the past that is part of your own cultural heritage. In an essay, describe this event, place, object, or person from the past and describe the meaning it holds for you today. ***Workshop 3***

A LAST WORD

If we are not familiar with our "roots," but we wish to discover our heritage, our families can help us do so. How can we look beyond our busy daily lives and learn about our heritage from family members who are near us every day?

CONNECTING

1. Walker writes about Dee's personal yearning for something better than life in the rural South. "It's really a new day for us," Dee proclaims. She tells her sister, "You ought to try to make something of yourself, too, Maggie." Gather information about the civil rights movement in the United States from its beginning stages to the present. What leaders, laws, events, or actions made it possible for minorities to hope for "a new day"? How much freedom do minorities enjoy now? Write a report and prepare a time line. ***Workshop 18***

2. Although they are sisters, Maggie and Dee differ greatly—in the way they look, walk, dress, read, and regard their heritage. Both Maggie and Dee will presumably have to work for a living. Think of four qualities that good workers should possess. Compare your list with those developed by two of your classmates. As a group, produce a final list of the traits that define good workers. Discuss how Maggie and Dee measure up against your group's view of qualities necessary in a good worker. ***Workshop 12***

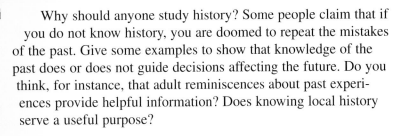

from *Growing Up*

EXPLORING

● ●

Why should anyone study history? Some people claim that if you do not know history, you are doomed to repeat the mistakes of the past. Give some examples to show that knowledge of the past does or does not guide decisions affecting the future. Do you think, for instance, that adult reminiscences about past experiences provide helpful information? Does knowing local history serve a useful purpose?

THEME CONNECTION...
PARENTS AND CHILDREN

As Russell Baker sits at his mother's bedside, he regrets not having long ago asked her to tell him about her youth. Baker explains that the more children know of their parents' early experiences, the better these children will understand themselves. "We all come from the past, and children ought to know what it was that went into their making."

TIME & PLACE

In "Who We Are" Russell Baker remembers his mother. He describes visiting her first in a Baltimore hospital after she had a serious fall in 1977, and later when she was bedridden in a nursing home. He regrets that her senility makes it impossible for him to connect with her. He regrets that he did not seek to learn about her youth years earlier, when she might have told him a great deal. As he visits his ailing mother and contemplates her condition, Baker recognizes his mother's special strengths, foibles, and uniqueness. He also meditates on the past, the suffering of old age, and the links that should connect parents and children.

THE WRITER'S CRAFT

SOUNDING NATURAL

Russell Baker is a Pulitzer Prize-winning journalist. As a journalist, he must capture and hold the reader's interest. The reader will toss aside the newspaper if its sentences are unfamiliar and confusing. Baker's sentences, even long ones, are uncomplicated, as in this example: "She ran after squawking chickens, an axe in her hand, determined on a beheading that would put dinner in the pot." His dialogue sounds natural and realistic. Notice the mother's familiar way of talking: "Guess where I came from today? . . . All the way from New Jersey . . ." Like E. B. White, Baker seeks simple, exact words and sentences to communicate what he observes and thinks.

● ●

from *Growing Up*
Who We Are

Russell Baker

About the Author

Russell Baker won the 1982 Pulitzer Prize for biography/ autobiography with his book *Growing Up*. His life began in the rural mountains of Virginia in 1925. He spent his boyhood in a number of locations, barely a step ahead of adversity during the Depression, as his widowed mother raised him and his sister to "make something" of themselves. In eleventh grade, Baker discovered his calling as a writer. After college and a stint in the Navy, Baker got his first job as a newspaper reporter on the *Baltimore Sun*. He became a regular columnist in 1962 and has won a number of journalistic awards and honors.

formidable—having qualities that discourage approach or attack

t the age of eighty my mother had her last bad fall, and after that her mind wandered free through time. Some days she went to weddings and funerals that had taken place half a century earlier. On others she presided over family dinners cooked on Sunday afternoons for children who were now gray with age.

Through all this she lay in bed but moved across time, traveling among the dead decades with a speed and ease beyond the gift of physical science.

"Where's Russell?" she asked one day when I came to visit at the nursing home.

"I'm Russell," I said. She gazed at this improbably overgrown figure out of an inconceivable future and promptly dismissed it.

"Russell's only this big," she said, holding her hand, palm down, two feet from the floor. That day she was a young country wife with chickens in the backyard and a view of hazy blue Virginia mountains behind the apple orchard, and I was a stranger old enough to be her father.

Early one morning she phoned me in New York. "Are you coming to my funeral today?" she asked.

It was an awkward question with which to be awakened. "What are you talking

about, for God's sake?" was the best reply I could manage.

"I'm being buried today," she declared briskly, as though announcing an important social event.

"I'll phone you back," I said and hung up, and when I did phone back she was all right, although she wasn't all right, of course, and we all knew she wasn't.

She had always been a small woman— short, light-boned, delicately structured— but now, under the white hospital sheet, she was becoming tiny. I thought of a doll with huge, fierce eyes. There had always been a fierceness in her. It showed in that angry, challenging thrust of the chin when she issued an opinion, and a great one she had always been for issuing opinions.

"I tell people exactly what's on my mind," she had been fond of boasting. "I tell them what I think, whether they like it or not." Often they had not liked it. She could be sarcastic to people in whom she detected evidence of the ignoramus or the fool.

"It's not always good policy to tell people exactly what's on your mind," I used to caution her.

"If they don't like it, that's too bad," was her customary reply, "because that's the way I am."

And so she was. A **formidable** woman. Determined to speak her mind, determined to have her way, determined to bend those who opposed her. In that time when I had known her best, my mother had hurled herself at life with chin thrust forward, eyes blazing, and an energy that made her seem always on the run.

She ran after squawking chickens, an axe in her hand, determined on a beheading that would put dinner in the pot. She ran when she made the beds, ran when she set the table. One Thanksgiving she burned herself badly when, running up from the cellar oven with the ceremonial turkey, she tripped on the stairs and tumbled back down, ending at the bottom in the debris of giblets, hot gravy, and battered turkey. Life was combat, and victory was not to the lazy, the timid, the **slugabed**, the drugstore cowboy, the **libertine**, the mushmouth afraid to tell people exactly what was on his mind whether people liked it or not. She ran.

But now the running was over. For a time I could not accept the inevitable. As I sat by her bed, my impulse was to argue her back to reality. On my first visit to the hospital in Baltimore, she asked who I was.

"Russell," I said.

"Russell's way out west," she advised me.

"No, I'm right here."

"Guess where I came from today?" was her response.

"Where?"

"All the way from New Jersey."

"When?"

"Tonight."

"No. You've been in the hospital for three days," I insisted.

"I suggest the thing to do is calm down a little bit," she replied. "Go over to the house and shut the door."

Now she was years deep into the past, living in the neighborhood where she had settled forty years earlier, and she had just been talking with Mrs. Hoffman, a neighbor across the street.

"It's like Mrs. Hoffman said today: The children always wander back to where they come from," she remarked.

"Mrs. Hoffman has been dead for fifteen years."

"Russ got married today," she replied.

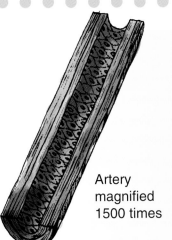

Artery magnified 1500 times

FOCUS ON... SCIENCE

Baker's mother was diagnosed as having "hardening of the arteries," also known as arteriosclerosis. Much more is now known about circulatory problems and their effects on memory and brain function. Working with biology students, find out about the various forms of arteriosclerosis and their causes, effects, treatment, and prevention. Write your findings in the form of a brief report, and include illustrations, if possible.

"I got married in 1950," I said, which was the fact.

"The house is unlocked," she said.

So it went until a doctor came by to give one of those oral quizzes that medical men apply in such cases. She failed catastrophically, giving wrong answers or none at all to "What day is this?" "Do you know where you are?" "How old are you?" and so on. Then, a surprise.

"When is your birthday?" he asked.

"November 5, 1897," she said. Correct. Absolutely correct.

"How do you remember that?" the doctor asked.

"Because I was born on Guy Fawkes Day," she said.

"Guy Fawkes?" asked the doctor. "Who is Guy Fawkes?"

She replied with a rhyme I had heard her recite time and again over the years when the subject of her birth date arose:

"Please to remember the Fifth of November,
Gunpowder treason and plot.
I see no reason why gunpowder treason
Should ever be forgot."

Then she glared at this young doctor so ill informed about Guy Fawkes' failed scheme

slugabed—one who stays in bed after his usual time of getting up

libertine—a person who is unrestrained by convention or morality

to blow King James off his throne with barrels of gunpowder in 1605. She had been a schoolteacher, after all, and knew how to glare at a **dolt**. "You may know a lot about medicine, but you obviously don't know any history," she said. Having told him exactly what was on her mind, she left us again.

The doctors diagnosed a hopeless **senility**. Not unusual, they said, "Hardening of the arteries" was the explanation for laymen. I thought it was more complicated than that. For ten years or more the ferocity with which she had once attacked life had been turning to a rage against the weakness, the boredom, and the absence of love that too much age had brought her. Now, after the last bad fall, she seemed to have broken chains that imprisoned her in a life she had come to hate and to return to a time inhabited by people who loved her, a time in which she was needed. Gradually I understood. It was the first time in years I had seen her happy.

She had written a letter three years earlier which explained more than "hardening of the arteries." I had gone down from New York to Baltimore, where she lived, for one of my infrequent visits and, afterwards, had written her with some **banal** advice to look for the silver lining, to count her blessings instead of burdening others with her miseries. I suppose what it really amounted to was a threat that if she was not more cheerful during my visits I would not come to see her very often. Sons are capable of such letters. This one was written out of a childish faith in the eternal strength of parents, a naive belief that age and wear could be overcome by an effort of will, that all she needed was a good pep talk to recharge a flagging spirit. It was such a foolish, innocent idea, but one thinks of parents differently from other people. Other people can become frail and break, but not parents.

She wrote back in an unusually cheery vein intended to demonstrate, I suppose, that she was mending her ways. She was never a woman to apologize, but for one moment with the pen in her hand she came very close. Referring to my visit, she wrote: "If I seemed unhappy to you at times—" Here she drew back, reconsidered, and said something quite different:

"If I seemed unhappy to you at times, I am, but there's really nothing anyone can do about it, because I'm just so very tired and lonely that I'll just go to sleep and forget it." She was then seventy-eight.

Now, three years later, after the last bad fall, she had managed to forget the fatigue and loneliness and, in these free-wheeling excursions back through time, to recapture happiness. I soon stopped trying to wrest her back to what I considered the real world and tried to travel along with her on those fantastic swoops into the past. One day when I arrived at her bedside she was radiant.

"Feeling good today," I said.

"Why shouldn't I feel good?" she asked. "Papa's going to take me up to Baltimore on the boat today."

At that moment she was a young girl standing on a wharf at Merry Point, Virginia, waiting for the Chesapeake Bay steamer with her father, who had been dead sixty-one years. William Howard Taft was in the White House, Europe still drowsed in the dusk of the great century of peace, America was a young country, and the future stretched before it in beams of crystal sunlight. "The greatest country on God's green earth," her father might have said, if I had been able to step into my mother's time machine and join him on the wharf with the satchels packed for Baltimore.

I could imagine her there quite clearly. She was wearing a blue dress with big puffy sleeves and long black stockings. There was a ribbon in her hair and a big bow tied on the side of her head. There had been a childhood photograph in her

SPOTLIGHT ON...
INTERVIEWING

In his essay, Baker laments not staying in touch with his mother more and not finding out about her past. One way to find out about a person is to conduct an interview. Here are some tips to keep in mind whether you are interviewing a member of the family or someone you hardly know:

1. What information do you hope to get from this interview? Make a list of questions.
2. Do your homework. List what you already know about this person.
3. Ask the person for the interview at a convenient time for both of you. If you wish to tape the interview, get the person's permission first.
4. Take notes during the interview, even if you are taping it. Note the person's mood or tone, humor, and so on.
5. Write a summary of the interview.
6. Be sure to thank the person for meeting with you.

bedroom which showed all this, although the colors of course had been added years later by a restorer who tinted the picture.

About her father, my grandfather, I could only guess, and indeed, about the girl on the wharf with the bow in her hair, I was merely sentimentalizing. Of my mother's childhood and her people, of their time and place, I knew very little. A world had lived and died, and though it was part of my blood and bone I knew little more about it than I knew of the world of the pharaohs. It was useless now to ask for help from my mother. The orbits of her mind rarely touched present interrogators for more than a moment.

Sitting at her bedside, forever out of touch with her, I wondered about my own children, and their children, and children in general, and about the disconnections between children and parents that prevent them from knowing each other. Children rarely want to know who their parents were before they were parents, and when age finally stirs their curiosity there is no parent left to tell them. If a parent does lift the curtain a bit, it is often only to stun the young with some **exemplary** tale of how much harder life was in the old days.

I had been guilty of this when my children were small in the early 1960s and living the affluent life. It galled me that their childhoods should be, as I thought, so easy when my own had been, as I thought, so hard. I had developed the habit, when they complained about the steak being overcooked or the television being cut off, of lecturing them on the harshness of life in my day.

"In my day all we got for dinner was macaroni and cheese, and we were glad to get it."

"In my day we didn't have any television."

"In my day . . ."

"In my day . . ."

At dinner one evening a son had offended me with an inadequate report card, and as I leaned back and cleared my throat to lecture, he gazed at me with an expression of unutterable resignation and said, "Tell me how it was in your days, Dad."

I was angry with him for that, but angrier with myself for having become one of those ancient bores whose highly selective memories of the past become transparently

exemplary—serving as an example or illustration

Growing Up

247

dishonest even to small children. I tried to break the habit, but must have failed. A few years later my son was referring to me when I was out of earshot as "the old-timer." Between us there was a dispute about time. He looked upon the time that had been my future in a disturbing way. My future was his past, and being young, he was indifferent to the past.

As I hovered over my mother's bed listening for muffled signals from her childhood, I realized that this same dispute had existed between her and me. When she was young, with life ahead of her, I had been her future and resented it. Instinctively, I wanted to break free, cease being a creature defined by her time, **consign** her future to the past, and create my own. Well, I had finally done that, and then with my own children I had seen my exciting future become their boring past.

These hopeless end-of-the-line visits with my mother made me wish I had not thrown off my own past so carelessly. We all come from the past, and children ought to know what it was that went into their making, to know that life is a braided cord of humanity stretching up from time long gone, and that it cannot be defined by the span of a single journey from diaper to shroud.

I thought that someday my own children would understand that. I thought that, when I am beyond explaining, they would want to know what the world was like when my mother was young and I was younger, and we two relics passed together through strange times. I thought I should try to tell them how it was to be young in the time before jet planes, superhighways, H-bombs, and the global village of television. I realized I would have to start with my mother and her passion for improving the male of the species, which in my case took the form of forcing me to "make something of myself."

Lord, how I hated those words. . . . ❖

ON THE JOB
HOSPICE WORKER

Trained medical personnel and social workers may specialize in working with terminally ill patients, either in hospices or in patients' homes. Terminally ill patients need special care to help them understand both their illnesses and the consequences of those illnesses. Patients' families also need extra guidance. Medical personnel, such as nurses or nurses aides, may need to teach family members about the illness and how to care for the patient. Social workers may help both patient and family members cope with the illness and the patient's death. Anyone who works with the terminally ill must be tolerant and comfortable around the patients as well as the patients' families. He or she should have a good sense of humor and a positive outlook on life.

ACCENT ON...
INFORMATION SYSTEMS

Russell Baker wants his own children to know what life was like in the time before television. How can people record some of their present experiences so that people in the future will understand the past? Design an information system that is easy to use: inputting information should take little time or effort, and accessing the information should be effortless as well. Use existing systems as a resource or create your own original system. Explain how your system would work and why it would be easy to use. Include a diagram or a model of your system along with your detailed explanation.

UNDERSTANDING

1.  Baker says there are "disconnections" between parents and children that prevent them from knowing each other. Locate in the text the reasons he gives for these disconnections.

   Feeling disconnected is a common human experience. For example, a member of a club, team, or activity may feel cut off from others in that group. Or a visitor to an unfamiliar place such as a rodeo, golf course, or factory may feel disconnected from those who know the place and understand the activity. Working with a partner, identify different situations in which a person might feel cut off from others. Then list at least five steps to follow to overcome isolation and connect with others. Share your group's ideas with the class.

2. Baker thinks the past is important. Locate in the text his comments about why the past is significant.

   At work the past is important in evaluating the performance of an employee. Look back at your performance at your job, on a club, or on a team. Analyze your performance in a one- or two-page essay. Stress the positives of your performance as well as recommending ideas for improvement. **Workshop 5**

A LAST WORD

When was the last time you asked one of your parents about his or her childhood? How will your life be richer if you ask adults to tell about their youthful experiences?

CONNECTING

1. Collaborate with classmates to write an illustrated history of your region. Base your history on interviews with people the ages of your parents and grandparents. Develop a list of interesting questions intended to reveal life in the past in your area. For instance, how was milk delivered? What were grocery stores like? Was there a curfew? What did people do for fun? What did the town look like? Include photographs and short biographies of those interviewed and illustrations of things discussed in interviews. **Workshop 2**

2. Today, the needs of elderly patients overwhelm long-term care facilities. How well does your region serve the elderly? What kinds of facilities exist to care for those with long-term illnesses? How well trained are those working in such facilities? Prepare an oral report on care for the elderly to present to community leaders. Use clear graphs and charts to express statistical data. **Workshop 19**

3. Locate issues of local and national newspapers published the day you were born, look at issues of magazines such as *Look* or *Life* published the week of your birth. Notice elements such as advertisements, cars, music, food prices, fashions, and anything else that interests you. Write an essay in which you compare and contrast the way these elements were on the week you were born with the way they are now. **Workshop 9**

Home Now

EXPLORING

At what age do you think people stop needing their parents, or do they ever stop needing them? For instance, if you worked full time, drove your own car, and lived at home only with your mother, think about whether you would want your mother at home when you returned after work. Would you want her to ask about your day and have your dinner ready? Sometimes one child remains at home after older brothers and sisters have moved away. Do you think the other brothers and sisters remain close to one another after they leave home, or is it natural and desirable for them to lose touch with one another? Consider your ideas about how family members do, or should, relate to one another.

THEME CONNECTION...
A CHANGED FAMILY

The moment Robert realizes he is approaching Little Tokyo, he remembers frequent and happy visits to this place with his dad. He decides right away to have "a proper dinner, the kind his family used to have together at home." Little Tokyo reminds Robert of the past— before his dad died and his brother and sister moved away, when family life was different. Now when he comes home from work, his mother just sits there, "not even looking up when he said hello." Robert longs to experience again the home he knew as a child.

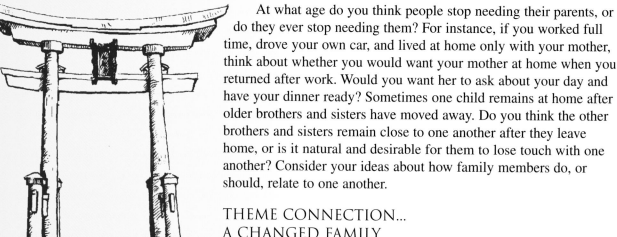

TIME & PLACE

"Home Now" takes place in the present, primarily in Little Tokyo, an ethnic Japanese district in Los Angeles. At the end of a working day, Robert is momentarily trapped in traffic. Leaving the freeway at an unfamiliar exit to escape the snarled traffic, he unintentionally finds himself in Little Tokyo, a neighborhood he and his father had once visited regularly. Transformed by investors, particularly those from Japan, the neighborhood consists of expensive restaurants, "boutiques, gift shops, clothing stores . . . even a baker whose signs were written in French." Robert's memories afford a contrast between old and modern Little Tokyo.

THE WRITER'S CRAFT
LIMITED OMNISCIENT POINT OF VIEW

Oba tells his story in the third person, using "he," "she," and "they" to describe what happens. This tactic makes it possible for authors to enter the minds of all their characters. They can tell what "she" or "he" feels or thinks. Because authors can tell everything about each character when they use the third person point of view, this point of view is called "omniscient," meaning "all-knowing." However, Oba limits this omniscience by entering only Robert's mind. This *limited omniscient* point of view centers attention on one figure's motives, emotions, and thoughts.

Home Now

Ryan Oba

t was five in the afternoon and already the sun was going down. A jackknifed tractor trailer two miles ahead had traffic backed up to where Robert's Honda was—stuck under an underpass, surrounded by other cars. Robert hated winter, hated freeways, hated being where a sudden earthquake could drown him under a pile of concrete.

He was going to be late for dinner—that is, if his mom cooked any. More likely she was making some **origami** something or other that she and the other ladies sold to each other at boutiques. She wouldn't notice if he was late.

Robert had driven fifty yards in the last half an hour. There was no sign of this jam being cleared up in the near future. An old man in a Lexus cut in front of him and braked. Robert honked his horn. The driver didn't even look back. Robert pounded his steering wheel. It was getting late and no one was going anywhere.

Then some movement ahead caught his attention. A few cars were skirting along the right shoulder to the next off ramp. Robert had never taken that exit, but what the hell? He was looking at a good hour and a half in this traffic jam and he didn't feel like going home anyway. Besides, he had a full tank of gas. With a shrug Robert cut to the freeway shoulder, to the off ramp, and into the city. . . .

Robert hardly visited the city. No reason to, really. A dirty place, full of gang members and bums. Yeah, he knew there were other things there, but he was mostly worried about the gang members and bums. He rolled up his windows and locked his door.

"My, what a beautiful part of Los Angeles," he muttered sarcastically. On both sides of the street was a tattered patchwork of warehouses and old brick buildings, some of them still burned out from the riots. He noticed a sign. Plain block letters on an orange Day-Glo background, it read IF YOU LIVED HERE, YOU'D BE HOME NOW. It was an ordinary sign, the sort of sign usually hung on a new apartment complex built next to any one of the various freeway interchanges. What made this one odd was that it was tied to a rusty chainlink fence surrounding an empty lot.

If you lived here, you'd be home now.

"Street artists at work." Robert snorted.

As he drove north, he began to feel strange. Somehow the buildings began to look familiar. He was sure he had never driven this way before. . . . Then he knew. Robert thought about the sign and began to smile. In a way, he was home. He remembered the area. Little Tokyo was just a few miles ahead.

Little Tokyo. Robert and his dad used to go there all the time. When Robert was young, they would walk up and down the street, looking at the Japanese stores and restaurants. His dad would tell Robert about the way the community used to be, before rich businessmen demolished the old shops to make room for their offices and hotels. **Sushi** was cheap back then; before the ***hakujins*** discovered it, you could get a plate for less than a dollar.

About the Author

Ryan Oba is the cofounder of the Asian American Playhouse established at Cornell University in New York. Many of his poems and short stories have been published in magazines and literary anthologies. Oba teaches English and writing at Santa Monica College in California.

origami—the art or process of Japanese paper folding

sushi—cold rice dressed with vinegar, shaped into small cakes, and topped or wrapped with garnishes (as of raw fish)

hakujin—Caucasian

tsukemono—pickles

Of course most of the stores were gone now, as well as the bowling alley and the Atomic Café. At least that's what his sister told him. The last time he went to Little Tokyo was before his dad got sick.

Since his father's death, Robert always found one reason or another to avoid the area. He wasn't clear why; it just didn't seem right.

But today was different. Little Tokyo was ahead, and it was all he could do to keep his mind on the road. Maybe it was just one-too-many nights of coming home to see his mother in the living room surrounded by a pile of paper frogs or cranes or Japanese carp. She'd sit there, no lights on except at her worktable, not even looking up when he said hello.

Jeez—her crafts were everywhere—in the kitchen, in the bathroom, along the hallway. Even in his room—once he found a mobile of colored paper balls floating over his desk. When he took them down, the look on his mom's face made him feel so guilty he not only put them back, he asked her to make a pencil holder and paper-clip tray for him too.

But now Little Tokyo was ahead. J-Town. Just south of City Hall. His mouth watered at the thought of curry rice, beef teriyaki, and **tsukemono**. He was going to have a proper dinner, the kind his family used to have together at home.

It was one of those rare clear days in Los Angeles County that makes it impossible to get lost. To the east and north there are mountains, while to the west and south is the beach. In the middle of it all is the city. Usually the smog hides everything, but today the air was clear as air should be. The setting sun gave the glass

● ● ● ● ● ● ●
If you lived here, you'd be home now.
● ● ● ● ● ●

skyscrapers a warm, otherworldly glow that made Robert think of revelation. He stopped at an intersection. This was different from the freeway. Seeing these golden buildings up close was almost like seeing the angels Los Angeles was named after.

Three streams of dirty water shot across his windshield.

"What the hell are you doing?" Robert screamed. He hit his horn and his accelerator at the same time and sped through the red light. In his rearview mirror he saw a bum holding a spray bottle and a wad of filthy newspaper.

As the figure shrank into the distance and it became obvious he wasn't going to shoot him, Robert felt safe enough to think.

"He was just trying to wash your windshield," he told himself. And then, to no one in particular. "Lucky I didn't hit another car! I could've been killed!"

For the rest of the way Robert carefully checked each person on the sidewalk. He only let up his guard when he saw the tall pagoda marking the entrance to Little Tokyo. He laughed out loud at the sight.

If you lived here, you'd be home now.

It was amazing how a few Japanese signs could set off a space so completely. One block away, Robert wouldn't have felt safe enough to roll down his window. Here, though, Robert locked his car, fed the meter a few quarters, and started walking.

But it was more than the signs; it was the place. The sounds. The aromas coming off from the restaurants made his stomach growl. By this time the day was reduced to a soft glow in the western sky. The store lights were on.

After the war, this was the only part of the city they'd let us live in. It was the oldest, dirtiest part of Los Angeles, his father would

Unit 6: Friendship and Family

say. Look what we did with it. Look!

Once he showed Robert the curb in front of an old noodle shop. There were iron rings coming out of the sidewalk. In the old days people would use these rings to hitch their horses. Robert forgot the name of the shop, and of course by now it had been demolished, but he looked for those rings anyway. He didn't find any.

Then his nose recognized a smell. A smell just like this one flickered from the past. It engulfed him, submerged him. Not teriyaki, nor candy, nor even perfume, it was the smell of old paper, incense, and mothballs. It was the smell of an old gift shop, where his dad bought him a book of Japanese fairy tales. "Momotaro." "The Rabbit in the Moon." And his favorite, "Urashima Taro." It had to be that shop; there was no other smell in the world like it. He felt a way he hadn't felt in a long, long time. He touched his cheek and realized he was crying.

For the better part of an hour Robert looked for that shop. Up and down First, Second, even Third Street, from Alameda all the way up to San Pedro. Nothing. New boutiques, gift shops, clothing stores . . . even a bakery whose signs were written in French. But no old gift shop. Robert frowned. It was like the ending of "Urashima Taro," when Urashima goes back to his home village after visiting the kingdom under the sea. Though it seemed like only a short visit, years and years have gone by. So when he returns, everything has changed and no one remembers who he is or any of his family.

FOCUS ON... HISTORY

In the story, Oba alludes to the way Japanese Americans were treated after World War II. Find out more about this period in United States history, about the Japanese internment camps and the attitudes and feelings that motivated them. Write a two-page report with factual information as well as a summary of the effects of these events on Japanese Americans.

◆◆◆◆◆◆◆◆◆◆◆◆◆◆

A cold breeze sent a shiver down Robert's spine. It made its way to his stomach, reminding him that he hadn't yet eaten. Where to go? Most of the restaurants were new, and much more upscale than the small places he remembered. Investors from Japan had poured quite a bit of money into the area. And the buildings looked great—ceramic tiles, sleek marble, and new masonry. . . . Even in his business clothes, he felt a bit underdressed. What would his dad say if he saw this place now?

Oh well, thought Robert as he entered the closest restaurant, what would he think of *anything* if he were alive today? Of his wife filling their house with so many crafts that you couldn't take three steps without running into a box. Of his fishing poles, stuck in the garden, being used to grow tomatoes. Of his son, crying out in the open, for everyone to see.

As soon as he set foot in the restaurant, Robert knew they served good food. It was a fresh smell, delicately intertwined with hot tempura oil and just the right hint of tea. He went through the curtains into the restaurant. Nice.

SPOTLIGHT ON...
STRATEGIES FOR TAKING
ESSAY TESTS

In the story, Robert feels isolated and lost. Students often feel this way when faced with obstacles, including essay tests. When you take essay tests, remember the following tips to keep from becoming lost:

1. **Skim the entire test**. Get a sense of the number of questions you need to answer.
2. **Allot your time.** Plan how much time to allot for each question.
3. **Follow directions.** Make sure you listen to the teacher's oral directions in addition to following the written ones.
4. **Read all questions carefully.** Answer the questions asked and do not go off the topic.
5. **Complete easy questions first.** Answer the questions you know; answers to questions you are unsure of may come to you later.
6. **Check your answers.** Go over the test to be sure you have answered all the questions.

---

irasshaimase—welcome

yonsei—fourth generation

Clean, like all Japanese establishments; paper lanterns were hanging from the ceiling. Energetic sushi chefs were busy rolling rice into California rolls.

"*Irasshaimase*!" greeted a waiter.

"Huh?"

The waiter looked puzzled. "Not Japanese?"

"Japanese American. I'm **yonsei**."

The waiter didn't acknowledge Robert's reply. Instead, his lip curled. "Not Japanese . . ." he repeated. He brushed him back into the lobby. "No room now! Wait."

Robert sat down and waited. A couple of Japanese tourists entered. They were very well dressed; their clothes looked like they were from France or Italy or someplace like that. The waiter greeted them and they were immediately ushered in.

"Maybe they had reservations," Robert tried to convince himself. He waited a little longer. The waiter peeked through the curtain and quickly looked away when he saw Robert still there.

The door swung open again. This time it was a Caucasian man dressed in a sweatshirt and blue jeans. The waiter ran over to him.

"*Irasshaimase!*"

The man looked puzzled and annoyed. "Do you have sushi here?"

"Oh! Sushi? You like sushi?" the waiter smiled a toothy grin. "Please come in, come in!"

Robert looked at the waiter in amazement as the other man was led into the bright restaurant.

If you lived here, you'd be home now.

Slowly Robert got up and walked out.

As soon as he left the restaurant, he heard someone approach him. He turned to see another homeless guy with his hand outstretched.

"Excuse me, sir, but I haven't eaten—"

"*Well, neither have I!*" Robert exploded. He stood there, surprised at the sound of his own voice. The homeless guy lifted his hands to cover his eyes.

"I'm sorry, man, I don't want no trouble."

Robert shook his head quickly, as if to clear the fog that had rolled into his mind. He pulled out a crumpled bill.

"Here, dude, take it," he offered.

"I don't want no trouble, man." The guy turned, then ran down the street.

● ● ● ● ● ● ●
"Not Japanese… No room now! Wait!"
● ● ● ● ● ● ●

Robert walked the streets of J-Town as if in a daze. A dollar bill still held loosely in his hand, the hunger seemed to have left his body. He looked at the lights, the signs of the businesses, all in Japanese, a language he couldn't read. He looked past J-Town, to the skyscrapers of Civic Center. Those glowing buildings were dark now, save for bright halos of neon. So huge, yet so distant.

And there was that smell again, like a pair of old hands, quiet, yet familiar. This time, though, he let the smell sail past him, to find someone else, maybe, more worthy to follow its path. He passed a mural dedicated to the Japanese Americans who gave their lives for this country. He didn't stop to read the words.

He got into his car and retraced his route back to the freeway. It would be empty by now, everyone safely home from work, perhaps to wives, girlfriends, husbands,

families. . . . His sister was probably painting in her studio, while his brother was in front of a computer somewhere. He thought of his mom, busy filling every emptiness with new children born of string, colored paper, and hot-melt glue.

The last thing he saw before the on ramp was that same orange sign, unreadable in the night. Still, he remembered what it said.

If you lived here, you'd be home now. As he drove, Robert expanded on the work of the artist—wondering how the sign would look in other places: in Japan, on a gravestone, in the kingdom under the sea . . . ❖

ON THE JOB
RESTAURANT MANAGER

Restaurant managers can learn about the business of restaurants in college, in vocational school programs, or through long-term training on the job. Running a restaurant requires a number of important skills. Being able to allocate resources, work with others, choose the proper equipment and procedures, and use resources and time effectively are all important to the successful operation of a restaurant. Knowledge of restaurant and health regulations is also part of the restaurant manager's job, as is familiarity with fair labor practices.

ACCENT ON...
CULINARY ARTS

In the story Robert knows when he enters the restaurant that it has good food. He recognizes the aromas of tempura, oil, tea, and sushi. Earlier he remembered the tastes of his childhood—those of curry rice, tsukemono, and beef teriyaki, all common Japanese dishes. What other types of Japanese dishes are common? In groups, research Japanese cookbooks or restaurants. Create a menu for a typical Japanese dinner. Write a brief description next to the name of each dish. If possible, create one or two of the courses to share with your class.

UNDERSTANDING

1. What kind of person is Robert? Examine what he says, thinks, and does to accumulate evidence about his qualities. Would these traits make him a stable and dependable colleague at work or on a team? Using your knowledge of Robert's qualities, prepare an evaluation in which you support or deny his request to be in charge of a group of people at work. *Workshop 5*

2. In "Home Now," Robert feels homeless. Find passages that show how Oba defines home. With several classmates, collect definitions of "home" from the real world. Investigate, for example, how magazines, newspapers, and real estate publications picture home. Collect illustrations that might supplement your findings. Your group should present its discoveries to the class, along with its own conclusions about what "home" means.

3. Robert is struck by differences between the Little Tokyo he once knew and Little Tokyo today. What details does he find the same? What changes have taken place?

   Robert receives discourteous treatment from a Japanese waiter. Imagine that you are in Robert's place and write a letter to the restaurant manager or owner stating your complaint. *Workshop 11*

4. Robert is unhappy. With a partner, accumulate information from the text to explain the causes of Robert's unhappiness. What are his problems? Having identified these problems, choose one to consider closely. Brainstorm to find solutions for this one problem. As you work to solve the problem, keep a written record of the steps you follow.

CONNECTING

1. Robert is dismayed by the changes in Little Tokyo. The question of how to use land is being hotly contested today in regions throughout the country. For instance, some people want to transform old neighborhoods into upscale shopping areas, while others oppose replacing old buildings and stores with new ones. Similarly, some citizens want to make undeveloped land available for new industries, while others wish to preserve the land and deplore bringing new companies into their community. Working collaboratively, gather information about a proposal or dispute concerning land use. Prepare an oral or written feasibility report describing what you consider to be the right course of action on this issue. ***Workshops 5 and 19***

2. The reference in "Home Now" to a book of Japanese fairy tales is significant. Robert compares his own experience in Little Tokyo with that of Urashima in the fairy story "Urashima Taro." This comparison sheds light on Robert's character.

   Gather collections of fairy stories. Read some of the stories to see how they comment on human experience. Write an essay pointing out the relevance of events in two fairy stories to actual experience. ***Workshop 1***

3. In "Home Now," Robert is troubled by such familiar conditions of modern life as congested traffic, aggressive panhandlers, the possibility of violent assault, and decayed neighborhoods.

   One or more of these conditions—or some different but equally disturbing circumstance—may exist in your own region. Working alone or with others, choose one of these or some other modern situation and investigate it thoroughly. Prepare a report explaining its causes and proposing ways to deal with it. ***Workshops 6 and 10***

The Japanese symbol for "home" is "uchi."

A LAST WORD

Ten years from now, how will your family or home life be different? Will you and your siblings have moved away and gone in different directions? What will your relationships with parents and other relatives be like once you are all grown? What might you do now to make sure you don't take the people around you for granted?

Looking for Work

EXPLORING

"Media," the plural of "medium," includes forms of mass communication such as newspapers, magazines, and television. The media, especially television, often suggest behaviors, goals and ambitions, dress styles, ways of speaking, gadgets to buy, and even foods to eat. All of us are affected by television, but children and young adults are especially impressionable. What effects has television had on teenagers and young children you know? Do they try to dress, talk, and look like characters in commercials or TV shows? How would they be different without the influence of television?

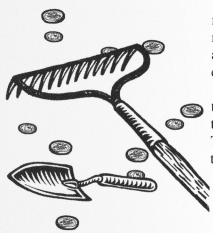

THEME CONNECTION...
FAMILY VALUES

The nine-year-old narrator in "Looking for Work" sees on television an affluent way of life he wishes he could experience. Impressed with the appearance and practices of television families, he asks his mother, brother, and sister to imitate these families. His story reveals, however, that his own family life does not need improvement. It offers, for example, freedom, a measure of independence, a work ethic, and laughter.

TIME & PLACE

This story portrays a Mexican-American family living in a predominantly white neighborhood, a situation that could occur in many places in the United States. The story takes place in the 1950s or early 1960s, a time when Mexican-American families were often misunderstood and unappreciated. At that time many families from minority cultures gave up their language, dress, food, and other customs to conform to the dominant culture. Later, in the 1980s and 1990s, this trend began to change. Today families from other nations increasingly preserve their original culture while at the same time adapting to the most widespread and dominant customs of American society.

THE WRITER'S CRAFT

ACTION VERBS

Soto's story is easy to read, primarily because it uses action verbs—verbs that portray something happening. These verbs show the subject of the sentence doing something. "I *skipped* off her porch, *fetched* my rake, and *crossed* the street." A sentence that shows the subject doing something is written in the "active voice." Thus the sentence "Mrs. Moore gave me a quarter" shows Mrs. Moore doing something; it is an active sentence with an action verb, *gave.* Action verbs make sentences easy to understand, and they also move events along and keep things going.

Looking for Work

Gary Soto

ne July, while killing ants on the kitchen sink with a rolled newspaper, I had a nine-year-old's vision of wealth that would save us from ourselves. For weeks I had drunk Kool-Aid and watched morning reruns of *Father Knows Best*, whose family was so uncomplicated in its routine that I very much wanted to imitate it. The first step was to get my brother and sister to wear shoes at dinner.

"Come on, Rick—come on, Deb," I whined. But Rick mimicked me and the same day that I asked him to wear shoes he came to the dinner table in only his swim trunks. My mother didn't notice, nor did my sister, as we sat to eat our beans and tortillas in the stifling heat of our kitchen. We all gleamed like cellophane, wiping the sweat from our brows with the backs of our hands as we talked about the day: Frankie our neighbor was beat up by Faustino; the swimming pool at the playground would be closed for a day because the pump was broken.

Such was our life. So that morning, while doing-in the train of ants which arrived each day, I decided to become wealthy, and right away! After downing a bowl of cereal, I took a rake from the garage and started up the block to look for work.

We lived on an ordinary block of mostly working class people: warehousemen, **egg candlers**, welders, mechanics, and a union plumber. And there were many retired people who kept their lawns green and the gutters uncluttered of the chewing gum wrappers we dropped as we rode by on our bikes. They bent down to gather our litter, muttering at our evilness.

At the corner house I rapped the screen door and a very large woman in a muu-muu answered. She sized me up and then asked what I could do.

"Rake leaves," I answered, smiling.

"It's summer, and there ain't no leaves," she countered. Her face was pinched with lines; fat jiggled under her chin. She pointed to the lawn, then the flower bed, and said: "You see any leaves there—or there?" I followed her pointing arm, stupidly. But she had a job for me and that was to get her a Coke at the liquor store. She gave me twenty cents, and after ditching my rake in a bush, off I ran. I returned with an unbagged Pepsi, for which she thanked me and gave me a nickel from her apron.

I skipped off her porch, fetched my rake, and crossed the street to the next block where Mrs. Moore, mother of Earl the retarded man, let me weed a flower bed. She handed me a trowel and for a good part of the morning my fingers dipped into the moist dirt, ripping up runners of Bermuda grass. Worms surfaced in my search for deep roots, and I cut them in halves, tossing them to Mrs. Moore's cat who pawed them playfully as they dried in the sun. I made out Earl whose face was pressed to the back window of the house, and although he was calling to me I couldn't understand what he was trying to say. Embarrassed, I worked without looking up, but I imagined his contorted mouth and the ring of keys attached to his belt—keys that jingled with each palsied step. He scared me and I worked quickly to finish the flower bed. When I did finish Mrs. Moore gave me a quarter and

About the Author

Gary Soto (1952–) writes about the Mexican-American experience in America, often basing his work on his own personal experiences growing up in the Central Valley area of California. After graduating from college, Soto began to teach and to write. He is best known for his award-winning poetry, which often depicts the poverty and despair of characters who yearn for something better. Soto also writes prose and autobiographical stories, including *Living Up the Street: Narrative Recollections*, which won the American Book Award in 1985. He teaches language and writing at the University of California at Berkeley.

egg candlers—people who inspect eggs by holding them up in front of a candle to check for embryos

Soto writes about earning a quarter for weeding a garden and a nickel for running an errand. What is the going rate for such jobs today? Business magazines publish data every year summarizing income levels in various lines of work. Make a list of several jobs or career areas in which you are interested. Then find out how much the annual salary is today. Create a computer-generated chart to compare the annual wages of several contemporary jobs.

◆◆◆◆◆◆◆◆◆◆◆◆◆◆◆◆◆◆◆◆◆◆◆◆

converged—to meet
or come together

two peaches from her tree, which I washed there but ate in the alley behind my house.

I was sucking on the second one, a bit of juice staining the front of my T-shirt, when Little John, my best friend, came walking down the alley with a baseball bat over his shoulder, knocking over trash cans as he made his way toward me.

Little John and I went to St. John's Catholic School, where we sat among the "stupids." Miss Marino, our teacher, alternated the rows of good students with the bad, hoping that by sitting side-by-side with the bright students the stupids might become more intelligent, as though intelligence were contagious. But we didn't progress as she had hoped. She grew frustrated when one day, while dismissing class for recess, Little John couldn't get up because his arms were stuck in the slats of the chair's backrest. She scolded us with a shaking finger when we knocked over the globe, denting the already troubled Africa. She muttered curses when Leroy White, a real stupid but a great softball player with the gift to hit to all fields, openly chewed his host when he made his First Communion; his hands swung at his sides as he returned to the pew looking around with a big smile.

Little John asked what I was doing, and I told him that I was taking a break from work, as I sat comfortably among high weeds. He wanted to join me, but I reminded him that the last time he'd gone door-to-door asking for work his mother had whipped him. I was with him when his mother, a New Jersey Italian who could rise up in anger one moment and love the next, told me in a polite but matter-of-fact voice that I had to leave because she was going to beat her son. She gave me a homemade popsicle, ushered me to the door, and said that I could see Little John the next day. But it was sooner than that. I went around to his bedroom window to suck my popsicle and watch Little John dodge his mother's blows, a few hitting their mark but many whirring air.

It was midday when Little John and I **converged** in the alley, the sun blazing in the high nineties, and he suggested that we go to Roosevelt High School to swim. He needed five cents to make fifteen, the cost of admission, and I lent him a nickel. We ran home for my bike and when my sister found out that we were going swimming, she started to cry because she didn't have the fifteen cents but only an empty Coke bottle. I waved for her to come and the three of us mounted the bike—Debra on the cross bar, Little John on the handle bars and holding the Coke bottle which we would cash for a nickel and make up the difference that would allow all of us to get in, and me pumping up the crooked streets, dodging cars and pot holes. We spent the day swimming under the afternoon sun, so that when we got home our mom asked us what was darker, the floor or us? She feigned a stern posture, her hands on her hips and her mouth puckered. We played along. Looking down, Debbie and I said in unison, "Us."

That evening at dinner we all sat down in our bathing suits to eat our beans, laughing and chewing loudly. Our mom was in a good mood, so I took a risk and asked her if sometime we could have turtle soup. A few days before I had watched a television program in which a Polynesian tribe killed a large turtle, gutted it, and then stewed it over an open fire. The turtle, basted in a sugary sauce, looked delicious as I ate an afternoon bowl of cereal, but my sister, who was watching the program with a glass of Kool-Aid between her knees, said, "Caca."

My mother looked at me in bewilderment. "Boy, are you a crazy Mexican. Where did you get the idea that people eat turtles?"

"On television," I said, explaining the program. Then I took it a step further. "Mom, do you think we could get dressed up for dinner one of these days? David King does."

"Ay, Dios," my mother laughed. She started collecting the dinner plates, but my brother wouldn't let go of his. He was still drawing a picture in the bean sauce. Giggling, he said it was me, but I didn't want to listen because I wanted an answer from Mom. This was the summer when I spent the mornings in front of the television that showed the comfortable lives of white kids. There were no beatings, no **rifts** in the family. They wore bright clothes; toys tumbled from their closets. They hopped into bed with kisses and woke to glasses of fresh orange juice, and to a father sitting before his morning coffee while the mother buttered his toast. They hurried through the day making friends and gobs of money, returning home to a warmly lit living room, and then dinner. *Leave It to Beaver* was the program I replayed in my mind:

"May I have the mashed potatoes?" asks Beaver with a smile.

"Sure, Beav," replies Wally as he taps the corners of his mouth with a starched napkin.

The father looks on in his suit. The mother, decked out in earrings and a pearl necklace, cuts into her steak and blushes. Their conversation is politely clipped.

"Swell," says Beaver, his cheeks puffed with food.

Our own talk at dinner was loud with belly laughs and marked by our pointing forks at one another. The subjects were commonplace.

"Gary, let's go to the ditch tomorrow," my brother suggests. He explains that he has made a life preserver out of four empty detergent bottles strung together with twine and that he will make me one if I can find more bottles. "No way are we going to drown."

> **That evening at dinner we all sat down in our bathing suits to eat our beans, laughing and chewing loudly.**

rift—alienation, hostility, or indifference

SPOTLIGHT ON...
RECOGNIZING BIASES

In Soto's story, the narrator alludes to cultural bias between whites and Hispanics. How can you recognize cultural bias and avoid it? Here are some ideas:

1. To recognize bias, you have to distinguish objective thinking from subjective thinking.
2. An objective statement or reaction is based on fact or direct observation. When you react objectively, you do not let your personal feelings or opinions bias your observations or reactions.
3. Cultural bias is caused by opinions and fears that are unwittingly inherited from living in a particular place (culture) at a particular time.
4. As you make conclusions about people and cultures, be objective. Rely on facts and observable information.

◆◆◆◆◆◆◆◆◆◆◆◆◆◆◆◆◆◆◆◆◆◆◆◆

chavalo—a young person

"Yeah, then we could have a dirt clod fight," I reply, so happy to be alive.

Whereas the Beaver's family enjoyed dessert in dishes at the table, our mom sent us outside, and more often than not I went into the alley to peek over the neighbor's fences and spy out fruit, apricot or peaches.

I had asked my mom and again she laughed that I was a crazy *chavalo* as she stood in front of the sink, her arms rising and falling with suds, face glistening from the heat. She sent me outside where my brother and sister were sitting in the shade that the fence threw out like a blanket. They were talking about me when I plopped down next to them. They looked at one another and then Debbie, my eight-year-old sister, started in.

"What's this crap about getting dressed up?"

She had entered her profanity stage. A year later she would give up such words and slip into her Catholic uniform, and into

squealing on my brother and me when we "cussed this" and "cussed that."

I tried to convince them that if we improved the way we looked we might get along better in life. White people would like us more. They might invite us to places, like their homes or front yards. They might not hate us so much.

My sister called me a "craphead," and got up to leave with a stalk of grass dangling from her mouth. "They'll never like us."

My brother's mood lightened as he talked about the ditch—the white water, the broken pieces of glass, and the rusted car fenders that awaited our knees. There would be toads, and rocks to smash them.

David King, the only person we knew who resembled the middle class, called from over the fence. David was Catholic, of Armenian and French descent, and his closet was filled with toys. A bear-shaped cookie jar, like the ones on television, sat on the kitchen counter. His mother was remarkably kind while she put up with the racket we made on the street. Evenings, she often watered the front yard and it must have upset her to see us—my brother and I and others—jump from trees laughing, the unkillable kids of the very poor, who got up unshaken, brushed off, and climbed into another one to try again.

David called again. Rick got up and slapped grass from his pants. When I asked if I could come along he said no. David said no. They were two years older so their affairs were different from mine. They greeted one another with foul names and took off down the alley to look for trouble.

I went inside the house, turned on the television, and was about to sit down with a glass of Kool-Aid when Mom shooed me outside.

"It's still light," she said. "Later you'll bug me to let you stay out longer. So go on."

I downed my Kool-Aid and went outside to the front yard. No one was around. The day had cooled and a breeze rustled the trees. Mr. Jackson, the plumber, was watering his lawn and when he saw me he turned away to wash off his front steps. There was more than an hour of light left, so I took advantage of it and decided to look for work. I felt suddenly alive as I skipped down the block in search of an overgrown flower bed and the dime that would end the day right. ❖

ACCENT ON...
ENTREPRENEURIAL ENTERPRISES

Gary Soto decided that one way to make money was to offer his personal services to his neighbors. Providing personal services can be a lucrative enterprise, since many people need assistance with various household chores such as laundry, grocery shopping, yard work, or walking pets. The first step for any entrepreneur is to make a business plan—a statement of what the business will be, how it will operate, and how it is being financed. Plan your own personal service firm. Decide on a service that you will provide and create a brief business plan. You may acquire a blank form from the library or from the chamber of commerce. Then create a logo for your firm.

ON THE JOB
EXECUTIVE ASSISTANT

An executive assistant must possess both secretarial skills and administrative ability. The executive assistant helps solve problems and negotiate decisions. Training for such a position includes a high school diploma, exceptional communication skills, and strong computer skills. Some college or business school training is also helpful. Maintaining databases, preparing mass mailings, and juggling several tasks at one time are some of the responsibilities of an executive assistant.

UNDERSTANDING

1. The narrator's efforts to earn money serve as more than a means of getting enough to buy admission to the swimming pool. What does he gain from these experiences that is more important than the money he earns?

   Brainstorm the experiences you have had with your own enterprises, such as baby-sitting or mowing lawns. Then write a story about a young person's efforts to earn money. This story should imitate Gary Soto's style. ***Workshop 2***

2. What kind of family life does the boy have? Although his family differs from families shown on *Leave it to Beaver* and *Father Knows Best*, does Soto's family present problems for him, or does it offer a positive environment for growing up? Explain your conclusions by providing specific details from the text.

   Working with several classmates, agree to watch one television show that depicts a family. Before watching the show, develop a list of questions to answer as you view it. For example, how do family members treat one another? What might a child conclude from watching this show? Working together, prepare a final written or oral report to share with the class. ***Workshop 5***

3. What indications are there that the narrator's family encounters discrimination? What evidence can you cite that shows acceptance by others?

   Have you ever felt discriminated against for any reason? People discriminate against others not only because of race, but also for such reasons as height, weight, athletic limitations, intellect, family income, age, clothing, and even hairstyles. Work collaboratively with two other classmates to identify and list forms of discrimination most commonly affecting teenagers in school and on the job. Propose solutions to the problem of discrimination. ***Workshop 10***

A LAST WORD

Television families are rarely realistic. It seems they are always funnier or happier or sadder than our own families are. How can you look at your own family objectively and explain how it differs from a television family?

CONNECTING

1. Opportunities to supplement school classes with work experience are increasingly available to secondary school students. Collect information about various work-experience programs, such as internships, apprenticeships, and cooperative education programs. Prepare a report for parents and school administrators explaining what these programs involve and why your school should or should not support them. ***Workshop 10***

2. Companies are helping employees learn to appreciate multicultural diversity in the workplace and to work with all kinds of people. Investigate the training efforts companies are making to promote an appreciation of diversity. Compile your information into an oral or written report. ***Workshop 19***

from *The Way to Rainy Mountain*

EXPLORING

"Tradition" is a manner of behaving or thinking that generations pass down to succeeding generations by word of mouth. Families, schools, and cultures have traditions that they pass on to the next generation. Identify as many traditions as you can. Notice, for example, social customs and superstitions. Which of these seem to be shared throughout the United States? What reasons might explain the existence of various social customs and superstitions? For example, why do you suppose it is becoming socially acceptable for women to invite men on dates?

THEME CONNECTION...
FAMILY TRADITIONS

Often grandparents keep alive stories of family tradition or history. They serve as our link to generations long since past. Momaday connects with his heritage and his ancestors largely because of his grandmother's influence. She taught him their history and religious beliefs, and at her home he observed gatherings of Kiowa leaders. Momaday's memoir shows one generation shaping the next with its lessons and insights.

TIME & PLACE

The Kiowa (KY uh wuh) tribe has about 8,000 members today, most living in Oklahoma, the land Momaday describes. Their legends say they originated in a land covered by snow much of the year. From this snow-covered land they traveled to an area near modern-day Yellowstone National Park. Then they went on to what are now eastern Wyoming and southwestern South Dakota. In 1867, defeated by the United States armies, they were sent along with the Comanche and other tribes to settle on a reservation in what is now Oklahoma. Today the Kiowa Indian Council, made up of all tribe members 18 years old or older, governs the Kiowa people.

THE WRITER'S CRAFT

DESCRIPTION

Effective written description awakens one or more of the reader's five senses—sight, hearing, taste, touch, and smell. By appealing to the senses, the writer enables the reader to re-create a scene or person in the mind's eye. Momaday's description of his grandmother emphasizes sight: "I see my grandmother . . . standing . . . turning . . . bent . . . looking down . . . going out . . . praying." And he describes the sound of his grandmother: "She began in a high and descending pitch. . . ."

from *The Way to Rainy Mountain*

N. Scott Momaday

About the Author

Born in Lawton, Oklahoma, N. Scott Momaday (1934–), half Kiowan and part Cherokee, grew up on Pueblo, Apache, and Navajo reservations in northern New Mexico. When he began writing in college, he started exploring the culture of Native Americans. In 1968 Momaday received the Pulitzer Prize for his first novel, *House Made of Dawn*, a story about a Native American caught between two cultures. This award was the first major recognition of a Native American literary work. *The Way to Rainy Mountain*, his best-known work, is autobiographical. Momaday is a professor at the University of Arizona.

wariness—care or caution

consummate—complete

deicide—the act of killing or destroying a god or divine being

 returned to Rainy Mountain in July. My grandmother had died in the spring, and I wanted to be at her grave. She had lived to be very old and at last infirm. Her only living daughter was with her when she died, and I was told that in death her face was that of a child. . . .

My grandmother had a reverence for the sun, a holy regard that now is all but gone out of mankind. There was a **wariness** in her, and an ancient awe. She was a Christian in her later years, but she had come a long way about, and she never forgot her birthright. As a child she had been to the sun dances; she had taken part in that annual rite, and by it she had learned the restoration of her people in the presence of Tai-me. She was about seven when the last Kiowa sun dance was held in 1887 on the Washita River above Rainy Mountain Creek. The buffalo were gone. In order to **consummate** the ancient sacrifice—to impale the head of a buffalo bull upon the Tai-me tree—a delegation of old men journeyed into Texas, there to beg and barter for an animal from the Goodnight herd. She was ten when the Kiowas came together for the last time as a living sun-dance culture. They could find no buffalo; they had to hang an old hide from the sacred tree. Before the dance could begin, a company of soldiers rode out from Fort Sill under orders to disperse the tribe. Forbidden without cause the essential act of their faith, having seen the wild herds slaughtered and left to rot upon the ground, the Kiowas backed away forever from the tree. That was July 20, 1890, at the great bend of the Washita. My grandmother was there. Without bitterness, and for as long as she lived, she bore a vision of **deicide**.

Now that I can have her only in memory, I see my grandmother in the several postures that were peculiar to her: standing at the wood stove on a winter morning and turning meat in a great iron skillet; sitting at the south window, bent above her bead-work, and afterwards, when her vision failed, looking down for a long time into the fold of her hands; going out upon a cane, very slowly as she did when the weight of age came upon her; praying. I remember her most often at prayer. She made long, rambling prayers out of suffering and hope, having seen many things. I was never sure that I had the right to hear, so exclusive were they of all mere custom and company. The last time I saw her she prayed standing by the side of her bed at night, naked to the waist, the light of a kerosene lamp moving upon her dark skin. Her long black hair, always drawn and braided in the day, lay upon her shoulders and against her breasts like a shawl. I do not speak Kiowa, and I never understood her prayers, but there was something inherently sad in the sound, some merest hesitation upon the syllables of sorrow. She began in a high and descending pitch, exhausting her breath to silence; then again and again—and always the same intensity of effort, of something that is, and is not, like urgency in the human voice. Transported so in the dancing light among the shadows of her room, she seemed beyond the reach of

time. But that was illusion; I think I knew then that I should not see her again.

Houses are like **sentinels** in the plain, old keepers of the weather watch. There, in a very little while, wood takes on the appearance of great age. All colors wear soon away in the wind and rain, and then the wood is burned gray and the grain appears and the nails turn red with rust. The window panes are black and opaque; you imagine there is nothing within, and indeed there are many ghosts, bones given up to the land. They stand here and there against the sky, and you approach them for a longer time than you expect. They belong in the distance; it is their domain.

Once there was a lot of sound in my grandmother's house, a lot of coming and going, feasting and talk. The summers there were full of excitement and reunion. The Kiowas are a summer people; they abide the cold and keep to themselves, but when the season turns and the land becomes warm and vital they cannot hold still; an old love of going returns upon them. The aged visitors who came to my grandmother's house when I was a child were made of lean and leather, and they bore themselves upright. They wore great black hats and bright ample shirts that shook in the wind. They rubbed fat upon their hair and wound their braids with strips of colored cloth. Some of them painted their faces and carried the scars of old and cherished **enmities**. They were an old council of warlords, come to remind and be reminded of who they were. Their wives and daughters served them well. The women might indulge themselves; gossip was at once the mark and compensation of their servitude. They made loud and elaborate talk among themselves, full of jest and gesture, fright and false alarm. They went abroad in fringed and flowered shawls, bright beadwork and German silver. They were at home in the kitchen, and they prepared meals that were banquets.

There were frequent prayer meetings, and **nocturnal** feasts. When I was a child I played with my cousins outside, where the lamplight fell upon the ground and the singing of the old people rose up around us and carried away into the darkness. There

sentinels—guards

enmities—deep hatred

nocturnal—happening at night

were a lot of good things to eat, a lot of laughter and surprise. And afterwards, when the quiet returned, I lay down with my grandmother and could hear the frogs away by the river and feel the motion of the air.

Now there is a funeral silence in the rooms, the endless wake of some final word. The walls have closed in upon my grandmother's house. When I returned to it in mourning, I saw for the first time in my life how small it was. It was late at night, and there was a white moon, nearly full. I sat for a long time on the stone steps by the kitchen door. From there I could see out across the land; I could see the long row of trees by the creek, the low light up on the rolling plains, and the stars of the Big Dipper. Once I looked at the moon and caught sight of a strange thing. A cricket had perched upon the handrail, only a few inches away. My line of vision was such that the creature filled the moon like a fossil. It had gone there, I thought, to live and die, for there, of all places, was its small definition made whole and eternal. A warm wind rose up and **purled** like the longing within me.

The next morning, I awoke at dawn and went out on the dirt road to Rainy Mountain. It was already hot, and the grasshoppers began to fill the air. Still, it was early in the morning, and birds sang out of the shadows. The long yellow grass on the mountain shone in the bright light, and a scissortail **hied** above the land. There, where it ought to be, at the end of a long and legendary way, was my grandmother's grave. She had at last succeeded to that holy ground. Here and there on the dark stones were ancestral names. Looking back once, I saw the mountain and came away. ❖

ON THE JOB
ENVIRON-MENTALIST

The landscape of the Kiowa was filled with natural beauty. Many such landscapes are in danger of being ruined by society's "progress" or lack of respect for the natural world. Environmentalists work to make sure that we don't forget how important it is to protect and preserve that natural world. Many colleges and universities offer programs in environmental studies. Environmentalists usually specialize in one area, such as water conservation, water quality, or wildlife or botanical preservation. The U.S. Forest Service and the federal government provide many jobs for environmentalists. Workers in this field need to be aware of the changing laws and regulations that affect the environment. For that reason, they may also need to be able to speak to the public either in support of or in opposition to those laws.

ACCENT ON...
ENVIRONMENTAL ARCHITECTURE

Architectural trends come and go just as clothing styles and dances do. Whereas several decades ago the architectural trend was toward sharp angles and lines, the movement in the 1990s is toward buildings that blend in with their surroundings. Consider the site of your own home, or of a place where you would like to build a home. Is it flat? Hilly? Treed or bare? You might check on styles such as earth houses (partly underground) or geo-domes to see if they fit your needs. Then design a home that fits your location. Include landscaping plans as you create a sketch of your enviro-home.

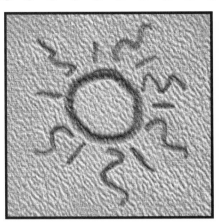

FOCUS ON...
SOCIAL STUDIES

Momaday mentions that the Kiowa worshiped the sun. Native American cultures and cultures the world over are rich with religions involving sun worship. In groups, research one or two cultures in which the sun played a central part in worship, or was worshiped itself as a god. Report back to class with your findings, using colorful details to make your report engaging.

UNDERSTANDING

1. When and why did the Kiowa cease the sun dance, their central rite of worship?
    Instead of trying to understand unfamiliar beliefs and customs, often human beings scorn them. For example, your school probably has traditions that might puzzle students attending other schools but make sense to you. Investigate the significance of a tradition in your school, community, or family. What is the significance, for example, of the name of the athletic team or the school mascot? Does your community have a parade, and if so, are there special reasons for certain events? Present your findings to the class orally or in writing. *Workshops 2 and 19*

2. Why does Momaday describe the land and its creatures in such detail in the last two paragraphs? How do these passages make you feel? What ideas do they raise?
    Select any space outdoors such as a natural woods, a cluttered alley, a backyard, or a beach. Observe it carefully. Using video technology, still photography, or words, prepare a report showing how this space looks and feels. Turn this report into a recommendation for city, township, or other community leaders as to what should or should not be done with natural areas. *Workshop 10*

3. Momaday favors balanced, rhythmical phrases. Notice, for example, "There were *a lot of* good *things* to eat, *a lot of laughter* and surprise. . . . I lay down . . . *and could hear the frogs* away by the river *and feel the motion* of the air." Beautifully balanced, too, is the description of the landscape: " . . . *I could see* out across the land; *I could see* the long row of trees by the creek, *the low light* up on the . . . plains, *and the stars* of the Big Dipper." Find additional examples of balanced phrases in the selection, and explain what they add to this autobiographical essay.
    In one paragraph, describe a person or natural scene using balanced words, clauses, phrases, and sentences.

The Way to Rainy Mountain

4. Find passages that indicate how Momaday views his grandmother and that show the kind of person his grandmother was.

Momaday makes the past sound attractive. Have you ever made the past sound not only attractive, but even better that it was? Think about how your memories affect the way you view your past. With your group, write a letter of inquiry and send it to four adults. Ask the adults to tell you their memories of the same important event—for example, details they remember about President Kennedy's assassination or the loss of the Challenger spaceship. Compare their replies to see if they give similar views of the same historical event. ***Workshop 9***

CONNECTING

1. Compile a genealogy of your family that goes back two or three generations. Design a genealogical chart showing how family members connect. Write an article to accompany the chart, and give some interesting facts about the people it represents. This may involve interviewing parents, grandparents, and other family members. Make copies of your work and send them to family members.

2. The conflict between the descendants of European immigrants and the Kiowa people is only one example of the hostility that continues to erupt between cultures with differing social customs, religious beliefs, and political structures. In the former Yugoslavia, for example, Serbian Christians and Bosnian Muslims wage war. In Northern Ireland the Protestants and Roman Catholics continue bitterly to oppose one another. Each side thinks it is right.

To think critically about conflicting points of view, hold a debate. You may debate about an existing confrontation between two opposing cultures. First you and your group members must decide on a resolution about which members will debate, such as "The British army should withdraw from Northern Ireland." Or you may debate about an issue that causes conflict among students at your school such as whether uniforms should be required. Assign two people to argue on one side, and two to argue on the other. Everyone will gather and share information to support both sides. Conduct the debate according to traditional rules. ***Workshop 19***

3. It is essential in this shrinking world to understand and appreciate cultures different from your own. How might your group or class help raise global awareness at your school? Brainstorm possible activities to spread information about the religious and social customs of various countries or ethnic groups. With your group, conduct research on such matters, for example, as dress, food, courtship practices, education, marriage customs, parent-child relationships, and the role of women. Compile your information in your report accompanied by appropriate illustrations. You may wish to share the information in your report by making an oral presentation to the class or to a larger audience, using overheads or slides to illustrate your points. ***Workshops 19 and 20***

A LAST WORD

Even if we don't ask questions of our elders, we can learn from them by observing and listening. What habits, mannerisms, or qualities do the adults in your life have? Do you have the same habits or qualities? What do you know about those adults as a result of observing their habits?

Family Harmony

- *The Phone Booth at the Corner*
- *I Ask My Mother to Sing*

EXPLORING

It has been said that to be happy, human beings need much more than food, shelter, and clothing. Among other things, close relationships and favorite places contribute to personal happiness. Why do you think relationships such as good friendships and strong family ties make people happy? Why might a particular place such as a familiar neighborhood, house, or park make someone happy?

THEME CONNECTION... FAMILIES FACE CHANGE

Both in Lee's "I Ask My Mother to Sing" and in Delgado's "The Phone Booth at the Corner" children observe adults dealing with change. Lee's narrator observes his mother and grandmother sing of faraway China where once they had been happy. Their song expresses the loss that comes from exchanging an earlier way of life for a new one. The narrator, who has never lived in China, loves to hear his family's song. In Delgado's poem, the narrator captures the impact of change on his Spanish-speaking, sixty-year-old grandfather.

TIME & PLACE

In "The Phone Booth at the Corner," Juan Delgado recalls his boyhood. He presents a time when his grandfather, visiting the United States for the first time, is bewildered by a phone booth.

Li-Young Lee's poetry is very personal. A Chinese-American poet who lives in Chicago, Lee came to the United States with his family in 1964 after years of persecution and wandering. "I Ask My Mother to Sing" was composed after the death of Lee's father. In the poem, Lee captures the moment when his mother and grandmother sing of places in a faraway country. He describes their song as if it were happening right now in his presence.

THE WRITER'S CRAFT

IMAGERY

Just as sculptors make images out of stone, so poets make images out of words. A combination of words that makes you respond with any one of your five senses is called imagery. A poet's imagery pictures how something looks, feels, sounds, tastes, or smells. Li-Young Lee's poem, for example, shows exactly what a water lily filling with rain looks like. Juan Delgado uses imagery in describing a caged parrot and a man trapped in a phone booth. He also gives the reader images of sounds: the parrot's whistle, the grandfather's Spanish, and laughter.

The Phone Booth at the Corner

Juan Delgado

About the Author

Juan Delgado has had poems published in a variety of magazines and other publications, most notably the *Best New Chicano Literature 1989*, an annual collection recognizing the works of emerging writers. Delgado also wrote *My Green Army*. He attended college at the University of California in Irvine.

Grandfather took a walk
down to the neighborhood bar.
That day mother had placed me
under his care—
at sixty he was visiting us
for the first time.

We stopped near a phone booth.
Outside the bar in a cage
a parrot whistled back at us.

The phone began to ring.
Grandfather pushed the door,
forgetting he spoke only Spanish.
He raised the phone to his ear:
there was nothing he could do.

Again, he pushed the door.
He didn't understand
it was divided by hinges
and would only open by pulling in.
He pushed even harder—I could see
the fear in his face grow with his effort.

We were both unable to speak
as we pushed for what seemed minutes.
He finally stopped—exhausted
and the door opened.

He stepped out laughing.
I began to laugh with him
and the bird whistled.
All three of us
broke the air with our voices. ❖

I Ask My Mother to Sing

Li-Young Lee

About the Author

Li-Young Lee (1957–) was born of Chinese parents in Jakarta, Indonesia, where his father was jailed for nineteen years as a political prisoner. The family fled in 1959, spending several years on the move until they made their way to the United States. Lee has studied and taught at a number of universities and has received several awards, grants, and fellowships in recognition of his writing.

She begins, and my grandmother joins her.
Mother and daughter sing like young girls.
If my father were alive, he would play
his accordion and sway like a boat.

I've never been in Peking, or the Summer Palace,
nor stood on the great Stone Boat to watch
the rain begin on Kuen Ming Lake, the picnickers
running away in the grass.

But I love to hear it sung;
how the waterlilies fill with rain until
they overturn, spilling water into water,
then rock back, and fill with more.

Both women have begun to cry.
But neither stops her song. ❖

FOCUS ON...
GEOGRAPHY

In Lee's poem, the speaker refers to places in China that he/she has never seen. Find out about these places. Write two or three paragraphs that describe the city of Beijing, Kuen Ming Lake, and the Summer Palace. You may also wish to prepare a map that illustrates the location of these places.

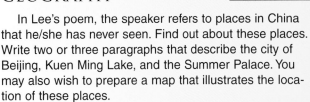

UNDERSTANDING

1. Juan Delgado's poem tells a brief tale. Outline the plot of the tale. Then retell the plot in the form of a short story. Make up your own events, characters' names, ages, physical characteristics, thoughts, and feelings. *Workshop 1*

2. Since poets work with relatively little space, they must select details carefully. When poets include specific objects or events, they have reasons for doing so. In the second and final stanzas of "The Phone Booth at the Corner," a caged bird is mentioned. Why do you think Delgado put a bird in his poem? What purpose does the bird serve?

   When you make lasagna or use a power tool, you know the reason for each thing you do. Choose an activity and explain to a small group the reasons for the steps it involves, or choose a simple piece of equipment and explain its construction and operation. *Workshop 4*

3. "I Ask My Mother to Sing" expresses powerful emotions. Working with a partner, decide on the feelings expressed and point out the passages that convey them.

   Having mixed feelings is a common experience. Perhaps you have had mixed feelings about an amusement park ride that you simultaneously feared and loved. Or perhaps a horror movie made you scream and yet laugh at its bizarre events. Select a controversial current affairs issue about which it is possible to have mixed feelings. Write a report explaining the controversy and giving reasons to support each side. Conclude with a recommendation. *Workshop 10*

A LAST WORD

Children learn from watching and listening to adults. Do you think that children acquire definite attitudes and ways of dealing with change from the adults around them? Consider the attitudes you have acquired from your own family. Why is it important that we stay open-minded to the ideas of other people?

ACCENT ON...
MUSIC TECHNOLOGY

Either of these poems could be set to music. Use any instrument or a software program you are familiar with to create your own music to accompany one of the poems. Think about the narrator's emotions and your own emotions as you read the poem. Try to make your music express these same emotions. The poem may also suggest a certain rhythm for your composition. Write out or memorize your final version, then perform the music or play an audio recording for the class.

CONNECTING

1. The women in Lee's poem like to sing. Everyone enjoys special activities unrelated to work or school. For example, we fix cars, hike, plant flowers, play an instrument, race, surf the Internet, lift weights, bike, cook, and take pictures. Prepare an annotated list of reading materials that explain one of your favorite activities. Include this annotated bibliography in a manual. Your manual should supply directions for beginners on how to practice this pastime, as well as any other information that might interest the reader.

2. Both poems present vivid scenes using words. It has been said, however, that a picture is worth a thousand words. "Picture" includes not only photographs and paintings, of course, but also photocopies, posters, transparencies, videotapes, slide presentations, charts, noteboards, and so on. Using a variety of visual aids, create a graphic exhibit for your school that tells the story of one ethnic group in the United States. ***Workshop 20***

3. Lee and Delgado remind readers that members of different generations can enjoy being together. In some cultures, the extended family is vanishing. In others, the family consisting of a mother, father, and child is also disappearing. Work with several classmates to investigate the attitude of one particular culture toward family. Find out, for instance, if girls and boys are held in equally high esteem and if they receive the same opportunities. Discover typical attitudes toward grandparents, as well as information about where grandparents live and how they are treated. Prepare a written or oral report on the family for social workers, counselors, and teachers who need information to understand the ethnic groups they encounter. ***Workshops 2 and 19***

from *Reparation Candy*

EXPLORING

At times people have probably asked you to do things you did not want to do at all. What made you decide to run an errand, wash the dishes, eat an exotic food, or do something else you knew you would dislike? Identify the influences that caused you in the past to put another person's wishes ahead of your own. When you put someone else's desires first, did you ever find yourself in an embarrassing situation? How did you handle the embarrassment?

THEME CONNECTION... MOTHER AND DAUGHTER: CULTURE CLASH

In "Reparation Candy," a mother who has not many years ago emigrated from China insists that her traditional habits and beliefs are correct. Her American-born daughter challenges these views, however, with ideas that reflect her own exposure to Western attitudes. Cultural differences between mother and daughter as well as the mother's inflexible will combine to embarrass the daughter.

TIME & PLACE

Maxine Hong Kingston was born to Chinese parents who had arrived in America not long before her birth. The excerpt from "Reparation Candy" presents the frustration and embarrassment she experienced as a child belonging simultaneously to two different cultures. When the local druggist's delivery boy erroneously delivers medicine to her home, the mother regards the event as a curse that will bring illness on the entire family. She believes that only if the Stockton, California, druggist makes amends in a specific way will the curse be lifted. The daughter disagrees.

THE WRITER'S CRAFT

DIALOGUE

Dialogue, or the conversation between two or more characters, helps readers understand these characters better through the characters' own words. Maxine Hong Kingston's handling of dialogue is realistic and lively. The daughter's conversations both with her mother and with the druggist sound like ordinary exchanges between real people. They also help convey the outlook and character traits of mother and daughter.

from *Reparation Candy*

Maxine Hong Kingston

e were working at the laundry when a delivery boy came from the Rexall drugstore around the corner. He had a pale blue box of pills, but nobody was sick. Reading the label we saw that it belonged to another Chinese family, Crazy Mary's family. "Not ours," said my father. He pointed out the name to the Delivery **Ghost**, who took the pills back. My mother muttered for an hour, and then her anger boiled over. "That ghost! That dead ghost! How dare he come to the wrong house?" She could not concentrate on her marking and pressing. "A mistake! Huh!" I was getting angry myself. She fumed. She made her press crash and hiss. "Revenge. We've got to avenge this wrong on our future, on our health, and on our lives. Nobody's going to sicken my children and get away with it." We brothers and sisters did not look at one another. She would do something awful, something embarrassing. She'd already been hinting that during the next eclipse we slam pot lids together to scare the frog from swallowing the moon. (The word for "eclipse" is *frog-swallowing-the-moon*.) When we had not banged lids at the last eclipse and the shadow kept receding anyway, she'd said, "The villagers must be banging and clanging very loudly back home in China."

("On the other side of the world, they aren't having an eclipse, Mama. That's just a shadow the earth makes when it comes between the moon and the sun."

"You're always believing what those Ghost Teachers tell you. Look at the size of the jaws!")

"Aha!" she yelled. "You! The biggest." She was pointing at me. "You go to the drugstore."

"What do you want me to buy, Mother?" I said.

"Buy nothing. Don't bring one cent. Go and make them stop the curse."

"I don't want to go. I don't know how to do that. There are no such things as curses. They'll think I'm crazy."

"If you don't go, I'm holding you responsible for bringing a plague on this family."

"What am I supposed to do when I get there?" I said, **sullen**, trapped. "Do I say, 'Your delivery boy made a wrong delivery'?"

"They know he made a wrong delivery. I want you to make them **rectify** their crime."

I felt sick already. She'd make me swing stinky **censers** around the counter, at the druggist, at the customers. Throw dog blood on the druggist. I couldn't stand her plans.

"You get **reparation** candy," she said. "You say, 'You have tainted my house with sick medicine and must remove the curse with sweetness.' He'll understand."

"He didn't do it on purpose. And no, he won't, Mother. They don't understand stuff like that. I won't be able to say it right. He'll call us beggars."

"You just translate." She searched me to make sure I wasn't hiding any money. I was sneaky and bad enough to buy the candy and come back pretending it was a free gift.

"Mymotherseztagimmesomecandy," I said to the druggist. Be cute and small. No one hurts the cute and small.

About the Author

Maxine Hong Kingston (1940–) was the oldest of six children. Her father had been a scholar and teacher in China. He and his wife, a doctor, owned and operated a laundry in Stockton, California. Hong Kingston worked there as a youth. Her first book, *The Woman Warrior* (1976), is a collection of autobiographical essays about the influence of her female ancestors on her own life. This book along with *China Men* (1980), the novel *Tripmaster Monkey: His Fake Book* (1989), and essays, stories, and poems have established Hong Kingston as a highly respected Chinese American voice.

Ghost—Chinese term for caucasians

sullen—gloomy, in an ill humor

rectify—to set right, remedy

censer—a vessel for burning incense

reparation—something done or given to make amends

FOCUS ON... LITERATURE

Hong Kingston writes that the word for eclipse is "frog-swallowing-the-moon"—the Chinese mythical explanation for the natural phenomenon of an eclipse. Research another legend in Chinese mythology or mythology from another culture that explains an event in nature. Present the myth orally to the class. Draw an illustration to accompany your retelling.

"What? Speak up. Speak English," he said, big in his white druggist coat.

"Tatatagimme somecandy."

The druggist leaned way over the counter and frowned. "Some free candy," I said. "Sample candy."

"We don't give sample candy, young lady," he said.

"My mother said you have to give us candy. She said that is the way the Chinese do it."

"What?"

"That is the way the Chinese do it."

"Do what?"

"Do things." I felt the weight and immensity of things impossible to explain to the druggist.

"Can I give you some money?" he asked.

"No, we want candy."

He reached into a jar and gave me a handful of lollipops. He gave us candy all year round, year after year, every time we went into the drugstore. When different druggists or clerks waited on us, they also gave us candy. They had talked us over. They gave us Halloween candy in December, Christmas candy around Valentine's day, candy hearts at Easter, and Easter eggs at Halloween. "See?" said our mother. "They understand. You kids just aren't very brave." But I knew they did not understand. They thought we were beggars without a home who lived in back of the laundry. They felt sorry for us. I did not eat their candy. I did not go inside the drugstore or walk past it unless my parents forced me to. Whenever we had a prescription filled, the druggist put candy in the medicine bag. This is what Chinese druggists normally do, except they give raisins. My mother thought she taught the Druggist Ghosts a lesson in good manners (which is the same word as "traditions"). ❖

UNDERSTANDING

1. "Reparation Candy" contains a series of cause and effect connections. Outline its pattern of cause and effect links, showing how one event leads to the next.

   To ask why something has turned out a certain way is to ask about causes. People often analyze causes when they consider incidents in their own lives. Select a recent event in your life, such as joining a club, getting a job, or taking a trip. Write an essay examining its causes. *Workshop 6*

2. The child confronts the druggist and demands candy. How does the druggist respond and why? What motive or motives does the narrator assign to the druggist?

   Suppose someone were to make an unreasonable demand of you, as the child did when she asked the druggist to give her candy. Imagine, for example, that you manage a grocery store that closes at 10:00 P.M. It is now 10:25 P.M. and you are about to go home. Before you can leave, however, a customer enters the front door you had neglected to lock. She demands to shop, even when you tell her the store is closed. What will you as manager do? Describe in writing your encounter with this customer. *Workshop 2*

3. What do the episodes of the candy and the eclipse have in common? What do they reveal about Hong Kingston's childhood?

   A dutiful child, Hong Kingston obeyed her mother. Cases may arise, however, when you believe orders must be resisted. They may outrage your principles, for example, or your common sense. Working in a small group, choose one famous person who refused on principle to obey orders. Consult newspapers, magazines, history textbooks, autobiographies, biographies, and other sources to gather information about this person's stand against authority. Collaborate to present information about this person to the class. Explain who your figure is, why he or she resisted, and the consequences of refusing to submit to orders. *Workshops 7 and 18*

4. Hong Kingston tries to persuade her mother that her views about the curse and the eclipse are wrong. What arguments does she use, and why does she fail to change her mother's mind? Base your answer on passages in the text.

   Persuasion is a useful skill. Identify one thing you would like to see changed at school or work. Develop a persuasive written argument for making this change. The audience for your argument is the person in a position to make change happen. *Workshop 10*

ACCENT ON...
COMPUTER TECHNOLOGY

The druggist in the story erred in having a delivery sent to the wrong party. Pharmacists must be very careful to give the correct medicine, in the correct dosage, to the right person. Today, computer databases store these records. Find out about database software, perhaps with the help of a student of business information systems. Develop a directory that lists information for each student, such as grade level, homeroom, extracurricular activities, and interests. Use the information in the databases to help plan extracurricular activities or to schedule speakers for events. Update the database as needed.

CONNECTING

1. Hong Kingston's Chinese upbringing required her to obey her mother. Do today's American teenagers typically obey their parents or guardians? If so, why? If not, why not? Work with your class to develop a questionnaire for teenagers. Include in the questionnaire five to ten "yes/no" or "true/false" questions. Draw conclusions from the results and make your findings available in writing for your class.

2. As a Chinese-American, Hong Kingston had to adjust to holding views different from those of her mother. As a Chinese-American, she undoubtedly had to make other adjustments as well. Everyone must adjust to new, difficult, or surprising circumstances at some time or other. When have you had to get used to change? Work with a small group to prepare a brochure listing methods of adjusting to change. *Workshop 21*

3. The narrator's mother does not grasp her daughter's point of view. Investigate and write a research paper on the mother's cultural background. What would life have been like for a girl in China from 1915 to 1940? *Workshop 2*

WRAP IT UP

UNIT 6

1. Russell Baker says that "We all come from our past, and children ought to know what it was that went into their making." In other words, children should know about their past as well as their parents' background. Think about the characters in "Home Now," "Reparation Candy," and the excerpt from *Growing Up*. How do Robert, the narrator of "Reparation Candy," and Russell react to the situations that rise before them? How do their family backgrounds, culture, and parents influence their actions?

2. In "Everyday Use," the excerpt from *The Way to Rainy Mountain*, and "I Ask My Mother to Sing," certain traditions are kept alive. Identify the traditions, and explain their significance in relation to the stories.

Each family and culture keeps its traditions alive through succeeding generations. Interview members of your family and identify three traditions that date back from two generations or more. Explain the significance of these traditions to your family.

WORKSHOPS

WORKSHOP 1
The Writing Process

WHAT IS THE WRITING PROCESS?

Think of a piece of writing you completed recently. What steps did you take in writing the piece? No two writers write exactly the same way, but there are several stages in the *writing process* that are common to everyone.

POINTERS

Every writer has a different work style, but all writers go through the same five stages of the writing process. As you write, you may move back and forth among the stages.

1. **Prewriting** Prewriting is everything you do before you begin to write your essay. Prewriting occurs when you plan, ask questions, make notes, and narrow your topic. When you explore ideas about your topic, gather information, and organize your ideas, you are prewriting.

   During this stage you should identify your purpose and audience. Before you write, determine what your readers know, what they need to know, and why they need to know it. Knowing your audience will influence your purpose, tone, and presentation.

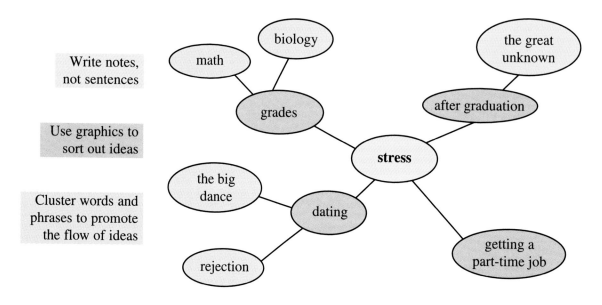

2. **Drafting** Getting your ideas down in rough sentences and paragraphs with a beginning, middle, and end is the drafting stage of the writing process. If your prewriting plan is highly detailed and well organized, your rough draft may be fairly complete. If your prewriting notes are loosely organized, your draft may be exploratory and somewhat unstructured. The important thing to remember when writing a draft is to get your ideas down in an understandable and logical form, with a beginning, a middle, and a conclusion.

Rough Draft Sample

<table>
<tr>
<td>Writer begins paragraph with a solid topic sentence</td>
<td rowspan="2">Adults often tell us that this is the best time of our lives, but high school is full of stress. One source of stress is presure to get good grades, even in tough courses, like biology. And everyone expects us to decide right now what we're going to do with the rest of our lifes! Some kids have part-time jobs—and money to spend—but they don't have much time for anything else, like dating. Dating is another source of stress. When everyone else is going to the big dance you feel left out if you stayed home. But what if you asked someone to the dance and get turned down? If our parents could spend a day with us, they would remember how stressful high school is!</td>
</tr>
<tr>
<td>Writer gets the ideas down without worrying about spelling, grammar, and mechanics</td>
</tr>
</table>

3. **Revising** The revising stage involves evaluating and improving your draft. In revising, focus on the organization of your ideas. Use clear sentences with strong supporting details and active verbs.

4. **Editing** In this stage, review your sentences and paragraphs for clear, correct construction and smooth transitions. Proofread your work word-by-word for errors in grammar, usage, and mechanics. (See *Workshop 17* for proofreader's marks.) To polish your writing, leave it for a day or two, then carefully read it. You may evaluate your own draft, or you may choose to ask a peer reviewer to read it and make constructive comments. Then incorporate any necessary changes.

Revised and Edited Draft

<table>
<tr>
<td>Writer has added detail and improved some phrasing</td>
<td rowspan="3">Adults, especially our parents, often tell us this is the best time of our lives, but they seem to have forgotten that high school is full of stress. One source of this stress is pressure to get good grades, even in difficult courses like biology and math. Another source of stress is planning what we will do with the rest of our lives. There are so many decisions to make and so much we don't know yet. Some high school students have part-time jobs—and more spending money—but they don't have much time for anything else, like dating. Dating also causes stress, especially when everyone except you is going to the big dance. The stress increases when you ask someone and are turned down. If our parents could spend a day with us, they would remember how stressful high school is!</td>
</tr>
<tr>
<td>Errors in mechanics and spelling have been corrected</td>
</tr>
<tr>
<td>Errors in verb tense have been corrected</td>
</tr>
</table>

5. **Presenting/Publishing** The manner in which you present or publish your work depends on your audience and purpose for writing. For example, you may present or publish in the form of a class report, a news article, a letter to the editor, or a computer bulletin board memo.

PRACTICE
Complete one of the following assignments using the five steps of the writing process.

1. Write an article for the school newspaper that discusses the advantages and disadvantages of having a part-time job.

2. Write a memo to your supervisor explaining why the company should provide you with a certain kind of computer training.

WORKSHOP 2
Descriptive Writing

WHAT IS DESCRIPTIVE WRITING?

Effective *descriptive writing* includes precise, vivid details organized in an appropriate way, such as chronological order, order of importance, spatial order, or order of impression. Descriptions use sensory, colorful language and transition words and phrases to achieve logic and unity.

POINTERS: DESCRIPTIVE WRITING

In all writing, ideas must be connected to one another, or the work will not be logical. In writing a description, the writer must decide how to arrange the details for the best effect. Refer to the following suggestions to choose a method of organization.

1. **Chronological order** To write in chronological order, arrange details and events in the order in which they occur. Time sequence is often used to describe a process or tell about a series of events. Use transition devices to help show temporal, or time relationships. Here are some useful transition words and phrases: *first, next, before, after, during, again, then, meanwhile, second, finally, soon,* and *last.*

2. **Order of importance** Another way to organize your writing is to arrange details in order of importance, either from most important to least important, or from least to most. Some transition words that show degree of importance are *first, mainly, best, worst, second, third,* and *last.*

3. **Spatial order** Spatial order presents details by their physical location. Spatial order may be helpful in describing objects or places. In showing spatial relationships, use transition words and phrases such as *above, under, below, around, in front of, behind, on the left,* or *on the right.*

4. **Order of impression** With this method, details are in the order a character notices or perceives them, or simply in the order of the impression the writer is trying to convey to the reader. This approach might combine spatial order with chronological order, for example, to create a mood.

Sample Descriptive Writing

Chronological order provides a coherent description of the experience	Painting my bedroom took more preparation than I had expected. First, I had to put away all my stuff, shove my bed into the middle of the room, and drag the rest of my furniture into the hall. The next step was filling tiny holes in the walls with white, clay-like material called spackling.
Transition words and phrases clarify the temporal relationships	While the spackling dried, I put masking tape around the window frame and the door frame and along the baseboards. (Masking tape allows you to paint close to the edges without getting paint on the wrong surfaces.) After I spread a clear plastic drop cloth on the floor, I was finally ready to open the paint can.

PRACTICE

Here are some ways you can practice using different methods of organization in your descriptive writing.

1. Describe a magazine you would recommend, using order of importance.

2. Describe a new pizza shop you just visited, using order of impression.

3. Describe an event you witnessed recently, using chronological order. (Do not share information that is personal or would embarrass others.)

284   Workshop 2

POINTERS: JOB DESCRIPTION

A *job description* tells employees what a job involves. An employer might refer to it when setting the salary for that position and when evaluating an employee's performance. Employees in new positions are often asked to write their own. Here are some guidelines to follow in writing a job description.

1. **Identify the supervisor for a person in this position.** If a person in this position supervises others, explain who they are.

2. **Outline the main responsibilities of a person in this position.** Start by brainstorming everything for which the person is responsible. Then list the responsibilities in order of importance. Examples of responsibilities include taking customer orders, ordering new parts, and answering telephone inquiries.

3. **Describe the specific duties of the position.** Start each duty with a verb and be specific. For example, instead of writing "Use the computer," write "Enter new orders into the computer."

4. **List the qualifications for the position.** This could include required education, training, licensing, or experience. The list of qualifications should closely match the responsibilities and duties of the position.

Sample Job Description

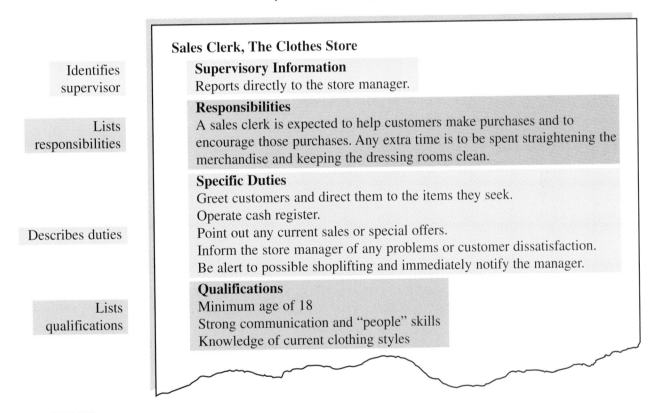

Sales Clerk, The Clothes Store

Identifies supervisor

Supervisory Information
Reports directly to the store manager.

Lists responsibilities

Responsibilities
A sales clerk is expected to help customers make purchases and to encourage those purchases. Any extra time is to be spent straightening the merchandise and keeping the dressing rooms clean.

Specific Duties
Greet customers and direct them to the items they seek.
Operate cash register.

Describes duties

Point out any current sales or special offers.
Inform the store manager of any problems or customer dissatisfaction.
Be alert to possible shoplifting and immediately notify the manager.

Lists qualifications

Qualifications
Minimum age of 18
Strong communication and "people" skills
Knowledge of current clothing styles

PRACTICE

Prepare a job description for a position below or for a position you have held.

1. Counter person in a fast-food restaurant

2. Receptionist in an office building

3. Lifeguard

WORKSHOP 3
Narrative Writing

WHAT IS NARRATIVE WRITING?

A *narrative* tells what happened in a personal experience, an event at work or school, history, or a short story. Knowing the elements of narration is important as you observe what happens on the job, track the progress of a project, or write reports to share with co-workers.

POINTERS: NARRATIVE WRITING

Narrative writing describes an event or series of events that have taken place. A narrative uses specific details about time, place, people, and feelings or impressions. Keep the following pointers in mind when using narration.

1. **Sketch out a timeline to establish the key events or incidents about which you want to write.**

2. **Choose a method of organizing the details and the events.** Often, narrative writing calls for chronological order. Spatial order or order of importance may also be appropriate.

3. **Start with a purpose or thesis statement.** This statement identifies the subject of your account, your central or controlling idea, and your viewpoint.

4. **Begin the narrative with the problem or conflict.** The middle should expand on the situation using details and events, and the end should bring the issue to a final solution.

5. **Use transitional words and phrases to clarify the order and relationship of details.**

6. **Conclude your narrative with a resolution or a summary of the events.** Explain how they relate to your initial thesis statement.

Narrative Writing Sample

Thesis statement introduces the central idea and viewpoint

"Problem" is introduced at the beginning

Transitions help establish chronological organization

Concluding sentences summarize the resolution of the initial problem

My first job interview was full of surprises. I had put a lot of thought into what I would wear, but I hadn't thought about the questions I might be asked. The first thing the interviewer, Ms. Pelagro, asked me was why I wanted to work for her company. I wasn't expecting her question, but I mumbled that some of my friends worked there and really liked it, so I wanted to work there, too. She nodded, so I relaxed a little. Then Ms. Pelagro asked why she should hire me instead of others who had applied for the same job. At first, I couldn't think of any reasons. I finally told her that, from what I knew about the job, she needed someone who was used to working hard and paying attention to details. She said it looked as if I had a clear picture of what was expected. The next day, I was hired!

PRACTICE

Use one of the following assignments to help you practice your narrative writing skills.

1. Describe an early memory from your childhood.

2. Write an account of a personal experience that has affected your outlook on life.

3. Choose a narrative from the reading selections, such as "Obituary of a Bone Hunter" or "Polar Bear Pass." Write a different ending for the story, using the same method of organization as in the original.

POINTERS: OBSERVATION REPORT

In an *observation report,* you simply describe what you see. For example, you might describe a physical object, the results of an accident, possible sites for a new store, or an employee's performance. Observations are part of many kinds of reports, so you need to know how to write them. Here are some guidelines to follow in writing an observation.

1. **Describe only what you see, without making judgments or expressing your own opinion.** For example, instead of writing that an employee is wasting time with personal phone calls, you would describe what you see: the employee calls home nearly every afternoon at 3:00.

2. **State your observations objectively.** Do not try to influence others' decisions by using subjective words in your report. For instance, you might write that you observed only three cars pass by one possible site during your half-hour visit. That is more objective than stating that the site is out in the "boonies."

3. **Include only information you have determined to be truthful and accurate.** For example, an employee might tell you that "everyone" is having trouble with a certain procedure. Determine whether this comment is true before including it in your report.

Sample Observation Report

Begins with central idea

Uses objective words

Reports facts

> On Tuesday, November 14, I visited potential store Site A from 10:10 to 10:53 AM. Site A is located in the Eastland Shopping Mall at the intersection of Routes 34 and 123. (See attached map with Site A marked.) This site includes 2,500 square feet and is being operated as a candy store. According to Gregory White, the mall manager, Eastland includes twenty-three other small stores and three anchor stores: Sears, JCPenney, and Lazarus (a clothing chain). He reports that all store sites are occupied, but the mall does not include any other auto part stores. The interior of the mall was clean and well lighted, with padded benches in three areas for shoppers. A security guard patrolled the mallway.
>
> The parking lot has space for 2,000 cars, according to Mr. White. He says the lot, which included a number of potholes, will be resurfaced next week. A steady stream of traffic came in the two entrances during my visit.

PRACTICE

Complete one of the following assignments to practice writing an observation report.

1. Describe a piece of machinery or equipment using spatial organization.

2. Observe another person's actions for five minutes and describe what you see. (Be sure to ask the person for permission to observe.)

3. Describe an accident you observed. Explain what happened without assigning responsibility for the accident.

WORKSHOP 4
Process Explanation

WHAT IS A PROCESS EXPLANATION?

Have you ever had to explain how to do something that seemed fairly simple—and then realized as you got into the explanation that you had left out a step? *Explaining a process* is a task you will be called upon to perform regularly in daily life, especially on the job.

POINTERS: EXPLAINING A PROCESS

To describe a process, the writer explains a sequence of events or steps to instruct or inform the reader. As you write process descriptions, refer to the following guidelines.

1. **Know your audience.** Find out what your readers know about the topic. What information do you need to explain? Customize your writing to the readers' experience.

2. **Know your purpose.** Make sure you know what use your readers have for the process.

3. **Start with a clear thesis statement.** Let your readers know what process you are explaining.

4. **Define unfamiliar terms.** Remember that your audience may not be as familiar with the topic as you are.

5. **Never use technical jargon for a general audience.** Technical terms may discourage your audience.

6. **Divide the process up into manageable pieces.** Use short, succinct sentences that describe the steps in an easy-to-follow manner.

7. **Arrange the steps in your process in chronological order.** Use transition words and phrases to signal a move to the next step or stage. Words such as *first, second, next, after,* and *last* help your reader follow the progression of the steps.

8. **Check the steps in the process for accuracy.** Make sure you know the process thoroughly, either from reading, observing, or experiencing it firsthand. Double check the steps you have included to make sure nothing is missing or misleading.

9. **Use diagrams, charts, and other visual aids.** When appropriate, help the reader understand the process by using visuals as well as written text. A diagram can clarify nearly any process description.

Sample Process Explanation

Thesis statement identifies the process

Transition words make the chronological order clear

Writer avoids technical jargon

With all the breeds of dogs available today, how can you choose the best pet for you? First, go to the library and check out books about dogs. After skimming the books, list four or five breeds that appeal to you because of their size, appearance, or other factors. Consider how much time and space you have for a dog. Then narrow your choice to the breeds that fit your requirements and read more about each one. Write each breed as a heading on a sheet of paper and underneath list the information you gather. Also consider whether you want a purebred dog. If you do not plan to enter dog shows, a mixed breed might be a good choice.

Next, visit animal shelters, breeders, or pet stores and spend some time with the breeds that interest you. Remember that a certain dog's personality may differ from others of the same breed. By this time, you will have a clear idea of the breed—or even the dog—that's best for you.

PRACTICE

Use one of the following exercises to practice explaining a process.

1. Explain how a process such as writing a letter could be done more efficiently.

2. Explain how members of a certain team, council, or committee are chosen at your school.

POINTERS: INSTRUCTIONS

A process explanation is written so readers will understand the process, not necessarily so they can carry it out. *Instructions* are meant to be carried out by readers. These guidelines will help you write instructions.

1. **Begin with an introduction.** Explain in one or two sentences who should follow the instructions, when they should be followed, and what they accomplish. Also list any supplies that should be gathered or special training that is required before someone follows the instructions.

2. **List the instructions in numbered steps placed in chronological order.** Begin each step with an action verb, such as *press, add,* or *list.*

3. **Consider what your readers know and what they need to know.** Include all necessary steps, but omit obvious ones, such as "Seat yourself in front of the computer."

4. **Indent explanations.** Readers appreciate explanations of what should happen, such as "The screen will show a menu." Indent the explanation under the numbered step to which it refers.

5. **Include pictures and diagrams if they would be helpful.**

Sample Instructions

How to Send a Fax

Begin with introduction
You will need the recipient's fax number and the information to be sent, printed clearly on flat (not curled or folded) 8½" × 11" sheets of paper.

Numbered steps in order
1. Place the sheets of paper face down in the top tray.
2. Program the machine with the recipient's fax number.

Explanations indented
Numbers will appear in the window on the right side. Be careful not to use the recipient's phone number.

3. Compare the numbers in the window with the recipient's fax number.
If they are different, push the "clear" button and repeat Step 2. If they match, proceed to the next step.

4. Push the "start" button.
The machine will dial the number. Once the connection is made, the pages will start to move through the machine.

5. If the machine stops, read the message in the window and follow the instructions.
Check the transmission report to verify that all pages were sent.

6. Remove the sheets from the bottom tray after they have been sent.

PRACTICE

Complete one of the assignments below to practice writing instructions.

1. Tell readers how to get from the school to your home. (Write instructions instead of drawing a map.)

2. Explain how to plant a tree, change a tire, bathe a baby, or another task of your choice.

WORKSHOP 5
Analysis

WHAT IS AN ANALYSIS?

An *analysis* is the examination of a problem, question, or issue. A written analysis clearly states an issue. It then proposes a solution, with the support of other documents, expert opinion, and so on. An analysis of an issue presents the writer's opinion and draws on other sources to add weight to that opinion.

POINTERS: ANALYSIS

When preparing an analysis, follow these guidelines.

1. **Know your subject.** Thoroughly research your subject or issue before you begin to write. Your analysis will help you understand all sides of the issue.

2. **Identify your assumptions.** What is your viewpoint? Do you have any biases? What are they? Try to look at the issue objectively. Determine the most reasonable position to take.

3. **Gather information.** Sources of information might include books, newsmagazine articles, CD-ROMs, the Internet, or people themselves who might be interviewed.

4. **Collect and organize evidence.** Collect evidence that supports your view. Make an outline of your position. For each point you make, cite at least one source or reference that supports that point.

5. **Draft and revise your analysis.** Write an analysis based on your outline. Proofread carefully and revise the draft as needed.

Sample Analysis

States the question

Examples support writer's opinions

States the conclusion

In "The Chrysanthemums," Elisa's husband is surprised at how quickly her mood changes. Why does she change from her usual self to a stronger person and then back to his uncertain wife? Elisa is still trying to gain an identity for herself. When the itinerant repairman stops at the ranch and praises her chrysanthemums, she feels strong and competent. She eagerly gives him sprouts for "a lady down the road" and explains in detail how to care for them. Elisa believes she has a special skill in growing things, and she feels good about herself. Later, though, she sees that the man has thrown away her sprouts. Elisa assumes she has nothing to offer after all. Her shifting self-confidence causes her changing moods.

PRACTICE

Complete one of these assignments to practice writing an analysis.

1. Study a character or author from one of the selections. Write a short analysis explaining why this person made certain choices. For example, you might analyze why Michael Jordan stresses commitment.

2. Research a question your community faces, such as whether to build a new school or tear down an old one. Analyze the reasons for and against the proposed action. Then recommend what you consider to be a wise plan of action in this situation.

3. Analyze a question you face, such as whether to try out for a team or which job to apply for. Explore at least two possible options and reach a conclusion about which is the better one for you.

POINTERS: PERFORMANCE EVALUATION

Most supervisors analyze and evaluate their employees' performance once or twice a year. These evaluations are usually shared with the employees to help them improve their performance. *Performance evaluations* are often considered in promoting or terminating an employee. Sooner or later, you will need to evaluate someone's job performance. These guidelines will help you.

1. **Begin with an overall assessment.** Emphasize the positive, but do not overlook problems. Everyone likes to be praised, but if an employee is not doing acceptable work, praise is not in order.

2. **Describe both strengths and areas for improvement.** Few evaluations will be all positive or all negative. Be specific so employees can make any needed changes. If you write that Sam needs to improve his time management, he might not know where to start. Instead, point out that Sam arrived late for work four times during the past month. Now Sam knows how he can improve his time management.

3. **State specific goals.** Instead of asking Sam to be on time more often, ask that he arrive on time every day. Other employees might be asked to reduce their word processing errors by 50 percent or to assemble one more widget each hour.

Sample Performance Evaluation

Performance Evaluation for Brittany Kellogg

Overall assessment
> Brittany, your ability to deal with customers is excellent. The only change I would recommend is staying longer to help with closing tasks.

Strengths
> You listen carefully to customers and show them you care about their order. You always apologize for mistakes, even those caused by other employees. I have seen you handle a long line of people with patience and good humor.

Weaknesses
> However, last Tuesday, you left at 10:15 P.M., but the rest of us stayed until 10:35 P.M. to finish cleaning up. Last Thursday, you left at 10:10 P.M. These were school nights, but other employees are students, too. We can all go home earlier if we share the work.

Goals
> Please stay until all the closing tasks are completed, unless you have informed me of special circumstances that require you to leave early. I am pleased with your work, Brittany, and hope you will remain on our team.

PRACTICE

Complete one of these assignments to practice writing a performance evaluation.

1. Write a performance evaluation for someone who has worked on a class project with you. Ideally, this person will also write a performance evaluation for you. Talk over your comments and recommendations.

2. Evaluate work you have done for pay or as a volunteer.

3. Make up a "problem employee" and evaluate his or her work. Be objective as you describe incidents and suggest improvements.

WORKSHOP 6
Cause and Effect

WHAT IS CAUSE AND EFFECT?

You have been explaining *cause and effect* your entire life. At school you might be asked to identify the causes of the Civil War or the effects of smog in the air. At work you might describe the cause of a decrease in sales or the effect of using safety glasses in assembly-line work.

POINTERS: CAUSE AND EFFECT REPORT

In a report on causes and effects, you will focus on cause (what makes something happen) and effect (the result). As you write a cause-effect report, keep the following in mind:

1. **Choose a topic and decide whether to describe cause, effect, or both.** For example, you might describe the cause of a character's actions and the effects of those actions.

2. **State your topic as a question.** Suppose you were writing a report on Barba Nikos and decided to focus on cause. You might ask "Why did the narrator throw a plum at Barba Nikos?"

3. **Brainstorm possible causes or effects that answer this question.** Put these causes or effects in a logical order. You might describe them chronologically or by order of importance.

4. **Add supporting details.** Your support could include examples, definitions, or dialogue from the story.

5. **Include transitional words to help show relationships.** Words and phrases such as *but, however, just as, like, on the other hand,* and *unlike* will help make your comparisons clear to the reader.

6. **Check your logic.** Make sure the cause-effect relationship you describe is not just a coincidence—two events that occur close together in time but have no real relationship to each other.

7. **Write a conclusion about the main cause and/or effect.** Summarize your main point clearly and creatively.

Sample Cause and Effect Analysis

Question introduces the topic	Why was the main character in "I Find Food Gold" so quick to believe he had struck gold? He had only his own opinion to rely on—he was
Causes listed in order of importance	afraid others might steal his treasure if he told them about it, so he did not seek anyone else's opinion. He wanted to impress the more experi-
Supporting details	enced miners by dramatically displaying his find after they had decided that there was no gold in the area. As a result, he was easily fooled by the
Transition words	shiny mica. His desire to strike gold and become rich was so great that it
Main cause described	clouded his judgment.

PRACTICE

Complete one of the following assignments to practice describing cause and effect.

1. Explain why the daughter in "Reparation Candy" does not want to do as her mother commands.

2. Explain why the doctor in "The Use of Force" feels justified in examining the child against her will.

POINTERS: ANALYTICAL REPORT

An *analytical report* identifies and examines the probable causes of a problem or the probable effects of a proposed action. To analyze causes, the report might be organized as: (a) problem; (b) causes; and (c) solution. To analyze effects, the report might organized as: (a) proposed action, (b) probable effects; and (c) conclusions and recommendations. Below are guidelines for writing an analytical report.

1. **Clearly define the problem or the action being considered.** Your topic sentence should be the question you will answer.

2. **Be objective.** Offer statistics and other factual data, not your personal opinion. For example, avoid statements such as, "Safety glasses might be okay for some, but I think they cut down on my vision."

3. **Choose reliable resources.** If you interview just a few assemblers who are annoyed by wearing safety glasses, their opinions may not represent the majority of the assemblers.

4. **Explain your findings.** Don't just list data; tell readers what it means in relation to your main point.

5. **Draw logical conclusions.** Do make sure the information in your report supports your conclusions.

6. **Make recommendations for the next steps or for further study.** If a specific action was being considered, state whether or not you think this action should be taken. If several solutions to a problem were offered, recommend one.

Sample Analytical Report

Question to be answered	If our plant club raises the price we charge for poinsettias, will our profits increase? We usually charge $6.99, but people have to order our plants and come to the school to pick them up.
Objective statistics from a reliable resource	According to our recent survey of 100 customers, 82 said if they cannot save money by buying our plants, they might pick up a poinsettia while they are shopping at a supermarket.
Explanation of statistics	If we raise our prices but sell fewer plants, we could lose money.
Conclusion	Since we can't offer the convenience of picking up a plant on the spot, we need to keep our prices low to attract customers.
Recommendations	I recommend that we find ways to sell more plants rather than raising our prices.

PRACTICE

Complete one of the following assignments to practice describing cause and effect.

1. Your state legislators are considering raising the minimum age for drivers to 18. Write a report explaining the probable effects of that action.

2. Explain to your supervisor why your work has not been up to your usual standards this week.

WORKSHOP 7
Summary

WHAT IS A SUMMARY?

A *summary* is a shortened version of an original text. A *paraphrase* summary helps clarify the difficult vocabulary and concepts in the original writing. It can be as long as the original or somewhat shorter.

You might be asked to write a summary at school to show that you read and understood certain material. At work you might be asked to present your ideas in a shortened, easy-to-understand form. Strengthening your skill in summarizing is a good idea, as you will use this skill often.

POINTERS: PARAPHRASE SUMMARY

A paraphrase summary of a literary work should be brief and clear. This provides an excellent way to study a piece of writing, especially when you must compare it with a similar work. When you write a summary, keep the following pointers in mind.

1. **Read the original work carefully.** Make sure you understand it yourself before you try to explain it.

2. **List the main ideas in the original writing.** Keep them in the same order and use phrases instead of whole sentences.

3. **Write your first draft.** Refer to your list of main ideas when you write the summary. If you encounter difficult words, you might define them in your summary or explain the same concept without using the difficult word. You can add examples to a paraphrased summary if they will help the reader understand complicated ideas. Write as concisely as possible.

4. **Reread the original and your draft.** Compare them to make sure you included the important ideas in a logical order in your summary. Also determine whether you stressed the same ideas as the original. Avoid emphasizing a point more in your summary than the original author did.

5. **Revise your summary.** Look for more words or concepts that readers might not understand and find ways to explain or eliminate them. If possible, have a partner read your summary and point out anything that is still confusing. Eliminate any unnecessary words, phrases, or sentences, but do not delete words that add polish to writing, such as articles *(a, an, the)*.

6. **Edit your summary.** Make sure you have included transitional words and phrases so that each sentence leads smoothly to the next. Check your grammar, spelling, punctuation, and so on.

Original Passage from the Declaration of Independence

Unimportant words and phrases deleted

When in the Course of human events, it becomes necessary for one people to dissolve the political bands which have connected them with another, and to assume among the Powers of the earth, the separate and equal station which the Laws of Nature and of Nature's God entitle them, a decent respect to the opinions of mankind requires that they should declare the causes which impel them to the separation.

Summary

Difficult words replaced with simpler ones

When one group of people chooses to separate from another group and become equal to that group, those who choose to separate should explain the reasons for their action.

PRACTICE

Complete one of the following assignments to practice your skills in summarizing. If a passage has few difficult words or concepts that need to be explained, focus on writing concisely.

1. Summarize a different section of the Declaration of Independence.

2. Summarize the excerpt from *The Speech of Chief Red-Jacket.*

3. Summarize how Kathy Wright became a nurse, as explained in the excerpt from *Exploring Careers.*

POINTERS: EXECUTIVE SUMMARY

A business report that runs several pages or longer often begins with an *executive summary.* This type of summary is a synopsis that explains what the report covers and includes any recommendations made in the report. After reviewing this summary, the busy reader can decide whether to read the entire report. Like many other summaries, an executive summary is written in nontechnical language so most readers will understand it. Below are guidelines for writing an executive summary.

1. **Begin with a clear statement of the topic.** Business people appreciate writers who get right to the point.

2. **Make sure your summary includes the essential information in the longer report.** A reader should understand the main points in the original report after reading your executive summary.

3. **Do not add anything to the summary that was not in the original.** This includes your own opinion about the writer's recommendations.

Sample Human Resources Department's Report

With the recent expansion of Pennsylvania Company, it has become more and more difficult for employees to learn about our many products and services. They have no opportunity to meet top executives and find out how their department fits into the total picture. A new approach, such as a formal day of orientation scheduled every month, would help. A representative from each division of the company would deliver a presentation, and a human resources staff member would provide information about personnel policies and employee activities. Special sessions of particular interest, such as company history, could be added as well. . . .

Sample Executive Summary

Gets to the point

Includes essential information

Because of the recent growth of our company, we need a more structured, day-long employee orientation that would be offered each month. Top executives and other employees would make brief presentations about company history, products, organization, personnel policies, and employee activities.

PRACTICE

Complete one of the following assignments to practice summarizing.

1. Summarize a class lecture. Then compare your summary with that of another student who summarized the same lecture.

2. Summarize a newspaper or magazine article about an event, discovery, or other topic that interests you.

3. Watch a television news program and summarize its content.

WORKSHOP 8
News and Feature Writing

WHAT ARE NEWS WRITING AND FEATURE WRITING?

News writing and feature writing often can be found in the same newspaper or magazine. News writing provides readers with the most current information, while feature writing focuses on information of general interest. News writing involves the objective and concise reporting of facts, but feature writing is creative and attempts to involve readers emotionally. A feature deals with real events but focuses more on people, lifestyles, and uniqueness. The skills involved both in news reporting and feature writing will help you in many other writing assignments at school and at work.

POINTERS: NEWS WRITING

News articles are written as inverted pyramids. The first sentence, or lead, gives the most important information, and each of the following sentences offers facts of less importance. When you write a news article, keep the following pointers in mind.

1. **Answer the basic questions first.** Write the words *who, what, why, when, where,* and *how* on a sheet of paper. Answer these questions in as few words as possible. (If any of these questions is not important to your article, omit it.) Combine your answers into one or two sentences.

2. **Decide which other details to include.** Brainstorm a list of details readers might want to know, such as the impact of a certain event. If you interviewed someone, consider any quotations you gathered. Then choose as many details as you have space to include in your article.

3. **Arrange the details in decreasing order of importance.** If the article must be shortened, the editor will cut from the end of the article first.

4. **Aim for conciseness and objectivity in your first draft.** Omit opinion words such as *good, poor, easy, incorrect, unfortunately,* and *hopefully.*

5. **Revise and edit your article.** Make sure you have included explanations as needed and used terms that readers will understand. Consider whether you have answered the readers' probable questions. Use transitional words and phrases so that one sentence leads smoothly to the next. Check your grammar, spelling, punctuation, and so on. Make sure your writing is factual and objective so readers will not realize your personal feelings about the event.

6. **Check your facts.** Make sure times, locations, dates, people's titles, and the spelling of their names are correct. Check to see if you have overstated or understated anything.

News Writing Sample

Lead sentence answers basic questions	Student Council President Nestor Colon announced that a new dress code will go into effect Friday, November 6. In response to student and staff concerns, the following will no longer be acceptable: t-shirts and
Objective terms used	sweatshirts with any advertisement, shorts shorter than mid-thigh, see-through clothing, and hats. According to Colon, a student will receive a warning for the first violation of the code. The student's family will be notified for a second violation. A third violation will result in detention.
Least important fact is last	A council committee has been working on this dress code since early September.

PRACTICE

Complete one of the following assignments to practice news writing.

1. Write a news article about a positive event in your school or community. Keep your writing factual and objective.

2. Write a news article about a recent change in your community that you and others opposed, such as a reduction in city services or the clearing of a wooded area for a parking lot. Again keep your writing objective so readers will not guess you opposed this action.

3. Rewrite a reading selection, such as "Train Time," as if it were a news article.

POINTERS: FEATURE WRITING

The topic of a feature article might relate to a news story, but a feature is not written as an inverted pyramid. Instead, its organization depends on the subject matter. Below are guidelines for writing a feature.

1. **Select a topic that will interest your readers.** Consider bringing out the human side of a recent news story. For example, you might base your feature on a visit to a disaster site or an interview with a person who won an award or survived an ordeal. Or you might write about the success or continuing struggle of an ordinary person in your community. You might consider a historical feature explaining the history of a school or community event.

2. **Gather information.** This information may come from interviews, library research (especially for a historical feature), or other sources. If you write the entire feature without doing any research, you might actually be writing an opinion column.

3. **Follow the rest of the writing process to complete your article.** Now write your first draft, revise it, edit it, and perhaps arrange to have it published in the school or local newspaper. Make sure your finished article begins with an anecdote or fact that will encourage readers to continue reading. Also check to see that any facts or other information you have included is accurate.

Feature Writing Sample

Begins with a sentence that attracts readers' attention	Tamika Gresham is a modern-day Mozart who composes to a rock beat. Tamika has been writing songs since she was in the seventh grade. Last year she started her own band. Known as Ursa Major, the band consists of Tamika, her brother Demetrius, and friends Cindy Sherman and Julian Moore. Though they occasionally play popular songs, Ursa Major focuses on Tamika's music. The odds against succeeding in the recording industry may be great, but Tamika is as determined as she is talented, according to Cindy. Julian adds that it is only a matter of time before the music world learns the name Tamika Gresham.
Focuses on the human aspect of the story	

PRACTICE

Complete one of these assignments to practice writing a feature story.

1. Interview an older person in your family or neighborhood about his or her life as a teenager. Then write a feature story for your school or local paper. (You could also interview someone in a nursing home.)

2. Brainstorm a list of human-interest topics that would interest students in your school. Then choose one and write a feature story about it. Gather any necessary information.

WORKSHOP 9
Comparison and Contrast

WHAT IS A COMPARISON AND CONTRAST REPORT?

In a *comparison-contrast report*, the writer shows how two or more things are similar (*compare*) and how they differ (*contrast*). School assignments often involve comparing and contrasting events, ideas, information, and people, such as the painting styles of two Impressionist artists. At work, you might compare and contrast two software programs being considered for purchase. Knowing how to organize a comparison-contrast report is a valuable skill.

POINTERS: COMPARISON AND CONTRAST

Comparisons identify issues common to both things being compared and are organized in two ways. The **whole-to-whole pattern** compares one whole topic to another by describing all elements of one entire topic before going to the next. The **part-to-part pattern** first compares one element common to both topics, then a second common aspect, and so on. After choosing a pattern, follow these guidelines:

1. **Decide which aspects of the topic to discuss and put them in order.** For example, if you choose to compare Robert from "Home Now" and Russell from *Growing Up*, pick three traits of a character and explain in order of importance how each trait applies to each character.

2. **Write a topic sentence or thesis.** Your thesis should describe the general subject of your report and your conclusions. How similar or different are the two topics you are comparing?

3. **Write your first draft and make revisions.** If you chose a confusing organizational pattern, try another pattern. Check for problems in the elements being compared or the order in which you discuss them. Organize the body of your report, and end with a summary sentence or paragraph.

4. **Edit your report for grammatical correctness.** Aim for smooth transitions as you compare or contrast different aspects of your topics.

Sample Comparison/Contrast Essay

Thesis

Organized on the part-to-part pattern, discussing knowledge of each character's family and past, then going on to discuss the possibility of each character's learning more about his past

The main characters in "Home Now" and *Growing Up* both want to know more about their families and past, but one character seems to have a much better chance of reconnecting with his family. Robert in "Home Now" is searching for a restaurant he vaguely remembers from his youth, a place where he thinks he will feel at home. Russell in *Growing Up* sits with his senile mother, trying to patch together information about her youth and his family background.

Robert's mother waits for him at home and might help him reconnect with his Japanese heritage. His brother and sister, too, might be of help. On the other hand, Russell's mother no longer lives in the real world. It's too late for her to help him reconstruct his family background, and he does not mention any siblings that might fill in the missing pieces.

PRACTICE

Complete one of the following assignments to practice writing a comparison-contrast report. You can choose either organizational pattern.

1. Compare and contrast the two daughters in "Everyday Use."

2. Compare and contrast the son in "Those Winter Sundays" with Roger in "Thank You, M'am."

3. Compare and contrast the outlook expressed in the poem "I Hear America Singing" with the account in "Steelworker."

POINTERS: FEASIBILITY STUDY

In business writing, the compare-contrast approach is often used in feasibility studies. A *feasibility study* compares two or more alternatives to help a company decide, for example, whether to purchase a certain type of equipment or to change a procedure. By explaining what time, effort, and/or expense would be involved in each proposed action, a feasibility study provides information a reader can use to make an informed choice. A feasibility study might be organized on a whole-to-whole pattern or a part-to-part pattern.

Sample Feasibility Study

Thesis

Organized on the whole-to-whole pattern, discussing pesticides first; report would go on to discuss biological methods

Using pesticides in city parks is initially less expensive and more effective than using biological methods. However, pesticides threaten the health of a significant portion of the population that uses the park, along with the health of some pets.

The most commonly used pesticides kill the target insects within 48 hours and cost less than $10 an acre to purchase and apply. Nevertheless, studies by the state health department indicate that these pesticides can cause respiratory difficulties for about 15 percent of the population. Certain breeds of dogs are also sensitive to the chemicals used in the most common pesticides.

For an analytical feasibility study, see Workshop 6.

PRACTICE

Complete one of the following assignments to practice writing a feasibility report.

1. Write a report comparing and contrasting two companies that sell compact discs through the mail.

2. Write a report comparing and contrasting exercise programs offered by the local government or YMCA versus those offered by a private health or athletic club.

3. Write a feasibility report comparing two options a group is considering. For example, let's say that school rules forbid students from driving to away games. You could compare chartering a bus versus asking parents to drive.

WORKSHOP 10
Persuasive Writing

WHAT IS PERSUASIVE WRITING?

On Monday you talk a friend into helping you shop for a new jacket. On Tuesday you debate with friends over which movie to see. On Thursday you explain to your parents your reasons for choosing Apple Valley Technical College over Harkins Community College. In all three of these situations, you are engaging in the art of *persuasion.* You probably use this skill frequently, so it is important to know how to use it effectively.

POINTERS: PERSUASIVE ESSAY

In a persuasive essay, the writer wants to convince the reader to think or act in a certain manner. Topics for persuasive essays vary. As you write your persuasive essays, keep the following guidelines in mind:

1. **Select an appropriate topic.** Any topic you choose should lend itself to objective study. It should have at least two distinct "sides." The topic should interest your audience.

2. **State your position.** Include a thesis statement that clearly states the main idea of the essay.

3. **Support your opinion with evidence.** Gather statistics, facts, expert opinions, examples, or observations and develop each with appropriate details. Your sources must be reliable and suitable for the topic.

4. **Know your audience.** Direct your arguments to a specific group. Use what they already think or know about the issue to help persuade them to adopt your position.

5. **Address possible opposing arguments.** Anticipate opposing arguments in a balanced, unemotional manner. Use precise language to emphasize the points you make.

6. **Avoid errors in logic.** Do not use stereotypes, oversimplifications, generalizations, or false analogies.

7. **Organize your information.** Arrange your paragraphs in a logical order. Perhaps you will present your most important points first. You might consider refuting opposing arguments at the beginning, or you may put these arguments at the end. In any case, include a strong introduction and conclusion to strengthen your essay.

Sample Persuasive Essay

Thesis statement	Dicey, the main character in *Homecoming*, is only 13, but she has enough "street smarts" to take care of her younger sister and brothers. After
Supporting arguments	their mother abandons them, Dicey keeps her siblings calm and plans how to handle the situation. She buys them dinner, calls to check on the bus
Supporting opinion	schedule, and evades a mall security guard. In fact, she seems better able to plan ahead and take care of the children than her mother does.

PRACTICE

Use one of the following assignments to help build your persuasive skills.

1. Persuade Juan and Rosa in "Martinez' Treasure" that they don't need the treasure they think they have hidden.

2. Persuade the men in *Trifles* that they should have more respect for the women's concerns.

3. Persuade Feld in "The First Seven Years" to let his daughter go out with Sobel instead of Max.

POINTERS: PROPOSAL

A *proposal* is a business report used to persuade someone (usually an employer or supervisor) to act on information you have provided. Below are guidelines for a business proposal.

1. **Begin with a solution.** Answer a question or solve a problem at the outset. Your opening paragraph should state the action you are proposing. This statement is similar to a thesis in a persuasive essay.

2. **Give readers a reason to comply.** List the reasons why the company or department should follow your recommendation. Begin with the most important reasons. Include evidence to support your reasons.

3. **Respond to possible objections with logic.** Businesses want to know the bottom line—how much money they will save (or earn) in the long run. As you anticipate objections, do so by comparing products and costs and emphasizing the savings or additional earnings for the company.

4. **Recommend alternate solutions.** For example, if you are proposing that all ten computers in the Art Department be upgraded, you might offer a plan for replacing the computers gradually, over a six-month period. You might also suggest a way to "recycle" the old computers.

5. **Conclude with a strong summation.** To remind the audience what needs to be done, briefly summarize the proposal you made in the opening paragraph.

6. **Check for errors.** Review your proposal for errors in logic, grammar, and organization.

Proposal to Start a Partners Program

Solution

Reason

Advantages

A "Partners Program" would help welcome new employees and raise morale for everyone. This is a large company, so it's easy for new staff to feel lost. In a Partners Program, each new employee would be assigned a staff member, who would help the employee become familiar with the building (including the cafeteria and parking areas), meet other employees, and learn about sources of help, if necessary.

The assigned partners would also benefit because they would develop a stronger bond with the company and have the satisfaction of knowing they are contributing to another employee's success. The program would cost very little—just two or three hours of the staff member's time during the first month or so of the new person's

Summation

employment. With your approval, I will set up this program as part of Human Resources' commitment to the well-being of our employees.

PRACTICE

Complete one of the following assignments to create a proposal.

1. Persuade your employer to purchase or lease a new copier. (The old copier keeps breaking down and interfering with your efficiency.)

2. You have been working part-time as a sales clerk during the school year. Persuade your employer to hire you full-time for the summer.

WORKSHOP 11

Business Letters

WHAT IS A BUSINESS LETTER?

A *business letter* is a professional piece of correspondence aimed at a particular audience (usually an outside organization), and designed to provide a permanent written record of a business transaction.

POINTERS: WRITING A BUSINESS LETTER

When drafting a business letter, follow these guidelines:

1. **Include the basic parts of a letter.** The heading, often printed on letterhead stationery, gives the sender's address. Under the heading, write the complete date, and the name, title, and mailing address of the recipient. Next, the salutation or greeting includes the recipient's title and last name followed by a colon. The body consists of the message and ends with a closing such as *Cordially* or *Sincerely yours* on a separate line. Follow the closing with a comma, and sign the letter under the closing. Type your name under your signature.

2. **Type business letters in block form or modified block form.** To use block style, place each part of the letter flush left (aligned at the left margin). To use modified block style, place the heading, date, closing, and signature to the right of center. The other parts of the letter remain flush left.

Letter of Inquiry or Request

A *letter of inquiry* asks for information. Be as polite and specific as possible. Explain what you would like to know, what you intend to do with the information, and where to send the information. Thank the recipient for taking the time to read and respond to your letter.

Heading, date, and address appear at the top of the letter	24 Madison Lane Woodlin, MN 78012-3721 November 12, 199- Admissions Director Interlochen Center for the Arts P.O. Box 199 Interlochen, MI 49643-7200
Include a salutation	Dear Director:
Ask for information in the body of the letter	I am a high school junior who is interested in attending your Summer Arts Camp. I would especially like to know more about your new jazz guitar ensemble. Please send me a brochure about the camp and an application form.
Express your thanks ahead of time	I look forward to learning more about Interlochen and perhaps attending camp there this summer. Thank you for sending the information.
Closing, your signature, and your typed name appear at the end	Sincerely, *Karen Shao* Karen Shao

Letter of Application

A *letter of application* indicates a person's interest in a specific position. It should be limited to one page and include information not found in the applicant's résumé, his or her availability for an interview, and how he or she can be contacted.

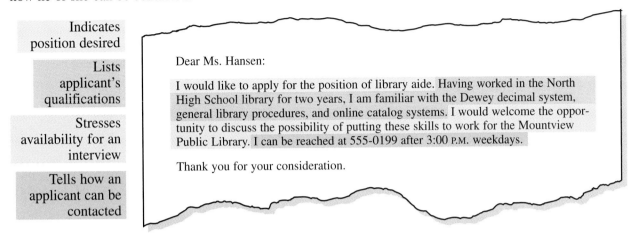

Indicates position desired

Lists applicant's qualifications

Stresses availability for an interview

Tells how an applicant can be contacted

Dear Ms. Hansen:

I would like to apply for the position of library aide. Having worked in the North High School library for two years, I am familiar with the Dewey decimal system, general library procedures, and online catalog systems. I would welcome the opportunity to discuss the possibility of putting these skills to work for the Mountview Public Library. I can be reached at 555-0199 after 3:00 P.M. weekdays.

Thank you for your consideration.

Letter of Recommendation

A *letter of recommendation* explains to an employer why he or she should hire a particular person. It is usually written by a former or current employer or supervisor. A letter of recommendation outlines the employee's qualifications for the job and includes the writer's recommendation.

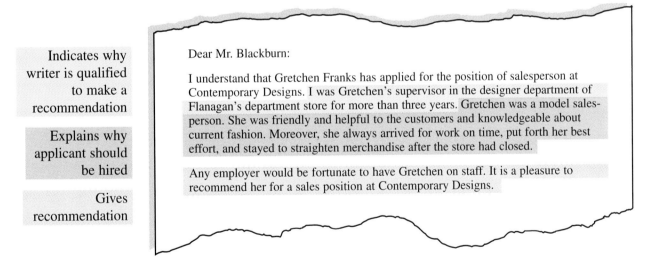

Indicates why writer is qualified to make a recommendation

Explains why applicant should be hired

Gives recommendation

Dear Mr. Blackburn:

I understand that Gretchen Franks has applied for the position of salesperson at Contemporary Designs. I was Gretchen's supervisor in the designer department of Flanagan's department store for more than three years. Gretchen was a model salesperson. She was friendly and helpful to the customers and knowledgeable about current fashion. Moreover, she always arrived for work on time, put forth her best effort, and stayed to straighten merchandise after the store had closed.

Any employer would be fortunate to have Gretchen on staff. It is a pleasure to recommend her for a sales position at Contemporary Designs.

PRACTICE

Complete one of the following assignments to practice writing a business letter.

1. You have heard about a course offered locally that interests you, such as sailing, rappelling, car repair, or another topic. Write to the organization that offers it, asking for more information.

2. Write a letter of application for a part-time job advertised in the classified section of a local newspaper.

3. Write a letter of recommendation explaining why a friend would make a good employee.

WORKSHOP 12

Definition

WHAT IS A DEFINITION?

A *definition* explains what something means. For example, a specialized term in an automotive class will need definition. To help us understand abstract ideas and concrete experience, dictionaries define thousands of words. Dictionary definitions are "formal." Formal definitions follow a set pattern: first, they state the term to be defined; second, they place the term in a general class; finally, they distinguish the term from other members of this general class.

POINTERS

You can use the dictionary to find the basic definition of thousands of words and phrases, but for more complex ideas and concepts, such as what a spreadsheet is or can do, a dictionary may not provide enough information and details. Formal and informal definitions are used to explain what something is or is not. In your writing, consider the following guidelines as you define terms and ideas:

1. **A formal definition explains or describes the characteristics or qualities of a subject.** Whenever you decide to define a term, begin with the dictionary. Make sure you understand exactly what the formal dictionary definition is.

2. **To write a paper that defines, a brief definition could serve as your thesis statement of an essay or the topic sentence of a paragraph.**

3. **In a complex definition, identify the features or characteristics of the subject that either make it unique or make it like other subjects.**

4. **When defining an abstract word such as "freedom" or "honor," you may wish to extend the dictionary definition with your own ideas and create your own informal definition.** As long as your definition does not contradict the dictionary, it will be convincing.

Definition of Photosynthesis

Begin with a strong thesis statement

Characteristics that make the subject different

Photosynthesis is the process that green plants use to produce their own food. Photosynthesis begins as the chlorophyll in plant cells absorbs radiant energy from sunlight. The energy is used to combine carbon dioxide from the atmosphere with water absorbed by the plant roots. This combination produces sugar, a form of chemical energy that the plant stores and uses as food. During photosynthesis, oxygen is also released into the atmosphere.

PRACTICE

To develop your skill in writing definitions, choose one of the following assignments.

1. Explain the "information super highway" and how it might affect your generation.

2. Develop your own definition of "talent" by using the dictionary and examples from your own experience.

3. Define paradise, according to Sarah in "A Paradise Lost."

WORKSHOP 13

Memo

WHAT IS A MEMO?

A *memo* is a brief message usually written from one company employee to another. It may be from a supervisor to a subordinate, from a subordinate to a supervisor, or from one co-worker to another. The purpose of a memo may be to express, to inform, to request, to instruct, or to persuade.

POINTERS: MEMO

All memos generally follow the same format, which enables workers to communicate efficiently. When preparing a memo, follow these guidelines:

1. **Begin with a heading.** Include who is receiving the memo, who is sending it, the date, and the subject.

2. **State your main point.** Long introductions are unnecessary; give your main point as soon as possible.

3. **Be concise.** Since a memo is intended for individuals who work for the same company, background information is often unnecessary. Provide only the information the recipients do not already have.

4. **Be clear.** Many memos announce a policy change or request that a certain action be taken. Strive to make clear your expectations of the recipients. What exactly do you want them to do or to know?

5. **Vary the tone.** Different audiences and purposes require different tones. A memo to a supervisor would have a different tone from a memo to a co-worker. Ask your supervisor for style guidelines and, if possible, read other recent memos before writing one.

Memo

Heading

To: Karl Wojcicki
From: Jennifer Duguid
Date: March 20, 199-
Subject: Flexible scheduling

Main point

Starting April 5, all employees will be able to choose their own work schedules. You may come in any time between 7:00 A.M. and 9:00 A.M. and leave any time between 4:00 P.M. and 6:00 P.M., as long as you work eight hours daily. Please discuss your schedule preference with your supervisor, who will ensure that any critical hours are covered in your department.

PRACTICE

Complete one of the following assignments to create a memo.

1. Write a memo to your employee, approving his or her choice of working hours.

2. In a memo, explain a change in the areas where eating is allowed at your company.

3. Write a memo to announce a new company softball team.

WORKSHOP 14

E-Mail

WHAT IS E-MAIL?

E-mail, or electronic mail, is a message sent through a computer network. E-mail is delivered to the recipient's computer memory almost immediately, making it a speedy way of communicating. (See **Workshop 18** for information concerning on-line databases.)

POINTERS: E-MAIL

You might send e-mail to an employee or to a group of people within your company. Or you could send e-mail to someone in another company or even in another nation. To create an e-mail message, follow the guidelines for a memo by getting to the point and being concise. In addition, keep the points below in mind.

1. **Find out your recipient's computer network address.** You can send messages only to others on the same network or a connecting network, and you must know the person's exact address. Your company may also have an address that allows you to send a memo to a group of people.

2. **Use an appropriate tone.** Remember that the reader cannot see your face and realize that you are joking or being sarcastic. A reader might be offended by a comment you meant to be funny. Be sensitive to how your message might affect your reader.

3. **Remember that others may read your e-mail.** E-mail seems friendly and informal, but some e-mail messages can be accessed and read by others. Most e-mail can be printed and distributed to others. Don't write anything that would be embarrassing if it were read by the "wrong" person. Fix spelling and grammar errors, and avoid offensive language.

4. **Avoid sending e-mail when you are angry.** Go ahead and write down your feelings, but don't send them until you feel calm and are sure you really want to share that message.

5. **Use upper- and lower-case letters.** ALL CAPITALS MAKE ANYTHING DIFFICULT TO READ.

Sample E-Mail Message

Internet addresses	To:	president@whitehouse.gov
	From:	terrysmith@FranklinCo.com
Optional memo heading	Date:	December 1, 199-
		Dear President Clinton:
Main point		Congratulations on vetoing that tax bill! I agree with you completely!

PRACTICE

Complete one of the following assignments to practice using e-mail. Make up addresses, if necessary.

1. Use e-mail to invite a co-worker to a meeting.

2. Use e-mail to announce a company picnic.

3. Use e-mail to check on the delivery of an order in Japan.

WORKSHOP 15
Active Listening

WHAT IS ACTIVE LISTENING?

When you listen to a teacher, talk to a good friend, or watch a television show, you should listen actively. *Active listening* means thinking critically, carefully, and considerately about what one hears. Your job as a listener is to understand and evaluate the speaker's words.

POINTERS

Active listening is essential for effective communication. Follow these guidelines to sharpen your active listening skills.

1. **Identify the main idea.** What is the speaker's subject? What is his or her position on the subject? Some speakers begin by explaining their main point; others wait until later in the speech to reach their main point.

2. **Concentrate on the topic.** As you listen to someone, think about what is said. If you mentally follow a speaker's train of thought, you will not be easily distracted. If possible or practical, take notes.

3. **Ask questions.** Clarify the points you do not understand by asking questions of the speaker. If you are unable to address the speaker, ask yourself the questions. Then predict what the speaker will say, as if you and the speaker were having a conversation.

4. **Notice verbal cues.** Transition words help listeners follow what the speaker is saying. Words such as *furthermore* and *next* indicate that the speaker is going to make another important point. *On the other hand* lets you know that the speaker is about to make a contrast with a previous point. Other transition words include *but, however, like,* and *similarly.*

5. **Watch for nonverbal cues.** Facial expressions, hand gestures, and other kinds of body language might emphasize important points, enliven a speech with humor, or provide additional insight as to the speaker's attitude toward the topic.

6. **Keep an open mind.** If you do not agree with a speaker's opinions, do not let your emotions get in the way of hearing what is said.

7. **Separate fact from opinion.** A fact is a piece of information that can be proven or verified. It is neither good nor bad. An opinion is an individual's view of a situation or fact. When evaluating a speaker's message, consider the facts separately from the opinions expressed.

PRACTICE

You should use your active listening skills all day long. Here are some ways you can practice.

1. Listen to a classmate's oral presentation. Afterwards, write a summary of the presentation. Include the speaker's main points as well as a description of the speaker's verbal and nonverbal cues and how they made the content of the presentation easier or more difficult to understand.

2. Listen to a speech delivered in person or on television. If possible, record the speech on audio or video tape. Summarize the speech for your classmates, then review the tape to determine if your summary covered the main points the speaker made.

WORKSHOP 16
Critical Thinking

WHAT IS CRITICAL THINKING?

Critical thinkers examine their own thinking and the thinking of others to see if it makes sense. Critical thinking includes a number of skills that help people discover truth, such as analysis, cause-and-effect reasoning, comparison and contrast, paraphrasing, and summarizing.

POINTERS

To examine an issue, a critical thinker does the following:

1. **Describes the real issue or problem.** Before a critical thinker can try to solve a problem, he or she must be able to describe it. For example, in "Train Time" the question is not how to help Native American children succeed in the white world. Instead, the question is why the Major and others think these children *need* to succeed in the white world.

2. **Raises relevant questions.** After reading "Everyday Use," a critical thinker might ask what role, if any, the father of Maggie and Dee had in shaping their vastly different outlooks on life.

3. **Recognizes his or her own biases and those of others.** The critical thinker tries to put aside his or her own preferences and look at an issue objectively. For example, he or she may not read science fiction by choice but can still carefully analyze the characters in "The Wife's Story." The critical thinker also looks for signs of bias when considering others' opinions.

4. **Questions assumptions.** In "The Use of Force," the author does not seem to doubt that force was necessary. A critical thinker might ask whether the doctor's need to control the situation was even more important than his need to protect the child from diphtheria.

5. **Is open to new ideas and other points of view.** The critical thinker knows that a closed mind shuts out new information—including truth. He or she tries to listen with an open mind to others' opinions.

6. **Carefully weighs new information.** The critical thinker evaluates information—and its sources—before accepting it as true. This thinker does not try to make new information fit his or her previous conclusions, but considers whether new evidence means that those conclusions should be adjusted.

7. **Considers implications and possibilities.** As "The First Seven Years" ends, Sobel seems to have agreed to wait two years to ask Miriam to marry him. A critical thinker might ask if Miriam, who is only nineteen, will still feel the same about the aging Sobel in two years.

8. **Supports opinion with evidence.** The critical thinker does not expect his or her opinions to be accepted without support. The thinker is able to explain logical reasons for his or her conclusions.

PRACTICE

Answer one of the following questions to practice using your critical thinking skills.

1. After reading "The Story of an Hour," do you think Kate Chopin justifies Mrs. Mallard's reaction to her husband's miraculous escape from death?

2. In "The Scotty Who Knew Too Much," why does Scotty have so much trouble dealing with the world?

3. In "Looking for Work," what assumptions does Gary make about the way other people live? Why does he think he's correct? (Be sure to support your conclusions with examples.)

WORKSHOP 17
Using the Dictionary

POINTERS

Dictionaries include much more than definitions and spellings. Whether in print or on-line, dictionaries generally contain these components:

1. **Guide words.** The first and last words on each page are printed at the top of the page and called guide words. If the word you seek is alphabetically between the guide words, it will be on that page.

2. **Main entry.** The main entry shows each word's spelling, syllable division, pronunciation, part of speech, and definition. A guide to pronunciation and pronunciation symbols is usually provided in the front.

Sample Definition

Main entry

Pronunciation

Part of speech

Earliest known definition appears first

im•pose \im-ˋpōz\ *v* **im•posed; im•pos•ing 1 a:** to establish or apply by authority **b:** to establish or bring about as if by force **2 a:** place, set **b:** to arrange (as pages) in the proper order for printing **3** to force into the company or on the attention of another

3. **Reference Lists.** Abbreviations, foreign words and phrases, biographical names, geographical names, colleges and universities, signs and symbols, and punctuation and style guides are included in the back of dictionaries.

4. **Proofreaders' Marks.** Found near the main entry for *proofread,* these symbols are used to show what corrections need to be made to a document. Following are the most frequently used proofreaders' marks.

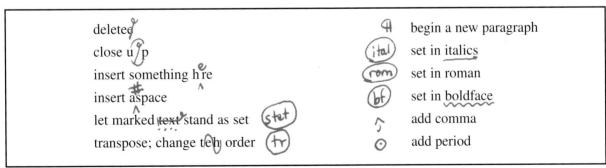

PRACTICE

Complete one of the following assignments to practice finding information in a dictionary.

1. Find the definition of the word *philanthropist.*

2. Identify the adjective form of the word *injury.*

3. Use proofreaders' marks to edit a paper you have written.

WORKSHOP 18
Using an On-line Library

WHAT IS AN ON-LINE LIBRARY?

Computer on-line databases allow you to access a whole library of information with your computer. These databases often include newspaper, magazine, and journal articles and abstracts (summaries); encyclopedia entries; CD-ROM databases on current affairs, business, health, and other topics; maps; indexes of periodicals; and other resources. Many of these databases are linked through a computer network called Internet. Some of these databases are available to people with home computers who subscribe to CompuServe, Prodigy, America Online, or other commercial on-line services. People with home computers can also access Internet through a commercial service. However, many school and community libraries subscribe to Internet and to on-line services that are not available to the average person. The libraries then offer Internet and the other services to patrons at a small charge or no fee. It is possible to use a home computer to connect with a library computer service, which then allows the home user to connect with Internet at no charge.

POINTERS

A librarian, another knowledgeable person, or a user manual can help you learn the most efficient way to use the various on-line services. The guidelines below are a starting point.

1. **Get organized before logging on to the database.** Don't waste valuable computer search time thinking about which topics you want to research.

2. **Take advantage of free services.** In addition to using the available services of your library, take advantage of free Internet services such as WAIS, MOSAIC, and VERONICA, which allow you to search a wide range of databases by asking questions or choosing items on menus. GOPHER is another free navigation tool that can help you access Internet menus and services.

3. **After you choose a database, narrow your search by using combinations of key words.** This approach is called a Boolean search. By entering key words at the prompt, you tell the computer to search for certain combinations of concepts. For example, let's say you want to know about the jobs available in the travel industry. If you enter *travel*, the computer will give you the titles of hundreds of articles that include that word. If you enter *travel industry and employment*, the computer will offer a shorter list of articles that include both terms and are much more likely to be helpful.

4. **Find out the most cost-effective way to download and print the information you locate.** Commercial services may charge for each document you download, along with the time you are on-line. Get to know short-cuts that can save time and money.

PRACTICE

Complete one of the following assignments to practice carrying out a computer on-line search.

1. Find out who won the Pulitzer Prize for literature this year (or the last year that it was awarded).

2. Identify four American poets who write (or wrote) about nature.

3. Find out how the population of your state has changed over the past five years.

WORKSHOP 19
Oral Presentations

WHAT IS AN ORAL PRESENTATION?
An *oral presentation* conveys information to co-workers, students, or customers and is often accompanied by visual aids. Many employees give oral presentations, whether to explain a process to co-workers, inform a supervisor of progress on a particular project, or sell a product to customers.

POINTERS
Many people find public speaking stressful. To avoid feeling nervous, carefully plan your oral presentation.

1. **Know your subject.** At work or school you may be asked to give a presentation. Sometimes, however, you will receive only a broad topic. You may need to narrow that topic to a single subject. In addition, you may need to do some research in order to familiarize yourself with the topic. If possible, choose a subject you are already knowledgeable about and one that will appeal to your audience.

2. **Analyze your purpose.** What are you trying to accomplish? You may want to provide information, persuade others, or motivate people.

3. **Analyze the audience.** Is the audience familiar with your topic? Will they understand any jargon you might use? If your purpose is to persuade, think about the attitudes, education, and beliefs your audience may hold.

4. **Organize your presentation.** Plan ahead of time the order in which you will cover your points; otherwise you may ramble or repeat yourself. Prepare an outline that includes all your major points and some brief details about each. If you plan to use notecards during your talk, arrange them according to your outline.

5. **Prepare visuals.** Visual aids will make your presentation more interesting and easier to understand. Graphs, drawings, photographs, models, videotapes, or actual equipment are types of visuals you may want to use. Be careful not to use too many visuals. Choose visuals that will convey your points most effectively. Make sure they are clear and visible to the audience. (See Workshop 20 for more information on visuals.)

6. **Rehearse.** Practice your presentation to determine if you need to make any changes in content or length. Ask a friend or family member to critique your presentation to see if you are speaking clearly and loudly enough and if you are maintaining eye contact. You may wish to videotape the presentation and critique it yourself.

7. **Deliver the presentation.** Remember what you rehearsed. Direct the audience's attention to your visual aids at the appropriate times. Refer to your notes when necessary. Follow your outline and speak naturally.

PRACTICE
Prepare an oral presentation for one of the situations listed below.

1. You have been asked to prepare an orientation for three new employees at a company where you work (or would like to work). Include a visual to show how the company is organized.

2. You have an idea for a new product. Prepare a presentation for your supervisor, encouraging her to suggest the product to upper management. Create visuals to help explain the product's benefits.

3. You have been asked to convince middle school students to stay in school and graduate. Interview people who did and did not graduate and incorporate their comments and advice into your presentation.

WORKSHOP 20
Creating Effective Visuals

WHAT ARE EFFECTIVE VISUALS?

Information can be communicated in many different ways. One of the most successful ways is the use of *visuals,* such as tables, charts, graphs, and maps.

POINTERS

Follow these guidelines to create organized, attention-getting visuals:

1. **Form tables.** A table displays data arranged in columns or rows. Each column has a short heading that quickly tells what can be found in that particular column.

Roosevelt High School Enrollment

	Grade 9	Grade 10	Grade 11	Grade 12
Female	345	402	394	347
Male	361	398	382	320
Total	706	800	776	667

2. **Construct graphs.** Graphs show how numbers relate to each other. A line graph lists one set of numbers along a horizontal line and another set of numbers along a vertical line. By plotting points where the two lines meet and connecting the points together, you can show how the two types of data work together. In a bar graph, instead of plotting points, you draw a bar the length or height of the amount you wish to show.

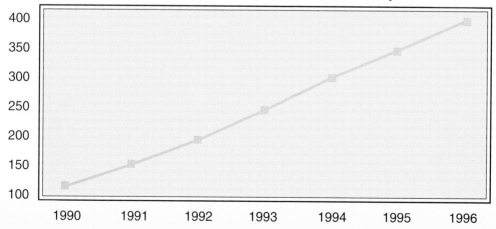

3. **Make charts.** An organizational chart can show the positions in a company and their relation to one another. A flip chart will show only the information you are currently discussing; flip to the next page of the chart to show your next point. Use pie charts to show percentages. To show how a company spends its money, for instance, use sections of the pie to represent each expenditure.

Organizational Chart

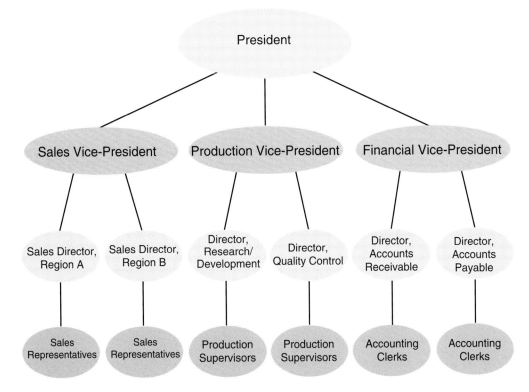

4. **Prepare maps.** When making a map, label each feature clearly and include only those features necessary for your purpose. Include a scale to give readers an indication of the map's proportions.

5. **Write outlines.** Sharing your outline with the audience makes it easier for them to follow your reasoning and remember your main points. You can place your outline on posterboard, create a transparency to use with an overhead projector, or use a computer projection panel to display your outline.

PRACTICE
Choose one of these assignments and select the best way to communicate the information visually. (Make up amounts and figures for your visuals.)

1. Show the total expenditures for your company, including categories such as salaries, raw materials, new equipment and vehicles, property rental, and office supplies.

2. Compare the average salary that five banks pay to their tellers.

3. Show how the average rainfall or snowfall in your region has varied over the past five years.

WORKSHOP 21
Brochure

WHAT IS A BROCHURE?

A *brochure* often advertises products or services, as do flyers and pamphlets. Less formal than a letter, a brochure employs colorful graphics and an eye-catching format to draw a reader's attention. Its folded sections make it easy to hold or carry.

POINTERS

1. **Make an outline.** Decide what information you will include and organize it in an outline. For example, if you are writing to advertise a landscaping business, you should include a list of your services, a brief description of each, and how customers can contact you.

2. **Write engaging copy.** Use colorful, inviting language to describe your product or service. Emphasize the benefits to the customer.

3. **Arrange information in an attention-getting way.** Use small paragraphs, numbered or bulleted lists, and short direct sentences to make your brochure easy to read.

4. **Add visuals.** Interesting photographs and simple charts can emphasize the written information and draw more attention to it.

5. **Choose an appealing design.** The lettering, paper quality, and color of the brochure can encourage or discourage people to pick it up and read it. Select the best quality paper available to you, add color where possible, and use lettering that stands out and is easy to read.

PRACTICE

Complete one of the following assignments to create a brochure.

1. Create a brochure that describes a product or service that you are selling for a club at school. Explain what your group does and why people should buy your product or service.

2. Create a brochure aimed at junior high school students that will help them succeed in high school.

GRAMMAR WORKSHOP

Pronouns

POINTERS

1. A pronoun must agree with its antecedent in number and gender.

> **Angela** showed **her** supervisor the progress report.

The antecedent, *Angela*, is singular and feminine, so the pronoun *her* is used. Sometimes, however, the gender of the antecedent is not provided.

> A **manager** is sensitive to his employees' morale.

Since the manager could be male or female, you have three possible options. You can include both gender pronouns.

> A **manager** is sensitive to **his** or **her** employees' morale.

You can reword the sentence so that the antecedent is plural.

> **Managers** are sensitive to **their** employees' morale.

You can reword the sentence so that the pronoun is unnecessary.

> A **manager** is sensitive to employees' morale.

2. A singular indefinite pronoun antecedent takes a singular pronoun. Common singular indefinite pronouns include *anybody*, *each*, *either*, *everyone*, *everything*, *neither*, and *somebody*. A common error is to choose a pronoun that agrees with a noun in the sentence instead of the indefinite pronoun antecedent.

> Incorrect   **Neither** of the men can bring **their** truck.
>
> Correct   **Neither** of the men can bring **his** truck.
>
> Incorrect   **Each** of the women inserted **their** timecard.
>
> Correct   **Each** of the women inserted **her** timecard.

3. *You* and *they* are always definite pronouns. Another common pronoun error is the indefinite use of *you* and *they*. If one of these words is used without referring to anyone in particular, replace it with a noun.

> Incorrect   To earn a promotion, **you** must do outstanding work.
>
> Correct   To earn a promotion, employees must do outstanding work.
>
> Incorrect   In the company cafeteria, **they** have a wide variety of food.
>
> Correct   The company cafeteria offers a wide variety of food.

PRACTICE

Find and correct the pronoun error in each sentence.

1. They have a sale at the computer store today.

2. A nurse has many responsibilities, so she must plan carefully.

3. Everyone in the meeting wanted to explain their ideas.

4. A bus driver must be able to maneuver his bus through heavy traffic.

GRAMMAR WORKSHOP

Adjectives and Adverbs

POINTERS

1. Adjectives modify nouns and pronouns. Do not use an adjective without a noun or pronoun, and do not use an adjective to modify a verb, an adverb, or another adjective.

> I will put this report in a **large**, **yellow** folder. (*large* and *yellow* describe the noun *folder*)

> This **detailed** report begins with the history of the problem. (*detailed* modifies the noun *report*)

2. Adverbs modify verbs, adjectives, and other adverbs. Adverbs tell *when*, *where*, *how* or *to what extent* about the words they describe. Adverbs often end in *-ly*.

> The new procedure worked **efficiently**. (*efficiently* tells how the procedure worked)

> Put the report **there**. (*there* tells where to put the report)

> **Soon** we will need to replace the copier. (*soon* tells when the copier should be replaced)

3. Some confusion arises with the modifiers *good, bad, well, and badly*. *Good* and *bad* are adjectives; *well* and *badly* are adverbs. *Well* can be an adjective, but only when referring to someone's health.

> Joan did a **good** job on this proposal. (*good* is an adjective describing *job*)

> The new product is selling **badly**. (*badly* is an adverb describing how the product is selling)

> He felt **well** enough to come to work today. (*well* is an adjective describing *He*)

4. Comparative and superlative forms are sometimes misused.

The comparative of an adjective or adverb compares two things and is formed by adding *-er* to the end of the word or by using the word *more*.

> These cookies are **sweeter** than the cookies I made.

> This algebra problem is **more complicated** than the one we had yesterday.

When comparing three or more things, use the superlative form. The superlative is formed by adding *-est* to the end of the word or by using the word *most*.

> This is the **fastest** I have ever worked.

> The **most complicated** part is figuring out how to save money.

5. Some adjectives and adverbs have irregular comparison forms. Practice using these forms to help you remember what they are. When in doubt, consult a dictionary.

PRACTICE

Find and correct the adjective or adverb error in each sentence.

1. Kevin was certainly that he would be chosen.

2. Complete surprised, I rushed quickly into the office.

3. The change we made on the new product is working good.

4. This is the more orders we have ever received in one month.

GRAMMAR WORKSHOP
Prepositions

POINTERS

1. **A preposition connects a noun, a pronoun, or a group of words acting as a noun to another word in the sentence. A preposition often shows the location of something.** The word being connected is called the object of the preposition. A preposition combined with the object of the preposition forms a prepositional phrase.

> Your report is jammed **in the copier**.

In is a preposition. *Copier* is the object of the preposition. *In the copier* is the complete prepositional phrase, showing the location of the paper.

2. **Learn which words are prepositions.** Following is a complete list of prepositions. Study this list so that you can recognize prepositions easily.

aboard	at	by	inside	outside	toward
about	before	concerning	into	over	under
above	behind	despite	like	past	underneath
across	below	down	near	pending	until
after	beneath	during	of	regarding	unto
against	beside	except	off	respecting	up
along	besides	excepting	on	since	upon
among	between	for	onto	through	with
around	beyond	from	opposite	throughout	within
as	but	in	out	to	without

3. **The placement of a preposition is important.** Sometimes a preposition comes after its object. This is especially true in spoken English. For formal writing, it is best to avoid this construction.

> Informal   I am not sure where to put the paper **in**.
>
> Formal   I am not sure **in** which slot to put the paper.

Sometimes a prepositional phrase is misplaced. Do not position a prepositional phrase too far from the word or words it modifies.

> Incorrect   The salesperson placed an order **in the blue suit**.
>
> Correct   The salesperson **in the blue suit** placed an order.

PRACTICE

Write a sentence for each prepositional phrase below, using the example as a guide.

> Example   until four o'clock
>
> Sentence   The meeting will not be over until four o'clock.

1. at the bottom
2. by Tuesday
3. through the air

4. for three dollars
5. on a whim
6. with Tanya and Sean

GRAMMAR WORKSHOP

Complete Sentences

POINTERS

1. A sentence needs two basic parts to express a complete thought: the subject and the predicate. The subject includes the key noun or pronoun and all the words that modify it. The predicate includes the verb or verb phrase and all the words that complete its meaning.

```
┌──────── subject ────────┐┌────────predicate───────┐
The manager of our department has posted a new schedule.
```

2. Some sentences do not follow the usual subject-predicate order. Some place the subject after the verb.

```
┌──────────predicate──────────┐┌──────subject──────┐
In the computer's memory was stored the essential data.
```

In imperative sentences, the subject *you* is understood rather than expressed.

```
┌subject┐┌──────────predicate──────────┐
(You)    Please start with the files on my desk.
```

3. A sentence fragment lacks a subject, a verb, or both. Every sentence must contain a verb. Unless the subject is understood, it must be included in the sentence.

Fragment	Told me to start on Tuesday. (lacks a subject—who told you?)
Better	Karen told me to start on Tuesday. (includes a subject—*Karen*)
Fragment	The safety glasses. (lacks a verb—what about the safety glasses?)
Better	The safety glasses **protected** my eyes from sparks. (includes a verb—*protected*)

4. A run-on sentence is two or more complete sentences written as if they were one sentence. Incorrect punctuation causes run-on sentences. When only a comma separates two main clauses, a comma splice occurs.

Run-on	I sent my résumé to four companies, only one replied.
Better	I sent my résumé to four companies, but only one replied.

Another type of run-on sentence is two main clauses with no punctuation between them.

Run-on	I sent a cover letter with my résumé the company that received it responded.
Better	I sent a cover letter with my résumé, and the company that received it responded.

PRACTICE

Indicate whether each item below is a fragment or a run-on sentence and correct each.

1. I was appointed team captain, I will set up our schedule.

2. Jennifer will be in charge of materials Jonah will take care of quality control.

3. Late the next day.

GRAMMAR WORKSHOP

Phrases and Clauses

POINTERS

1. A phrase functions as a single part of speech. It can be a preposition, a noun, an adjective, an adverb, or a verb. A clause is a group of words that contains both a subject and a predicate. A main clause can stand alone as a sentence. A subordinate clause depends on the rest of the sentence and cannot stand alone.

┌─verbal phrase─┐┌main clause┐┌─phrase──┐   ┌subordinate clause┐┌─main clause─┐
Waiting for Stan,   we stood   by the elevator.   When we saw him,   he was smiling.

2. A subordinate clause is usually joined to the rest of a sentence with a subordinating conjunction or a relative pronoun. Common subordinating conjunctions include *after*, *although*, *when*, and *while*. Relative pronouns include *what*, *whatever*, *who*, *whoever*, *which*, and *that*. *Why* and *how* can introduce noun clauses.

┌──────main clause──────┐┌────subordinate clause───┐
We will be trying a new procedure because the old one took too long.

┌─subordinate clause─┐
The procedure that we had been using was outdated.

3. Do not leave a phrase or a clause dangling. A dangling modifier is a word or group of words that does not seem to modify any word in a sentence.

| Incorrect | **Eating lunch,** the bus pulled into the parking lot. (*Eating lunch* does not modify anything in the sentence, since a bus does not eat lunch.) |
| Correct | **Eating lunch, we** saw the bus pull into the parking lot. |

When you use a phrase or a clause to modify another word, be sure it is clear what the phrase or clause modifies.

4. Phrases and clauses can be misplaced. Do not place a phrase or clause too far from the word it is meant to modify.

| Incorrect | The pilot gave the weather report **in the helicopter.** (*in the helicopter* is misplaced) |
| Correct | The **pilot in the helicopter** gave the weather report. |

PRACTICE

Revise each of the following sentences.

1. Rushing to meet the deadline, two pages of the report were left out.

2. No invoices will be distributed by clerks that are out of date.

3. Dennis likes his job in his blue jeans because he can work.

GRAMMAR WORKSHOP

Subject-Verb Agreement

POINTERS

A verb must agree in number with its subject.

1. Make sure the verb agrees with the subject and not the object of a preposition.

Incorrect The **employees** of this company is dedicated.

Correct The **employees** of this company **are** dedicated.

2. A sentence may contain a predicate nominative, which is a noun or pronoun that follows a linking verb and describes the subject. The verb still agrees with the subject.

Incorrect **Charts** is the best visual to use in this case.

Correct **Charts are** the best visual to use in this case.

3. Watch for sentences in which the subject comes after the verb. The verb still should agree with the subject.

Incorrect In the outer office **was** two worried **employees**.

Correct In the outer office **were** two worried **employees**.

4. When a compound subject is joined by *or* or *nor*, the verb agrees with the subject that is closer to it.

Incorrect Neither the manager nor the **employees knows** about it.

Correct Neither the manager nor the **employees know** about it.

5. Watch for intervening expressions. Expressions such as *in addition to*, *as well as*, or *together with* do not change the number of the subject.

Incorrect **Karen Smith**, together with her staff, **are working** on the project.

Correct **Karen Smith**, together with her staff, **is working** on the project.

6. Indefinite pronouns may be singular or plural. Some indefinite pronouns, such as *anyone*, *everything*, and *each*, are always singular. Others, such as *few*, *both*, and *many*, are always plural. A few (*some*, *all*, *most*, and *none*) can be singular or plural. Determine the number of the indefinite pronoun. Then make the verb agree with it.

Incorrect **Everyone** in the office **are going** to the meeting.

Correct **Everyone** in the office **is going** to the meeting.

PRACTICE

Correct the agreement error in each sentence.

1. In the second group is Beatrice and Lamar.

2. Either Sheryl or Samuel are going to call the supplier.

3. The first shift, in addition to the second shift, have asked for longer breaks.

GRAMMAR WORKSHOP

Capitalization

POINTERS

1. Capitalize the first word of a direct quotation if the quotation is a complete sentence.

> The principal said, "We have spent a great deal of time planning the program for Career Day."

2. Titles that are used before a proper name or in direct address are capitalized.

> At the airport, Mayor Cummings greeted Vice-President Gore.

> I learned that Grandpa Gonzalez fought in the Korean War.

Titles that follow a proper name or are used alone are not capitalized.

> My uncle will be visiting us this weekend.

3. Capitalize the names of organizations, firms, and companies.

> I will be an intern for the Environmental Protection Agency.

> I hear that Habitat for Humanity needs more volunteers.

> My neighbor works in the shipping department of Macro Industries.

4. Capitalize the names of ships, trains, planes, and spacecraft.

> The *Endeavour* space shuttle is landing today.

> The *Delta Queen* has pulled into the dock.

5. The titles of works such as books, magazines, songs, and stories are capitalized.

> Have you read all of *The Joy Luck Club*?

The article preceding a title is capitalized only when it is actually part of the title.

> Did you read that article in the *Time* magazine that came out this week?

6. Capitalize proper adjectives. A proper adjective is formed from a proper noun. Do not capitalize the noun it modifies unless the noun would be capitalized when used alone.

> Did that new Thai market open yet?

> Who is the new White House spokesperson?

7. Days of the week and months of the year are always capitalized.

> Our current deadline is Monday, October 12.

PRACTICE

Find and correct the capitalization errors in these sentences.

1. Why do they call the train *swift arrow*?

2. Have you ever donated blood to the red cross?

3. I danced with uncle Manuel at my Aunt's wedding.

4. We bought french pastries at the Bakery on the corner.

GRAMMAR WORKSHOP
Commas

POINTERS

1. Use a comma after an introductory participle or participial phrase (a verb or verb phrase that functions as an adjective).

> Frowning, Jessie read the report twice.

> Inserting the disk carefully, Jonathan began the procedure.

2. An introductory prepositional phrase requires a comma only if it is particularly long or would be misunderstood without one. If a sentence begins with more than one prepositional phrase, a comma should be used.

> In front of the locked door, Karl found a package.

3. Use a comma after an introductory adverb clause.

> While waiting nervously, Kayla planned what she would say.

Use a pair of commas to set off an internal adverb clause that interrupts the flow of a sentence.

> This heading, when used correctly, should include the date.

4. Use commas with nonessential elements. Nonessential participial phrases, infinitive phrases, and adjective clauses all need to be set off with commas. A phrase or clause is nonessential if it is not necessary to understand the meaning of the sentence.

> Mr. Joseph, speaking calmly, explained that the company was in bankruptcy.

> Azalea, who is in charge of the event, has called a meeting.

5. Use commas to separate three or more words, phrases, or clauses in a series.

> His duties included answering the phones, greeting visitors, and accepting packages.

> April is responsible for keeping inventory records, Juan will order any needed parts, and Jermaine will create new forms.

6. Use commas when writing dates and addresses.

> I will graduate on June 3, 1997, and start work the next week.

> Thirteen Front Street, Memphis, Tennessee, is the location of our central branch office.

PRACTICE

Add commas to each sentence where needed.

1. We need to order paper binders and notepads.

2. Approaching rapidly the deadline loomed over our heads.

3. Send that package to 14 North Tatum Street Phoenix Arizona.

4. In order to be accepted you will need to fill out an application.

5. Presto Print which is just off Schrock Road offers the lowest prices.

GRAMMAR WORKSHOP

Colons and Semicolons

POINTERS

1. Use a colon to introduce a list. Phrases such as *these*, *the following*, or *as follows* signal the beginning of a list.

> These people attended the conference: Amber, Oscar, Michael, and Tamika.

However, if the list immediately follows a verb or a preposition, a colon should not be used.

> The conference was attended by Amber, Oscar, Michael, and Tamika.

2. Use a colon before a formal quotation. *This*, *these*, *as follows*, or *the following* can signal the beginning of a formal quotation. Place the colon outside the opening quotation marks.

> Franklin Roosevelt cheered Americans with these words: "We have nothing to fear but fear itself."

3. Place a colon after the salutation of a business letter. In a personal letter, the salutation is followed by a comma; however, a colon is used for business letters.

> Dear Human Resources Manager: Dear Professor Henry:

4. A semicolon is used to separate two main clauses that are not joined by a coordinating conjunction. If a coordinating conjunction joins lengthy clauses that already contain several commas, then a semicolon is used.

> In the morning, I met with a representative from the contractor; in the afternoon, I toured the facility and the grounds.

5. Use a semicolon to separate main clauses that are joined by a conjunctive adverb. A conjunctive adverb is an adverb that joins two independent clauses.

also	consequently	however	meanwhile	still
besides	finally	instead	moreover	then
certainly	further	likewise	nevertheless	therefore

> The problem seemed overwhelming; **nevertheless,** Janis looked calm.

> I sent out twenty-eight carefully written résumés; **consequently,** I received quite a few responses.

6. When the items in a series contain commas, use a semicolon to separate them.

> The company has offices in Rockridge, New Hampshire; Watertown, Massachusetts; and Portland, Maine.

> Also attending were Shantel, from the records department; Morgan, claims department; and Preston, human resources.

PRACTICE

Add colons and semicolons where needed.

1. Gabriel worked at Fisher Foods last summer he expects to work there again this year.

2. Joan will start in the claims department however, she will soon transfer to accounting.

3. The available dates are Wednesday, September 6, Thursday, September 14, and Monday, September 25.

GRAMMAR WORKSHOP

Spelling

POINTERS

1. **Spelling counts.** Misspelled words may lead your reader to believe you are careless or not prepared for the writing task involved. Spelling errors on a résumé or job application could cause a potential employer to consider your work sloppy and hire someone else. Also, misspelled words can make it difficult for a reader to understand your message.

2. **When revising a piece of writing, proofread it once solely to look for spelling errors.** Computer spelling checks can alert you to certain mistakes, but not to all possible mistakes. For example, if you spelled the word *hear* when you meant to spell *here*, a computer spelling check would not alert you to this fact.

3. **Learn specific spelling rules.** Though there are exceptions, learning spelling rules will help you improve the accuracy of your spelling. You probably know the saying "Write *i* before *e* except after *c* or when sounded like *a* as in *neighbor* and *weigh.*"

| niece | believe | feign | freight | deceive | receipt |
| diet | grief | eighth | sleigh | ceiling | conceit |

4. **Make a list of words you are likely to misspell.** Most of us have trouble remembering how to spell certain words. Keep track of the words that you find difficult. Use these words in your writing, and learn to spell them correctly so that you can cross them off your list.

5. **Do not be confused by homonyms or similar-sounding words.** Two words can sound the same—or nearly the same—and be spelled quite differently. Be careful not to write one word when you intended to use another. For example, an *effect* is a result; *affect* means to influence or to have an effect upon.

Example 1   I like the **effect** of these new headings.

Example 2   The appearance of your résumé can **affect** how many responses you receive.

It's is the contraction for *it is*; *its* is the possessive form of *it*.

Example 3   **It's** time for us to review what we've done.

Example 4   This box has lost **its** label.

Who's is a contraction of *who is*; *whose* shows the possessive form of *who*.

Example 5   **Who's** going to be in charge of collating?

Example 6   **Whose** message is that?

PRACTICE

Correct the spelling or word-choice errors in each sentence.

1. What are the frieght charges on there order?

2. Whose responsible for filling out this receipt?

3. I beleive its on the fourth floor.

4. This low cieling may effect the height of the doors.

NDEX

AUTHOR/TITLE INDEX

GENRE INDEX

Autobiography

Technical Writing

Poetry

ENERAL INDEX

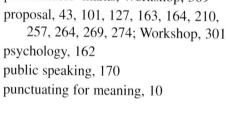

ACKNOWLEDGMENTS

PHOTO & ILLUSTRATION CREDITS

Illustrations on pages 4, 10, 13, 16, 18, 24, 34, 40, 46, 54, 55, 59, 62, 66, 68, 75, 82, 100, 106, 108, 113, 118, 121, 126, 133, 145, 153, 154, 159, 167, 168, 174, 178, 180, 188, 197, 203, 206, 211, 216, 219, 222, 227, 228, 234, 237, 245, 250, 252, 258, 260, 265, 269, 271, 275, 276, and 278 were created by Learning Design Associates, Inc., Columbus, OH. All other illustrations are in the public domain.

iv–xiii © Corel Professional Photos CD-ROM; **3** Courtesy of the Honorable Janet Jackson; **6** © Corel Professional Photos CD-ROM; **7** © National Portrait Gallery, Smithsonian Institute, James Barton Longacre, after Bass Otis and John Singleton Copley/Art Resource, NY; **12** © Super Stock; **14** © Elliot Varner Smith, International Stock; **19** © The Bettmann Archive, Mathew Brady; **20** © The Bettmann Archive; **26** © Super Stock; **29** © Corel Professional Photos CD-ROM; **37** © Stan Reis, International Stock; **38** © Michael P. Manheim, International Stock; **41** © Scott Thode, International Stock; **45** © Corel Professional Photos CD-ROM; **48** © Super Stock; **49** © Super Stock; **57** © Corel Professional Photos CD-ROM; **58** © Corel Professional Photos CD-ROM; **61** © Ohio Historical Society; **64** © Tom Carroll, International Stock; **70** © Lou Manna, International Stock; **72** © Bob Stern, International Stock; **73** Image provided by © 1994 Photodisc, Inc.; **77** Image provided by © 1994 Photodisc, Inc.; **78** © Elliot Smith, International Stock; **80** © Charles Steiner, International Stock; **87** © Red Wing Shoe Co., Inc. (314 Main St., Red Wing, MN 55066); **88** © Super Stock; **93** © Corel Professional Photos CD-ROM; **94** Image provided by © 1994 Photodisc, Inc.; **97** © Corel Professional Photos CD-ROM; **99** © Peter Tenzer, International Stock; **105** © Super Stock; **110** © Super Stock; **111** Image provided by © 1994 Photodisc, Inc.; **116** © Corel Professional Photos CD-ROM; **119** © James Davis, International Stock; **123** © Bill Stanton, International Stock; **127** © Super Stock; **131** © Jay Thomas, International Stock; **135** © The Bettmann Archive; **137** © Jay Thomas, International Stock; **138** © South-Western Educational Publishing; **141** © Jose L. Pelaes, The Stock Market; **144** © The Bettmann Archive; **146** © International Stock; **151** © Bill Tucker, International Stock; **160** © Corel Professional Photos CD-ROM; **162** © National Museum of American Art, Washington D.C./Art Resource, NY; **163** © Super Stock; **169** © Buddy Mays, International Stock; **170** © Johnny Stockshooter, International Stock; **172** © George Ancona, International Stock; **176** © National Museum of American Art, Washington, D.C./Art Resource, NY; **179** © International Stock; **181** © Super Stock; **185** © Super Stock; **191** © Super Stock; **194** © Norris Clark, International Stock; **195** © Scott Thode, International Stock; **199** © Super Stock; **201** © Ronn Maratea Photography, International Stock; **204** "The Scotty Who Knew Too Much" by James Thurber. Copyright © 1940 James Thurber. Copyright © 1968 Rosemary A. Thurber. From *Fables for Our Time* published by HarperCollins; **209** © Corel Professional Photos CD-ROM; **214** © Corel Professional Photos CD-ROM; **221** © Super Stock; **223** © Scott Thode, International Stock; **230** © Manny Millan, *Sports Illustrated;* **233** © Corel Professional Photos CD-ROM; **238** © Super Stock; **240** © Dan Brevick, LDA, Inc.; **241** © Ryan Williams, International Stock; **247** © Super Stock; **248** © Stan Pack, International Stock; **253** © The Bettmann Archives; **254** © Corel Professional Photos CD-ROM; **255** © Corel Professional Photos CD-ROM; **256** © Mark Bolster, International Stock; **262** © Patrick Ramsey, International Stock; **263** © Super Stock; **267** © Super Stock; **268** © John Zoiner, International Stock; **273** © Corel Professional Photos CD-ROM.

South-Western Educational Publishing has made every effort to locate copyright holders and to make full acknowledgment for the use of the photographs and illustrations used in this book.

338